Russia Discovered

Nineteenth-century Fiction
from Pushkin to Chekhov

Russia Discovered

Nineteenth-century Fiction
from Pushkin to Chekhov

ANGUS CALDER

HEINEMANN · LONDON

BARNES AND NOBLE BOOKS · NEW YORK
(A division of Harper & Row Publishers, Inc.)

Heinemann Educational Books Ltd
LONDON EDINBURGH MELBOURNE AUCKLAND TORONTO
SINGAPORE HONG KONG KUALA LUMPUR
IBADAN NAIROBI JOHANNESBURG
LUSAKA NEW DELHI KINGSTON

ISBN 0 435 18099 1

Published in the U.S.A. 1976 by
Harper & Row Publishers, Inc.
Barnes & Noble Import Division
ISBN 0–06–490924–7

Published in Great Britain by
Heinemann Educational Books Ltd
48 Charles Street, London W1X8AH

Photoset and printed by Interprint (Malta) Ltd

CONTENTS

FOR JENNI

FOREWORD

If you like, one 'discovery' this book is about is my own. It is an attempt by a reader with no Russian at all to interpret and evaluate the major nineteenth-century Russian writers of fiction as we know them in English. Like so many other people, I have found that these writers, muffled though they must be by translation, move and provoke me far more than most novelists in my own language. I can't imagine what life would be like without them.

My own discovery of them took place, as it happened, in Nairobi, where the chance came up to teach a course on them at the University there. Like 'Africa' in general, 'Kenya' is 'emerging'. People are still trying to find out what the country, and the continent, are, in human and geographical terms, and where they can and should go. In this discovery, it is realized, writers will have to play an important role. We have forgotten how Chaucer and Shakespeare discovered England and how Burns and Scott explored and mapped the meaning of Scotland. But in this island also, writers have helped to give people an idea of who they were by observing places and manners and bringing their observations together into one plausible vision—a 'new edition of human nature', as someone said of Scott's fiction.

There are important books to be written on the part played by literature in the morphology of nationalism. But I am not trying to push a thesis through this one. I simply take it for granted that in that nineteenth century which saw the burgeoning, for good and ill, of modern national-ism, writers in Russia (like writers in Africa now) were aware of themselves as discoverers, reporting to Russians themselves, and of course to the outside world as well, what their country was like, how it compared with Western Europe, why its landscapes were beautiful, what its future might be. Their vision is so fresh, I believe, because they were frontiersmen. The territory which they explored was one which they, by artistic means, could control, but which the Tsars, by political means, in the end couldn't; it was full of people who were subversively free. The glory of Russia is that its novelists and poets have made themselves spokesmen for all the free thought and humane feeling which Tsarist and Stalinist regimes have denied, that they have accepted a very dangerous role with proud dedication to the cause of illegal truths. The tragedy of Russia, of course, is that they had to be so brave.

II

I am concerned with books written between 1824, when Pushkin started *Onegin* and 1904, when Chekhov died and Tolstoy completed *Hadji Murad*. I can't for my own part understand novels except in terms of their historical context, and biography is the indispensable link between art and history. I have tried to gather from secondary sources in English the kinds of information which help me to understand the work of Pushkin, Gogol, Lermontov, Turgenev, Dostoevsky, Tolstoy and Chekhov, seven writers who seem indisputably great, and also of three, Goncharov, Saltykov and Leskov, whose best known fiction seems worthy to stand beside theirs. Rather reluctantly, I decided to mention only briefly an undoubtedly major writer, Gorky, whose early work falls before 1904 but who went on writing for a quarter of a century after Tolstoy's death. I know only enough about twentieth-century Russian fiction to understand that it is a rich and complex subject, not to be ventured into lightly.

Because nine of the ten writers covered were adults well before his reign ended, I have decided to root the book in the Russia of Nicholas I (1825–1855), which I describe in some detail in my first chapter. Thereafter I mention historical facts and trends only in passing until the eighth chapter, where it seemed essential to sketch, however, briefly, the Russia of Alexander III in which Chekhov found his feet as a writer. Towards time and the generations my attitude is Turgenevan. I believe that the historical sense is the mother of all understanding, and have therefore spliced Dostoevsky with Tolstoy in such a way that *War and Peace* takes its proper chronological place before *The Brothers Karamazov*, and have dealt with Chekhov's stories before confronting the last main works of Tolstoy.

The asides between my chapters—one might call them inter-chapters or indefinitions—are attempts to clear fussy terminological juggernauts off the highway I have tried to move fast on. Synopses of stories, clumsy though they may seem, are things I have found that I need myself if I am to get anything from discussion of books which I haven't recently read. I would like people to read this book right through from cover to cover, though as an habitual skimmer of other people's critical studies, I am not fool enough to suppose that many will do so. But I hope each bit in turn is useful.

III

Superlatives heaped on the great Russians are as redundant as stilts on a peak. Tolstoy and Dostoevsky seem to be the largest names in fiction and as it happens I think (at this moment, when I have read mainly Russians for some years) that among British novelists only Dickens and perhaps Emily Brontë can be compared to these two without unfairness. James, Stendhal and Balzac, I think, are three more nineteenth-century writers who can achieve important effects outside any great Russian's range. I am pretty clear that no other prose literature can have flanking its two greatest masters four or five contemporaries almost as great; rereading Gogol and Chekhov, I almost retract the almost. (And I am left, I must confess, with an uneasy feeling that I haven't done justice to Turgenev here. There is no writer whom I find more seductive. I am afraid that in resisting his charm so as not to gush I may have seemed to miss the point; and I wish there had been some way, in the space available, of paying adequate tribute to his supremely fine 'long short stories' while engaging with the historical and artistic importance of his 'novels'.)

Of course, discoverers can't and don't start from scratch. Without French, German and British writers to challenge and instruct them, these men couldn't have done so much. I hope my scattered comparative observations don't seem too glib; it seemed to me important to focus, however poorly, the context in European culture which the great Russians moved in as uninvited but later honoured guests. I am, not to be bashful, extremely glad that my reading for this book has seemed to confirm the extreme importance of Byron, Scott and Dickens in European literary history. No doubt a Frenchman, with equal justice, would have mentioned Balzac, Flaubert and Zola more often.

I am aware that I may seem unready to bring my ideas about the writers I cover to conclusions, either general or particular. So I am. I don't like, I will confess, either the Whig-Bolshevist view of Russian fiction which tends to see novels in terms of their contribution to the cause of Progress and their spadework for the Revolution, nor to that Cold War Liberal view which puts rational humanists into the unbecoming position of acclaiming Dostoevsky's more reactionary aspects because religious fervour is thought to be incompatible with Stalinism. (Which, of course, it isn't; Dostoevsky's Shatov might well have made one of that man's most fervent admirers.) I am also deeply allergic to general theses about hedgehogs and foxes, wounds and bows, mirrors in roadways and pistol shots in concerts. Let the reader supply his own over-view, if he must; I am concerned to report as accurately as I can what these writers seem to be up to, what they are saying, what they have discovered, and a more disparate bunch of people could hardly be imagined. If I appear to be arguing that Gogol is both a fantasist and a realist, Turgenev both subjective and objective, Dostoevsky both authoritarian and anarchist, Tolstoy both a conservative and a radical, well, that is indeed what I am arguing. Their work seems to me to be inherently contradictory. Let paradoxes flourish. Life is like that. Tidiness is the refuge of frightened minds, as we found when *bien-pensant* Western liberals were so comically shocked to discover that Solzhenitsyn, Hero of Liberalism First Class, was in very truth a conservative nationalist; and no less fine a writer, I will insist, for that. Without contraries, there is no progression, said Blake. And elsewhere, to generalize is to be an Idiot.

But, lest I am sounding like some butterfly aesthete, let me affirm my belief that the great Russians were and are great because they were and are so tensely aware of life's political dimension. This is true even of Pushkin and Chekhov. To tell the truth about life in Russia was and is a form of political action. The great nineteenth-century Russians are so important for us now because they were ready and able to expose and tackle the most explosive social and philosophical problems and because they have a unique moral and political urgency. Making discoveries in Russia, they told people abroad new things about man's nature and about the human world. They seem to me to share with Shakespeare and Milton and their best contemporaries a capacity, within a society moving through intellectual and social revolutions towards a political one, to think freely and bravely about human relationships with other people, with nature, with time and with 'God'.

But I don't read Hobbes or Kant in a railway train for fun. If I were about to be shot into space for the rest of my life with a single suitcase of books, I would take (along with plenty of Shakespeare, Milton and Herbert, Scott, Byron, Dickens and Yeats), *Dead Souls, Sportsman's Sketches, War and Peace, Anna Karenina, The Brothers Karamazov*, a fat selection of Chekhov tales and, as a light-hearted afterthought, Leskov's *Enchanted Wanderer* as well. Their job would be to remind me how good life on earth had been. I can't imagine why writers so full of sunlight and hay-smell, steppe flowers and glittering snow have ever had a general reputation for 'pessimism', grimness and wistful grieving. They are so profound, of course, not because they maintain that Anglo-Saxon virtue, 'a sense of proportion', but because their zest for life is as exorbitant as their sense of outrage. (After the period covered here, Babel and Sholokhov take to an almost amoral extreme the tendency in Russian fiction to admire and relish life even when it is at its most vicious and frightening.) The sticky buds of spring, delicious home-made jams, beautiful sensuous women, ludicrous rumours, farcical set-tos and fiery sunsets—these are things to lure us back again and again.

The history of Russia is fearful for outsiders to think of. Nowhere else has tyranny at so many stages in history taken cruelty, deception or both to such extremes. Life loved in spite of war, epidemic and famine, the flogging serf-owner, the town of N, Peter the Great, Nicholas I, secret policemen, inflammable wooden slums, civil war, Joseph Stalin and Nazi occupation is life celebrated in spite of whatever threatens life most. These great writers have so much to teach us about the use of time, the search for the full potential of every second, and the obligatory rage against whatever denies that to us. And no other reading, surely, is less a waste of time.

IV

No one else but me should bear any blame at all for whatever mistakes and fatuities I have committed to print. But I have many people to thank for helping me to get this book written. George Steiner, to begin with, hasn't seen a word of it yet, but when as an undergraduate I was callowly disillusioned with the study of literature, his range and his enthusiasm helped to restore my faith, and his *Tolstoy or Dostoevsky?* is, of course, one of the most exciting critical texts. Another indirect debt is to Jim Stewart and Andrew Gurr, who let me play my own hand for a couple of years with a class of students who took the 'Shakespeare-Tolstoy' option at the University of Nairobi. To those students, to Helen Aswani and Simmi Chima, Joan Deming, Julia Howe, David Krival, Geoffrey Kuria, Mary Matingu, Esther Mukuye, Richard Ndirango, Stephen Nduhiu, Samuel Ngugi, Selma Patwa, Liz Wafula, Chris Wanjala and Mrs Waichungo, I owe the gratitude for their ideas and above all for their scepticism, which any teacher owes to keen collaborators. Arnold Kettle, then at Dar es Salaam, helped me over a hefty step by pointing out to me that Dostoevsky is often an extremely funny writer and saved me from the dismal sham of talking over-earnestly about books which make me snigger aloud, and I have since gained a lot from teaching part-time the Open University course on the nineteenth-century novel which he organized. Talking about *Anna Karenina* and *On The Eve* with mature students, mostly women, was rewarding for me and I hope it was for them.

Without the interest and encouragement of Tony Beal of HEB, I would never have mustered the bravado to project or write this book, and I am very grateful for his patience with my delays. Without the very long-suffering staff of the National Library of Scotland and the kindness of the Librarian of Edinburgh University who let me use his many shelves, my work would have been much more difficult. I must also thank David Daiches for his helpful comments on Chapter Five and W. F. Mainland for some stimulating correspondence about Schiller and Dostoevsky. Mary Mackintosh helped me to tidy the book up.

The two biggest debts remain. Nikita Lary took enormous trouble with my manuscript and made scores of salutary criticisms; any acknowledgement here seems embarrassingly inadequate. Finally, Jenni Calder, the critic I'm married to, has helped me to patch over certain vast gaps in my knowledge of nineteenth-century fiction and has given all kinds of help and encouragement besides putting up with my brooding, snarling and thinking aloud. I hope it seems a good enough book to dedicate to her.

Edinburgh, 1975

RUSSIA

This book is concerned with fiction written in the 'Russian', that is, in the 'Great Russian', language. Within the 'Russian Empire' there were other literatures. In 1847 the police of the 'Third Section' rounded up a group of Ukrainian nationalists which included the serf-born poet Taras Shevchenko (1814–1861) whose work 'formed a landmark in the creation of a literary Ukrainian language' (Seton Watson 271). Ukrainian ('Little Russian') separatism has been a factor in 'Russian' politics since those days. But Gogol, born a 'Little Russian', wrote in Russian, as nearly a century later did Isaac Babel, a Jew born in Odessa.

It is always worth remembering that the masters of Russian fiction partook of an imperialist culture. It is hardly stretching a point to suggest that the situation in the countryside, where clean-shaven lords in European dress ruled bearded peasants in 'Russian' garb, was more like that in Ireland than that in England and France; Gilbert Phelps some years ago pointed out the affinities between the great Russian writers and those Irish writers, Maria Edgeworth and Joyce. Beyond this, Kipling is bound to spring to mind when we read Lermontov, Tolstoy or even Chekhov on the activities of Russians in the Caucasus. But major Russian fiction has by and large more to say about 'Empire' than major British fiction at the same period—no doubt for the obvious reason that the British conquests were made far overseas, whereas Russians expanded their frontiers on land.

Readers who know of so many descendants of Russian Jews now living abroad, and of the recent manifestations of anti-Semitism in the USSR, may be puzzled that so few Jews appear in nineteenth-century Russian fiction. The fact was that Jews were confined within a 'Pale' which in 1835 was redefined as an area of fifteen provinces in the West and South of the Empire, and great novelists rarely took their characters there. Poles are more in evidence, because they moved more freely, though it is impossible to think off-hand of a sympathetically conceived Polish character. The presentation of Tartars, who fitted easily into the well-worn stereotype of 'noble savage' is, by contrast, stylized but fair-minded. The most important ethnic minority from the novelist's point of view were the loyal and highly educated Baltic Germans who were so prominent among officials and professional men, and on balance even Dostoevsky gives them reasonably generous treatment; they were more often melted in the Russian pot than Poles, and educated Russians knew Germany and German culture well.

1
PUSHKIN'S RUSSIA

In March 1790, a young Russian traveller named Nikolai Karamzin arrived in Paris. France was in the first stage of her great revolution, but Paris remained the fairy-tale capital of luxury and culture. Karamzin was dazzled and afflicted by the contrast with his native land. A French lady asked him about Russia:

> In your land (he reports himself replying) spring sets in slowly, almost imperceptibly; in ours it falls suddenly from the heavens, and the eye cannot follow its swift course. Your Nature seems wasted and weak; ours has all the flaming vitality of youth.[1]

So a patriot could find comfort. Russia, in torrents like its own rivers in the spring thaw, would release a new force upon the world. But it could not show anything yet to match the middle class comfort of England, which Karamzin visited next. England's revolution was industrial. The air reeked of coal. But the road was crowded with modern coaches and rolled past fields of amazing fertility. 'Not one object from Dover to London,' Karamzin wrote, 'reminded me of human poverty.'[2]

Fiction in Russia rose quite suddenly to a prodigious maturity in the period which saw the double growth in Europe of modern democratic and revolutionary ideas and of modern industrial society. In a backward country on the fringe of Europe hurrying to catch up with France and England, the issues confronting modern man presented themselves more drastically and, perhaps, with greater clarity than they could further West even to a Dickens, a Stendhal or a Balzac. '. . . In the second half of the nineteenth century', writes George Lukács, 'Raskolnikov came from far-off, unknown, almost legendary Russia to speak for the whole civilized West.'[3] Like Shakespeare earlier in a country which had come late to its Renaissance, Tolstoy and Dostoevsky would project with unparalleled power the crisis of human nature in an age of dissolving institutions and expanding horizons.

Karamzin's short novel *Poor Liza*, published in 1792, is traditionally regarded as the first significant work of Russian prose fiction. The author was heavily influenced by such Western writers as the great Englishman

Sterne and the greater German, Goethe, pioneers of 'sentiment' in literature. Half a lifetime would pass before Karamzin's young friend Pushkin would create fiction to equal any Western contemporary. To the outside world, in 1790, Russia seemed to have no literature. Its educated men took seriously only what they read in French. The Empress Catherine the Great, herself German by birth, confronted those of her subjects who tried to write with a sage fear that free expression would bode no good for her autocratic power. She posed as an enlightened 'philosopher', but now that the French had rebelled against their King and were extolling Jean-Jacques Rousseau as a prophet of liberty, the dangers of enlightenment were very clear.

About the same time that Karamzin was awe-struck by his vision of the Dover road, Alexander Radishchev, chief of the St Petersburg Customs House, was exiled to Siberia for daring to describe, in the manner of Laurence Sterne, a fictionalized *Journey from St Petersburg to Moscow* (1790). The ideas he expressed were mostly French. The Russian style he wrote in was clumsy, or so we are told—it would be left to Karamzin to create an adequate Russian prose. But both his message and his fate pointed to the future.

In Radishchev's book, Russia appeared as a moral slum, dominated by a ruler who was prevented by the flattery of sycophants from seeing the horrible truth. Corrupted noblemen governed, as little despots, their squalid slaves. Rhetorically, Radishchev warned of, but almost seemed to favour, revolution. Inept as his rhetoric was, it seemed sincere. In his worship of man's inner light, his conscience, and in his readiness to see oppression behind all bland appearances Radishchev—by his own account, he couldn't sip a cup of coffee without thinking of the 'sweat of unfortunate African slaves'— was a precursor of Leo Tolstoy. And at one point he anticipates Gogol's epigraph to his *Inspector General*; 'Look in this mirror,' he tells overdressed city women, 'and whosoever recognizes herself in it, let her scold me unmercifully.'[4]

The idea that an imaginative writer should be the conscience of his generation, exposing to the public eye evils which men less brave didn't dare speak about, would help to give the Russian novel its unique moral seriousness and intellectual daring. Catherine detected the enemy at once. Radishchev's book was suppressed (though Pushkin, amongst others, would know and admire it); a new edition was burnt as late as 1902. Catherine said that its author was 'a rebel, worse than Pugachev'.[5]

Pugachev was the Cossack who, in 1773, had headed a peasant revolt in the Eastern provinces. This had been quite quickly quelled, but the rich lived in fear of a repetition.

Catherine was an effective ruler, who extended and consolidated Tsarist autocracy, and thrust Russia's power out to new boundaries in the South and West. Her generals and admirals were renowned. The surface of her rule glittered over the poverty of Russia. An Englishman named

Parkinson took Radishchev's road from Petersburg in 1793. He noted that the Empress had made a point of 'embellishing' as many places as possible along this main highway with stuccoed brick houses and 'shewy' churches of neo-Classical design. 'The contrast,' he observed, 'between the wooden huts of the Russians and these gay specimens of Grecian Architecture is very striking and almost ridiculous.'[6]

Even by the standards of a Europe, still largely feudal, in which major landowners enjoyed great freedom, the nobility of Russia were amazingly free. Their powers over their serfs were at a peak. Well over half the Empire's people were the property of a small class of nobles. Certain newspaper advertisements are famous: 'For sale; girl of sixteen, exemplary conduct, and also slightly used carriage.' While a pedigree puppy might fetch three thousand roubles, a serf girl might be worth no more than three. Serf life was cheap. The nobleman's power to punish was almost unchecked and men were flogged to death for petty offences. Sergei Aksakov in his *Family Chronicle* (1856), one of the many important works of Russian literature which live on the borderline between document and fiction, describes a landowner of Catherine's day given to unspeakable orgies who took pleasure in watching murderous beatings administered to his most devoted attendants and imprisoned his wife in a cellar when she protested. This does not seem to have been an exceptional case.

Cruelty co-existed with ignorance under at best a brittle veneer of 'culture'. In Denis Fonvizin's play, *The Minor* (1782), the first classic of the Russian stage, a country lady asks, 'Now, what's the use of studying geography?' A wise man tells her, 'it is useful, because when you want to travel somewhere, you know where you are going.' She retorts, 'Why, my dear sir! But what are the cab drivers for? That's their business. . . . A nobleman just says, "Take me yonder", and they take you wherever you wish.'[7] Fonvizin was too clever; under Catherine, he died in disgrace. But he had satirized indelibly the backwoods nobility. Skotinin ('Mr Brute') boasts he hasn't read a line since he was born and so loves pigs that he dreams of owning all the pigs in the world. His sister, Mistress Prostakova, is more pretentious; she hires a German tutor for her son, but the man turns out to be a coachman by profession.

This was a standard joke. Those nobles who wished to be polished, looked abroad for the wax. A German coachman, or a French barber, could easily pass for the missionary of enlightenment. The French *philosophe* Voltaire had praised Catherine, and Catherine's nobility liked his sceptical, hedonistic writings, which might help them to feel emancipated from traditional religious sanctions. But up-to-date ideas did not turn them against serfdom. What was read was not made to refer to Russian reality; it merely served to widen still further the gap between lord who could read and peasant who could not. The educated lord became a mimic man. Reality for him was somewhere else—in France, land of fashion in clothes and ideas, England, home of trade and of novel techniques in farming and industry, or Germany, advancing in philosophy and literature. He posed in Russia as a European; he was scorned in Europe as an Oriental.

For someone who read books, reality could not be here, in the melancholy, formless steppes, over which he floated weightless on the magic carpet of his rank, given by his birth a freedom without meaning and hard to distinguish from mere whimsy. From Fonvizin, Karamzin and Radishchev onwards, Russian writers had somehow to balance their hatred of ignorance against their suspicion of imported ideas and their fitful appreciation of the virtues of a Russian peasantry which still maintained an ancient folklore, communal values and luxuriant Christian superstition. One of their tasks was to make real, by describing it in a significant way, the life of their shapeless unknown country; they had to salvage Russia for reality.

Nikolai Gogol presents an extreme case. Theoretically a devoted patriot, he spent half his adult life abroad, and loved Italy deeply. He wrote there his greatest book, *Dead Souls* (1842) and in it he apostrophized his homeland:

> Russia! Russia! I behold thee—from my alien, beautiful, far-off place do I behold thee. Everything about thee is poor, scattered, bleak; thou wilt not gladden, wilt not affright my eyes with arrogant wonders of nature, crowned by arrogant wonders of art, cities with many-windowed, towering palaces that have become part of the crags they are perched on . . . . All is exposed, desolate and flat about thee; like specks, like dots are thy low-lying towns scattered imperceptibly over thy plains; there is nothing to entice, nothing to enchant the eye. But just what is the incomprehensible, mysterious power that draws one to thee? Why does one hear, resounding incessantly in one's ears, thy plaintive song, floating over all thy length and breadth, from sea to sea? What is there in it, in this song of thine?[8]

II

Russia had spread out like a blot over a vast plain, swept by long winds, hardly broken by low plateaux, between the Carpathian Mountains and the Urals. Its history had been shaped by its huge slow rivers.

From a watershed in the Valdai hills, the Western Dvina flowed to the Baltic Sea, the Dnieper to the Black Sea, and the Volga, immensely, to the Caspian. This watershed coincided with the wedge of mixed forest between the dense conifer forests to the North and the treeless, but potentially fertile, 'black earth' steppe to the South.

The steppe was a natural route for nomadic invaders—Huns, Magyars, Turks—galloping towards Europe from arid central Asia. Tartar hordes in the mid-thirteenth century sundered the first Russian realm established around Kiev. The 'Little Russians', Ukrainians, were split from their Slav brothers to the East while 'Great Russia', centred ultimately on

Moscow, fell under the so-called 'Tartar yoke'. In the woods, Muscovy became, over centuries, a warrior state under autocratic rulers. The 'Yoke' was thrown off before the end of the fifteenth century and Tsar Ivan the Terrible (1533–1585) fought down to the Caspian. But Germans, Poles and Swedes blocked his way to the Baltic. Russia remained cut off from the outlets of its rivers, except in the frozen North through which Ivan opened up trade with the England of Elizabeth. Cherishing a Greek Orthodox faith, and without easy access to the West, Russia could not share in the Renaissance which transformed the intellectual life of Latinized Western Europe.

The Romanov dynasty of Tsars, which came to power in 1613 and was destined to rule for 304 years, governed a 'warfare state' shaped by constant fighting against Tartars, Swedes and Poles and by the need to maintain large armies to defend and extend its amorphous frontiers. In Western Europe, the relations between great landholders and monarchs were generally governed by law. In Russia the Tsar's will was law. During the seventeenth century, when it had virtually disappeared in Britain, serfdom established an iron grip on Russia. The serfs were tied to the land and ruled by the landholders; the autocrat ruled all.

But because there were steadily expanding frontiers to the South and East, some Russians could escape growing enslavement to enjoy simple freedom. On the Dnieper and the Volga, runaways, fishermen, border warriors, frontiersmen of the Wild East, formed the unique communities of Cossacks. Such men also struck lonely paths across the vast landmass to the East, and in the seventeenth century Russians acquired control over Siberia as far as the Pacific Ocean.

The Romanovs now called in foreigners to give them technical assistance. It was in the 'German suburb' of Moscow that the boy king Peter the Great (1682-1726) developed his obsession with modernity.

He grew up a huge man, given to the most revolting orgies. The left side of his face twitched. His eyes protruded, rolling. He was always on the move, drinking deep, living rough and dressing like a Dutch seaman. In 1695, defeating the Turks, he established the first Russian port giving access to the Black Sea. Then he went on his famous trip abroad. In Holland, England and elsewhere he examined shipyards, factories, museums, restlessly curious about new techniques and ideas.

He came back having recruited hundreds of foreign experts. On the day after his return, he shaved the traditional long Muscovite beards off his courtiers. He forced his nobility to wear foreign clothes and insisted that their wives, hitherto secluded in an Asiatic fashion, should attend mixed dances. Having hacked his way through the Swedes to the Baltic he invented, in 1703, a new capital for Russia. Thousands of workmen perished to create, on marshy ground flat as a gravestone, St Petersburg, a 'window on to Europe.'

Russia began to resemble a modern police state. The independence of the Church was destroyed. Countless peasants fled into the forests or steppes to escape compulsory military service for twenty-five years and other tyrannical innovations. It was decreed that all nobles must serve the state. In 1722 Peter established his famous table of ranks. All official appointments, civil and military, were arranged in fourteen parallel grades (hence that slightly bewildering Russian figure, the civil service 'General'). From now on, Russians would be obsessed with rank and medals.

But few of Peter's innovations were so enduring. He created an Academy of Science, but students as well as lecturers had to be imported from Germany. Russians did not take to education; nor could Peter stimulate in Russia industries to match those of the West, though he started scores of iron works. But he left ample material for myth. His appalling figure would haunt his compatriots, most memorably in Pushkin's narrative poem *The Bronze Horseman* (1833). For the critic Belinsky he would be no less than 'a deity who has called us into being and who has breathed the breath of life into the body of ancient Russia, colossal but prostrate in deadly slumber.'[9]

The nobility, a diverse class ranging from Princes with ancient titles to recent recruits of many nationalities commenced, after Peter's death, to get rid of their duty to serve the state while, contrary-wise, they increased their privileges. In their heyday under Catherine their only obligation, as Mirsky pleasantly puts it, was to shave their faces.[10]

Not all Russian peasants, then or later, were downtrodden. The lot of those who farmed state-owned land might be very much better than that of those owned by the nobility. The noble was free to exploit his peasants either by exacting from them compulsory labour on the portion of the estate which he farmed on his own account—this was known as *barshchina* —or by demanding a money payment, *obrok*, which came to be regarded as a more 'liberal' arrangement. The nobles could arrange marriages between their serfs, could chain them, knout them or deport them to Siberia. *Obrok* serfs, encouraged by their masters to work as craftsmen or traders, so that they could pay more *obrok*, might even grow rich. Some serfs actually bought serfs. But all they owned was owned in the name of the master. There were serf capitalist millionaires in the cotton textile industry which serfs created, but such men could not assert their enterprise and independence like the pioneers of industrialism in North West England. Meanwhile, the nobility pampered by *obrok* and *barshchina*, had little incentive to improve their extremely backward methods of cultivation. Russia stagnated in an age of rapid economic change. Her foreign trade was in foreign hands.

The complacency and laziness of the nobility was to prove its undoing as the Tsars strove to organize Russia so that it could compete as a military power with Western countries. An expanding empire needed a central bureaucracy, and this could only recruit sufficient staff if it went outside the often reluctant nobility—to the merchant class and to the class of married priests.

As Catherine's successors sought to found their power on obedient, but well-trained, bureaucrats, two trends were set in motion which do much to explain the character of nineteenth-century Russian fiction. On the one hand the old nobility, challenged by upstarts, became prone to disgruntlement. It dared not kick against the system too hard—any change might blow the lid off the fury of the peasants, and Pugachev was not forgotten. But from this class came a small but important group of writers—including Pushkin, Turgenev and Tolstoy—who were not friendly towards the bureaucracy. The nasty portrait which Tolstoy draws in *War and Peace* of Mikhail Speransky, a priest's son, who became an architect of a modernized government system, clearly reflects the disdain felt for a jumped-up nobody and handed down, to Tolstoy by older members of his own class.

Secondly, to educate your civil servants, as the Tsars found, might be dangerous. Universities imparted ideas. Ideas came from outside Russia. Ideas wouldn't stay still and wouldn't be servile. The new schools and universities bred a rebellious intelligentsia drawn in great part from the sons of priests and of impoverished minor noblemen. Angry literary critics of plebeian birth would, by the middle of the century, be found busy challenging and egging on writers of wealthy noble lineage. One is talking about small minorities here; but great writers, while always in a minority, never escape from the social situation they are born into.

The career of Alexander Pushkin, who was born in 1799, and who is generally considered by Russians to be their greatest writer of all, demonstrates rather neatly both the factors just mentioned. A further factor, of course, was the involvement of Russia in an explosive period of European history. When Pushkin was a few months old, Napoleon came to power in France.

III

The Russian monarch then reigning was the mad Tsar Paul. It is said that when Pushkin was passing Paul in his baby carriage, the Tsar sternly reprimanded his nurse for not taking the infant's cap off. The nobility, dismayed by Paul's passion for discipline, felt avenged when he was murdered in 1801, with the connivance of his son Alexander.

Alexander and his brothers inherited their father's hobby, drilling men. The new Tsar used to say that if there were anything finer in the world than the sight of 1000 identical men all performing exactly the same movement, it was the sight of 100,000 men performing it. His brother Constantine complained, more endearingly, that war dirtied the soldiers' clothes and was bad for discipline. Of a third brother, Nicholas, there will be much to say later.

But Alexander had been introduced to 'liberal' ideas by a French tutor, and his closest friends and advisers were, at first, 'liberals'. Almost all the 'liberal' tsar dared to achieve, however, were some minor reforms in the institution of serfdom and an overhaul of the bureaucracy to bring it closer to the French model. (French police methods were then much admired.)

Meanwhile, Alexander fought Napoleon, allied with him, and fought him again. In 1812 the French Emperor invaded Russia with an army of 420,000 men. He occupied a deserted Moscow after a murderous confrontation with the Russian army at Borodino. But the wooden city caught, or was set on, fire. Napoleon was stranded without adequate supplies as the notorious Russian winter began to creep in. He raced back to the border and crossed it, finally, with a mere 5000 troops. The Russian climate and, perhaps above all, the sheer size of Russia, had defeated him, but the valour of the Russian army and the actions of guerillas against the retreating French made, and make, 1812 a focus of national pride.

In a sense, the Russian nation had been born, to join the French, Germans and British in a new era of self-conscious nationalism. The 'people' had beaten Napoleon. Rich and poor had fought and endured together. To Napoleon himself, it had seemed that the Russians were in effect two races. He shrank from inciting the peasants to rise against their masters because these shaggy creatures seemed to him hardly human.[11] Yet as the Russians became conscious of themselves as one 'nation', serfdom was bound to seem illogical; if all were equally Russian, why should some Russians be the property of others?

Russians who read books were bound to be infected with the mystique of the common people present in Western Romanticism. But Romanticism also exalted the exceptional man. The great exemplar was Lord Byron. The handsome, brooding Byronic hero, steeped in mysterious sins, a restless wanderer alienated from his own society who was also, politically, a liberal, had immense appeal all over Europe. This appeal was perhaps greatest of all in Russia, where the intellectual was so very much an outsider, and very likely an aristocrat into the bargain. To borrow a term from Dostoevsky (who was still reflecting the influence of Byronism in the 1870s) Byron was Napoleon's 'double'. And though Russian armies pursued the retreating French emperor across Europe and entered Paris as conquerors, they were fascinated by the myth of the man they helped to humble.

Napoleon had risen from obscure origins, Napoleon had led a revolutionary nation and had carried, like a secular messiah, the gospel of liberation wherever his armies had gone. The English radical writer Hazlitt, among others, was 'prostrated in mind and body' (a friend wrote) by Napoleon's final defeat at Waterloo. 'Hazlitt's principle was that crimes, want of honour, want of faith, or want of every virtue on earth, were nothing on the part of an individual raised from the middle classes to the throne, if they forwarded the victory of the popular principle whilst he remained there.'[12] Fifty years later Raskolnikov, in Dostoevsky's *Crime and Punishment*, would echo and expand that 'principle'. An ancient political order in Europe had been destroyed by Napoleon. A traditional morality based on belief in the hereafter was meanwhile succumbing to the assaults of the free intellect. Individualism, capitalism and amoralism advanced now together. With his insatiable ambition and his bottomless cynicism, Napoleon was an apt hero for the new age dominated by a rapacious bourgeoisie. He represented the heroic and triumphant will of the self-justified man of talent to whom everything was, or should be, permitted. He was a supreme 'realist' in a period when reality—the actual condition of humanity—was being transformed at unprecedented speed by new inventions and by a new science of economics which seemed able to justify almost anything if it contributed to 'progress'.

The 'Liberalism' for which Napoleon seemed to stand out as prophet was used to justify wars of novel bloodiness and the ruthless treatment of the emerging working classes of Europe. But it was genuinely 'liberating' in its assault on traditional class systems. The 'popular principle' exemplified by the French Revolution now threatened every established political order.

Even the old-fashioned 'State serfs' of North Russia were stirred by Napoleon. A German who travelled there in 1843 found a portrait of Napoleon in every substantial peasant's house. 'No name,' he wrote, 'no historical figure is better known and more popular with the common Russian than Napoleon. ... He has now become the hero of popular story, a fabulous mythical hero; every trace of hatred has vanished.'[13]

The young Russian officers who entered Paris with Tsar Alexander's conquering army were embarrassed and ashamed by the contrast that city made with the Russia they returned to. It was 'unbearable', one of them wrote, to 'look at the empty life in Petersburg and listen to the babbling of the old men who praised the past and reproached every progressive move. We were away from them a hundred years.'[14]

Alexander's own 'liberalism' had been an inspiration. But the Tsar now lapsed into an obscurantist Christian mysticism; his right hand was now a faithful, reactionary and ruthless minister named Arakcheev. Small secret societies appeared among the cream of the rising generation of officers and intellectuals. One, the Northern Union, wanted a constitutional monarchy, but the Southern Union, led by an officer named Pestel, was out for a democratic republic.

When Alexander died suddenly in 1825, it was not clear which of his brothers, Constantine or Nicholas, would succeed him. In an atmosphere of uncertainty and rumour, the Northern Union, on 14 December, was able to muster 3000 soldiers in Senate Square in Petersburg, calling for 'Constantine and Constitution.' Pro-Nicholas forces dispersed them. The leaders, who had never been very clear what they were up to, were arrested, along with many others who were thought to have been implicated. 116 men were exiled to Siberia. Five were hanged. Since capital punishment was not normal practice in Russia, the executioners were inexperienced. The nooses were not tight enough and at the first try three of the arch-rebels simply fell down when the stools were pulled from under their feet. One, who broke his legs, is said to have exclaimed, 'Poor Russia, she cannot even hang decently.'[15]

From one point of view, the 'Decembrist' rebels of 1825 were almost reactionaries, who were trying to maintain the tradition whereby in the eighteenth century noblemen, through the guards regiments, had controlled the succession to the throne. But their confused idealism gave their attempted coup an aura of true revolution. Martyred in Siberia, their memory lived on to inspire future rebels.

IV

When Nicholas I arrived thus on the throne, Belinsky and Gogol were sixteen, Goncharov was fourteen, Lermontov eleven, Turgenev seven and Dostoevsky four. Tolstoy was born three years later. It was in Nicholas's reign of thirty years that the architects of Russian fiction grew to maturity. It was against his view of the world that they had to set theirs.

Nicholas girded up his guts so tight to perfect his military carriage that his stomach was pushed up into his chest. A French observer, the Marquis de Custine, wrote: 'An unlucky fly, buzzing in the Imperial Palace during a ceremony, mortifies the Emperor: the independence of nature appears to him a bad example: every thing which he cannot subject to his arbitrary laws becomes in his eyes as a soldier, who in the heat of battle revolts against his officer.'[16] The whole state should work like a well-drilled army unit. Nicholas could see that reform was desirable—in the endemic peasant unrest of his reign, he saw the threat of a fresh Pugachev rising, of real revolution. But granted that the nobility were against it and the bureaucracy was hopelessly corrupt, he thought that it was, in effect, impossible. 'There is no doubt,' he once said, 'that serfdom, in its present form, is a flagrant evil . . . yet to attempt to remedy it now would be, of course, an evil even more disastrous.'[17]

Russia could not and did not remain completely torpid, and in fact enormous changes were in progress. For the first time, as internal and external trade expanded, most Russians were adjusting to a money economy. But Russia mostly exported such things as grain, flax and timber —'primary' products. What she imported, for her richer classes, were manufactured goods, mainly from Britain. Her production of iron doubled while that of Britain increased thirty times.

It was growingly thought that serfdom was choking the growth of industry—free labour, modern-minded thinkers supposed, would be more mobile and more efficient. But mobility was one of the things the Tsar's ministers feared—one of them opposed the building of railways on the grounds that it would endanger 'public morals' by encouraging 'frequent, purposeless travel' and thus 'fostering the restless spirit of our age.' By the end of Nicholas's reign, Russia had a railway system only one fifth the size of that of France.[18]

In only one respect was Russia 'ahead' of the rest of Europe; in the growth of bureaucracy and the subordination of its people to an army of civil servants ranging upwards from starvelings in the lower ranks to sumptuous senators in scarlet who might, nevertheless, be open to a modest bribe. The system was clogged by the very paper it produced; it is recorded as a fact, not invented by Gogol, that once ten waggons-full of paper dealing with a single case of fraud on a contract were sent from Moscow to Petersburg; and, furthermore, that they disappeared on the road.[19] Inefficiency abetted corruption. 'The administration of justice in Russia', acknowledged an experienced English traveller, 'is little better than a system of cheating and bribery...'[20]

To rise up through the system, you had to flatter. At the top, the Tsar himself moved in 'a permanent conspiracy of smiles.' No unpleasant truths were told him. Even so, Nicholas mistrusted his bureaucrats. He brought in soldiers to command several key ministries; he even appointed one to control the Holy Synod of the Orthodox Church. His own personal Chancellery, which mushroomed, included the Third Section, the secret police, under Count Benckendorff.

Russia was a 'police state', though an inefficient one. Spies were everywhere. An English dandy who visited Petersburg in 1829 was surprised when a clever, well-travelled Russian to whom he was talking in a restaurant disagreed violently with him when he criticized the city, and launched into wild praise of it. When they rose, he took the Englishman aside and told him why—two people nearby had been listening—'I have no doubt they were spies.'[21]

The newspapers, of course, could not report most of the news. Neither injustice nor disaster might be mentioned. The censorship was erratic but exasperating. At its worst point, in the year 1848 when revolutions all over Europe made Nicholas unusually nervous, even phrases like 'forces of nature' were deleted from textbooks on physics. A brilliant dandy named Chaadaev wrote an essay critical of Russia which appeared in print in 1836; an important document in Russian intellectual history which opened the debate between 'Westerners' and 'Slavophiles'. The journal was suspended. The editor was exiled. Chaadaev was declared insane, and had to endure regular visits from a doctor.[22]

V

Under Nicholas Russia's imperialist expansion continued, rapidly into Central Asia, slowly in the mountains of the Caucasus, where hill tribes resisted stubbornly. The Great Russians of the Muscovite heartland already dominated a multitude of other peoples.

'Great Russia', stretching from Finland to the Urals and from the Arctic Ocean to the northern fringe of the steppes, was already a vast country. But dialects differed little over its expanse, and though the area was more than six times that of Germany, Baron von Haxthausen found only one basic peasant costume, compared with his own country's hundreds of local garbs. The people, Slavs who had absorbed aboriginal Finnish stock, tended to fair hair, blue eyes and rosy complexions.

In 1835 the population of the Empire was 60,000,000 men *and* women. Of the *men* nearly 11 million were serfs owned by the nobility; $10\frac{1}{2}$ million were State serfs.

The peasants wore beards. They smelt, in their homespun woollen smocks and sheepskin coats, of onions, cabbage and greasy leather. They wore shoes of treebark. In their log huts the most prominent feature was usually a huge brick stove, five feet high, six or eight feet square, big enough to sleep on. Their lives were governed by the rhythm of the Russian seasons—long, snowclad, icebound winters and hot dusty summers. Typhus was endemic, syphilis common, famine frequent. But the peasantry were incredibly hardy. They lived mainly on rye bread supplemented by cabbage soup, buckwheat gruel, vegetables, mushrooms and berries, and washed down by *kvass*, a drink of fermented rye. Tea was becoming a national drink and the tea-urn, *samovar*, a feature of the peasant hut. On his minimal diet, the peasant could labour fourteen hours a day in the summer and in winter make journeys of hundreds of miles, sledging fast over the snow, to sell his wares in the big cities— sleeping five hours, driving five, in severe frost. He was a jack of all trades, who could amaze foreigners by his ingenuity with a hatchet, but villages often specialized in particular handicrafts. A commune of stone masons, for instance, might hire other serfs to farm its land in summer, troop off to Moscow, and return in winter.

A law of Alexander's enabled serfs to buy their freedom, but by 1855, after 52 years, only 100,000 had done so, often at huge cost. One of them was Anton Chekhov's grandfather.[23] Peasants could express their revolt against misery only by flight—difficult but not impossible in a land where passports were required for internal travel—by arson or by murderous riot. Russia had 1500 peasant risings in the first sixty years of the nineteenth century. Between 1835 and 1854, 144 proprietors, including Dostoevsky's father, were murdered by their serfs. 'During the three decades of Nicholas's reign the frequency of disturbances steadily increased.'[24]

But where the landlord was the State, or a nobleman who didn't interfere too much, the villager's life might seem tolerably independent. For the peasant, indeed, the landlord seemed really a parasitical intruder between himself and his father, the Tsar. To him, it seemed, the whole of Russia was one vast commune, one *mir*, where the Tsar, as head of the family, distributed the land, as the elders did in that smaller *mir*, the village. The *mir's* roots were not so deep as some romantics supposed, but there it was, the commune which regulated farming, shared the land in strips equally, enforced patriarchal authority over wives and arranged marriages. The peasants' proverbs extolled the *mir*. 'Throw everything upon the *mir*, it will carry it all.' 'No one in the world can separate from the *mir*.'[25] Agriculture under the *mir* was conservative and inefficient, but traditional community had its compensations.

Another bearded class of Russians, the merchants, were also deeply conservative, preserving the old dress and customs of Muscovy which Peter the Great had attacked. Their wives, still closetted strictly indoors, emerged on festival days in lavish national costume, headdresses heavy with pearls and gems. The men were organized in three guilds, each with its greater or lesser privileges. Change moved among them slowly, and they still married their own kind, but some were now educating their daughters in the hope that they would marry civil servants and rise into the gentry.

While the sons of priests, the 'seminarists', were also tending to break out of their class, the Orthodox church itself remained slumped in intellectual torpor. Its hold over the people was still powerful. Pilgrims thronged the roads to such holy places as the city of Kiev and the more famous monasteries. One foreign traveller was amazed to see an elegant young dandy fall on his knees before a holy relic, touch the ground with his forehead, and humbly kiss it. The church's rituals, shared by all classes, provided a unifying and softening element in Russian life. But its subservience to the autocracy alienated it sharply from those who wished for secular reform. Dissenters from this state religion were persecuted.

Nevertheless, there were millions of them. The 'Old Believers', who were strong among the Cossacks, the merchants and the state serfs of the North, clung to the ancient rituals of the church which had been reformed in the seventeenth century, and were noted for thrift, frugality, and literacy. Other sects showed the extremes to which Russians might take the quest for salvation. One group of 20 or 30,000, the *skoptsy*, castrated themselves. Others refused to speak, or burnt themselves to death, or whipped themselves. The wandering *stranniki* who denounced Tsardom as the devil's rule and refused to carry passports or pay taxes were to make a great impression on Leo Tolstoy, as were the Dukhobors, a quaker-like pacifist sect which was repeatedly persecuted.

But very few of the nobility were drawn towards such doctrines. They still had too much to live for. Merchants might now own serfs, but the majority still belonged to the nobility. Most 'nobles' were petty; some were even poor. A man owning over 500 male serf 'souls' was certainly well off. The 1858 count showed about 100,000 serf-owners. Of these 40 per cent had twenty souls or less. 2421 proprietors each owned between 500 and 1000 souls; and the 1382 magnates who each owned over 1000 souls between them possessed three out of every ten serfs in private hands.[26]

Nicholas flattered the nobles, called them 'my police' and tried to use them by making their local assembly the arm of the state in each district, where they collected taxes, supervised recruitment to the army, and generally ran things under the Governor's eye. But the whims of autocracy chafed even its instruments. Foreign travel was restricted, and pressure put on young nobles to enter the Tsar's service was often resented. And the tiny steps sometimes taken towards the reform of serfdom were enough to worry the serf owners.

For the nobility, serfs were almost their whole capital—serfs even provided the tools they themselves worked the land with. Some nobles farming the rich black earth lands to the south might be able to accept or even welcome a form of emancipation which would replace servile with hired labour and would give them all the land and the peasants none; the export of grain could be a rich trade. But in the scantier soil around Moscow, serfs, with the *obrok* they provided, were all that could pay for the high living which nobles, imitating Europe, increasingly sought for. Increasingly, the nobility lived in the cities, mortgaging their peasants with the state to pay for imported luxuries. By the mid nineteenth century, two-thirds of all privately-owned serfs had thus been mortgaged.

But granted the gap between Russia and Western Europe, the alternative to imitation might seem to be mere barbarism. French was the social language of the urban aristocracy; it was possible to meet aristocratic Russians who spoke their native language badly. And even the major poet Fedor Tiutchev (1803–1873) used French, Henry Gifford tells us, as 'the language of most daily transactions, in which the conventional self—husband, father, friend and public servant—could move at ease. For his deepest intimacies and supreme perceptions Tiutchev reserved Russian.'[27]

If the hegemony of French culture was challenged, it was by German rather than native ideas. Nicholas himself admired German discipline and efficiency; young intellectuals (including Belinsky, Turgenev and Dostoevsky) were bowled over by German literature and philosophy. Both the regime—with its slogan, 'Orthodoxy, Autocracy and Nationalism'—and the intellectuals wanted Russia to make an independent mark on Western civilization. But when Nicholas ordered that no French be spoken at court, people complied only till his back was turned. And his own capital, Petersburg, was a city whose very buildings defied the culture of the nation which had erected them.

VI

Petersburg, as many foreign travellers testify, was superbly impressive to the eye. Its imposing granite quays fronted huge buildings in neo-

Classical style. Summers at this most Northern of great cities provided a spectacle of uncanny beauty—the famous 'white nights' when the sun barely set and its floating reflection made the river Neva shine like mother of pearl, while gilded turrets and steeples glimmered in a vaporous twilight. But by day the gigantic squares and streets wore a depressing air of silence, almost of vacancy. Their scale was anti-human. The city was dominated by soldiers, by the court and by the civil service. In it, an insecure, 'detribalized' lower middle class was coming into existence, mixing junior officers, students, clerks and tradesmen. And its declassed intelligentsia in which merchants' sons mingled with the children of nobility and the sons of priests and serfs, was to provide Russia with a breeding ground for rebels.

To anyone used to the comforts of the West, the verminous hotels of Petersburg were appalling. The streets were easy to race on while they wore their winter covering of snow. In spring, they dissolved into mud, and if the traveller pressed on into the interior he would find that on Russian roads sand gave way only to morasses, stones and tree-stumps, floods or dust. Pushkin joked in his *Onegin* about the Russian blacksmith 'blessing the ruts and ditches of the Fatherland' as he earned his pay for repairing yet another fancy carriage rashly ventured. Jolted and jarred, cursing the bed-bugs and mosquitoes, the traveller found no relief in the landscape. Its unstartling undulations, its sparse fields, its fir forests or birch groves varied little from province to province. Turgenev had not yet revealed beauty in them, and they gave hardly more delight to the untutored eye than the roadside villages, regular lines of sombre grey huts with their gable ends always facing into the street. But suddenly, from a broad monotonous plain, there sprang a view of Moscow, its innumerable steeples with their copper crosses glittering, churches, palaces, monasteries, strange onion-shaped domes, enamelled, golden green, flashing fire above a sea of red housetops. This was a holy city, Mother of Russia. After the fire of 1812 it had been rebuilt with a more regular layout, but it remained anarchic, in the greatest possible contrast with Petersburg. Noblemen's town mansions, set in extensive leafy grounds full of birdsong, were interspersed with the wooden homes of the common people. Away from the Tsar, people were freer in their manners. Here the nobility was still dominant; here eccentricity flourished. Rich youngsters who dressed their coachmen in exquisite clothes and revelled with the gypsy girls boasted of their bad behaviour before amused and tolerant elders. To Leo Tolstoy, once such a young reveller, Moscow would seem as real as Petersburg was sham.

From Moscow radiated outwards the lesser towns of the empire, its provincial capitals and district capitals. From a distance, with its halo of church spires, each might promise something, but on arrival each would turn out much the same: a square and a few streets of neo-Classical buildings giving way rapidly to log huts; 25,000 people or so, including the poorer nobility who wouldn't live on their estates but couldn't afford to live in Moscow; unpaved streets, perhaps an ill-attended theatre; perhaps also a few drunken army officers ready to liven the place up with petty orgies; always, however, dreadful boredom. This was Gogol's grotesquely mediocre town of N; this was the muddy milieu where Dostoevsky set his horribly farcical *Devils*; here Turgenev's provincial virgins yearned for a real man to come so that they might love him; here characters in Chekhov would waste their lives playing cards.

But the broad Volga led towards the frontier and Asia. In such a riverside town as Saratov, the noblemen's carriages drove through exotic tribesmen, Bashkirs and Kalmuks. Cossacks mingled, with their fur hats; they had now been disciplined by the state into a cavalry force, but were excused taxes in return for military service and remained horsemen, masters of the wide horizon.

If one pressed southwest from Saratov towards the Black Sea one crossed the exorbitantly fertile steppes which Catherine had conquered and populated with colonists of many races—Ukrainians, above all, but also Germans, Armenians, Greeks, Jews, Serbians, Bulgars and Moldavians. To gather a rich yield of wheat, the farmer had merely to scratch the black earth. Where this had not been done, the rolling plain, broken only by gullies and ravines, burgeoned innumerable flowers. At first there would be very few trees; further south, no trees at all; and Chekhov, who would grow up by the Black Sea, would be almost obsessed with the need to plant trees.

The Black Sea port of Odessa was the outlet for the grain trade, a boom town now that Europe was eager for Russian grain. Italian was the language of commerce, and foreign merchants listened to the latest operas. Cutting north again, one passed through the Ukraine, 'Little Russia', made culturally distinct from Great Russia by hundreds of years of separate history. The contrast was expressed in its brisk and lively dances, compared with the slow serious measures of Muscovy, and in the crooked streets of Ukrainian villages, with their whitewashed wattle houses and fine fruit trees. Kiev, more ancient than Moscow and yet more holy, housed amongst other relics the shrivelled remains of hermits dead for centuries. Around it, the nobility were Polish catholics. Russia had acquired under Catherine a large share of the old Polish territories; the rest had gone to Prussia and Austria. The Polish gentry, impoverished and rebellious, were deeply loathed by nationalists like Gogol and Dostoevsky. Nicholas had to suppress one of their outbreaks in 1830. But the German barons of the Baltic provinces also acquired in the eighteenth century were, by contrast, firm props of Tsarism, providing Russia with good generals and with some of its least corruptible civil servants. Perhaps because they were efficient and conscientious, they were often mocked and resented, and so great a humanist as Tolstoy hardly overcame his prejudice against them. Subject peoples were legion. The Tartars of the Crimea and the Volga, tribes of Finnish and Siberian hunters, a medley of cultures in the Caucasus mountains, nomads on the steppes, Jewish traders in the towns of the South-West, preserved more or less tenaciously their own customs and languages, even when surrounded by Russians on all sides. The growing list of such peoples (governed, very often, by methods of 'indirect rule') posed a threat to order which could be met only with a vast army and diligent repression. Great Russians themselves suffered under authoritarian methods designed to hold down non-Russian peoples. They too supplied many of the convicts who helped to colonize Siberia, which was already a grim byword in Europe.

One great writer, Dostoevsky, took that long road, and described his detention in *The House of the Dead*. But to free settlers, and freed prisoners, Siberia might seem a relatively easy-going place, where the long arm of autocracy could barely reach. 'The common people,' wrote one Decembrist exile, 'seemed to me much more free, more clever, even more educated than our Russian peasants. . . Here they better appreciate human dignity. . .'[28] Fugitives saw Siberia as a place to escape to; and prospectors yearned for its fabled gold.

As this indicates, stereotypes may be misleading. Nicholas I's Russia was as complex as it was huge. One word, 'autocracy', couldn't cover it. If its serfs were regarded as less than human, so were the slaves of the USA, and the former were liberated sooner. The poor in industrial Britain could hardly laugh long or loud at the Russian peasant, and if Russia's state educational system was perverted by despotism, at least it *had* such a system many years before England.

Russia was a country where the 'knout', a vicious long whip which could kill a man with a couple of stripes, was so commonly employed that its use in the street excited no interest. Yet beggars never went short of charity, and even hostile foreign travellers were impressed with the gentleness of Russian speech, by the civility and kindness expressed in the stranger's greeting 'God be with you', and by the richness of the language in terms of endearment. In scenes unthinkable in Paris or London, rich men kissed syphilitic beggars at church on Easter Sunday, and a Grand Duke would embrace his soldiers at a public parade. The Tsar's cavalcade hurtled down the roads with reckless disregard for anything in its way, yet the same Tsar threw his palace gardens open to vast, orderly crowds of people of all classes to celebrate the Tsarina's birthday.

Nowhere did the law tie people more strictly to one place; nowhere were they fonder of wandering. The roads tempted pilgrims and beggars; proprietors short of labour asked a fugitive few questions. 'Freedom,' said the bird in the Russian proverb, 'though the cage is a golden one.'

And 'freedom' in Russia under Tsarist tyranny perhaps meant more than 'freedom' anywhere else, for two reasons. The vast land gave men space to range over. The peasant forced to pay *obrok* to a lazy champagne-swiller was the same man who sledged a thousand miles to sell the wares he had made. The soldier forced into the army fought, perhaps, on the bracing frontier of the Caucasus. The exile in Siberia confronted almost limitless expanses of virgin land. The nobleman who for having the wrong friends might suddenly be hurled without trial into prison could hunt all day, like Tolstoy's heroes, in an unspoilt wilderness.

But another proverb said 'Obey and then reason.' For the great writers of Russia, as for other intellectuals and rebels, freedom was also defined, with acute vividness, by its obvious absence. This thrust men into extremes of resistance. No other regime so mistrusted ideas; nowhere else did a passionate minority value ideas so highly. Nowhere did revolutionaries make such reckless gestures. Nowhere were men and women more prone to reject all authority, that of morals along with that of the State. Russia in the late nineteenth century was notorious for harbouring two irreconcilable political ideas—despotism and anarchism. Europe thought the Russians wild people, given to extremes of cruelty and kindness, rashness and servility. And with some of the great Russian writers themselves, we are aware of acute self-contradictions. In Tolstoy the landowner tyrant co-existed with the anarchist saint; in Dostoevsky the Tsarist propagandist met the rebel.

The position of women was also paradoxical. While peasant women were strictly subordinate, in the higher classes it was normal for married women to own property, even landed property, at a time when this was difficult in England. 'On the front of every house in Moscow and St Petersburg', reported Haxthausen in the 1840s, 'is written the name of the proprietor, and before every third house at least the name is that of a woman.'[29] An English doctor was shocked, in the 1820s, by the 'openness' with which 'even unmarried females' spoke of 'pregnancy, of confinement, of the diseases of childbirth, and even of those changes which are peculiar to the sex, in the presence of males. . . .'[30] Scheming, domineering, inquisitive and, by reputation at least, free with their sexual favours, Russian women of the nobility were already, under Nicholas I, offering some foretaste of their outbreak in life as in literature which would lead the English critic Saintsbury in 1907 to refer to that 'singular Russian specialty, the revolutionary girl.'[31]

The best known heroines of Russian fiction can't often be matched in Western work. They are both charming and pushful, fresh and wilful. And Pushkin's Tatiana is the first of them.

VII

Pushkin's ancestry set him apart in two ways. In the first place, his lineage was authentically ancient; he was proud to trace it back 600 years. Secondly, his maternal great grandfather, Abram Gannibal, had been an African, probably from Ethiopia. He had been purchased in Constantinople for Peter the Great, who had given him an education. Pushkin's skin was fair, but his features showed this African descent. He was proud of it, but highly self-conscious about it.

His Uncle Vasili was a talented poet and his father also dabbled in literature. Karamzin and other leading writers came to the Pushkin home when Alexander was a child and the boy early devoured the French books which filled his father's library. It was not, however, for this reason that he was nicknamed 'Frenchy' when he went to school in 1811. That was because there was a current joke about Frenchmen being like monkeys, and Pushkin's appearance was unusual. The Lycée at Tsarskoe Selo which he attended was one of Alexander I's more 'liberal' creations. Its aim was to train an élite, drawn from the highest ranks of the nobility, for the highest offices of state. Ironically, its first pupils, Pushkin's classmates, tended to emerge from it either poets, or rebels, or both. Several of them wrote verses of high standard even at school. By 1814, Pushkin himself was publishing poems; by the time he left the Lycée in 1817 he was acknowledged as a rising star by Russia's best writers.

His father's life was that of a nobleman of middling means, hard up, in and out of the service, living above his income. When Pushkin rejoined his family, their flat in an unfashionable suburb of Petersburg was, for all their ancient lineage, 'always in a state of chaos,' as a neighbour described it: '. . . numerous ragged and always drunken house-serfs; large ramshackle coaches with gaunt old jades, gorgeous dresses and a perpetual shortage of everything beginning with money and ending with glasses.'[32] Pushkin, who was officially a junior civil servant, devoted himself to literary talk, to drinking, gambling, and wenching. At the theatre he made loud remarks mocking the Tsar. Among his friends, he circulated poems extolling liberty, lampooning Alexander and attacking serfdom. Young nobles of the Decembrist generation read them avidly, and one claimed that 'there was scarcely a literate ensign in the army who did not know them by heart.'[33] In 1820 Alexander I packed him off to exile in the South of Russia, initially to the recently conquered territory of Bessarabia.

This wasn't a bad fate. Pushkin travelled to the snowy peaks of the Caucasus, bathed in the warm Black Sea, engaged in numerous sexual adventures with women of various races, read Lord Byron, and absorbed at first hand details which he used in the Byronic narrative poems he was now writing. In 1824 the authorities, annoyed by approval of atheism which he had expressed in a letter to a friend which they had opened, switched his exile to his family's estate at Mikhailovskoe, in west-central Russia. His father agreed to spy on him. There was a furious quarrel, and Pushkin was left alone with his sister's old nurse, who told him folk-tales in the dreary evenings and put him in touch with the popular imagination.

In December 1825, he nearly broke his exile to set off for Petersburg, then didn't, luckily for him. Dear friends as well as many acquaintances were among the Decembrists who were hung or exiled. He was summoned to Petersburg in September 1826. Nicholas I interviewed him personally.

Pushkin freely admitted that if he had been around in December, he would have stood with the rebels. Nicholas, deploying all his considerable charm, offered Pushkin his permission to reside in the capital. There was one condition; the Tsar himself would be his censor. The Tsar's censorship, however, was in fact exercised through Benckendorff, the head of the notorious Third Section.

Pushkin's new relationship with Nicholas dismayed or disgusted people who sympathized with the Decembrists. His cool nobility-style 'liberalism' put him quite out of touch with the rising generation of intellectuals in whom the universities were breeding an ardent German-influenced idealism. His marriage in 1830 to a society beauty who had no money put him still more at the Tsar's mercy. To his rage, the Tsar gave him the rank of Gentleman of the Bedchamber—which was usually reserved for mere striplings—so that his desirable wife could attend court balls. In return for substantial privileges—permission to conduct historical research in the state archives, as well as lavish loans from the Tsar which helped to meet the mounting debts incurred by his own gambling and by his wife's expensive tastes—Pushkin was made to appear a tool and a fool. He wrote, as he complained, under double censorship, that of the Tsar as well as the normal one. It is not too strong to say that frustration and disillusionment drove him to his death.

Pushkin, formerly an avid cuckolder himself, was, of course, jealous in respect of his luscious, empty-headed wife. A young Frenchman named D'Anthès flirted with her. Society gossiped. Pushkin forced D'Anthès to fight a duel with him. D'Anthès wounded him mortally. Pushkin died, with great courage, two days later, on 29 January 1837. Trapped in the inanities of Russian high society, from which the Tsar would never let him escape, as he wished, to travel in the free world of Europe, he had finally beaten himself to death against his cage. The Tsar, as he was dying, wrote to him, 'I forgive you,' and provided his widow with a pension; later he may have made her one of his many mistresses.

High society sided with D'Anthès. The press was forbidden to publish any but the barest notice of the poet's death; one editor, who went a bit further and also set the announcement in a black border, was asked by the authorities, why give this honour to a man who had not been an official? Nevertheless, crowds of men and women of all classes, even some in rags, came to pay homage as the poet lay in state. The church where his funeral was held proved too small, and one diplomat who did get in said to Karamzin's daughter Sofia. 'It was only here that we realized for the first time what Pushkin meant to Russia. . . . None of you ever told us that he was your national pride.'[34]

The fact that people had set such store by a mere writer worried the authorities. Afraid of demonstrations, the police smuggled the body away hugger-mugger, to be buried almost without witnesses near Mikhailovskoe. On the surface, Pushkin's was not an especially impressive personality.

He was so unreliable that the Decembrist conspirators dared not entrust him with their secrets. A cuckolded gambler of five foot three inches with a funny face was not going to dazzle Petersburg society, which neither knew nor cared about the hours of inspiration which he lived for. But the writer who, as he lay dying, turned towards his books and said 'goodbye, my friends', is now generally regarded as the greatest Russian of his day. He didn't exactly 'found' Russian literature, and he could not have achieved so much had not others, notably Karamzin, done a great deal before him. But he stands in relation to his country's literary history as Shakespeare does to England's or Goethe to Germany's; his work is the moment of full sunrise.

VIII

About two-thirds of the books he owned were foreign. He read mostly in French. This was inevitable Modern Russian literature had made an indecisive beginning only in the eighteenth century, when the figure of Lomonosov (1711–1765), son of a White Sea fisherman, mathematician, scientist and grammarian as well as poet, stood on the beach-head of a new culture. He was followed by uncertain writers who in Catherine's reign established neo-Classicism, on French lines, as a literary orthodoxy. Karamzin (1766–1826), friend and mentor of the young Pushkin, left behind him as literary monuments his early *Travels* and also the incomplete history of Russia to which he devoted more than twenty years of his life. The example of his style, in verse as well as prose, was important. Freely introducing words from French, he created a style in which men of his own class could work easily and precisely. There was an influential counter-tendency in favour of truly colloquial, earthy Russian, found in the verse fables of Krylov (1769–1844), which began to appear from 1809, and in the one major work of Griboedov (1795–1829), the famous comedy *Woe From Wit* (1825). Both men gave many proverbial sayings to Russia. They were associated with the reactionary Admiral Shishkov who founded, in 1811, a 'Concourse of Lovers of the Russian Verb'. Karamzin himself was by now an unashamed apologist for Tsarism and serfdom, but in the literary squabbles of the period Pushkin was on his side against Shishkov.

So was Vasili Zhukovsky (1783–1852) who, as tutor to Nicholas I's son and heir, was able to give Pushkin much help in his friction with the authorities. Zhukovsky produced few original poems, but his translations from English, German and Greek have independent status as Russian classics, and his smooth sweet style was an important example before the young Pushkin and others of his generation who created, in the 1820s, the 'Golden Age' of Russian poetry.

Pushkin's narrative poems of the 1820s were much admired, and were financially successful. In the 1830s, his popularity was waning. But even before this, he was dissatisfied with the literary situation in Russia. He longed for a critical journal to match the famous *Edinburgh Review*, but this would require more freedom of comment than the Tsar would permit, and several promising publications were stifled in the 1830s. Meanwhile, the *Northern Bee*, edited by Pushkin's arch-enemy Bulgarin, who was in the pay of the secret police, had official favour. Pushkin complained to Benckendorff that because it was allowed to publish political news, it had 3000 subscribers, but others, restricted to literature, couldn't get more than 300. When Pushkin was at last allowed, in 1836, to publish his own journal, *The Contemporary*, that mustered a mere 700.[35]

Readership was largely restricted to the nobility. It was reported that for the second edition of Karamzin's history, there were 406 subscribers; only five of these were clergy, 40 were merchants, and three peasants.[36] But the nobility still preferred foreign books. Pushkin made a lady narrator say in an unfinished story written in 1831:

> The fact is that we would be delighted to read Russian; but it seems that our litera-ture is no older than Lomonosov, and still extremely limited. It offers us, of course, several excellent poets, but one cannot ask of every reader an exclusive passion for verse. As for prose, we have only Karamzin's *History*; the first two or three novels appeared two or three years ago, while in France, England and Germany books follow one after the other, each more remarkable than the last . . . . We are forced to cull everything, news and ideas, from foreign books; and so we think in a foreign language (at least those do who do think and follow the thoughts of the human race).[37]

As the response to Pushkin's death would show, the flowering of Russian poetry had not passed unnoticed. But to liberate Russia from the need to 'follow the thoughts of the human race' in foreign tongues, several more steps were required. Pushkin attempted in his *Boris Godunov* (1825), based on a section of Karamzin's *History*, to write a truly national drama which would help to oust imitations of French classicism from the stage. The Tsar wouldn't let him publish it; Bulgarin, who on this ocsasion did the censor's job for him, suggested it would go better as a historical novel like one of Walter Scott's.

Pushkin in other works helped to meet the need for Russian fiction. He used foreign models, as he had to do. It was part of his greatness that, for all his occasional chauvinist outbursts, he was never a narrow national-ist. He reacted against French literature only after learning a great deal from it. He turned instead to English literature, declaring that he preferred it to the 'timid and over-refined' influence from France, and was deeply influenced by Shakespeare, Scott and Byron. He knew the work of Goethe, his great German contemporary, just as he knew the music of Mozart, so often compared to him as an example of apparently effortless genius.

But he went beyond imitation. John Bayley suggests that he is 'unique among great writers . . . in his attitude to literary forms. All his works are an examination—often amounting to an inspired parody—of one or another of them.'[38] Without his interest in technique, and mastery of it, he couldn't have given Russian fiction its first masterpieces.

IX

In his narrative poem *Gypsies* (1824), Pushkin used a Byronic story so as to create the first of the many important 'superfluous men' of Russian fiction.

Spotting 'superfluous men' in the work of Pushkin's successors is only a little less boring and unproductive than discussions of 'the nature of Russian realism'. To suggest as some have done that Gogol's marvellously self-satisfied Chichikov has something of importance in common with Chekhov's nervous little 'heroes' because they are all 'superfluous men' is to broaden the term so as to make it worthless. But since this 'type' is so often referred to, and since it does suggestively indicate a link between the nature of much Russian fiction and the reality of life in Tsarist Russia, it is worth examining it at its point of origin.

The secular cult of Napoleon had infected the youth of Europe with egotistic ambition. Byron's heroes, and also the heroes of certain French novels, had propagated the notion that a man of deep intelligence or true genius must be unhappy in society. In Russia the idea was easily received. The official attitude to bright young men was exemplified by Benckendorff's reply to Pushkin, when rejecting proposals which the latter had sent him, at the Tsar's request, for reforming the education system:

> His Majesty was so good as to observe that the rule you seem to accept, namely that enlightenment and genius are the only prerequisites for perfection, is a dangerous rule which has dragged you to the very brink of the abyss and has led to the undoing of a large number of young men. Morality, loyal service and industry must be preferred to enlightenment that is inexperienced, immoral and useless.[39]

The best qualities of mind and spirit were 'superfluous'. The Decembrists, for all their intelligence and goodwill were, as the Tsar had proved by getting rid of them, 'superfluous'.

The title of Griboedov's important play from the 1820s is variously translated as *Woe from Wit, The Misfortune of Being Intelligent, Wit Works Woe, The Trouble with Reason*, etc. etc. In every case however the main point is clear. The play is about the alienation of its clever hero Chatsky from the stupid people he meets in Moscow society; they include a high civil servant, Famusov, who says that the only way to stop the young from getting silly ideas is to burn all books and his sycophantic secretary Molchalin who admits to two talents only—being quite correct and knowing his place. Chatsky, a young man who has quit the service and travelled abroad, argues with such people, and the rumour goes round that he is off his head. Utterly disgusted, he leaves Moscow for the country.

Pushkin was a penetrating literary critic, and one of his comments was that the really clever man was Griboedov himself, not Chatsky. Chatsky is a fool, for talking cleverly to fools and passing on to them his friend Griboedov's clever ideas.[40] The rather complicated points which arise seem important to grasp if one is to understand *Onegin*. The superfluous man cannot be truly heroic. All he can do is rant, pose or take out his alienation on other people by nasty behaviour. He is a 'hero' only by default—unlike others, he has qualities which could redeem society, but since he can't use them they are something worse than useless. Lilies that fester smell far worse than weeds. The real hero is the writer. He does something. He writes. That is action.

Gypsies was published before Griboedov's play, which was banned by the censors, and began to circulate in manuscript. In previous poems Pushkin, excited by Byron, had experimented with 'Byronic' heroes. But his mind and sympathies were too capacious to accept the stereotype. Aleko, in *Gypsies*, is conventionally Byronic in so far as he has a 'secret cause of sorrow' and is the prey of tumultuous passions which drive him restlessly on, a wandering exile. He is a nobleman who has thrown up high society. He loves, and is loved by, a gipsy girl named Zemfira. For two years he is happy as a wandering gypsy. The fully Byronic hero would betray such an artless girl. Instead, demonstrating the sheer *incapacity* which is one hallmark of the superfluous man, Aleko waits till he himself is discarded. Simply and spontaneously, Zemfira falls in love with someone else. Aleko murders both her and her lover, showing himself unfit for the natural, 'peaceful' life of the gypsies.

The ironies in *Eugene Onegin* are more complex. It is one of the most moving love stories ever written, but anyone who dared discuss it as if it were essentially a 'romance' between an artificial young man and an artless, 'natural' country girl would expose a naive ambition to reduce major fiction to the level of a novelette.

This novel-in-verse, published in separate chapters from 1825 to 1832, took Pushkin over eight years to write. Its form, like that of Byron's *Don Juan*, is leisurely; digressions on the theatre, on girls' pretty feet, on Pushkin's own life and art, and so on, are as much a part of it as the simple story which Pushkin tells. But unlike *Don Juan*, the finished product is graceful. As Vladimir Nabokov says, 'Its eight chapters form an elegant colonnade.'[41] The ending is inconclusive, yet seems appropriately final— in this Pushkin anticipates later masters of Russian fiction. Gogol never completed *Dead Souls*; Dostoevsky saw *The Brothers Karamazov* as only the first part of a mightier novel; Tolstoy left the characters in *War and Peace* suspended long before the point where he had once intended to begin. Yet all these books seem 'finished'. The artistry which leaves the future open, as it always is in life, may satisfy us more than that which neatly marries or kills off the leading characters and cries halt.

Onegin himself is a bored young Petersburg beau who cannot settle down to writing or study or any useful course of action. On the death of his uncle, he inherits an estate in the country. Living there, he makes the acquaintance of Lensky, a youthful poet in the German Romantic fashion. Lensky is in love with Olga, the daughter of a 'simple' country squire, now dead. ('Simple' though they are, the Larins must be assumed to own several hundred serfs.) Through this connection, Eugene meets Olga's sister Tatiana, a bookish girl, who falls in love with him and touchingly confesses her love in a letter to him. Eugene doesn't take the chance of seducing her; instead, nobly, as it might seem, he explains to her that his nature is such that he can never make a good husband in a happy marriage. Later, at a party at the Larins, he flirts with Olga. Lensky picks a quarrel. The friends fight a duel and Onegin kills Lensky. He leaves the neighbourhood and travels widely in Russia. Olga quickly marries an officer. Tatiana, taken to Moscow by her mother, finds a distinguished suitor. Returning to Petersburg, Eugene sees her at a ball, and is dazzled—the country maiden has become a perfect society lady. He now falls for her, and he in his turn writes her a pathetic letter. She doesn't reply. Finally, he bursts into her home. She explains that she still loves him, but must remain faithful to her husband. The story ends there with the clink of her husband's spurs heard outside the door.

This archetypally simple love story, as Pushkin handles it, includes a mocking commentary upon itself. Eugene, Tatiana and Lensky are all people influenced greatly by what they have read. One of the main themes of *Onegin*, perhaps the most important of all, is the damage which books can do to people. It combines obvious 'Romantic' features with dry, much-amused anti-romanticism. It explores the two-way relationship between fiction and reality.

Who, for instance, is Onegin? As Nabokov points out, his physical aspect—that of a dandy after the English fashion—is perfectly clear, but his inner life is obscure. To Tatiana, soaked in French and English novels, he looks like the hero of such a novel. But when, after his slaughter of Lensky, she makes her way into his deserted house and examines his study, with its bust of Napoleon, with its works of Byron, with its fashionable

> novels in which the epoch is reflected
> and modern man
> rather correctly represented
> with his immoral soul,
> selfish and dry,
> to dreaming measurelessly given,
> with his embittered mind
> boiling in empty action.

—she asks herself, being truly intelligent, 'Can it be, he's an imitation . . . a glossary of alien vagaries, a complete lexicon of words in vogue?—Might he not be, in fact, a parody?'[42]

In the country, Onegin is an outsider, a puzzle to his neighbours—but in Petersburg, surely he is a conformist, just another young man aping foreign fashions. His gifts are nothing beside those of Pushkin, who, as his friend, is in effect a character in the novel. Even the mediocre Lensky is creative by comparison. The only capacity Onegin shows in the novel is a gift for flirtation. Once he decides to captivate Olga, it costs him no effort to make her simper—but then, she is a flighty girl anyway. When he goads Lensky, he has no better motive than rage at the boring party which his friend has brought him to. And he kills out of sheer blundering impulse, as if he had lost the control over himself which a man of the world should possess. He turns up late for the duel, without a proper second. As the allegedly offending party, he should coolly receive Lensky's fire, then, if alive, discharge his pistol in the air; instead, he shoots first and shoots to kill.

Yet Lensky 'really' dies, and it hurts Onegin to remember it. Pushkin toys with his 'hero', jacking him up a little towards heroism, letting him down with a bump, then jacking him up again—but he never aims to make us hate him, nor do we hate him. Perhaps the essential point is that (like Chatsky) he isn't clever enough; he is a victim of the fashions of his day because he lets himself be a victim. By contrast with the true Byronic hero, in whom Pushkin, in one of his digressions, sees a 'hopeless egotism', Onegin still seems decent, unwilling to act badly, though he does act badly.

Lensky, unlike Eugene, has a capacity for happiness, but he too is at heart a conformist—made for marriage, Pushkin suggests. Fatuously, this young idealist falls 'Romantically' in love with the very girl whose father had agreed with his that they should marry.

Tatiana is the most fully 'developed' of these characters, as we usually apply the word to people in novels; that is, she seems to be the person we know most intimately. She likes to think of herself, later, when she gets to Moscow, as having been an artless country lass, but she is in fact a noblewoman, who can't write letters in the Russian language, though she is superstitious enough to accept much peasant folklore. In spite, one might say, of her own efforts to turn herself into a stereotype, into the heroine of a novel, she is too complex to be merely a 'type'. She is the finest product of Pushkin's irony, and the crowning irony is that her destiny is to be a society beauty, a heroine of the boring and trivial 'real world'. When Onegin meets her again, it is her now who seems to him a 'faithful reproduction' of the very type of ballroom queen, though we know by now that she is more than that. Is it this apparent stereotype that Eugene, the conformist, now falls for? She accuses him of wanting her now because she will be a credit to his powers of seduction—and we ask ourselves whether she isn't right. But then, when she says at the end that she still loves Onegin, we asks ourselves further, what is it that she loves? Is it still, perhaps, the impossible hero of her girlish dreams? Is it really her own youth that she has lost, and loves?

At bottom the answer is probably yes. What, asks Pushkin, for humans, is paradise without forbidden fruit? Isn't it precisely because Tatiana is now inaccessible that Eugene loves her? Pushkin applies this ironic insight to himself, in the first chapter, when he longs to travel:

> and sigh, 'mid the meridian swell, beneath the
> sky of my Africa,
> for sombre Russia, where
> I suffered, where I loved,
> where I buried my heart.[43]

To want to be a long way away so that one can yearn to be at home is typically 'Romantic' but illustrates absurd realities of human nature. To try to have it both ways (be both 'African' and 'Russian') is also common enough. But Pushkin, who is the true hero of the story, understands, accepts, masters and laughs at traits in himself which his characters succumb to. And Tatiana is a true heroine because she is prepared at the end to go on with a marriage which won't satisfy longings which could never be satisfied.

Pushkin makes play with parodies of other poets who had written in various languages and, as we have seen, juggles with stereotypes of the Romantic period. But the fiction he thus produces grounds itself firmly in reality.

In Chapter Seven, over 'real' bad roads, the Larins jolt to Moscow. Their cousin Aline greets them. She is so overjoyed that, like any ordinary person for whom great emotion is something normally found only in fiction, this consumptive old lady says, 'I'd swear the scene is from a novel.' Then she breaks out coughing and cries. The coughing and the tears are 'real'. Life can be like a novel, like this novel.

X

Scott, from 1814 onwards, had given the novel a historical dimension and had therefore given it, in the modern sense, a social dimension. (We see society as a product of its own growth, and cannot make sense of its conflicts except in 'historical' terms.) Pushkin's understanding, in *Onegin*, of the interaction within Tatiana between 'modern' literature and ancient superstition exhibits already the new grasp of history which the Romantic period was achieving. Pushkin began as an artist in prose with a shot at the historical novel. *The Negro of Peter the Great* (1827) was based on the life of his own great grandfather, Abram Gannibal. What he wrote of it isn't very good; Abram himself is almost wholly unconvincing and Peter is more like one of Scott's genial eccentric lairds than the cruel creator of Petersburg could have been. Otherwise, all the numerous fragments of unfinished fiction which Pushkin produced have some of the charm of major art. The essence of his mastery in prose was his ability to bring a world to life in a few swift strokes. It was the brisk opening of one of his fragments which gave Tolstoy the inspiration to plunge straight into *Anna Karenina*.

But the *Tales of Ivan Belkin* form a set of five brief masterpieces, thoroughly finished. Appearing in 1830, they made an apt start to the decade in which prose would take over from poetry as the dominant medium of Russian literature.

Pushkin had theories about prose long before he tried to use it in fiction. 'Precision and brevity—these are the two virtues of prose,' he wrote in 1822. 'It demands matter and more matter—without it brilliant expressions serve no purpose. In this it differs from poetry.'[44] His style, accordingly, was curt, concise and unadorned. Its merit—borne out by all critics and translators—is that it packs in enough 'matter' to be vivid, without a hint of rhetoric.

However, the tales of Belkin achieve some of the intricacy of *Onegin*. Pushkin borrows a device from Scott—he himself claims to be not their author but their editor, and pretends that they were written by a young landlord, recently dead. 'Belkin' himself, however, takes his stories from other people, and it is the point of view of a *third* party through which we see the events.

The Shot is 'told' by a military man, and to complicate matters still further he hears the end of the story from a *fourth* party, a great nobleman. What, it may well be asked, does all this achieve? In this particular case, a great deal. *The Shot* hinges on the furious sense of social inferiority felt by the main character, Silvio, a retired army officer of moderate means, towards the 'fourth party', this dazzling nobleman, to whom all graces and good fortune seem to come naturally. The fact that the 'third party' narrator is also uneasy when he meets the great man, and that we hear how Silvio took his revenge from the latter, deepens our sense of the social relationships underlying the tale. Pushkin anticipates the subtle combination of varying viewpoints by Lermontov and Tolstoy.

Two farcical anti-romantic love stories, and a neat ghost story, reveal Pushkin's range, but *The Postmaster* is best of all. (It seems to have made a particularly strong impression on Dostoevsky.) A stuffy civil servant is the 'third party' narrator. At a certain post house he gets to know the master, a man with a delightful daughter. From the old man's own lips ('fourth party' again) the civil servant hears how this girl was stolen from her father by a gay young city nobleman, how he found her with her lover in Petersburg, and how the latter promised to be faithful to her and thrust the old man out with a gift of money. Against the odds, sentimentality is avoided throughout the tale; at this point, the old man spurns the notes, but then thinks better of it, retraces his steps, and finds that a well-dressed young man has made off with them. From other witnesses, long after, the narrator learns how the old man took to drink and died and how his daughter came to weep over his grave. She came in a coach-and-six and had three children with her; we infer that her lover had not deserted her. The story is not depressing at all, because its theme, strangely, turns out to be the good nature of the postmaster, of his daughter, and of her lover— which impresses in turn the narrator and softens him. The world of Belkin, in fact, is one without villains. Feuding neighbours are reconciled. Deaths, including Belkin's own, are palliated by the affection of the survivors. Belkin himself, frank, warm-hearted, naive, and not very clever, is Pushkin's tribute to the rural nobility.

Even Pushkin's famous ghost story, *The Queen of Spades* (1834), is too playful and self-amused to be really alarming, though it creates a remarkable atmosphere, both intensely real and extremely macabre. Hermann, a German of mediocre background, hears from a rich acquaintance that the latter's grandmother has the secret of certain success at cards. To find it out, this methodical young man callously makes advances to the old lady's poor, bullied young companion, Liza, who duly falls for him. With her help, he gets admission late at night to the Countess's rooms. After pleas fail, he threatens the old woman with a pistol. She dies of shock. At her funeral, however, the corpse seems to wink at him. In a dream or vision, she tells him her secret. Hermann plays and wins, plays again, and wins. Poised on the brink of unthinkable wealth, he forgets himself and plays the wrong card, the Queen of Spades, which seems to wink at him. Hermann goes mad.

The force of the story lies in the contrast between Hermann, obscure thruster of the new age of Napoleonic greed (he is a prototype, in fact, for Raskolnikov) and the ancient Countess who lives with her memories of Catherine's day, when she was a famous beauty. Pushkin combines his secure grasp of social relationships with a fable not far in spirit from a folk-tale, and colours the result with cryptic but suggestive prose symbolism. When Hermann enters the wicked old lady's apartment every detail tells—the ancient icons, the old fashioned armchair, the tassels on the cushions which have lost their gilt, and amidst them a portrait of the Countess in her dazzling youth with 'a rose in the powdered hair drawn back over her temples.' Brittle and falsely coloured as the playing card with which she is linked, she seems to personify the shallow brilliance of Catherine's court, a culture now in its final decay. Catherine, we remember, took lovers in her sixties, and Hermann, in his quest for wealth, might be prepared to make love to this Countess. This gives appalling suggestiveness to the scene where, hidden, he watches her undress. 'Pins showered about her. The silver-trimmed yellow dress fell at her puffy feet. Hermann witnessed the hideous mysteries of her toilet.' The puffy feet are enough to evoke the whole aged body. Our imaginations are deftly prodded to supply not only the absent details of this scene, but also those of others which Pushkin does not describe, but which must be present in Hermann's imagination; the many moments when others have embraced that body.

Pushkin's usual charity is absent from *The Queen of Spades*. The story is as cold as ice, or emeralds. By contrast, *The Captain's Daughter*

(1836) is full of warmth and light and air. It is easy to read, easy to love, hard to forget, and much more profound than it seems at first sight. The short crisp sentences suit its narrator, Grinev, a more active Belkin from the recent past. As a very young man, he is caught up in Pugachev's rebellion of 1773. Like Scott's *Waverley*, the novel is set 'sixty years since', in time of civil war, and like young Waverley, Grinev, though essentially straightforward, is forced into a position where he has to take both sides.

He is a middling nobleman brought up in a household full of love, and his faithful manservant Savelich is there at his side to remind him of it wherever he goes. His father, an old soldier, sends him into the army with clear injunctions: 'Obey your superiors; do not try to curry favour with them; do not put yourself forward, but never shirk a duty, and remember the maxim: "Look after your clothes when they are new and your honour from your youth up." '[45] The fortress to which he goes on the Eastern frontier is commanded by another honest, endearing old man, Captain Ivan Kuzmich Mironov. The Captain's wife is a second mother to the boy, and though they are poor, Grinev falls in love with their daughter, Masha.

On his way to the frontier, Grinev was lost in a blizzard. A peasant Cossack appeared and led him to safety, a calm, resourceful man with sparkling eyes never still. In the sledge, driving to the safety of a Cossack hut, Grinev dreamt that he was going home. He found his father dying:

> I knelt down and fixed my eyes on the sick man. But what's this?... Instead of my father, a peasant with a black beard is lying on the bed, looking at me merrily. I turn to my mother in perplexity, and say: 'What does it mean? This is not my father. And why must I ask this peasant's blessing?' 'Never mind, Petrusha', replied my mother. 'He is taking your father's place for the wedding; kiss his hand and let him give you his blessing....' I refused. Whereupon the peasant jumped out of the bed, seized an axe from behind his back and began flourishing it about. I wanted to run away—and could not. The room was full of dead bodies; I kept stumbling against them, and my feet slipped in the pools of blood—The dreadful peasant called to me in a kindly voice: 'Don't be afraid', he cried. 'Come and let me bless you—' Horror and bewilderment possessed me—And at that moment I awoke.[46]

The dream illustrates Pushkin's mastery of the unstated motive and the ungiven explanation. He does not tell us that the boy dreams like this because he has had a day beginning with his first hangover and ending with the danger of death in the snow; he leaves us to grasp that for ourselves and, further, to infer that the nightmare stems from the novel sense of insecurity felt by a loved and loving son and that this pattern, love set against violence, is basic to the novel. The use of a dream to make at the same time complex psychological points and thematic points was a device often exploited by Pushkin's successors in Russia. While not unknown in fiction from other countries, it has an especially important place in Russian fiction. Pushkin could adopt it here, as Tolstoy would later in *Anna Karenina*, to express an idea which the censors wouldn't have liked if it had been stated directly. The guide who saves Grinev is Pugachev himself, not yet a rebel leader. The peasant in the dream seems to spring from this masterful guide who has undertaken the role of protection hitherto filled by Grinev's father. There are, or, should be, equalising bonds of gratitude and respect and love between nobleman and peasant which no man of Grinev's class can easily acknowledge. Bloodshed ensues.

Pushkin, speaking around Grinev rather than through him, is able to imply that the rebel who proclaimed himself Tsar ('father' of the Russian people) was as fully a part of the human family as the Tsarist forces. Grinev's mother accepts the impostor-father. It is somehow Grinev's fault (the fault of his class) that the peasant causes such carnage. Grinev is brave, generous and candid. But he is not as clever as Pushkin; he cannot fully expound the secret sympathy he feels for Pugachev, or the guilt he feels towards the peasants.

Grinev, next morning, rewards his guide. He doesn't see him again till the rebels have captured the fort, have hung Ivan Kuzmich, and have murdered his wife:

> 'Silence the old witch!' said Pugachev. A young Cossack hit her on the head with his sword and she fell dead on the steps. Pugachev rode away. The crowd rushed after him.[47]

Never is Pushkin's curtness more terrible, and we are not allowed to forget that loyal corpse. But Pugachev, for old time's sake, spares Grinev, and later helps him to rescue Masha from an unscrupulous rival who has joined the rebels. Pugachev is a very cruel man, but his yearning for freedom is movingly presented. And the facts as Pushkin tells them speak for themselves. The rebels are able to take over even the fort commanded by the lovable Ivan Kuzmich because people there accept them without a struggle. ('The crowd rushed after him.') They are able to defeat regular forces over a long period. Such a revolt can only have had a basis in powerful popular feeling.

There is every reason to suppose that Pushkin agreed with Grinev's view—'remember that the best and most enduring of transformations are those which proceed from an improvement in morals and customs, and not from any violent upheaval.'[48] He didn't have the temperament of a radical polemicist and a phrase like 'compassionate yet detached objectivity' would be needed to describe his 'position' as a writer. Even then, we would still have somehow to add the word 'ironical.'

One might well find such a 'position' unappealing, and young radical critics remained cool towards Pushkin for years after his death. One not only might, but must, criticize the end of The Captain's Daughter. Grinev has been imprisoned and condemned to exile for having been involved with Pugachev. Masha goes to Petersburg and pleads his case with Catherine herself. Masha is not a strongly drawn character, and the idea of her journey is plagiarized from Scott's Heart of Midlothian. Catherine's generous pardon seems to be there merely to balance the generosity shown towards Grinev by Pugachev. It is a great disappointment. But the novel's warm characterization and cryptic insights help us to forgive Pushkin for making, for once, the mistake of ending a tale too cosily. Through Grinev's parents, and through the captain and his wife, Pushkin reveals fine human qualities on the 'loyal' side; but Pugachev, with his fits of idealism, with his humour, with his moving fatalism, is also a very positive human being.

Pushkin is to the tip of his pen an aristocratic writer, at least in his prose fiction. He does not flatter high rank, because he has it himself; he does not patronize the poor, because that would be beneath him. His people, whether noble or not, are all, with the exception perhaps of Tatiana, conceived as being far more limited in scope and intelligence than the writer himself. His modest, if kindly estimate of human nature would seem wholly 'realistic' (in one sense) if we didn't get a much more exciting picture of it from other great 'Russian realists'. His most impressive creation is his own literary personality, which can convince us at the same time that he has a perfect knowledge of life and a perfect skill in presenting it.

He isn't, on face of it, very close spiritual kin to the turbulent people who wrote Russian fiction after him. Yet the force of his influence is beyond question—not only on Tolstoy, whose artistic restraint would match Pushkin's own, but on Dostoevsky, a verbose and extremist writer as different from his acknowledged master as one could imagine. Perhaps the real source of his authority was that he was the first man to create masterly fiction in Russian, but that he left ample scope for his successors, as well as innumerable hints for them to work on. Turgenev could compose his many variations on *Onegin* while Dostoevsky, with more vehemence, expanded and made much louder themes from *The Postmaster*, and neither would get much in the other's way.

FREEDOM

I don't think that 'freedom' is a salient theme in nineteenth-century British fiction. Though Emily Brontë's windy moors offer absence of restraint, though Dickens's prisons may seem to be symbols of social repression in general and though George Eliot's moralism implies a belief in free will, the abstract concept need never be used in discussing their work or that of their contemporaries. With the great Russians we can't really avoid it. Underlying this contrast, of course, is the contrast between two very different societies.

The British, after their seventeenth-century revolutions, had come to take 'freedom' for granted as the birthright of all islanders. Serfdom (except in Scottish coalmines) had died out by the seventeenth century. No 'Briton' could think of himself as a 'slave', as the National Anthem proudly points out. There is no need to explain how different things were in Russia, even after the serfs were emancipated.

The word 'freedom' covers concepts which must be distinguished philosophically yet must overlap psychologically. The 'autonomy' of the will, to use Kant's term, if we regard it as a basic attribute of all human beings, must theoretically be enjoyed by a female slave locked up in a cupboard; in that sense she is still and always 'free'. Women might be 'emancipated' enough to follow 'freely' all professions and customs but a determinist would still have to insist that their wills were not autonomous. Political 'liberty' may seem to have nothing much to do with the 'independence' of a man who holds his own land or is 'free' to wander on to virgin ground and to stake his claim, until we remember the way the American frontier brought 'liberty' and 'independence' together.

A man who respects himself as 'autonomous' will of course tend to chafe against political tyranny and may well seek a place where he may have 'independent' control of his own life. If we attribute to slaves and women the same 'autonomy' of will as ourselves, this suggests that they should have equal chance to express it.

For Gogol, 'independence', the Cossack goal, is the greatest good; neither 'autonomy' nor 'liberty' interests him at all. To Turgenev, 'liberty' and 'emancipation' are the beckoning lights. For Dostoevsky 'autonomy' is the prime concern, but he is acutely conscious of the insult to free-willed man offered by law courts, prisons and capital punishment and thus tends to yoke 'liberty' with 'autonomy'. Without a belief in 'autonomy', Tolstoy's appeals to men to perfect themselves would be meaningless, but though he denounces despotism so fiercely, Tolstoy values 'emancipation' little. He tends at times towards arguments like those used by early Christians to condone the existence of slavery; he implies that a 'freed' peasant or a 'liberated' woman may still be the 'slave' of evil passions. However, he is greatly attracted by the 'independence' of the wandering pilgrim, tramp or hermit. To judge from Chekhov's account of the 'savage' who lives on the open steppe in his story of that name, he would see 'independence' as a likely recipe for barbarism. 'Emancipation' of people from stupid and shackling customs would seem to be his main interest.

Since the comparison of Russia and America is a time-hallowed critical ploy, I hope I'll be forgiven for wondering how each great Russian would have reacted to the typical situations of Hollywood Westerns. Gogol, of course, would have favoured the lone saddle-tramp. Turgenev would go for the girl who rides and shoots like a man, but spare a tear for the Southern dude who breaks down in a crisis. Dostoevsky would feel most at home with the rebel outlaw, the Jesse James of myth, enemy of oppression who turns brigand but cannot escape the law. Tolstoy's hero would be the sensitive cavalry officer whose conscience revolts at last against massacring Indians. Chekhov would save his sympathies for the doctor, teacher or lawyer who tries to avoid gunplay and gets on with the task of creating civilization. But all of them (in relation to Tsarist Russia) are intellectual and moral frontiersmen who insist upon 'freedom' of one kind or another.

2
LITERATURE AND SERFDOM
Gogol, Lermontov and Goncharov

Obviously, the bleak reign of Nicholas I must produce its own sterile literature of patriotic bombast and officially approved sentiment. The world outside Russia has never known anything about it. What it does know of and respect is the challenge to empty rhetoric which came from a few brilliant men. Turgenev, in a lecture given after the death of Nicholas had seemed to ease Russia of an intolerable muddy burden of despotic mediocrity, exulted over the moment when the official Goliath had been confronted by three unlikely Davids: by a society dandy serving in the hussars, by 'an obscure Ukrainian teacher with his terrifying comedy' and by a 'similarly obscure student, who had not finished his course at the university, but who had the audacity to declare that we had not yet had a literature.'[1]

The 'obscure student' was Vissarion Belinsky, born in 1811, the son of a poor army doctor, who, in 1829 entered the University of Moscow, from which he was dismissed before he took a degree. Alexander Herzen (1812–1870), one of his contemporaries there, points to the paradox that until 1848 the Russian universities were free from the exclusiveness and snobbery of educational institutions in England (though of course serfs weren't admitted). 'Young men of all sorts and conditions coming from above and below, from the south and from the north, were quickly fused into a compact mass of comrades.'[2] And in the atmosphere of Moscow, relatively always less stifling than that of Petersburg, students and graduates came together in 'circles' which ardently discussed new ideas. The 'circle' in which Belinsky moved, dominated by a gently idealistic nobleman named Stankevich, for the moment interpreted the German philosophy which it doted on in a quietist and even a conservative sense. But another 'circle', led by one Sungurov, was broken up by the authorities in 1834 and its members sent to serve as common soldiers in the army. Herzen, whose own group was influenced by French Socialist ideas, was exiled to the Eastern borderlands in 1835.

Sir Isaiah Berlin has claimed that 'scarcely one single political and social idea to be found in Russia in the nineteenth century was born on native soil.'[3] The dialectical philosophy of Hegel gave the young idealists of the thirties and forties what Herzen called 'the algebra of revolution', and the schemes of the French Utopian Socialists, St Simon, Fourier, Cabet were available to provide their radicalism with projects and a name. Ideas imported from abroad were taken to drastic conclusions by thinkers whose very isolation in a country where intellectual debate was almost nonexistent made them all the more passionately attached to theory and bound them together, in spite of their quarrels, into a disputatious brotherhood. (Though the emancipation of women was on Herzen's agenda, there weren't any prominent sisters yet.) Pavel Annenkov, one of the brothers, wrote that in the days of the circles 'Any sign of a morally doubtful sentiment, evasive talk, dishonest ambiguity, empty rhetoric, insincerity, was detected at once, and provoked immediate storms of ironical mockery and merciless attack.'[4]

Like Herzen, who helped to convert him to 'Socialism', Belinsky emerged as a 'Westerner' in the intellectual wars which followed the publication of Chaadaev's famous *Philosophical Letter* of 1836. Chaadaev argued that Russia had no civilization of its own—'We have given nothing to the world, we have learnt nothing from the world . . . we have contributed nothing to the progress of the human spirit . . .'[5] The circles divided over the question of whether Russia should now seek to form itself in accordance with modern 'Western' ideas (of liberalism or of socialism) or should revert to its own past traditions. The 'Slavophiles', who extolled the Russian customs which Peter the Great had sought to abolish, and acclaimed the Orthodox Church, were hardly more congenial to Nicholas and his regime than the Westerners, and they too had trouble with the censors. They tended towards a kind of 'Conservative anarchism' standing by 'the primacy of the moral and religious law, of ancestral tradition, and of the spontaneous sense of the right and just over the written laws and regulations of the State',[6] and many of their beliefs would ultimately find expression in the works of Fedor Dostoevsky. For the moment, however, there was no Slavophile writer to match Belinsky or Herzen. The latter, a brilliant talker and the author of memoirs, *My Past and Thoughts*, whose candour and vivacity place them among the literary classics, left Russia for good in 1847 and became in exile a major figure in European Socialism. Generous in his loves and unswerving in his contempt for tyrants great and small, he is perhaps the most attractive of all revolutionaries—only a very remarkable man could have earned the respect both of Dostoevsky and of

Tolstoy. Neither he nor Belinsky (who knew no German) had had much notion of what Western Europe was like, and what Herzen saw abroad convinced him ultimately that the bourgeois West was revoltingly decadent and that the Russian peasant commune provided a basis on which his own fatherland could move straight from backwardness to Socialism. It is not very easy, as this shows, to pigeonhole Russian writers as 'Westerners' or 'Slavophiles'—the 1830s and 1840s established a kaleidoscope of ideas which could combine in many different patterns. But one real and striking difference between the two camps was that the Westerners were atheist, or at their vaguest, deist.

For the emerging Russian 'intelligentsia', the fervour which could not be released through the church would express itself through writing and, ultimately, through political action. Sir John Maynard writes, '. . . The influence of religious tradition and habit upon their whole moral and mental make-up is unmistakeable. There is the sick conscience, the sense of sin and the passion for expiation, the moral austerity, the readiness for martyrdom—all surviving the belief in God and the hope of immortality.'[7]

Belinsky, shy, clumsy, overworked and consumptive can be called, without absurdity, a 'saint' of literature. 'Our lot puts the cowl on us,' he wrote. 'We must suffer, that life may be easier for our grandchildren.'[8] Herzen describes how fury could seize him in argument till 'The dispute would often end in blood, which flowed from the sick man's throat . . .', and Turgenev relates that intellectual doubts deprived him even of appetite: ' "We haven't yet decided the question of the existence of God," he said to me once with bitter reproach, "and you want to eat." '[9]

Belinsky achieved enormous authority as a literary critic in various journals. Poetry and fiction were a relatively innocent-looking subject for discussion, and the way Belinsky used literary journalism as a vehicle for radical ideas which could not have got past the censors in a more straightforward form made him as much a founder of Russian socialism as of Russian criticism. He simultaneously gave literature a central place in political debate and impressed writers with the idea that fiction must serve the cause of political advance.

He did an important job in demolishing both 'pseudo-classicism' and 'romanticism' and advancing instead the claims of 'realism'. He proclaimed the greatness of Lermontov and Gogol and recognized the early promise of Dostoevsky, Turgenev and Goncharov—while these judgements now seem inevitable, major writers were not then so easy to pick out from the minor mediocrities. In his articles on *Dead Souls* in 1842, he argued that Gogol was the first writer to have looked boldly at Russian reality and that he was more significant than Pushkin because his work was more 'social' and more in tune with the spirit of the times. Next year he went further, to press the dubious argument that Pushkin was out of date, and if *Onegin* did *not* yet seem obsolete, this would only show that the world it described was imaginary. How could it be worthwhile to discuss such a poem? But unlike some of his followers, he didn't suppose that sound ideas about topical matters were sufficient in themselves to create important literature. 'With whatever beautiful ideas a poem is filled,' he wrote, 'and however much it deals with contemporary problems, if it has no poetry in it, it can contain neither beautiful ideas nor any problems.'[10]

Belinsky's consumption killed him in 1848 (saving him from almost certain imprisonment or exile). But his reputation and influence survived. From him stemmed an important school of critics, like himself men of relatively humble birth. Both Dostoevsky, whose first novel he praised, and Turgenev, whose dearest friend he became, would in effect carry on arguing with him for the rest of their lives. As Maynard points out, his declaration that if he could climb to the highest rung of self perfection he would call upon Hegel to answer him for all the victims of life and history —otherwise he'd throw himself off the ladder—anticipates the quarrel between Ivan Karamazov and God.[11] His moral passion was perhaps both the key to his influence and his greatest legacy.

II

The dandy serving in the hussars was Mikhail Lermontov, who managed in his brief and unhappy existence to earn himself a place as Pushkin's successor among Russian poets and to write one great novel, *A Hero of Our Time*.

Lermontov's mother came from a famous and wealthy family which opposed her marriage to an impecunious ex-officer. The child born in Moscow in 1814 became after his mother's death three years later the victim of a struggle for custody between his father and maternal grandmother. The grandmother won, which meant that the boy got the best education money could buy, but was condemned from the outset to restless unhappiness. A childhood illness left him stoop-shouldered and somewhat bow-legged and sensitivity about his appearance also helped to make him a natural outsider. From the age of fourteen, he poured out poems. An English tutor taught him to read Byron in the original, and while it was common at that time for young writers to fall under Byron's spell, Lermontov was unusually well placed to sympathize with his hero's own unhappy childhood. He went to Moscow University, but held aloof from his fellow students and left prematurely to join the Guards. He then discovered that his Moscow connections were not enough to give him entry into the higher circles of Petersburg society and strove to attract attention by cynical philandering and practical jokes. It was Pushkin's death in 1837 which brought him notoriety, and recognition as a poet.

Lermontov wrote an elegy for his idol to which he added a bitter supplement blaming as the murderers those 'standing in a greedy crowd around the throne, hangmen of Freedom, Genius and Fame.'[12] This outburst circulated round the capital, and Lermontov was thrown into jail. He was ordered South to serve in the Caucasus; the territory of his most famous poems and also of *A Hero of Our Time*.

The situation there recalls both the North-West Frontier of Kipling's India and the 'Wild West' wars of the US Cavalry. The Caucasus mountains and the 'Transcaucasian' area beyond it sustained an intricate patchwork of peoples, both Christian and Muslim. Russian interests conflicted there with those of Turkey and Persia, and committed successive Tsars in the nineteenth century to a struggle against the Muslim peoples of Circassia and Daghestan. The savage methods of the legendary General Yermolov, appointed to command in 1816, roused the resentment of the Avar and Chechen mountaineers, and from the 1830s Russia had to contend with a powerful movement combining hatred of foreigners with intense religious zeal, which came under the leadership of a remarkable man named Shamil. After ceaseless guerilla war, Shamil was only defeated in 1859; Tolstoy as well as Lermontov would have occasion to taste in the Caucasus an exhilarating cocktail of wonderful mountain scenery, strange Asiatic customs, the free and easy ways of the Cossacks used as frontier guards, and always imminent danger.

Soon ordered back to Petersburg, Lermontov became a literary lion, and was involved in a secret group known as 'the Sixteen' which met to discuss philosophical and political questions. At a New Year Ball in 1840, he managed to insult the Tsar's daughters, and then on top of that he fought a duel with the son of the French Ambassador. The Tsar, with apparent leniency, ordered his transfer to an infantry regiment where the mortality rate from battle and disease was running around 50 per cent—so that in fact the writer was being sent to his death. But the commander in the Caucasus, when he got there, assigned him to cavalry operations. Leading Cossacks into action on a white charger, Lermontov so distinguished himself that he was recommended for high decorations. Nicholas refused to award them to him, and insisted that he must now transfer to the infantry. But Lermontov got himself put on the sick list. In 1841, at the watering place, Piatigorsk, where he had set much of his novel, one of the butts of his vicious wit, a Byronic poseur named Martynov, challenged him to a duel. Lermontov was killed outright. He was only twenty-six. The Tsar is plausibly said to have commented 'A dog's death for a dog'.

Lermontov was hardly an attractive personality: Turgenev remembered that 'His swarthy face and large, motionless dark eyes exuded a sort of sombre and evil strength, a sort of pensive scornfulness and passion'.[13] His most famous narrative poetry is characteristically 'Romantic', making free use of the supernatural and expressing a deep love of nature. He died at an age when most young writers have barely started to escape from youthful imitation and self-indulgence; this makes it all the more remarkable that *A Hero of Our Time* should be the book it is—not only very exciting in its incidents, but original in its form, realistic in its psychology,

and utterly unsentimental. Its handling of the native peoples of the Caucasus is stylized, but entirely convincing. Its hero, Pechorin, stands up
superbly well to comparison with such French precursors as Constant's
Adolphe (1816) and Stendhal's Julien Sorel (*Scarlet and Black*, 1831). His
obvious Russian predecessor is Onegin. The River Onega is a cold one in
Northern Russia; the River Pechora flows still farther north. But if
Pechorin has dandyism and restlessness in common with Pushkin's un-
heroic hero, his calculating decisiveness and sheer courage are beyond
Onegin's range. Both odious and attractive, he crackles with energy:
physical energy, intellectual energy—and even, in a paradoxical fashion,
with moral energy, since he is acutely aware of the harm he does to others.

Lermontov certainly used his own character and experience to the full
in creating Pechorin. But we must not imagine that he approves of him.
After the book came out in 1840, some critics saw it as autobiographical.
For the second edition next year Lermontov wrote a preface in which he
rebuked those who took the novel 'literally'—thus hinting that it contained
meanings which the censorship might not have let him express openly—
and he made two claims which echo through subsequent Russian 'realism'.

He saw Pechorin as a 'type', representative of many young men, but
not timidly copying the humdrum surface of their lives:

> It is a portrait of the vices of our whole generation in their ultimate development.
> You will say that no man can be so bad, and I will ask you why, after accepting all
> the villains of tragedy and romance, you refuse to believe in Pechorin?. . . Perhaps
> he comes too close to the bone?

Secondly, he emphasized the moral value of truth-telling, and, in selecting
an analogy with medicine, suggested a role for the novelist combining
'scientific' detachment with 'artistic' sensitivity and with indispensable
social function:

> You may say that morality will not benefit from this book. I'm sorry, but people
> have been fed on sweets too long and it has ruined their digestion. Bitter medicines
> and harsh truths are needed now, though please don't imagine that the present
> author was ever vain enough to dream of correcting human vices. . . . Let it
> suffice that the malady has been diagnosed—heaven alone knows how to cure
> it.[14]

A Hero of Our Time is not explicitly a 'political' book. But when we
compare it with Emily Brontë's *Wuthering Heights*—which came out soon
after and was also the sole fictional masterpiece of a precocious author,
offering a comparable combination of 'romantic' story with 'realistic'
detail—we are aware of elements of topicality, of satire, of apparently
casual generalization, which make the Russian novel seem part of a
debate while the English one is a self-sufficient statement. In Nicholas's
Russia, to criticize a generation was, after all, to criticize the state which
wished and claimed to control all significant life.

In technique, however, the two books are suggestively similar. In each case the literary device of multiple narrative voices sustains a tantalizing combination of deep, 'subjective', commitment to the 'Romantic' hero and of cold 'realistic' objectivity about him.

III

The six sections of *A Hero of Our Time* are nothing like the 'chapters' of a novel of its period. As Donald Davie has pointed out,[15] the book is amazingly 'modern', anticipating effects which James and Conrad began to exploit in English fiction half a century later.

From the vantage point of the second section, in which the 'I' who begins the narrative (but is not to be confused with Lermontov himself) actually meets Pechorin, all the other episodes might be seen as 'flashback'. In 'Bela', the first episode, the narrator, who is travelling about the Caucasus making notes for a travel book, meets a fifty-year-old army captain named Maxim Maximych, and draws from him reminiscences of the kind often included in travel books. These in a 'natural' way lead into the tale of Maxim Maximych's friendship five years before with a rich young officer, Pechorin, who was sent to serve at his fort.

The old man's narrative exposes both his wondering affection for his dazzling junior and his inability fully to understand this creature, jaded with the love of women of fashion and disillusioned with reading and study. Maxim Maximych knows nothing about Byronism and other fashionable fads. When Pechorin arranges the abduction of Bela, the beautiful daughter of a local chieftain, and brings her into the fort as his mistress, Maxim Maximych sees not a typically 'Byronic' quest by a bored sophisticate for happiness in the arms of an unspoilt girl but a profound sexual passion between two young people whom he loves and admires. After describing how Bela, at first sullen, finally yields to Pechorin's expert hand, he confesses, 'I was upset that no woman had ever loved me like that.' Bela is captured from Pechorin by a native admirer, who stabs her in the back when chased to a halt; her painful death two days later is described with most unromantic thoroughness.

Coming fresh to 'Bela' the reader will be as interested in the Circassian tribesmen as in Pechorin and probably more interested in Maxim Maximych, the archetypal frontier soldier who is also, in Mirsky's words, 'the simple, humble and casual hero of duty, kindness and common sense.'[16] But the landscape dominates everything else. Lermontov's descriptions of snowy peaks, starry skies, deep ravines and glistening torrents are splashed with bright colours and swept by fresh air. While Turgenev's justly famous evocations of landscape often have the inert effect of fine, framed paintings, because landscape is what the characters, like the readers, *look at*, Lermontov's landscapes (and the same is true of Tolstoy's) are there to be *moved through*—they are experienced as the characters and the reader proceed together, and bad weather is described as zestfully as fair weather.

The second episode, 'Maxim Maximych', relates the travel-book-writer's unexpected second meeting with the old soldier in a small frontier town. They learn that Pechorin has arrived, and the veteran is overjoyed. The travel-book-writer's eye, that of a city-bred intellectual, sizes up the 'hero's' figure which gives a contradictory impression; his physique is strong but his fingers are astonishingly slender, his smile is childlike but his eyes don't laugh when he laughs and shine with the 'cold, dazzling brilliance of smooth steel'. The presentation is cautiously objective—the narrator admits that he might have assessed the man differently if he hadn't known something about him already, and his eye is clinical, but not unsympathetic. What swings our sympathies against Pechorin is his cold reception of Maxim Maximych. The old soldier has, for perhaps the first time in his life, neglected his official duty, rushing to see his friend. He arrives gasping for air, pouring with sweat:

> Strands of wet gray hair sticking out from his cap clung to his brow. He was about to throw his arms round Pechorin, but Pechorin rather coldly held out his hand, though he gave him a friendly smile.[17]

With a few swift strokes—the wet gray hair is especially telling—Lermontov is able to make us feel the old man's boyish enthusiasm, the young man's elderly reserve, and to make the encounter hurt us. Pechorin is on his way to Persia. He refuses to stop and chew over memories with the old man, and we and the narrator are left with the grief and humiliation of Maxim Maximych turning into anger against the stuck-up dandy whose memory had been so important to him.

Since Maxim Maximych is far and away the most lovable character in the book, and has so far taken the centre of the stage from the 'hero', this scene makes it impossible for us to love, or wholly to forgive, Pechorin, let alone judge him on his own terms. Yet paradoxically, since the old man has been, as it were, 'in love with' Pechorin, it shows us how profoundly the hero affects people, how attractive he can be.

The rest of the book is made up of 'papers' of Pechorin's which the old man passed on to the travel-book-writer. The latter explains that Pechorin died on his way home from Persia, so he can now print them without inhibition. They are extracts from Pechorin's journal and formally they compose a triptych—two 'short stories' flanking a longer one.

Both Tolstoy and Chekhov admired 'Taman', the first short story, immensely. It describes an adventure of Pechorin's on his way to the Caucasus and so is biographically the earliest episode in the novel. The 'hero' puts up for a couple of nights in a hut in a Black Sea port and is nearly murdered by smugglers because he knows too much. The tale confirms Pechorin's lust and recklessness, but since he tells it, we are also made aware of more attractive elements in him—his love of nature and his self-questioning. Ironically, the behaviour of the smuggler Yanko towards a blind boy shows a callousness as great as Pechorin himself could reveal, and the smuggler's girl plays with his feelings as he himself plays with those of other girls, and all but destroys him. Pechorin is shown up as gullible, vulnerable, and also as perhaps the agent of a 'fate' which he sees as beyond his control.

The longest section of the book, 'Princess Mary', is presented as a 'diary' kept by Pechorin at the watering place, Piatigorsk, where he stayed before proceeding to join Maxim Maximych and abduct Bela. Here we see Pechorin in relation to 'society'—to an empty, mediocre world of gamblers and well-to-do nonentities. The more interesting people there bring out, by comparison, Pechorin's superiority. Grushnitsky, a cadet posing in a private's greatcoat as an officer demoted for duelling and as a man of 'romantic destiny'—his ambition, Pechorin notes, 'is to become the hero of a novel'—is a shallow fake, beside whom Pechorin's own depth is obvious. Dr Werner, a sceptical materialist who, with his wit and intelligence, has fallen foul of society, thinks he understands Pechorin completely —but his ultimate failure to do so is a measure of Pechorin's complexity. Then there are two women: Princess Mary, sojourning with her mother, and Vera, a married woman, the only person who ever understood Pechorin, whose arrival reawakens her attraction for him, but who is mortally ill.

Pechorin first behaves insultingly towards Mary, then makes her fall in love with him. He sleeps with Vera and destroys the relative amicability of her marriage. He arouses the hatred of Grushnitsky and kills him, in a fiercely exciting duel on a ledge over a ravine, during which he displays appalling coolness. Pechorin then finds that Vera has left and rides his horse to death in pursuit of her. The authorities pack him off at once to Maxim Maximych's fort. He parts with cruel candour from the lovesick Mary—'Princess . . . you know I was making fun of you.'

But *why* Pechorin does all this is not so easy to report. At times he he acts with total ruthlessness, at others he has to force himself to act coldly. At one point it seems that Mary's falling in love with him is almost as much an accident as Vera's arrival, which makes it necessary for him to cultivate the Princess, as he can meet Vera unobtrusively at her mother's house. At another, he seems to be calculating every move with a view to asserting his power over the woman and destroying Grushnitsky's pretences to her. When he fights his duel, he is glad that things work out so that he has every excuse to kill Grushnitsky, yet he himself runs a terrible risk, and still gives his opponent a last chance to save himself from certain death if only he will retract the slander which provoked the duel.

All Lermontov's main characters are complex. Princess Mary herself is marvellously well presented as both commonplace and spirited, both 'fair game' for a clever seducer and a human being who deserves our compassion. Even Grushnitsky is much more than a cardboard 'type'.

But these characters are made vivid 'from the outside'. What is both fascinating and baffling about Pechorin is that, even when he tells us so much about himself, and even though we 'see' him clearly, his essential character still eludes definition. We cannot be sure whether his confession, which awakens Mary's sympathy, when he tells her of an unhappy childhood and of how the world's misunderstandings of him have made him a 'moral cripple', is a sincere expression of a will to virtue thwarted. If it is, how do we square it with his Machiavellian exclamation in the privacy of his diary—'I love enemies, though not in the Christian way.' We can make sense of him only if we accept that (like Heathcliff, and like certain characters in Dostoevsky) he is a man in whom generous responses and vicious impulses coexist (and this is his cardinal quality) with unresting intelligence.

It is an intelligence which has cut through all the shams of society and has recoiled upon itself to cut away the will to shape any consistent course, to obey any routine, to be stable in anything. More positively, it is an intelligence which permits Pechorin to be as candid in admitting his own cruelties and inconsistencies as he is in exposing the faults of others. It is a wonderful medium through which we can explore the failures and pretences of human nature, and we must, after all, value any searching insights it can offer us. But it has no objectives. It precludes objectives. Like his creator, Pechorin stops short at diagnosis and does not aspire to cure.

Even 'freedom' has come to define itself for him negatively. He could not marry, he says: 'My heart would turn to stone, its warmth gone forever. . . . I'll hazard my life, even my honour, twenty times, but I will not sell my freedom.'[18] Freedom is by implication merely the state of being-not-tied. And the final episode of the novel confirms that Pechorin's problem is bound up with his inability to make valuable use of the more positive kinds of freedom which he is not completely sure that he has.

The self-accusations which recur in his diary, along with the occasions when he reports himself as consciously mastering his own feelings, show that he considers himself 'free'. Yet the evening before he goes out to kill Grushnitsky, he declares himself an 'axe in the hands of fate. Like an engine of execution, I've descended on the heads of the condemned, often without malice, but always without pity.'[19]

The last story in the book, 'The Fatalist', comes from Pechorin's time at Maxim Maximych's fort. An officer named Vulich puts a pistol to his head to prove that what happens to men is 'predestined' and pulls the trigger. It misfires, and Vulich wins his bet. But Pechorin, who has bet against him, has seen on his face that 'strange mark of inevitable doom' which soldiers claim appears a few hours before a man dies. And later that night, Vulich is murdered by a drunken Cossack. To put his own fate to the test, Pechorin risks his life to capture the killer. But nothing, of course, is 'proved'. 'I prefer to doubt everything,' Pechorin concludes. As for Maxim Maximych who has the book's last word, the whole subject of predestination means nothing to him. It is Pechorin's misfortune that his intellect is so developed that he belongs, even more than the rest of his godless and cynical generation, to a world in which the stars have been deprived of their role as arbiters of mankind and in which religious faith is disappearing. His generation, he says, 'drift through the world, without beliefs, pride, pleasure or fear, except that automatic fear that grips us when we think of the certainty of death. We can no longer make great sacrifices for the good of mankind, or even for our own happiness, because we know they are unattainable.'[20]

Pechorin is, truly, a 'moral cripple' because he has no faith in any pattern in or above life which might give shape and hope to his own existence. All that he can conceive is a blind and arbitrary 'fate'. Yet he cannot and does not consistently act as if he were merely 'fate's instrument'. As John Mersereau puts it, . . . 'His occasional recourse to a belief in the power of fate is an act of self-deception, a convenient way to blame an exterior power for the tragic results of the exercise of his will.'[21]

So he is a 'hero of his time' in a wider sense than we might suppose. He is an intellectual frontiersman acting with joyless irresponsibility in a world which has no God. He anticipates Turgenev's Bazarov and Dostoevsky's Raskolnikov, but his actions, unlike those of such later so-called 'nihilists', believers in nothing, have no direction whatsoever except that dictated by the impulse of the moment. Pechorin is *utterly* uncommitted. To draw this comparison, however, is to show his relevance to the Russia of 1840, when there was no 'political' activity except talk, when seduction and frontier fighting and duelling were the only outlets for frustration and when only a few young Hegelian idealists had any positive alternative to offer to a stultified Orthodox Christianity which was subservient to a mindless state. After all, this was the age of Gogol.

IV

The third of Turgenev's heroes, the 'obscure Ukrainian teacher', was Nikolai Gogol, and his 'terrifying comedy' was *The Inspector General*, a play still performed and loved all over the world.

Few writers present such problems to biographers and critics. He strewed his letters so thickly with lies and evasions that the facts of his life are hard to be sure of. The obvious incompleteness of his sex-life, and such tell-tale signs as his obsession with noses, not only invite but almost compel 'Freudian' interpretations of his work. And how was it that one of the most perfectionist of all prose craftsmen—by his own account, he thought nothing finished until he had rewritten it eight times—could misunderstand his own gifts so completely and project for himself a mighty literary task, aimed at nothing less than the regeneration of Russia, which was absurdly unsuitable to them? He has been praised as an inspired symbolist who created out of his own utterly unusual personality a disturbing world of his own; Mirsky claims that his 'satire' is not 'objective', but 'subjective' and his characters 'not realistic caricatures of the world without but introspective caricatures of the fauna of his own mind.'[22] Vladimir Nabokov, in his attractive study, takes such a line of argument still further. Yet Gogol was hailed in his own day and by generations of liberals and left-wingers thereafter as the supreme satirist of the Russia of Nicholas I as it 'really' was and as the founder, even more than Pushkin, of 'Russian realism'.

But how can we characterize Gogol's special contribution to world literature? That in spite of his own miserable life he was one of the most hilarious of all writers does not, perhaps, surprise us—the melancholy clown is after all a byword. But the terms we try to use don't seem to fit him. 'Humour', with its suggestion of warm-hearted tolerance of human foibles seems as inaccurate as 'comedy', which would imply a certain urbane detachment. Even 'satire' doesn't quite work, because Gogol himself seems to have been so unclear about what he was attacking. Only a bundle of words will begin to describe his best work. It is 'comic' yet has room for lyricism and 'Gothic' melodrama. It is extremely funny and yet profoundly disturbing in its presentation of an anti-human world where ludicrous yet somehow 'real' characters inhabit the same level of existence as walking corpses, as talking dogs, as pigs which rush out of respectable Petersburg houses, as hurdy gurdies with a will of their own, and as heaps of rotting grain, delicious Ukrainian foods and exorbitant overcoats.

Up to a point, it is like Dickens's world, and this is very strange, because the two writers formed their styles at roughly the same time, neither had read the other, and their respective countries were politically and socially, as well as geographically, as distant from each other as European countries could be. But real death, real problems of married life, real social questions realistically tackled, are present in Dickens's greatest achievements. Nowhere in Gogol's work do people really die. Nowhere is adult sexuality remotely sniffed. Nowhere do we find the least sign of a coherent intellectual grasp of political, economic or moral issues. The most difficult question of all is this: how was it that a man who never outgrew the mentality of gifted schoolboy was able to create works which have convinced generations of adults that they have something important to say about the 'real' world adults live in?

V

Gogol was born in 1809. His father owned just under 400 serfs, and had wealthy connections. He also wrote plays and acted in them. He died when Gogol was sixteen and the boy's mother Maria Ivanovna was the inadequate guardian fate left him. She had married at fourteen and was extremely naïve, not least about her son, whom she spoilt and idolized. His self-destructive belief in his own God-given genius clearly owed much to her, as perhaps did his morbid fear of Hell—she was superstitiously pious.

Gogol went to school in a town a couple of hundred miles from his parents' estate, and many references in his fiction show how important the experience was for him. He seems to see the civil authorities (and even God himself) at one moment as oppressive but silly masters to be out-witted, at another as just masters from whom punishment should be gladly accepted. He was a reserved and sickly boy, marked out from others by his large and unique nose—'most decidedly bird-like, pointed and long', as he described it himself. He used spiteful pranks and his gift for jokes and mimicry as a way of holding his own among schoolmates who nicknamed him 'the mysterious dwarf'.

Full of grandiose ideas about his destiny, Gogol left the higgledy-piggledy Ukraine in 1828 and went to Petersburg, with its regular streets and barrack-like atmosphere. The force of the contrast is surely felt in his best work, which seems to polarize the monstrousness of bureaucracy on the one hand and, on the other, the flashing flow of great rivers, the free-dom of the open road, and the drowsy life of the country estate. He told his mother he was going to get a job in the civil service. Instead, he tried to find employment as an actor and spent his money on printing a Romantic poem called *Hans Kuechelgarten*, set in Germany and Greece. Two critics reviewed it and both panned it. Gogol burnt all the unsold copies he could find and then fled abroad, directed, as he informed his mother, by 'God's invisible hand', and using money she had sent him to pay the interest on the mortgage of her estate. He seems to have been aiming for America, but got only as far as Germany, and after six or seven weeks came back.

He did now enter the service, and spent a total of fourteen months as a clerk in two Government departments. Meanwhile, having pestered his mother for details of Ukrainian sights and customs, he published short stories in magazines. Zhukovsky and then Pushkin befriended the promis-ing author. Through the influence of one of their friends, Gogol was given a job teaching in a girls' school, the Patriotic Institute for Young Ladies.

Two collections of stories, *Evenings on a Farm Near Dikanka*, came out in 1831 and 1832, and made him famous. Their colourful pictures of life in the Ukraine, full of superstition, peasant manners and horseplay, appealed to the 'Romantic' taste for exotic rustics and reflected Gogol's adoration of Sir Walter Scott. They reveal the roots of his art in folklore. The Ukrainian puppet theatre gave him its stock characters. Folk songs flavoured his idealized view of the jovial, hard-drinking Cossack. His notion that folk songs were the best source for national history did not, however, augur well when in 1834 he was appointed Reader in Medieval History at Petersburg University, after crawling before the reactionary Minister of Education. Ivan Turgenev, one of his students, recalled that 'even when he appeared in the lecture room, he did not so much speak as whisper something incoherently, and showed us small engravings of views of Palestine and other Eastern countries, looking terribly embarrassed all the time.'[23]

None too soon, he resigned in 1835. Meanwhile, major work had begun to appear. A volume of mixed stories and essays called *Arabesques* appeared in 1835 and included the famous *Diary of a Madman*, which brought him trouble with the censorship. *Mirgorod*, published later in the same year, was a show case exhibiting, in four long stories, a variety of wares. It contains *Old World Landowners*, a comic-pathetic sketch of the way of life of an elderly Ukrainian couple, dominated by eating and drinking and totally devoid of any intellectual or even practical interests beyond serving up and devouring the fruits of the earth. Gogol seems to delight in this paradise of sweet teeth and full bellies and yet, at the same time, to be revolted by it. *Viy*, an alleged 'folk-tale' in fact invented by Gogol, mixes Cossack fun with Gothic melodrama and culminates in a series of scenes both macabre and ludicrous in which an easy-going seminary student confronts the walking corpse of a beautiful witch and the monsters she summons up. The best of the four, *How Ivan Ivanovich Quarrelled with Ivan Nikiforovich*, is a masterpiece of disturbing farce. Two petty Ukrainian landlords go to law against each other when one calls the other a 'goose'. Gogol effortlessly decorates this heartbreakingly banal affair with unlikely and hilarious detail. The judge who keeps snuff on his upper lip so that he doesn't need to use a snuff box is as vivid as the serving woman who brings out an old gun to air it on the clothes line. But the story ends with Gogol brooding gloomily over the unending quarrel. 'It is a dreary world, gentlemen.'

The longest story, *Taras Bulba*, is the one through which Gogol has been mis-introduced to the world as the inspirer of Hollywood film epics. Though that normally astute critic, Mirsky, is moved to call it 'Shakespearian', it cannot, and should not, be taken very seriously. Taras himself is a Cossack chieftain of the fifteenth century. (Or is it the seventeenth century? Gogol is not concerned with precise historical fact.) He introduces his sons Ostap and Andrei to the life of the Cossack warrior—in which, according to Gogol, spells of raiding the Turks and Poles and fighting the Tartars are interspersed with long fits of drunkenness at the famous Zaporozhe camp on the Dnieper. To avenge the honour of the Orthodox Church the Cossacks go to war against their persecuting Catholic overlords, the Poles. When a Polish town is besieged, Andrei deserts to the other side because he is in love with the Governor's daughter. For this Taras, when chance arises, slays him with his own hand. Ostap is captured and executed after torture and the story ends with Taras, who has led his own band against the Poles in revenge, being burnt by them at the stake.

In mode the book moves from gestures towards historical realism recalling Scott, through the Gothic flummery of Andrei's defection via a secret passage, into self-conscious imitation of Homeric epic in the descriptions of pitched battles between Cossacks and Poles. Gogol's real strengths as a writer are seen only in some wonderfully exuberant descriptions of the steppes and a few passages of poker-faced quasi-satirical humour (one of them, oddly enough, the description of the Polish crowd awaiting Ostap's execution). For the most part, the story's only serious interest is that it shows us the boyish Romanticism and dismaying moral immaturity of a man who nevertheless was already a great writer.

Gogol thoroughly approves of his horrible Cossacks, who steal every-thing they can grab, shred their opponents like cabbages, burn women alive and spit children on spears. They represent the Russian Soul, he tells us—not least, we must assume, in their homicidal hatred of Poles and Jews. (As a prelude to fighting the Poles they massacre the Jews of Zaporozhe.) But Gogol gives his game away when he compares the renegade Andrei, confronted by his father, to a schoolboy suddenly caught by his teacher. He has already assured us that the Cossacks at Zaporozhe are like a bunch of schoolboys having a good time. And there is no question of co-education—Gogol would have us believe that there are no women in the camp. It would be humourless to argue that the drunken Cossack braves electing their new headman suggest not the natural democrats Gogol makes them out to be, but Hitler's brownshirts yelling in a beer-hall; they are more like the school second fifteen larking about on Saturday night. Gogol operates on the level of juvenile fantasy, and writes well enough to keep us contented on that level.

It is revealing that he makes Andrei, sensitive, scholarly, and his mother's favourite, into a traitor in love with an absurdly idealized Polish girl; Gogol himself was a spoilt child who was helplessly attracted to the Catholic culture of the West, and had to correct himself by going to unconvincing extremes of patriotism. Yet his archetypal Russians in *Taras Bulba* are natural enemies of all discipline. After their first unsuccess-ful rising against the Poles, the Cossacks, however, go to war as never before. They introduce bureaucracy into their army—quartermasters, transportation specialists, and, sinister word, 'scribes'. The Petersburg of Tsar Nicholas is, so to speak, on its way. After the headman has accepted a truce Gogol's hero Taras breaks away from this organized body and goes off to fight his personal battle against the Poles. As this suggests, Gogol could never reconcile 'Tsarism' with 'Russia', hard as he tried. His heart was out on the steppes, with the naughty boys playing truant.

And Khlestakov, the anti-hero of his great play, *The Inspector General*, is the spirit of naughtiness and truancy incarnate. In Mirsky's view, Gogol symbolizes in him 'the irresponsibility, the light-mindedness, the absence of measure, that was such a salient trait of his own personality.'[24] Everyone knows this story. Khlestakov, a Petersburg civil service clerk, is trapped in a provincial town after losing his money at cards. He is mistaken by the local officials for the Inspector General who is being sent to examine their doings. He dazzles them with enormous lies about his lofty connections. They flatter him and pour roubles into his palm. Just after he makes his escape, the mistake is uncovered; but then word comes that the real Inspector has arrived.

It is said that this play is remarkable because we can sympathize with none of the characters. The coarsely corrupt mayor and the mediocre impostor Khlestakov are relatively impressive figures compared to the judge who poses as an intellectual, having read 'five or six books', the empty-headed, pot-bellied landowners Bobchinsky and Dobchinsky, and the naïve good-natured postmaster who opens everyone's letters out of sheer curiosity. But surely the truth is that we 'sympathize', in effect, with all of them. They don't repel us. They aren't frightening at all. They're not people we can for a moment take seriously; they are far too stupid to do any real harm. They are like children who have been solemnly playing some forbidden little game, and the Inspector's arrival means that the game is up.

Nicholas I saw no harm in the play. He made Gogol a present of 800 roubles, and the play was put on with his personal permission in April 1836. And, incredible as this may seem, the civil servants of Petersburg and their spokesmen in the press were angered by it.

By bizarre coincidence, the schoolboyish daydreams of Gogol and the real life of Russia in his day matched each other. People really were that stupid. Pushkin, who had given Gogol the idea of *The Inspector General*, had himself been mistaken, in a leading provincial town, for a spy sent on a secret mission to report on local administration. Gogol's satire was accurate, and stung. Enough people enjoyed the play to make it a success. But Gogol was upset by his new notoriety. 'The prophet is without honour in his own country', he wrote to a friend. 'Everyone is against him. . . . Scoundrels are put on the stage and everyone is attacking me for putting them there. Let the scoundrels be angry; but those are angry whom I never took to be scoundrels. . . . To say of a rogue that he is a rogue is considered to be undermining the foundations of the state; to say something that is true to life means to defame a whole class of people and arm others in defence of it.'[25]

Gogol's game, like Khlestakov's, was turning serious. And, like Khlestakov, he fled.

He had now acquired, alas for him, a very earnest view of himself as a writer. Belinsky had praised in *Mirgorod* 'a feeling of profound sadness, a feeling of profound pity for the conditions under which Russians have to live.'[26] Even before his play had been performed, Gogol had expressed the view that laughter was a moral force which could restrain the wicked. After it went on the stage, he wrote to Pushkin to explain that Khlestakov was a 'type' representing a trait found in all human beings. Pushkin had been encouraging him to embark on a really long work, and had given him the idea for one; this would become *Dead Souls*. Gogol now had a sense of mission. His writings would reform Russia. But in order to write he had to escape from Russia.

He left in the summer of 1836 and, except for two periods of eight months each, spent the next twelve years abroad. He settled in Rome, a city in every respect unlike Petersburg; ancient, scruffy, sunny, and Romantic with a capital R. It was here that he heard of Pushkin's death. He wrote to a friend soon after, 'You ask me to return to Russia. What for? To share the fate of poets in our country?. . . What am I to come back for? Haven't I seen the precious gathering of our educated ignoramuses?. . . I shall not lay down my head in my native land.'[27] Gogol had always been a greedy guzzler of Russian delicacies. He now developed an exorbitant affection for macaroni.

He lived by sponging off his friends and by handouts from the Tsar. Hypochondria surfaced in his fits of morbid depression; at one point, he believed that his piles had spread to his stomach. An emotional crisis in his relationship with an old schoolfriend whom he met in Paris suggests one answer to the mystery of his sexual life, or lack of it—he may have been for a moment openly homosexual. Somehow he completed his masterpiece *Dead Souls*, or rather the first part of it, which he saw as the prelude to a 'colossal' masterpiece, only the 'front steps' of a palace. In later parts, Gogol intended to imitate the ascent of Dante (one of his favourite writers) from Hell through Purgatory to Heaven. The ludicrous Chichikov, central figure in the first part, would be redeemed. Characters full of ideal virtue would make their appearance. Russia, confronting them, would change its evil ways. 'You must do as I tell you,' he wrote to a friend, 'for henceforth my words are invested with divine power, and woe to him who does not listen to them.'[28]

The Moscow censors, however, refused to pass the first part of *Dead Souls*. Gogol took it to Petersburg and, at the price of some alterations, it got through the censors there. It appeared in 1842. While Belinsky hailed a realist masterpiece, several other critics denounced its coarseness and filth. Gogol retreated again to Italy. Like Leo Tolstoy in old age, Gogol now saw art and morality as inseparable and strove to give his religious ideals expression in his writing. But Tolstoy would never cease to be a great writer, even if he became a great propagandist. His religious ideals would arise from a long and painful confrontation with Russian reality. Gogol's, on the other hand, referred to his private fantasy world, in which he was alternately a second Messiah and a sinner doomed to Hell, and he ceased to write at his best level. In the fragments which survive of the second part of *Dead Souls*, one or two agreeable monsters worthy to consort with those in the first part are muddled up with boring and impossible creations—an enterprising landowner who turns everything he touches into wealth, a millionaire tax farmer who is a model of Christian piety—who are designed to demonstrate the heights which Russians can rise to.

Gogol wrote long letters to his friends lecturing them on their private morals. In 1847 he published *Selected Passages* from his letters. He had never been a 'liberal'. He had always been as obsequious in his direct dealings with the State as he had been irreverent about authority in his writing. But his public was shocked when the *Selected Passages* revealed the naïve reactionary views of Russia's greatest writer. Gogol had ordered copies to be sent to every member of the Royal Family. He hoped to convert the Tsar and through him save Russia. Instead even devoted admirers were scandalized when they found him dismissing the idea of teaching peasants to read as 'absolute nonsense' and expressing his contempt for 'European notions about justice'. The dying Belinsky was provoked to write his most important single essay. His 'Letter to Gogol', which circulated in manuscript, became a major document in Russian left-wing thought. . . . 'A great writer, who by his wonderful works of art has so powerfully assisted in Russia's self-realization and enabled her to look at herself as in a mirror, comes out with a book in which he teaches the barbarian landowner, in the name of Christ and the Church, to make more money out of his peasants! . . . Preacher of the lash, apostle of ignorance, champion of obscurantism, panegyrist of Tartar customs—what are you doing?'[29]

Gogol, after his book's humiliating reception, went on a pilgrimage to the Holy Land, but found that even there he couldn't meet God in prayer. He now fell under the influence of an Orthodox priest, Father Matvei, who dealt in warnings of hell fire and regarded art as a sin. He was still struggling with the second part of *Dead Souls*. In February 1852, under Father Matvei's influence, he burnt the finished manuscript in the dead of night. Aghast afterwards at what he had done, he attributed his action to the devil. Then he set about dying, refusing all food. His end was as macabre as anything in his own stories. The dying man's long nose was hung with seven big leeches. He was so emaciated that the doctors who attended him could feel his backbone when they pressed his stomach. He died screaming.

His funeral was an enormous public occasion. The Government forbade any mention of his name in the newspapers.

VI

The relatively small body of work on which Gogol's immense reputation and influence rest dates from his late twenties and early thirties. It includes, beside *The Inspector General* and part one of *Dead Souls*, some remarkable short stories: *Diary of a Madman* (1834), *The Nose* (1836) and *The Overcoat* (1842) are the most famous.

In the first, a middle-aged civil service clerk becomes infatuated with the daughter of his head of department and goes crazy; his diary tells us that he has detected and scrutinized a correspondence between his idol's pet and another dog. He comes to the conclusion that he is the rightful king of Spain and is committed to a madhouse. *The Nose* is that of a middle-ranking civil servant. It absconds, leaving his face perfectly smooth.

He catches sight of it wearing the uniform of a State Councillor, the rank being three grades above his own. He accosts it and it puts him coldly in his place. But the police catch it and return it to him wrapped up in a piece of paper. *The Overcoat* tells of a clerk whose only interest in life is pushing his pen (he even takes work home with him in the evenings). He finds he needs a new coat and saves up painfully for it. On the night after he first wears his resplendent new acquisition it is stolen from him. He goes to a high ranking official looking for help to get it back, and is snubbed. He is promptly taken ill and dies, but his corpse haunts Petersburg, snatching coats, until it finally seizes that worn by the official who rebuffed him.

Can we regard such tales as 'realistic', in any useful sense of the term? Proceeding crabwise, it is worth looking at the impressions of Russia recorded around the time when Gogol was finishing the first part of *Dead Souls* by a gifted French writer, the Marquis de Custine.

Other travellers beside Custine noted how Russian drivers, like Selifan in *Dead Souls*, were prone to talk to their horses; that some of the things Gogol describes were, as he claimed, 'typically Russian', is beyond dispute. But when Custine describes with comic horror the vermin found in provincial Russian inns—'multitudes ... of a kind I have never before seen: they were black insects, about half an inch long, thick, soft, viscid and tolerably nimble in their movements'—and when he writes, like Gogol, of Russian coaches dashing at marvellous speed, rushing through the air and seeming scarcely to touch the earth, we fancy we detect a special kind of literary imagination at work, an imagination rather like Gogol's.[30]

It seems, however, that this kind of imagination can make discoveries which are denied to more 'normal' observers. Custine, for instance, notices how the bureaucracy in Russia re-invents reality. Forests, he points out, often exist only on paper in a minister's bureau—like the *Dead Souls* Chichikov sets out to purchase. One day, Custine warns, the people of Russia will warm themselves 'by the fires made of the old dusty papers accumulated in the public offices; these riches increase daily'—and we think of Gogol's miser Pliushkin, hoarding useless trash. Of the petty bureaucrats of Petersburg, Custine writes that they are men 'acting under an influence which is not in themselves, in a manner resembling the wheelwork of a clock. . . The sight of these voluntary automata inspires me with a kind of fear: there is something supernatural in an individual reduced to the state of a mere machine. If, in lands where the mechanical arts flourish, wood and metal seem endowed with human powers, under despotisms, human beings seem to become as instruments of wood. . . . These machines, clogged with the inconvenience of a soul, are, however, marvellously polite. . .'[31]

Custine the Frenchman provides a bridge, if we want it, between Gogol and his contemporary Dickens. Dickens writes about an inventive society where the 'mechanical arts' flourish, but where men have been reduced to 'hands' to tend machines, to commodities bought on the free labour market and used. Men, animals, and objects therefore share a common vitality which is also a common deadness. The casts of hanged men on Jaggers's wall in *Great Expectations* are given as much 'expression' and life as many of Dickens's 'living' characters. Wemmick's pig, in the same novel, is part of the family, so it comes as a shock when he gets turned into sausages.

In Gogol, the portrait of Bagration on the landowner Sobakevich's wall seems to participate in the discussion with Chichikov about 'dead souls'. Ivan Ivanovich's pig acts on behalf of his master when he dashes into the courtroom to steal a legal document. Both these scenes have to do with *documents*—with meaningless but somehow powerful words. The bureaucratic machine in Russia burgeons at the same time as industrial capitalism in Britain. Both re-invent reality.* Both de-humanize men and confuse the levels of existence; the animal, the inanimate and the 'human' are hideously, if hilariously, mixed up. Bureaucracy and industrialism merging together create the modern state. Stalin's Russia, South Africa, any nation at total war, deprive men simultaneously of freedom and humanity by subordinating their reality to documents and by using them as if they were animals or machines. The odd little Ukrainian squireling who pushed his pen for a while in Petersburg offices was endowed with the kind of imagination which could grasp the essential nature of a society dominated by bureaucracy. Like that of Dickens his gleeful but despairing vision has all too much bearing on the realities of our modern world.

The focus of Dickens's hatred is hypocrisy, the vice of a callous and sanctimonious middle class. The focus of Gogol's hatred is *poshlost*, a vice prevalent among 'polite' officials. The English adjectives 'cheap, bogus, vulgar' help to define *poshlost*. Mirsky calls it 'self-satisfied inferiority, moral and spiritual.'[32] Nabokov helpfully shows us its emanation in the advertisements in modern magazines:

> a radio set (or a car, or a refrigerator, or table silver—anything will do) has just come to the family: Mother clasps her hands in dazed delight, the children crowd around, all agog, Junior and the dog strain up to the edge of the table where the Idol is enthroned; even Grandma of the beaming wrinkles peeps out somewhere in the background (forgetful, we presume, of the terrific row she has had that very morning with her daughter-in-law); and somewhat apart, his thumbs gleefully

---

* E. P. Thompson in *The Making of the English Working Class* (1963) pp 359–60, quotes Dr Andrew Ure's *Philosophy of Manufactures*, published in the 1830s. For Ure, the term 'factory':

involves the idea of a vast automaton, composed of various mechanical and intellectual organs, acting in uninterrupted concert for the production of a common object, all of them being subordinate to a self-regulated moving force.

It is with a shock, even now, that one realizes that the 'intellectual organs' in question are *human*.

inserted in the armpits of his waistcoat, legs a-straddle and eyes a-twinkle stands triumphant Pop, the Proud Donor. The rich *poshlost* emanating from advertisements of this kind is due not to their exaggerating (or inventing) the glory of this or that serviceable article but to suggesting that the acme of human happiness is purchasable and that its purchase somehow ennobles the purchaser.[33]

Chichikov, in *Dead Souls*, is the supreme representative of *poshlost*. And because he is, in his gruesome way, an enterprising fellow with shrewd ideas about making money and no scruples about how he does so, he embodies not only the ineffable banality of the official class which has nurtured him and which admires him, but also the intrusion into Russian society of the ethics of capitalism.

VII

What is involved in *The Diary of a Madman*, *The Nose* and *The Overcoat* is not the usual kind of 'realism', where the writer selects and combines elements from 'real life' to create a life-like 'world' more interesting and significant than our own but representative of it. It's not the realism of Tolstoy, nor even the realism of Dickens, because the latter selects from absurdities which have occurred or could possibly occur in a world tending towards the grotesque.

The *Diary* might seem 'realistic' as an account from the inside of a madman's fantasies if the letter-writing dogs weren't so unconscionably 'real' —they are just as plausible as the human characters, and not even the most gifted madman could have invented them so perfectly. *The Nose* is close to pure fantasy, yet this is not quite the world of Edward Lear or Lewis Carroll because the barber who finds the nose in his roll one morning and the policeman who brings it back, not to speak of Kovalev himself, the owner of the nose, conform to the rules of 'real life'. *The Overcoat* has been hailed for its sympathetic presentation of a clerk's struggles, but its central figure, Akaky Akakievich ('Dirty Dirtson', we might translate his name) is almost totally dehumanized. We are not told why he is so poor when his fellow clerks seem quite prosperous, and of course his walking corpse is Gothic invention. To complicate our responses, these stories make casual references to further oddities which Gogol, poker-faced, claims to have occurred in Petersburg. The madman tells us he read in the papers that two cows went into a shop and asked for a pound of tea. In *The Nose* Gogol refers casually to a *real* rumour which went round Petersburg about certain chairs in Koniushenny St, which had started jumping about.

Gogol doesn't select merely from actual or possible facts. He selects from and invents *rumours* of what *might* have occurred had the universe obeyed the laws which popular gossip and superstition suppose that it follows. Ill-educated Russia, with its rich and late-surviving peasant folklore, its abiding Orthodox superstitions and its inept and servile press was in fact a country in which ludicrous rumours were believed.

Thus the rumour-world which Gogol creates and which obeys its own laws provides a satirical commentary on the 'real' world which so many Russians, including Gogol's mother and, after a point, Gogol himself, failed so laughably to understand. The notion of Gogol's madman that he is King of Spain is hardly more absurd than Gogol's own idea that his *Selected Passages* might persuade Tsar Nicholas to live virtuously. Himself prone to fantasy, he was an ideal commentator on a society where the scientific outlook imported from Western Europe was in piquant conflict with the world-view of most Russians. But the life-denying aspects of modern rationalism also suffer at Gogol's hands.

Akaky Akakievich is from one point of view a rumour-man. No one, surely, could be quite so narrow, so stupid. From another, however, he is almost a model product of a world ruled by anti-human rationality. Bureaucratic Man, if he could exist in pure form, would be like this, and when he died, he, like Akaky, would leave nothing but 'a bundle of quills, a quire of white government paper, three pairs of socks, two or three buttons that had come off his trousers, and the "dressing gown" [his old overcoat] with which the reader is already familiar.' He is the Bosses' Man, the Loyal Kikuyu, the Good Comrade who, uncomplainingly, does what he's told and more. But even Akaky is not quite a spotless Bureaucratic Man. The splendid overcoat which he is going to buy is not only a physical necessity in the harsh Petersburg climate, it also represents the latent hankering for a fuller life of this 'voluntary automation', this disgusting monster of self-suppressed humanity. He starves himself to buy it, but he has 'spiritual nourishment' because he carries 'ever in his thoughts the idea of his future overcoat.' His 'whole existence' has 'in a sense become fuller, as though he had married, as though some other person were present with him, as though he were no longer alone but an agreeable companion had consented to walk the path of life hand in hand with him.' And that companion is 'none other than the new overcoat.'[34]

If an overcoat can be like a wife, then a woman can be an object, and only an object-like man could be satisfied either by such a woman or by the overcoat. Only a dog-like man could value a medal awarded by Tsar Nicholas. In the *Diary*, a dog reports on such a man, who lifts her up to look at such a medal. '"Look, Madgie, what's this?" I saw a little ribbon. I sniffed it, but could discover no aroma whatever; at last I licked it on the sly: it was a little bit salty.'[35] The human-like dog is sensible enough to value an object as food, as something useful; the dog-like man delights in the medal as the objectification of his own status.

The revenge of Akaky's corpse against the bureaucrat who treats him, to use an appropriate English saying, 'like dirt', must seem like the revenge of outraged human nature upon an inhuman system—if only after the system has succeeded in killing it. *The Overcoat*, the most profound of these stories, ends suspended between a 'serious' moral point (the Person of Consequence isn't just a monster and his confrontation with the corpse actually makes him behave better towards his subordinates) and zany inconsequentiality (the last scene has a stupid policeman mistaking a live robber for an apparition). But the final joke is just as 'serious' as the moral, because it confirms our view of Gogol's world as one in which people are, above all, *stupid*.

VIII

In *Dead Souls* Gogol quits Petersburg for the open road. We are some-where half-way between the monstrous alien squares of the capital and the unformed anarchic steppe-world of Taras Bulba. The novel is full of fresh air, an item present in Petersburg only in the form of icy winds. The first part, which we may as well simply call from now on *Dead Souls*, since what remains of the second is so disappointing, opens with Chichikov rolling into the town of N, and ends with him on the road running away from it. The people of N are much like those Gogol describes in his tales of Petersburg and the Ukraine; apart from a week he had spent once in the provincial town of Kursk, he had no particular knowledge of life in the Great Russian provinces. But they live in a sizeable town surrounded by countryside, and this permits Gogol to combine a vision of *poshlost*-ridden society with images of natural freedom.

Chichikov's project, suggested to Gogol by Pushkin, is to buy dead souls. Peasants were called 'souls'. Under the bureaucratic system, landowners still had to pay taxes on 'souls' who died between one census and another but remained 'alive' for a time on paper. They could however mortgage such dead souls as well as live ones if they wanted ready cash. Chichikov intends to amass dead souls by gift or cheap purchase and, when they are legally his, mortgage them. With the money he can thus raise, he intends to buy a real estate with some live souls on it.

Chichikov is a former customs official dismissed for corruption. But no one in N knows this. His *politeness*—he has the quality Custine noticed—charms the officials and squires who make up the 'society' of N. The fecklessly sentimental Manilov makes him a present of some dead souls vowing eternal friendship. The widow Korobochka (Mrs Littlebox), in one of the greatest scenes in fiction, drives a bargain, and the bear-like Sobakevich drives a harder one. The gambler and bully Nozdrev plays draughts with Chichikov for his dead souls and falls out with him, accusing him of cheating. The miser Pliushkin gives him dead souls and sells him live runaways for only 32 kopecks each.

But Chichikov is not quite clever enough. He displeases the town's ladies, all ogling him, by falling gawpfully for the Governor's daughter. Nozdrev blasts out at a ball the unspeakable truth that Chichikov tried to buy dead souls from him. Korobochka arrives in town convinced that she has been cheated and anxious to find out the real market price of dead souls. Rumours, of course, go on the rampage. Chichikov has been planning, it's said, to abduct the Governor's daughter with Nozdrev's help, using the dead souls as a cover. The Postmaster jumps to the conclusion that he is in fact a certain one-armed brigand named Kopeikin, until it is pointed out that Chichikov has two arms. The Chief of Police inclines to the view that he is Napoleon in disguise. The Public Prosecutor dies of sheer brooding about it all. But Chichikov is able to leave town.

The similarity of much of this to *The Inspector General* is obvious, but the novel is far more complex than the play. Gogol creates in it his vision of what is 'typically Russian' and transmits it to us through a unique combination of poetic prose with ludicrous types. The old English word 'humours', used by Ben Jonson, fits these 'types' pretty well; each demonstrates a particular ridiculous trait or set of traits which might be present in many human characters, exaggerated so as to dominate one character completely. The rich prose, both when Gogol's touch is light and when he seems in deadly earnest, conveys a taste of something akin to Homeric epic.

Gogol in fact called the book on its title page a 'poem'. The reader of translations misses, by all accounts, wonderful effects of rhythm and mimesis in the original. What he cannot miss in any decent translation is the expansiveness of Gogol's style. The ending of Chapter Eight provides a famous example, where in one paragraph we move from Chichikov sitting sleepless in his 'uneasy easy chair' after his misadventures at the Governor's ball, to his tallow candle which seems about to go out and plunge him into the black night peering in at the windows—*but* this in turn is about to 'turn bluish because of the approaching dawn', *so* we have far off cocks calling, then the silent slumbering town through which only a typical Russian drunkard *may be* weaving his tipsy way—*except that* a bizarre vehicle described as a 'round-cheeked bulging water-melon' and stuffed with calico pillows and various foodstuffs is carrying a travesty of a flunkey on its footboard—*and* its noise awakens a sentry at the other end of town who shouts 'who goes there' *then* seeing that no one is there catches and kills an insect on his collar and falls asleep again. (The 'watermelon', as we will learn in the next paragraph, bears Korobochka whose wild talk of her dealings with Chichikov will help to wreck his plans.) Gogol here, as elsewhere, builds up through detail, which seems to add to itself almost by free association, a comprehensive-seeming picture of a vast range of life. He comments on individuals we never meet again and crowds his novel with the generous detail which properly belongs to the epic mode, in which the mortal activities of men are set against the surrounding life of nature (the night, the cocks, the insect) and in which a catalogue of objects (Korobochka's coach-load of pillows and goodies) can help to convince us that the whole of life is present and accounted for. 'Satirical epic' isn't quite the right phrase to describe such writing. It is funny. It is also moving. It is in parts grotesque. It seems totally 'real', and at the same time it seems, through its interest in what is 'typical', to be capturing more of the world than a 'normal' view of reality could do.

The inn at which Chichikov arrives is 'precisely like all inns in provincial capitals, where for two roubles a day the transients receive a restful bedroom with cockroaches peeping out of every corner like black plums'.[36] The motherly but grasping Korobochka is, we are told, like other 'petty landed proprietresses'—and we furthermore learn, a few pages later, that her stubbornness and stupidity are also found among people who work in government departments and are 'perfect Korobochkas'. So Gogol gives ample armament to the school of critics stemming from Belinsky which examined characters as 'types', while anticipating the later concern of Turgenev and Dostoevsky to create significant 'types'. His 'types' mostly belong to the gentry and official classes but in Selifan and Petrushka, respectively Chichikov's drunken coachman and his smelly flunkey, he typifies hilariously the servant class.

Chichikov is Gogol's supreme 'type', He is a mediocre, ill-read, but fairly clever impostor. An utterly middling fellow, conventional in looks, 'neither too stout nor too slim' in Gogol's comic-epic repeated description, his chief gifts are lying, flattering and adaptability. Great stress is laid on his mean physical traits. When he blows his nose it rings out like a trumpet, when he snores he produces a high-pitched nasal wheezing. In jubilation he dances like a goat. Above all, he is obsessed with what present-day *poshlost* might call his 'personal hygiene'.

Before he goes out he spends hours attending to his face, scrubbing his cheeks with soap, plucking hairs from his nose. 'It is probable,' remarks Gogol, 'that so much time and energy was never expended on dressing since the very creation of the world.'[37] He is devoted to a special kind of French soap which imparts an unusual freshness and whiteness to the skin. And in the very middle of that travelling case which, as Nabokov observes, is 'the exact counterpart of Chichikov's horribly rotund soul'[38]—in the very centre, let's say, of his soul, we find a soap dish. The other contents, beside, of course, razors, include the bureaucrat's basic necessity, writing materials; things like visiting cards and old theatre tickets which are souvenirs of an utterly conventional social life; and money kept in a special secret drawer—if Chichikov's heart is soap, money is some unobtrusive vital organ, call it the liver.

But Gogol's Romanticism, involving a Romantic cult of nature, provides images of hope and wholeness which both criticize and extend the lives of the 'types' we meet. The great sixth chapter exemplifies this. It opens with one of the most Romantic of Gogol's digressions, in which he tells us how, during his youth he was full of curiosity while travelling and his imagination seized and explored the lives of people he passed. But now every village seems bleak and vulgar to him. 'Oh my youth! Oh my fresh vigour!' We then catch up with Chichikov, who is entering Pliushkin's ruined village. Huge stacks of grain, which the master won't use and won't sell, are rotting there. Pliushkin's house, with all but two of its windows shuttered or boarded over, is like a decrepit old man barely open to the world any more. Yet its garden, reverting to wildness, is beautiful, and

Gogol's rich paragraph describing it extols the healing power of nature which restores warmth and beauty to what man has created with too much 'measured purity and tidiness'. Gogol, as always, prefers anarchy to constriction.

Against this vigorous image which expresses both natural life and natural decay, is set the miser who surrounds himself with the filthy objects which he compulsively hoards:

> a lemon, so mummified that it was no bigger than a walnut; a broken-off chair-arm; a wine glass with some kind of liquid and three dead flies, covered over with a letter; a bit of sealing wax; a bit of rag picked up somewhere; two quills, stained with ink, and as emaciated as if they had consumption; a quill toothpick, perfectly yellowed, which its owner had probably been picking his teeth with even before Moscow's invasion by the French.[39]

These things are collected and preserved but not used; they are deprived both of human use and natural decay. Pliushkin's miserliness is especially horrible because it concentrates not chiefly on money, but on objects which others have used or could have directly used—it belongs to a psychological epoch before the dominance of the money economy, and is in this light characteristic of a dying pre-capitalist Russia. But Pliushkin, the most disgusting of Gogol's grotesques, is also the only one who can move us. He is presented not as someone who always was and always will be absurd, but as a decayed person who once enjoyed much fuller humanity and can still give his grandchildren, on a rare visit, an absolutely perfect ride on his knees.

By preceding Pliushkin's appearance with an evocation of the writer's own decay, Gogol 'universalizes' Pliushkin, inviting us to see that we are all potentially subject to the same ugly narrowing of the affections. It is harder to judge the implications of the Romantic garden; we might say that by evoking an undeformed and harmonious nature, Gogol gives us a standard by which to measure Pliushkin's deformity, but this would be over-neat: what is clear is that such a lyrical prelude helps to give the presentation of Pliushkin a pathos and depth of context unique in Gogol's work.

But a similar, if less obvious, humanization affects both Sobakevich and Chichikov himself. Neither in the last resort can be seen as wholly and solely a part of the world of 'dead souls' in which levels of existence are so gruesomely confused. Nozdrev is the most complete representative of that world. His hurdy gurdy goes on tootling of its own accord after he has finished playing it. Surrounded by his dogs Nozdrev, we are told, seems 'absolutely like a father in the midst of his family.' The bear-like Sobakevich at first sight seems his counterpart. All his furniture looks like Sobakevich, bear-like. Yet Sobakevich has a depth of imagination denied to the other people Chichikov meets. His drawing room walls are hung, not with portraits of bears, but with pictures of the Greek rebels of 1820s. And it is he who amazes even Chichikov by singing the praises of his dead serfs while holding out for a higher price for them.

Chichikov has an ampler imagination. At one point, after the Governor's ball, he inveighs against balls in general and the aping of French fashions in the manner of an authentic satirist. And it is his imagination, set in motion by Sobakevich's praises, which provides the most superbly epic passage in the novel. Going over the nicknames of the dead men sold to him, Chichikov conjures up for them fates and personalities. He moves on to men sold to him by Pliushkin who are not dead, but runaways. They have escaped to freedom, along the open road. No doubt he idealizes the 'free and reckless' life led by Habbakuk Phyrov as one of the Volga barge haulers, but it is for all that an effective image of vitality released. Gogol gives his novel about serfdom a whiff of liberation.

These runaways are in fact more 'alive' than the officials of the town of N. The irony is compounded by the death of the Public Prosecutor. Only when he dies, only when soul and body have parted, do his colleagues find out 'with regret' that he had a soul, 'although out of modesty he had never flaunted it.' But 'why he had died and why he had lived,' Gogol comments, 'that God alone knows.'[40]

The free life is that of the open road. Russia itself is discovered along the open road, and her true nature is alien to that of Western Europe and all imported customs; long before Tolstoy, we find Gogol exalting Nature over artifical Convention. The burly Sobakevich and his hefty serfs seem to typify the vigour of Russia which compensates for the refinements of the West and will make her, so Gogol seeks to convince himself and us, the greatest nation in the world. Chichikov also partakes of the freedom of the road. The last image of the book, where his troika metamorphoses into Russia flying at unmatchable speed past all other nations, is one of a stupendous release of energy, terrifying to men and inspired by God. The reader can admire Gogol's own energy while regretting his chauvinism. He must also note that for Gogol the essences of freedom are not to be found in choice and revolt but in escape and space. He stands by Cossack principles: run away and keep moving. Travel liberates man. There is more ground to cover in Russia than anywhere else. About freedom on a more than physical level he has nothing to say. But one must add that the racing excursions of his own imagination, which he prodigally bestows on both Khlestakov and Chichikov, are enough in themselves to give us an exhilarating sense of life and freedom. *Dead Souls*, as its gloomy-looking title suggests, is concerned with one of the gloomiest subjects conceivable, serfdom, and the sale of men and women as commodities. Yet it makes us laugh aloud, again and again.

IX

The other great comic novel produced by Gogol's generation is an extreme contrast to *Dead Souls*. Goncharov's *Oblomov* is sprawling where Gogol's masterpiece is compact and is as sluggish as *Dead Souls* is energetic. But its author was almost as odd and sad a man as Gogol.

In his life, and indeed in his writings, Ivan Goncharov must seem the least 'radical' of the major Russian novelists. In Professor Lavrin's words, he was 'the very picture of what might be called respectable conformity. . . . Intent on becoming a success both as a writer and civil servant, he marched towards this double goal in a deliberate, even somewhat calculated manner.'[41] Born in 1812 at Simbirsk on the Volga, he passed through Moscow University without mixing in the life of the circles. Drudging away for years in the minor post of translator in the Ministry of Finance, he found little time for writing. His first novel, *A Common Story*, did not appear till 1847, when Belinsky hailed it. His second, *Oblomov*, conceived in 1846 or 1847, was not published till 1859.

Its success was partly eclipsed by that of Turgenev's *Home of the Gentry*, and the most memorable stories about Goncharov relate to his ruptured friendship with Turgenev. He accused Turgenev of having plagiarized plots and situations from his own unpublished work. A committee of fellow writers was called in to arbitrate in March 1860, and of course exonerated Turgenev. The quarrel was patched up, but after Goncharov's retirement from the civil service in 1867, with the rank of State Councillor (he had worked for a number of years as an official censor), he became convinced that Turgenev was not merely using himself ideas he had stolen from him, but was passing them on to the French novelist Flaubert and the German Auerbach. Seeing Turgenev from afar in a park in Petersburg, Goncharov fled in the opposite direction, shouting 'A thief! A thief!'

His last years were lonely. After the cool reception of his third novel, *The Precipice*, in 1869, he wrote little apart from memoirs. He trusted no one but his valet, whose widow became his housekeeper, and when he died in 1891, he left his estate to her and to her children. In some ways, he was much like his own most famous hero.

Oblomov is the greatest sluggard in literature. In few major novels does so little 'happen'. The first part of this long book, well over a quarter of it, deals with only a morning and an afternoon in the life of Ilia Ilich Oblomov, and at the end of it he has still not got out of his dressing gown. He is an absentee landowner in his early thirties, living in a flat in Petersburg on the proceeds of an estate with 300 serfs which he hasn't visited for twelve years. He is looked after by a rude and slovenly servant, Zakhar, who is nevertheless devoted to his master and to the house of Oblomov. Today, two misfortunes prey on his mind—the money from his estate is falling off, and his landlord is forcing him to move. His reaction to both crises is to find reasons for doing nothing. When Zakhar tries to poke him into moving house, Oblomov paints for him an Apocalyptic picture of what such a drastic event would mean—the chaos, the mislaying of familiar objects, the horror of getting up in the morning in a new place:

'. . . Do you see now what you will let your master in for—hah?' Ilia Ilich asked reproachfully.
    'I see,' Zakhar whispered humbly.

'Then why do you suggest moving? Isn't it beyond the power of human endurance?'

'I was just thinking, well, other people, they're no worse than us, and if they can move, we can—'

'What? ... What?' Ilia Ilich exclaimed, rising from his chair in amazement. 'What did you say?'

Zakhar was confused. ... He did not reply.

'Other people are no worse!' Oblomov repeated in horror. 'So it has come to this! I now see that for you I am no different from "other people"!'

He made a mocking bow to Zakhar and looked deeply offended.

'Pardon me, Ilia Ilich, but did I compare you to anybody?'

'Out of my sight!' Oblomov commanded, pointing to the door. 'I can't even look at you! Hah!—"Other people!" Very well!'

Zakhar went to his own room, sighing deeply.

'What a life! Think of it!' he grumbled as he climbed on to the stove.[42]

Besides Zakhar (who is himself profoundly lazy) a string of callers try to rouse Oblomov and persuade him to go out. But none succeed until his friend Stolz arrives. Stolz had a German father and a Russian mother and combines alien thoroughness and energy with a taste for the old Russian virtues. He is a businessman, an insatiable traveller, organizer, philosophizer about 'life' and reader of books. Before he dashes off again to Western Europe, he introduces Oblomov to Olga Ilinskaia, a serious young girl who lives with her aunt. Oblomov falls in love with her, and more remarkably, she falls in love with him. Oblomov willingly moves house to the rustic outskirts of Petersburg so as to be near her, and they enjoy an idyllic summer which leaves him with a firm commitment to marry her as soon as he can set his affairs in order.

But he falls into the toils of a crooked sponger, Tarantev, who has found him lodgings in a scruffy suburb of the city, and in the third part his resolve breaks again. Confronted with his revived sloth, Olga gives him up, and the fourth part presents his grateful relapse into the arms of his plump landlady Agafia, a perfect housekeeper devoted to this embodiment of an aristocratic indolence and gentleness previously outside her reach. He drifts into marriage with her and has a child by her, before dying of the inevitable consequences of over-eating and lack of exercise. Meanwhile the energetic Stolz has married Olga, and Oblomov's son is brought up by them while Agafia and Zakhar are left to mourn their dead 'idol'.

Stolz sums matters up in the final chapter:

'He was as intelligent as anyone, and his soul was pure—clear as crystal. A noble and affectionate man, and—he's gone!'

'Why? What was the reason?'

'The reason—What a reason! Oblomovism!' said Stolz.[43]

This word, 'Oblomovism', gave an ideal opening to the critic Dobroliubov, one of Belinsky's successors. He applied it to the Russian educated classes in general:

> Even the most cultivated people, such as possess a vivid nature and a warm heart, in practical life very easily depart from their ideas and plans, very readily make their peace with the reality that surrounds them, though they do not cease speaking of it as low and contemptible. This means that everything of which they speak and dream is, in their case, foreign and external; but in the depth of their soul is rooted one dream, one ideal—a most undisturbed rest, quietism, Oblomovism.

Everywhere—among landed proprietors, in the civil service, in the army, even among liberal intellectuals, Dobroliubov saw the stamp of Oblomovism on Russia. Fine words, but no action, resentment of discipline and hard work, and inability to think in terms of what was to be *done*—these traits were typified by Goncharov's hero.[44]

We cannot, in fact, even now, help seeing him as the great fictional 'type' of the declining nobility. He is lovable, affectionate, even idealistic, but he is a helpless parasite, formed by childhood at his ancestral paradise of Oblomovka. The famous episode where he dreams of his early days there in which he was so pampered by parents who dozed and guzzled their lives away that he grew up unable to take his own boots off, presents us with an idealized image of a doomed way of life. Generations of parasitism must affect the will and capacity of the parasite class. Most of the nobility, by the point in the 1840s when Goncharov thought of his hero, had mortgaged their estates. And Stolz, an efficient civil servant, reforming 'capitalist' landlord and eager businessman, can be taken to represent the 'new men', modern-minded, provident and uncorrupt, who under the patronage of the Tsars emerged as the new rulers and leaders of Russia. His interest in making money by lawful industry is contrasted with the old-fashioned Russian corruption of Ivan Matveevich, brother of Oblomov's landlady, who takes his seven roubles a day in bribes as a civil servant and, a parasite preying on a parasite, tries (but fails) to fleece Oblomov of all he has.

Yet Goncharov's handling of the 'reality' of Russia in the 1850s (or is it the 1840s?), while it permits such broad generalizations as those above, isn't in fact very clear or very convincing. Judged as a 'social novel', *Oblomov* would be a failure. Its persisting fascination has some other basis.

To describe what the book is like isn't easy. It is usually called a 'comic' novel, and certainly the best of it is warm, charitable comedy in which the exchanges between Oblomov and his acquaintances soar to lark-like heights of delicious inconsequentiality. But long tracts of the book are devoted to psychological analysis. The love stories are told with obvious intention of awakening deep pathos. And some critics have seen Oblomov's final relapse into sloth as one of the grimmest episodes in literature.

What can be stressed without fear of contradiction is that the book depends to a very rare extent on a single character, and, furthermore, a character whose very nature prohibits him from doing anything active. Climbing a hill in a park to find Olga is his most extreme exertion in the novel. The narrative itself—beguiling but very sluggish and very wordy, sprawling, without a 'plot', slowly digesting its episodes—faithfully reflects the nature of its central character. This character is uninterested in current affairs and incapable of making an acute analysis of society— and the novel is like this, too. Goncharov shows a mastery of concrete detail in his descriptions of the rooms in which Oblomov slumbers— dusty mirrors, an ageing dressing gown, a luscious pie, the cook's plump ever-busy arms. But the society in which he dines at Olga's has no vivid particular presence at all, nor do the places she lives in; and the scenes in Western Europe in front of which she and Stolz fall in love hardly convince us even as stylized backcloths.

Nor are Olga and Stolz themselves at all interesting when we meet them apart from Oblomov. The long passages describing their romance and their marriage fall so far below the level of the rest of the book that readers can be advised, without qualms, to skim them rather than labour over them. The only characters who do have a vivid existence when they are not in Oblomov's company are Zakhar, the master's serf counterpart, and the lower middle-class rogues Ivan Matveevich and Tarantev, who are splendidly established on the level of Gogolian 'humours', and are made odious without forfeiting all our sympathy. These two also have features in common with Oblomov. Tarantev is childishly inadequate in action and 'proficient in nothing except talking', and Ivan Matveevich is an endearingly dedicated gourmet.

Goncharov's imagination simply evaporates when it stirs more than a hundred yards from his hero. He himself affirmed in a memoir, 'What has not grown within me, what I have not personally seen, observed, experienced, is inaccessible to my pen.'[45] Many writers would say the same, but a few can have written such a long book using such a short effective range. We look in vain for any insight into what Stolz is like as a man of affairs—all we get are generalizations, as abstract as the children Olga bears him. Oblomov at several points denounces the empty whirl of Petersburg society from which he has retreated, but we get no impression of what that 'whirl' might be like.

Gogol's imagination roams happily in every corner of Russian social life, inventing freely what it has not seen. Goncharov's stays with his hero. His streets are empty, his drawing rooms a blur. But in one respect he is very close to much of Gogol. Pretending to write about adults, he writes about childhood.

Though Oblomov is in his thirties, his point of view, which dominates the narrative, is childlike in its limitations. He is himself painfully aware at times of his 'own lack of development, his arrested spiritual growth.' We love him because he is childish. When he denounces Zakhar for comparing him to 'other people', we think of him not as a nasty snob but as a spoilt child. His craving for rich foods and his idleness are childlike, so is his morbid fear of crowds, so is his sensitivity to gossip, and so is his disarming honesty, which makes him unable to flatter Olga, but which in itself appeals to her. He is like a sensitive boy of fifteen on the edge of an adult world which he fears and cannot understand. He dreams, like an adolescent, of exalted yet harmonious love and of 'family life' in the same way as he pretends to himself that he will reform the conditions under which his peasants live or imagines himself as a great general or artist. And his love for Olga, which is made very vivid and psychologically convincing, is that of an adolescent idealist who thinks of sexuality outside marriage as an impurity, an abyss of shame—just as hers for him (she is only twenty and still very 'girlish') is that of an inexperienced creature dreaming herself into love for the first time. The moment when her sexual appetite, which is discreetly referred to as 'nerves' is aroused in her and resisted by him, one evening when they are alone, is among the most effective in the book.

Tarantev is no more than a surly, insecure school bully. And Stolz— this is where his portrait fails—can only ring true for us when he plays the role of a kind of clever head-prefect with a soft spot for the lazy fat boy who doesn't do his homework and won't play games. When he is with Oblomov, we recognize and respond to a bright, if condescending, above all boyish, charm. But when Goncharov tries to pass him off as a wise, ageing married man, this deception cannot fool us for a moment.

Oblomov is a child who is also a man. So, when we look at ourselves, are we. Within every adult, a child lives on, wondering when he is going to grow up; and with that child there is likely to live an idyll like Oblomovka, that out-of-the way Eden exempt from adult responsibilities, where letters are never answered even if, amazingly, they arrive, where the great events are birthdays and festivals and funerals and their attendant gorging and drinking, where cooking, eating and sleeping seem to be the main occupations and where a small boy is the idol of all who surround him, feed him and keep him from harm. This is the world of happy childhood everywhere. Those adults who are lucky enough to have lived in such a world carry its image around with them as a standard against which the callous, busy life of grown ups can always be judged and found wanting.

Even within the dream, Oblomov dreams, as children dream, of something better still, a grown-up world without problems. On a long winter evening, his old nurse tells him in a whisper:

of an unknown country where there was no night, no cold, and where miracles were always happening: there were rivers of milk and honey, no one ever worked, and fine fellows like Ilia Ilich and maidens more beautiful than those in fairy tales did nothing but make merry the livelong day. And there was a good fairy who would sometimes appear on earth in the shape of a pike, and she chose for her favourite a quiet, harmless man—in other words, some do-nothing that everyone else treated with contempt—and for no reason showered him with all sorts of good things; he had only to eat, to dress himself in fine clothes, and to marry an incredible beauty who was called Militrissa Kirbitevna.[46]

Under the influence of Stolz, after he goes to Petersburg, Oblomov learns to dream a more complicated fantasy, in which he is a reforming landlord, marries a fine woman and lives in cosmopolitan luxury rather than in the patriarchal simplicity of Oblomovka, where money was used as little as possible. He tries to fit Olga into this dream, but her 'nervousness' and intelligence are more than it can cope with—she would hate the vegetable life he craves. Agafia, with her motherly, irresistible bosom, helps him briefly to realize Oblomovka again, if only in the manner of a parody; she is both his good fairy and, alas, his true Militrissa Kirbitevna, childlike herself in her unquestioning devotion, with her little house in the Vyborg suburb where no 'news' ever comes. It is with only the tenderest of irony that Goncharov tells us he would need 'the pen of a Homer' to describe the wonders of her store cupboard filled with produce made available by the labour of Oblomov's forgotten serfs. The vision is truly delicious, but can't endure. Suburban Petersburg is not Arcadia. The old self-sufficiency has given way to an insecure parasitism. Oblomov's over-indulgence first ruins his health, then kills him.

Stolz and Olga, of course, regard Oblomov's delectable ménage with horror. Their own married life, surrounded by 'tasteful' bourgeois bric-a-brac, in which a still-dissatisfied Olga submits to her husband as a 'leader', which is what she thinks she has always wanted, seems to be offered by Goncharov as the model of a good working partnership, but strikes the reader as thoroughly horrible. Stolz is a kind of emotional engineer, working on people as he works the land he leases so as to extract the maximum from them in terms of his own ideal of unflagging productivity—just as he has been an emotional economist, saving up his resources for one great 'love', and is now in effect an emotional monopolist, engrossing Olga completely into his own life. Both Olga and Stolz, though they 'love' Oblomov, have always been trying to turn him into something he isn't, to impose on him their own vision of life as striving, struggle and endless movement. When Oblomov tells Stolz he has married Agafia, Stolz whispers 'Done for!' And he reckons there is now no point in telling his friend that Oblomovka itself, under Stolz's management, 'is no longer in the wilderness, that its turn has come at last, that the sun's rays have fallen on it. . . . In another four years there will be a railway station there and (Oblomov's) peasants will be working on the line. . .'[47] He resigns himself to engineering the right kind of person out of Oblomov's son.

In their final confrontation, we must surely *feel* ourselves to be on Oblomov's side against Stolz. The thought of Oblomovka's sleepy peasants sweating to build a railway which will open their land up to the exploitation of city merchants is not a winning one, even if the schools which Stolz proposes to start are thrown in as part of the deal. Ideologically, in this novel. Stolz wins completely, and Oblomov meets the kind of base death all slackers deserve. But emotionally, shy good-natured child-likeness is more appealing, as Goncharov presents things, than arrogant, insensitive busy-ness, convinced of its God-like power to alter the world as it thinks best. We are, most of us, up to the furthest possible point, Oblomovists.

But not, of course, all the way. Goncharov himself had grown up under an indulgent mother who was, however, a very practical businesswoman from a merchant background. He had luminous memories of old-style Russian life in a place remote from great events. But when he went home to Simbirsk after graduating, he couldn't settle down in a town which presented to him a picture of 'sleep and stagnation'. [48] Oblomov's ultimate ideal is a state of torpor—like childhood, like dotage, like death. 'Even in love', he finds, 'there is no peace; it, too, keeps going forward, on and on.' At another point he exclaims, 'Ah, life!. . . It won't let you alone—there is no peace! I wish I could lie down and go to sleep—forever.'[49]

Goncharov clearly felt acutely the conflicting claims of innocence and experience,. He poses the contrast between Stolz and Oblomov with a naïveté which is itself rather childlike. The strange and exceptional weighting of this book in favour of the dream of childhood which results from the novelist's failure with Stolz is, in effect, its greatest strength. It makes us take our dream of childhood more seriously than we would normally do, and judge it both more fully and more severely than we would otherwise do. It takes to great literary heights certain preoccupations which readers of English will find displayed in books more-or-less aimed at children themselves, like Kenneth Grahame's *Wind in the Willows*.

Although Olga's boldness and idealism, and her symbolic role as 'awakening' Russia, give her much in common with Turgenev's heroines, *Oblomov* shows how unfounded was Goncharov's crazy suspicion of his fellow-novelist. They were good at precisely opposite things. In *Oblomov* we detect a flawed personality turning inwards and exploring its own obsessions, finally achieving a kind of lop-sided balance. In Turgenev we observe another unhappy writer turning outwards to release his obsessions into complex social actuality, where they confront the most up-to-date political problems. And Turgenev had what Goncharov most lacked; a mature sense of history.

THE NOBILITY

No book on Russian fiction should be without a table of ranks instituted by Peter the Great showing which titles in the civil service equated with which positions in the army. The one I supply here omits grades 11 and 13 (Ship's Secretary and Senatorial Registrar) which fell into disuse in the first half of the nineteenth century.

1.	Chancellor	= Field Marshal
2.	Actual Privy Councillor	= General
3.	Privy Councillor	= Lieutenant-General
4.	Actual State (or Civil) Councillor	= Major General
5.	State (or Civil) Councillor	
6.	Collegiate Councillor	= Colonel
7.	Court Councillor	= Lieutenant-Colonel
8.	Collegiate Assessor	= Captain or Major

9.	Titular Councillor	= Staff Captain
10.	Collegiate Secretary	= Lieutenant
12.	Provincial Secretary	= Sub Lieutenant or Cornet
14.	Collegiate Registrar	

The first eight grades conferred hereditary 'nobility' on those who attained it. The other six carried only 'personal nobility', which was not transmitted to the holder's children. In 1875, official statistics noted 650,000 hereditary nobles (slightly outnumbered by the priestly classes) and 375,000 personal nobles, out of a total population of 78 million for the whole empire. (Mackenzie Wallace I, 437).

All 'nobility' in Russia stemmed, after Peter, from service to the State. The title of Prince (*kniaz*) belonged to certain families prominent in old Muscovite days. Peter had introduced the titles of count (*graf*) and baron, the latter held almost exclusively by Baltic Germans. But most 'nobles' had no titles.

Talk of African 'kings', Japanese 'feudal lords' and Chinese 'scholar gentry' often misleads the unwary into inane generalizations and comparisons across cultures. I use the term 'noble' to refer to the Russian *dvorianin*, whom some historians, critics and translators will call a 'gentleman'. The word *dvorianin* is not a synonym for *pomeshchik*, which means landowner. A non-*pomechchik* who reached the eighth rank became a *dvorianin*. After 1861 a non-*dvorianin* could own land.

I prefer to call the landowning *dvorianin* a 'nobleman' because the word lacks the special, cosy and wholly English flavour of 'gentleman'. Whatever the Russian *dvorianin* was like, he never resembled Jane Austen's Mr Knightley. The petty *pomeshchik* who owned a few serfs and a few acres was closer to the little lairds of Scotland. The more substantial *pomeshchik* nurtured in days of serfdom was in many of his attitudes nearer to the plantation owners of North East Brazil than to the English baronet or squire. 'Nobility' furthermore has the advantage of suggesting a legally defined class or 'estate' which the English gentry weren't. Most translators refer to 'marshals of the nobility' rather than 'of the gentry' when their texts present those figures whose role it was to preside over corporate assemblies.

But 'nobility' still isn't adequate. It gives an exaggerated impression of the status of a *dvorianin* like Raskolnikov from an impoverished family or of the 'breeding' of a priest's son who rose in the civil service. If we use it we must be content to discount the absurd notion of a civil service wholly composed of 'noblemen'.

Many holders of *chin* (official rank) came, of course, from landowning families. The *chinovnik* flourished while the *pomeshchik* declined; so the 'nobility' was both flourishing and falling at the same time. But there is, as Tolstoy shows us, a clearish distinction to be drawn between the *pomeshchik* who lives on his own land and regards himself as a countryman and the *dvorianin* of another sort who also owns land but who is essentially a townsman with life and interests centring round service rank and medals, and who uses the countryside only for profit and holidays. Alexander III in the 1880s proclaimed the abiding importance of the rural nobility as leaders of national life and pillars of Tsarism but 'for all these fine words from high places, the nobility was a declining force. . . The social group that benefited from the policies of these years was much less the landowners than the bureaucrats.' (Seton Watson 467).

3
FICTION AND POLITICS
The Art of Turgenev

The fiction of Pushkin, Lermontov and Gogol has the freshness and lightness of touch of the heyday of victorious Romanticism, when Mozart was still worshipped as much as Beethoven, or more. It belongs to a world of vivid green jackets and brilliant waistcoats, before the smoke of the steam train condemned respectable men to don black suits. It may at times seem rhetorical, but it is never fulsome; it may often seem cold, but it's rarely sentimental.

Turgenev, together with Dostoevsky, belongs to a generation bridging periods corresponding to those which in Britain are called 'Romantic' and 'Victorian'. In Britain, decades of war and social turmoil were followed by a long phase, from the 1850s of relative complacency. In Russia the contrasts were starker because change, long-delayed, came with a greater rush. The epoch of Nicholas I when only a few individuals represented the ideas of modern man against a regime frightened of change, gave way to that of Alexander II when a government which was rapidly 'modernizing' Russia was confronted with many more rebels from a much broader social basis. Whereas in England and France the new age of the railways saw the triumph of the bourgeoisie and its values after a long rise, in Russia capitalism and liberalism made sudden and shocking inroads into a hitherto rigid social system.

Though Turgenev, the liberal Westernist author of short novels, and Dostoevsky, the Slavophile maker of vast, sprawling books, may seem in most respects directly opposite, they were both writers who carried certain Romantic preoccupations with them into the new era, and the work of both men reflects an obsession with the topicalities of politics and social change. Both men, trying with prodigious success to cope with the challenge of the novel of political prophecy, can be accused at times of windy over-emphasis. But both use remarkable intellectual strength to come to terms with the new complexities of Russian, and indeed of European, life. Turgenev, as his younger contemporary the anarchist Peter Kropotkin (1842–1921) would one day admiringly put it, was the chronicler of a period when 'The leading types of the educated classes went through successive changes with a rapidity which was only possible in a society suddenly awakening from a long slumber. . . .'[1]

II

Ivan Turgenev was born in October 1818 in the province of Orel. His father was a handsome cavalry officer of ancient lineage but small property. His mother, Varvara Petrovna, owned 5000 'souls' and dominated her son's life. She was a plain woman of remarkable intelligence and quite appalling strength of character. Turgenev claimed in old age that as a child he had been flogged almost every day, and whether he was exaggerating or not there is no doubt that his mother, besides providing one basis for some of the most impressive female characters in literature, gave him a measure of natural fellow-feeling for serfs who like himself suffered under her capricious tyranny. For instance, when two young peasants failed to bow as she passed them, she ordered their deportation to Siberia. It was a serf with a passion for the bombastic rhetoric of Catherine's day who, when the young master was about eight, introduced Turgenev to poetry.

He attended the universities first of Moscow, then of Petersburg, but came to the conclusion that 'the source of new knowledge was to be found abroad.' In 1838 he left Russia to complete his studies at the University of Berlin—in his own words, written thirty years later, he 'plunged headlong into the "German Sea", which was to purify and regenerate me, and when I finally emerged from its waves, I discovered myself to be a "Westerner", and I have remained one ever since.'[2] Berlin was the fountainhead of Hegelian ideas. Among his fellow students there were several young men who were or would be important in Russian life and thought, including the future anarchist Mikhail Bakunin (1814–1876), and the amiable Nikolai Stankevich, formerly leader of an important Moscow 'circle.'* In his novel *Rudin* Turgenev would model Pokorsky on Stankevich and evoke the atmosphere of the ardent discussions he had had with his friends in Berlin:

> ... You should have seen all our faces, you should have heard our speeches! In all eyes there was rapture, and cheeks burned, and hearts beat, and we talked of God, of truth, of the future of humanity, of poetry—sometimes we talked nonsense, we were enthusiastic over trifles; but what of that? Pokorsky would sit with his legs tucked under him, resting his pale cheek on his hand; and his eyes would shine, would shine.[3]

* See Chapter 2

Turgenev shared rooms with Bakunin. He travelled in Italy with Stankevich. And when Stankevich died in a small Italian town, Turgenev wrote to another Berlin friend, the future historian Granovsky:

> ... must we believe that everything beautiful and sacred, that love and ideas are merely the cold irony of Jehovah? What then is our life? But no—we must not lose heart and give in. Let us gather together, join hands, close our ranks: one of us has fallen, perhaps the best. But others are arising, and will arise, the hand of God never ceases to sow in the soul the seeds of great aspirations, and sooner or later light will banish darkness.[4]

The self-indulgent lushness of this points forward to some of the least attractive passages in Turgenev's fiction; and certain ideas which will inform much of that fiction are already present. The malevolence of fate opposes what is noblest in human nature. But 'God', a vague Idea, is on the side of man and after new generations have arisen to carry on the struggle for ideals over the fallen bodies of the vanguard, humanity will triumph.

In 1841 Turgenev returned to Russia. An affair with a serf-girl produced a daughter whom he would later acknowledge; a metaphysical dalliance with Bakunin's sister produced only some psychological scars. But in 1843, the direction of his life was settled, not by his brief and inefficient tenure of a civil service post, but by a book, a friendship and a woman. His tale in verse, *Parasha*, derivative of Pushkin, was promising enough to please Belinsky. Critic and author became close friends, though it was as disciple rather than equal that Turgenev loved the older man. His memoirs dwell on Belinsky's passionate sincerity—'Belinsky was essentially *ein guter Mann*—he was a truthful and honest man.'[5] While Turgenev never became a 'socialist', Belinsky's memory helped to give him some sympathy with the radical young men who later claimed to be Belinsky's followers. The temptations of aestheticism were for Turgenev acute, but he would never forget his friend's rejection of 'art for art's sake', which was allied to what seemed to him an 'almost infallible' aesthetic sense.[5] As Frank O'Connor puts it, Turgenev 'scarcely wrote a significant story that is not political.'[6]

His *Sportsman's Sketches*, appearing individually from 1847 onwards, not only marked him out as a rising star of Russian literature but made him appear a pretty dangerous subversive. Their propagandist effect was compared to that of *Uncle Tom's Cabin*. The modern reader is surprised to hear of this. Perhaps what he most enjoys in these wonderful little pieces— hardly, for the most part, 'stories'—is the way they communicate how supremely pleasant it must have been to have hunted the woods and steppes of Central Russia as a young, rich, sensitive man gifted with the exceptional leisure and freedom which serfdom accorded the nobility. His mother kept Turgenev short of funds, yet he never experienced anything like want, and his success as a writer would provide him not with the basic means of life, which he had already, but with money to enjoy his tastes for travel and for works of art. The 'sportsman' of his sketches doesn't mind sleeping rough, but this is a holiday interlude for a body kept groomed and healthy by the labours of serfs. He is detached from the labouring world he describes so well, and the landscape which for serfs is the scene of daily toil is for him an object of aesthetic appreciation. (But how dazzlingly 'concrete', in spite of this, Turgenev's descriptions are, how rich in detail: he never merely says 'it was a fine autumn day'—each day, and every hour, is individual, as is each birch grove and each village.)

Such was Russia that simply to describe serfs as human beings, with virtues and vices, skills and even artistic gifts, loves and religious feelings, was equivalent to a protest against the social order which denied them freedom. The *Sportsman's Sketches* followed works by other writers describing the lives of the peasantry—this was a tendency which Belinsky had encouraged. Yet their author, so far from committing himself to struggle in Russia for the emancipation of the serfs, was when he wrote them living mostly abroad.

This was probably a choice which, like his friend Herzen, he would have made anyway. But a very specific motive for exile was provided by his obsession with a famous singer of Spanish parentage, Pauline Garcia-Viardot, whom he heard and met when she sang at Petersburg in 1843. She was not conventionally beautiful, but she was greatly talented, and Turgenev was by no means the only remarkable man to fall under her spell. His devotion persisted till his death in 1883. Her French husband became a friend and hunting companion; he sent his illegitimate daughter to be raised by her; he became an affectionate unofficial uncle to her own children. Whether he ever actually slept with her is a matter of dispute, and is anyway essentially unimportant. What does matter greatly is that he became outwardly dependent on a second powerful female personality. It is easy (too easy) to see in the writer himself, with his towering frame, impressive forehead, and 'weak' chin the prototype of heroes in his own fiction whose will is drained from them by fascinating, selfish women. Too easy, because one can see the relationship as being, like his creation of those particular characters, the product of Turgenev's own will. One might equally well suggest that Turgenev used Madame Viardot for his own ends. She gave a focus to his life in Western Europe, where he preferred to live. She provided him with the advantages of a settled 'family' relationship, but didn't tie him down—he had several liaisons and flirtations with other women. And he could excuse to others, and indeed to himself, his unpatriotic exile by invoking the Goddess Love. He once told another close lady friend, 'People lacking character like to invent their "fate", which frees them from the responsibility of a will of their own.'[7] Pauline absolved him from guilt—she was his 'Fate'—but his 'Fate' didn't stop him from making frequent trips back to Russia. Turgenev's life, like his work, was on the whole tidy. If he was, as some critics suggest, prey to morbid and unmanly obsessions, the clarity of his work is all the more remarkable.

Turgenev followed Pauline to Germany, England and France in 1847. He was in Paris when the February revolution of 1848 destroyed the monarchy of Louis Philippe. In his moving anecdote 'My Mates Sent Me', he later gave an account of the terrible 'June Days' when the new bourgeois government killed thousands of workers who had risen against it. But unlike Herzen, he didn't deduce from this slaughter of brave dreams the idea that the West was rotten.

1848 saw Nicholas in Russia react with predictable oppression to the 'year of revolutions', which also swept Metternich out of control in Austria and saw revolts by Italians and Hungarians against Austrian rule. He joined with gusto in the repression of the Hungarian uprising, and at home the censorship went to minute extremes. '. . . In 1851 a commission was appointed to examine all music for the discovery of possible conspirative ciphers. . . . Count S. Uvarov, himself the reactionary Minister of Public Instruction from 1833 to 1849, was not allowed to use the word *Demos* in his book on Greek antiquities, nor might he say that Roman emperors were killed, only that "they perished". . . . The censor Akhmatov stopped a book on arithmetic because between the figures of a problem he saw a row of dots.'[8] There were barely a few hundred naive 'Socialists' in Russia, but the authorities pounced with terrible force, early in 1849, on the Petersburg 'circle' led by Mikhail Petrashevsky.

Petrashevsky's debaters (who included Dostoevsky) were not solely aristocrats like the Decembrists of 1825; they included petty officials, students and schoolteachers. The leadership of Russian radicalism was beginning to pass to the 'plebeians' or 'classless men', the *raznochintsy*. Turgenev's style of aristocratic idealism was on the way to becoming old-fashioned. His mother died and left him a share of her lands. He returned to Russia in 1850 and took up his lavish inheritance. He substituted *obrok* quitrents for *barshchina* labour, but of course he didn't free his serfs. He was in Petersburg when Gogol died in 1852, and wrote an effusive, quite 'unpolitical' obituary. A Petersburg paper refused to print it. Turgenev sent it to Moscow, where the censor passed it and it was published. When Nicholas heard of this, he ordered the author to be imprisoned for one month and then exiled indefinitely to his country estate.

He wasn't badly treated in prison and his period at his Spasskoe home under police surveillance meant that he resumed touch with the life of his own class, the provincial nobility. This gave him the basis for the fiction with which, in the 1850s, he moved from the sketch and the short story to confrontation at greater length with the Russia he had grown up in and lived in. But not at so great a length as he had at first intended. In 1852/3, he wrestled unavailingly with a massive and ambitious work to be called *Two Generations*. He was aiming at the kind of scale now commonly achieved by Balzac, Dickens, Thackeray and others in the West. The great Russian fiction of the thirties and forties fitted in only at the margins of the novel form as France and Britain had now developed it (though another way of looking at it would stress that Russia had developed the form of the short story, and certain techniques of the 'modern' novel, far ahead of other literatures). The social range, the sweep, the complex intrigues of books like *Dombey and Son, Vanity Fair, Cousin Bette* had no counterparts among the wonderful miniatures of Pushkin and Lermontov, in the delicacy of Turgenev's own *Sketches*, nor even in Gogol's *Dead Souls*, which both in its epic and its picaresque aspects harked back to methods now old-fashioned abroad, though it was, of course, none the worse for that.

Yet when Turgenev did finally strike out in 1855, writing his *Rudin* in a few weeks, he himself projected it not as a 'novel', but as a *bolshaia povest*, 'large story'.[9] Even compared with the novels of Jane Austen, *Rudin* and most of Turgenev's subsequent fictions have little or no element of 'intrigue'; emphasis falls not on plot, but on character, on satirical portraiture, on political and philosophical debate, on landscape, and on details creating 'atmosphere'. Turgenev himself had toyed with the idea that social conditions in Russia were not at the moment right for the Western kind of four volume novel. There must have been truth in this. The complex, constantly shifting class structures of Britain and France gave Balzac and Dickens scope for intricate and exciting plots. Muddled societies are full of mysteries—where, for instance, did wealthy Mr X get his money? In Russia the answer to that question would be too obvious; 'from owning serfs' or 'from operating as a merchant of the second grade.' What we now call 'social mobility' is at the centre of much Western European fiction, and as characters move up and down between different class levels, unexpected and exciting catastrophes and confrontations are possible, and various kinds of interest and suspense which could not easily be matched in class-bound Russia. Of course, Russian novelists could have created 'plots', and Dostoevsky did so. But 'plot', if we see the term as having connotations of intrigue and mystery, doesn't exist in the work of Turgenev or Tolstoy. Apart from coincidence, without which a work of its length could barely have any shape, even *War and Peace* is free of 'novelistic' devices. Its interest arises not from complicated intrigue but from our affection for the characters, our excitement over battles and other historic occasions, and also from the kinds of atmospheric and suggestive detail which we tend to associate with the 'short story'.

Turgenev and Tolstoy belonged to a leisured class where boredom was generally a greater problem than insecurity; the problem was not that the kind of frictions illustrated by 'plots' as well as created by them were generally present, but that they were absent; nothing exciting was likely to happen. The repetitive patterns of marriages of convenience and accepted adulteries, the slow rise or fall of family fortunes, the routine pleasures and *ennuis* of life in the country at one season, in the city at another, the social structure kept so tightly reined in by the autocracy,—these can't without strain provide scope for the kinds of interest we get from the rise of Stendhal's Julien Sorel from social obscurity to high society, or the maze of unscrupulous schemings which in Dickens's novels links rich, middling people and poor. Turgenev's 'novels' are simple 'stories' given rich interest by the exploration of character and themes within a situation.

The situation in *Rudin* is a variation on one which Turgenev, in short stories, had used already, and which he would often use again. As Richard Freeborn shows, it can be derived from *Onegin*: while the hero is an intruder in a milieu which is in some measure unfamiliar to him, the heroine belongs to the milieu. Her love for him, says Freeborn, is a 'challenge to his character which he can either accept or fail to live up to, and the extent to which he succeeds or fails reveals the extent of his moral worth.'[10] This is to put it rather abstractly. The hero is himself a challenge to the values of the group he finds himself among; he churns up the sleepy shallows of life. The result may be tragedy, or bathos, or both, as people respond to a situation where, perhaps for the first time, a choice of values is offered to them. And the love story is made to carry a strong 'political' charge.

Here is part of a letter written by a 'provincial miss' (a descendant of the bookish Tatiana) in a short story, 'A Correspondence', which Turgenev began in 1844 and finished only in 1854. She had been 'awakened' to love, but the young intruder who roused her has bowed out of her life, and she is left with a dismal choice: she can marry one of two provincial mediocrities (both common Turgenev types, the dull decent squire and the ageing grumpy man who is believed a 'wit' by his neighbours); or she can accept the fate of an old maid. Maria Alexandrovna writes:

> I am talking about young girls, especially those who, like me, live in the wilds, and there are very many such in Russia. . . . Picture to yourself such a girl. Her education, suppose, is finished: she begins to live, to enjoy herself. But enjoyment alone is not much to her. She demands much from life, she reads and dreams—of love. Always nothing but love! you will say. . . . But that word means a great deal to her. I repeat that I am not speaking of a girl to whom thinking is tiresome and boring—She looks round her, is waiting for the time when he will come for whom her soul yearns—At last he makes his appearance—she is captivated; she is wax in his hands. All—happiness and love and thought—all have come with a rush together with him; all her tremors are soothed, all her doubts solved by him. Truth itself seems speaking by his lips. . . . Great is his power over her at that time!— If he were a hero, he would fire her, would teach her to sacrifice herself, and all sacrifices would be easy to her! But there are no heroes in our times . . .

Under the influence of her beloved, such a girl 'grows apart from her family, her circle of friends'. Dissatisfied with her life before, she has to endure a redoubled and compounded dissatisfaction when he leaves her. Her 'secret dreams' have been betrayed and now she has to suffer under 'the vulgar triumph of coarse common sense' in a milieu which seems to her a 'desert'.[11]

The 'awakening girl', in Turgenev's hands, is made wholly convincing as an individual whose over-ardent emotions in part reflect her youth, in part the prevalence of Romanticism, and in part the social situation of young women of the nobility to whom no careers are open and for whom love and marriage are the only focus of hope. But a girl of this 'type' can be made to symbolize Russia; the lover who lets her down can look like a radical thinker who comes to give her a lead but then loses his nerve. Love, in any case, is an emotion with wider significance than it usually has in English novels of the same period. For Maria Alexandrovna, 'happiness and love and *thought*' are all bound up together; in 'love' are concentrated all the noble aspirations for which the 'desert' of Russian upper-class life has no use. It transforms the personality as if it were a religious experience, and it gathers up into itself the will to self-sacrifice which Turgenev's generation of idealists had hoped to direct towards the transformation of Russian society. The 'awakening girl' seems oddly like a Belinsky without a pen, a Herzen without a formed political creed. She requires a 'hero' both intellectual and strong to give direction to her craving for a nobler existence.

What begins with the vague hopes of a bookish 'Romantic' girl will end, in Turgenev's fiction, with the drive towards martyrdom of the 'Revolutionary' woman. Turgenev's passionate heroines display an independence which we can rarely match in the English fiction of that time. Again and again, they take the initiative in love affairs, force the issue, even seduce men. Behaviour which in the world of Jane Austen or George Eliot would never be tolerated is overlooked until the point when it is too late for anyone to do much about it. While conventions are strong and even oppressive in Russia too, some factor—is it simply carelessness? or is it based on a greater acknowledgement of the right and capacity of women to make their own choices?—permits the appearance of women in literature and in life as men's equals in rebellion.

There were, of course, revolutionary men as well. One thing distinctive about Turgenev's fiction is the fact that the characters who impress us with their strength of will are in *so many* cases women. It often seems as if Turgenev has lost faith in the men of his own class (the *raznochintsy* are another matter) and has made the women carry burdens of conscience, commitment and 'sacrifice' to which the men are unequal. Both men and women are prey to fate, to that 'cold irony of Jehovah' which Turgenev had detected in the death of Stankevich. But the women tend to oppose fate with more conviction.

Rudin displays the fate of an intellectual of the 1830s. The novel is set around 1840. Into the rather superior provincial milieu of the widowed blue-stocking Daria Lasunskaia bursts, like sun and wind, the brilliant Dmitri Rudin, a nobleman around thirty-five, without much money, but a delicious talker. 'They all thought it strange and incomprehensible that such an intelligent man could turn up so suddenly in the countryside.'[12] Above all he impresses Daria's daughter Natalia and the good-hearted *raznochinets*, Basistov, who tutors Daria's sons. He instals himself as a kind of Grand Vizier in the household. But gradually it emerges that he can achieve nothing. His ideas on farm management aren't carried out. His article on 'the tragic in art and life' will never be written.

However, he 'awakens' the seventeen-year-old Natalia. He is incapable of love (one of his models, Bakunin, was physically impotent, though Rudin's incapacity may be no more than spiritual) but he believes himself for a moment happy. Her mother forbids marriage. In the finest scene of the novel, Natalia meets him at a symbolic site—a place where a pond has dried up and a farmstead has disappeared, near a withered oak-wood—and asks him what they must do now. He replies, 'Naturally, submit'. She rages at him bitterly. 'I was ready for anything,' she says.

Rudin drifts around from place to place, an incompetent hanger-on of the incompetent nobility. We meet him again years later, shabby and grey-haired, accusing himself of having done nothing; we finally hear that he died on the barricades of Paris in June 1848, as if he symbolized all the naïve hopes destroyed there. There are clear suggestions, however, that his influence will live on. 'A fine word is also a deed,' one old comrade tells him. Through their effect on Basistov, we gather, his words may survive and be useful.

Rudin anticipates the essential character of all Turgenev's major novels. It is a story of 'love' involving few characters, mostly from the nobility, and covering, except for its epilogue, only a couple of months. In spite of the fate of its hero, it is not depressing. An intelligent man marries a pleasant young widow and this almost idyllically lightens some of its later pages. Turgenev might well have been in an unusually optimistic frame of mind; on 2 March 1855, Tsar Nicholas had died.

III

Russia's predatory ambitions towards the decaying Ottoman Empire had brought her into conflict with France and Britain. In September 1854, troops of the Western allies landed in the Crimea. Within a week the main Russian army there was defeated, and the Russians were forced into a heroic but unsuccessful defence of the town of Sevastopol, which fell in September 1855 after nearly a year of siege.

So Nicholas's last days were spent in an atmosphere of mounting national shame. Russian conservatives, since 1815, had been able to believe that whatever was wrong with their nation she was at least a formidable military power. Defeat came as a shock, and even people long used to bribing and jobbery were revolted by the corruption of the commisariat. It took less time for an allied soldier to reach the Crimea from Western Europe than for a Russian to reach it from Moscow; such facts emphasized the economic backwardness of Russia. The higher army officers seemed stultified by long habits of unthinking obedience, and it was becoming clear that 'at the root of all the weaknesses and abuses was the supreme evil of serfdom.'[13] In almost every house among the educated classes, 'words were spoken which a few months before would have seemed treasonable, if not blasphemous.'[14]

Alexander II, Nicholas's son, arrived on the throne in a climate of opinion which made reform seem inevitable. Though he was deeply conservative in temperament and views, he was a milder man than his father, and he made clear in a speech of March 1856 that his conservatism was of the kind which sought to preserve the autocracy by admitting reform—'It is better', he said, 'to abolish serfdom from above than to wait until the serfs begin to liberate themselves from below.'[15]

Though Turgenev resumed his summers with the Viardots and his travels in Europe, the Crimean War had perhaps forced him to realize that in the last analysis he was and must be Russian. His second novel, *Home of the Gentry* (1859) is almost Slavophile in its direction. (No book has caused more problems to translators by its title: *A Nest of Gentlefolk*, *A Nest of Nobles*, *A Nest of Hereditary Legislators* and, simply, *Liza*, are among the English versions used.)

Rudin had been rather clumsy in structure—Turgenev had begun by throwing up rather more characters and cross-relationships than he could explore in the brief span of his tale. *Home of the Gentry* is even further from finding a neat form. After the bright and economical opening in the provincial home of a silly widow, Maria Kalitina, it may seem irritating and even tedious that nine chapters are then devoted to a complete family history of the hero, Lavretsky, from the mid-eighteenth century onwards, an account of his father's marriage to a serf girl and his own upbringing under his father's brittle 'Western' ideas, the story of his own marriage to the charming Varvara and his break with her after, in Paris, he discovers her adultery. All this seems unbalancing as an introduction to a very brief and 'short-story'-like love affair between Lavretsky and Liza, the widow's daughter, which is shattered when Varvara herself reappears, determined to batten on her husband's landed wealth.

Lavretsky, already almost middle-aged, at last devotes himself to becoming a good landlord, in accordance with the ideas he has advanced in the novel, against those of the Westernist Panshin, a clever, polished but shallow young bureaucrat. Liza, 'awakened' by Lavretsky so that she can't accept Panshin's offer of marriage demonstrates her own special kind of independence by entering a convent against the wishes of her family. Elsewhere in Turgenev, 'Love' itself seems to be a kind of religion; here Religion is explicitly offered as substitute for Love. Liza is much less interesting than most of Turgenev's heroines, and we may suspect him of insincerity when he turns a girl he means to be charming in the direction of the Orthodox church. But even if the top-dressing of political debate here favours the Slavophiles, the essential 'politics' of the novel clearly condemn, as usual, the inanity of life among the nobility which deprives the fine qualities of a girl like Liza of any social outlet. By contrast, the 'Western' Varvara is a brilliantly sensual portrait of a woman whose dynamism can affect this sleepy world, if only in a destructive way.

Liza's fatalism—'happiness,' she says, 'depends not on us but on God'—drives her out of society altogether. But Turgenev gives the decision of even this wispish heroine a rather stiff political charge. Not only conventional piety (guilt that she has loved a married man) but the immoralities of her milieu drive her into the convent. Her father was both an official and a businessman, dedicated to making money, and therefore presumably corrupt in one role and a grasping exploiter in the other. 'I know everything,' Liza says, 'both my own sins and others', and how papa made all our money. . . . It all has to be paid for by prayer, wiped away by prayer.'[16]

The novel is set in 1842, though Lavretsky's predicament is, by symbolic interpretation, that of Turgenev's own generation, whose contacts with the West (represented by Varvara's expensive and immoral life in Paris) have diverted them from the intimate problems of rural Russia. The time is not yet ripe for a young Russian woman to expiate social sins by political action. *On the Eve*, published a year later in 1860, takes us forward more than a decade, to the 'eve' of the Crimean War, and shows us Turgenev's most attractive heroine caught up by a craving for action.

This is arguably, in its construction, the neatest of Turgenev's 'novels'. He never found a better opening than its richly atmospheric first chapters. The sultry heat of the Russian countryside where we meet a young sculptor and a student, discussing nature, love and a girl named Elena prepares us to meet a heroine who is, like these men, 'on heat'. Nowhere else does Turgenev so successfully combine landscape, ideas and character; the natural setting, from ants to horizon, is brought before us as the contrasting personalities of sculptor and scholar are developed and as they discuss enormous concepts—Beauty, Nature, Life and Death. The sexual drives of youth are harnessed with the intellectual and moral aspirations of young people.

The heat makes itself felt again in Chapter 17. Elena has always puzzled her conventional parents by her attitudes. 'From her childhood she had longed for action, for active goodness; the poor, the hungry and the sick concerned her, worried her, tortured her.'[17] Now she has fallen in love with a poor Bulgarian, Insarov, whose total commitment to the cause of his own people, oppressed by the Turks, raises him above the level of the young Russian intellectuals she knows. Insarov doesn't want to be distracted. He shies away, and decides to leave the neighbourhood. She expects him one hot morning to come and say goodbye, and when he doesn't come her impatience is intolerable. She slips out of the house and rushes to find him. As she walks towards his cottage, the thunderstorm latent in the air bursts. She hails him from the shrine where she has taken shelter; she tells him she loves him and so gives him no chance to escape. This initiative, taken in a fury of sexual as well as moral energy, binds to her a man who has already shown himself capable of strong and decisive physical action; in every way she surpasses Natalia, the girl in *Rudin*.

Turgenev combines in Elena two motifs which elsewhere he keeps separate—the pure 'Love' of the just-awakened girl and the destructive power which women can exercise over men. Insarov, in order to secure a false passport for his wife-to-be, has to compromise himself with Russian corruption by going to see a certain ex-official who can fix such things. With a symbolism which may seem unsubtle, he contracts in the process the tuberculosis which will finally kill him. Elena, visiting him boldly after the first phase of his illness has abated, 'gives herself' sexually to the sick man, pressing herself upon him in spite of his reluctance. After he dies in Venice, having failed even to complete his return journey to Bulgaria, Elena, in a letter, accuses herself—'Who knows, perhaps I killed him'—and this can be interpreted as a recognition of the strain which her bold sexuality has placed on the sick man. When we see her in Venice, her whole body has blossomed out—even her hair seems to be growing more thickly—whereas Insarov is now a complete wreck; it is almost as if, like a vampire, she has stolen life from his body.

In spite of this, Elena remains so appealing that some critics have accused Turgenev of sentimentality in portraying her. But her struggle against her own limitations has tragic stature. Perhaps her chief flaw is that she is not an intellectual—she is all ardour and fresh impulsive response, uncontrolled by careful thought. Both her sexual drive and her compassion are out of her control. For all her unconventionality, she is Fate's plaything—she has no true independence. She strikes out for a man who appeals to her instinct for self-transcendence and uncritically accepts his cause. Without theories about the rights of small nations or a considered attitude to revolutionary violence, her apparent self-sacrifice is really a form of self-indulgence and her sexual and political objectives are tragically confused. As a 'type' she represents a new kind of woman emerging in the 1850s, but like Rudin she is limited by the inadequacies of her own understanding of life as well as by the narrow range of options open to her.

Almost all critics see Insarov as a literary failure. Mirsky calls him a 'strong, silent puppet, at times almost ludicrous'.[18] Such judgements are unfair if they fail to take account of one of the most impressive features of Turgenev's fiction, its almost naive literal-ness. He can't invent characters without some factual basis; and he found one for On the Eve in a true episode told him by a young landowner who had himself played the role of by-passed suitor given to Bersenev in On the Eve. The real life girl actually went off with a Bulgarian lover, and Turgenev, who had already formed the concept of Elena as a new 'type' of heroine found in this anecdote the 'hero' he had been looking for as her foil. As a conscientious realist, he was unable to use a Russian of the same type, because in the 1850s revolutionary Russians simply weren't in evidence; but since his hero is, and must be, Bulgarian, he cannot develop his psychology in any depth. He knew nothing at first hand about Bulgaria. Insarov, sketchy though he is, performs two indispensable functions adequately. He is just convincing enough as the kind of man an Elena would need to arouse her courage and dedication and turn her energy outwards into action rather than inwards as neurosis; and as a foreigner of this kind he demonstrates, by contrast, the absence in Russian society of such men.

The main 'political' points in the story are given to the sculptor, Shubin, one of the sharp-eyed, gossipy, sharp-tongued but rather ridiculous men whose role in Turgenev's fiction is the double one of revealing the sterility of intelligence without passionate commitment and of expounding what seem to be the novelist's own judgements. (The roles of Potugin in *Smoke* and Paklin in *Virgin Soil* are similar.) Shubin is friendly to the gross, somnolent Uvar Ivanovich who functions, perhaps rather crudely, as a symbol of the indolent, passive and inarticulate Russian nation—Shubin hails him as 'spirit of the black earth!', and says to him after Elena's marriage:

> 'We haven't got anyone among us, no real people, wherever you look. It's all either minnows and mice and little Hamlets feeding on themselves in ignorance and dark obscurity, or braggarts throwing their weight about, wasting time and breath and blowing their own trumpets. Or else there's the other kind, always studying themselves in disgusting detail, feeling their pulses with every sensation that they experience and then reporting to themselves: "That's how I feel, and that's what I think." What a useful, sensible sort of occupation. No, if we'd some proper people among us, that girl, that sensitive spirit, wouldn't have left us, she wouldn't have slipped out of our hands like a fish into the water. Why is it, Uvar Ivanovich? When is our time coming? When are we going to produce some real people?'
>
> 'Wait a bit,' Uvar Ivanovich replied, 'they'll come.'[19]

But the fact that Insarov was more 'real' than any Russian contemporary didn't mean that the Bulgarian nationalist movement was going to be immediately successful: Bulgarian independence didn't come until 1878, and then incompletely. The title of *On the Eve* seems to have three kinds of topical connotation. The book is about events on the eve of the Crimean War in which the Balkan peoples were involved in a struggle from which their independence might, with Russian help, have emerged. On one level, it prophesies the coming arrival of a new kind of Russian man who might satisfy an Elena. But also, since it was published in 1860, it relates to the 'eve' of the Emancipation of the serfs and of a new phase in Russian history.

IV

After Alexander had spoken of reform things were bound to move, by Russian standards, fast. Herzen's *Bell*, published in London, though officially banned, circulated widely, and Herzen and other radicals for the moment looked hopefully to the new Tsar. The nobility who had, of course, to be consulted, couldn't resist the movement towards emancipation. From several years of politicking there emerged a settlement, proclaimed in 1861, which, while it could not prevent the gradual ruin of many landowners, ensured that the Russian peasant would remain one of the most exploited creatures on earth. While labour was 'freed' for terrible toil in factories, the man who stayed on the land was shackled with new bonds and would become prey to new exploiters, including his own more successful brethren.

The peasants themselves reacted against the proclamation. They had always tended to believe that they really owned the land they worked— 'We are yours but the land is ours.' Now they were being made to pay the landowners, in instalments which would continue for a lifetime or beyond, for land which they had regarded as theirs by right. Since the nobility took large tracts for their own use, peasants' holdings were reduced in size. A new form of exploitation based on money replaced the old quasi-feudal system. And while the peasant could now own property and go to law, his freedom of movement and choice of occupation were still restricted by the communes which replaced the landlords as rural authorities and which had the power to flog offenders and to grant and withhold passports.

As, through the 1860s, the complicated settlement proceeded, it was amply clear that social justice had not come to Russia. Other reforms followed. In 1864 the *Zemstvo*'s were created—elected district and provincial councils, dominated by the nobility, which had powers to raise taxes for roads, bridges, schools and other local improvements. In the same year public trial by jury on the Western model was introduced, as part of a generally modernized system of justice. But Alexander stopped short of the creation of a national assembly which would have restrained his own power by constitutional debate. Russia after the reforms was a more up-to-date place, where industrialists made their power felt, where the nobility began to look more like English 'gentlemen', where the bureaucracy was less blatantly corrupt and was open to moderate 'liberal' ideas, and where arts and sciences reached peaks undreamt of under Nicholas. The era of Oblomov was over, and with it the days of Pechorin and Rudin. But gross social and economic injustice persisted, along with the violent methods of a police state, and in an atmosphere of disillusionment, young radicals were ready to use violence in their turn. In 1866 an extremist shot at the Tsar and the routines of repression reappeared over the press and the universities.

Turgenev's fourth 'novel', *Fathers and Sons*, appeared in 1862. Its setting in 1859 brought it closer to the present than any of its predecessors, and in its hero, Bazarov, Turgenev paid what may be interpreted as guarded homage to the rising generation of radicals. But his presentation of Bazarov reflected his own ambiguous relationship with new ways of thought which could be seen as stemming from the radicalism of his own generation, but went far beyond it.

The new ideas had been formed largely by the literary critics N. G. Chernyshevsky (1828–1889) and N. A. Dobroliubov (1836–1861). They were *raznochintzy*, both sons of priests and they used the *Contemporary*, which Pushkin had founded, to advance a materialist ideology which included a utilitarian aesthetic.

Chernyshevsky was a 'socialist', acknowledged as a precursor by Lenin himself. But he was in reaction against the romantic idealism of Herzen's generation, a devotee of science and rationality. In the words of E. H. Carr: '... it was that once famous bible of materialism, Büchner's *Kraft und Stoff*, published in Germany in 1855 and quickly circulated in Russia in illicit translations, which satisfied the young Russians of the 1860s that human life and human behaviour were to be explained in material and physiological terms, and that the reform of society was in the strictest sense a scientific problem. Rather surprisingly, Chernyshevsky dismissed Comte as superficial, and was shocked by the deductions which some social thinkers were beginning to draw from Darwin's survival of the fittest. But this was because he felt himself to possess a simpler and more direct key to the problems of society. The question of morality seemed to him to have been solved once for all by the English Utilitarians, known to him principally through John Stuart Mill, whom he translated. Nothing else could be expected, and nothing else was needed, than the pursuit by every individual of his rational and enlightened self interest.'[20] He believed that enlightened self-interest would lead men and women awakened to rational thought into a cooperative way of life. His own saintly idealism of character is undisputed. But to Turgenev, and still more to Dostoevsky, it seemed that he and his followers (who were greatly augmented in and after 1864 by the publication of Chernyshevsky's moralizing novel, *What is to be Done*, which became a bible for young radicals) were introducing immoral doctrines which tended to undermine the dignity of man.

Music, for Chernyshevsky, was at its best when it was 'natural', in bird song for instance. Poetry was too vague to be useful. Novels excelled police gazettes only in their 'rhetorical amplification' of the facts. Gogol could be praised as the founder of the 'critical tendency' of Russian fiction, but only at the expense of the 'pure artist' Pushkin. In 1858 Chernyshevsky pitched into Turgenev's own liberalism and the love stories he provided. 'Goodbye erotic questions! A reader of our time, occupied with problems of administrative and judiciary institutions, of financial reforms, of the emancipation of the serfs, does not care for them.'[21]

Dobroliubov's critique of *On the Eve* was a prime example of the use of fiction-reviewing as an outlet for political sermons. Its reading of the novel still seems perceptive, and Dobroliubov was fully sensitive to the delicacy of Turgenev's art as well as to his gift for grasping up-to-date political topics.[22] Turgenev, however, thought the review 'harsh and unjust' and tried to persuade the editor of the *Contemporary* not to print it. In 1861, his connection with the periodical was publicly severed. But whereas Dostoevsky would react with wholesale disapproval to the ideas of the new critics and their followers, Turgenev retained a cautious but sympathetic interest in the radical young and their notions.

He defended himself against the charge that he had 'lampooned' Dobroliubov in his creation of Bazarov, by claiming that he had simply based the character of his hero on that of a young provincial doctor whom he had met briefly and who had since died, and on his observation of 'people like him.' He went further to say that 'with the exception of Bazarov's views on art, I share almost all his convictions.'[23] Indeed, angry conservatives accused him of favouring Bazarov at the same time as some, though not all, of the young radicals decried his travesty of themselves. Reality played its own hand in the controversy. The term 'nihilist' applied to Bazarov in the novel was seized and attached to the unknown perpetrators of a number of mysterious fires which occurred in Petersburg in 1862 and were attributed, on no sure grounds, to revolutionaries. Certainly, small revolutionary groups were now busy distributing provocative leaflets. In the Government's efforts to wipe out its enemies, Chernyshevsky himself was exiled to Siberia in 1864, and remained there for nearly twenty years.

Turgenev was bruised by the reception of his book; it seemed to him that only Dostoevsky and a couple of others had grasped his intentions. At the same time, he came under attack from his old friend Herzen. The scorn Herzen now poured on the corrupted West stung Turgenev into a controversy with him in which he reaffirmed his own faith that Russians were in fact Europeans and must travel the same road as their fellows. In spite of these disagreements, Turgenev was charged, along with dozens of others, with having trafficked with Herzen and the 'London propagandists'. He was at the time in France. Panic-stricken, he wrote to the Tsar in fulsome style to proclaim his loyalty and in written replies to the Senatorial committee which was set up to investigate the matter he went to unseemly lengths in dissociating himself from his former friends. Summoned nevertheless to appear before the committee, he went back to Russia early in 1864 and was able to clear himself. But meanwhile Herzen jeered in *The Bell* at this 'gray-haired Magdalene (of the male sex) who wrote the Emperor that she was losing sleep and appetite, white hair and teeth, because she was tormented by the fear that he did not know of her repentance. . .'[24] And some of his fellow-defendants were sentenced to years of hard labour.

It is easy to understand the impatience of younger men with Turgenev's brand of 'liberalism'. One student, about this time, defined a Liberal as 'a man who loves liberty, generally a noble. . . . These men like looking at liberty from windows and doing nothing, and then go for a stroll and on to theatres and balls.'[25] Turgenev, an ageing dandy with a high-pitched voice, was an easy target for such jibes from those who were, or thought themselves, more down to earth. Leo Tolstoy veered from intense affection for him to profound contempt, and there is a whiff of Bazarov in the comic account of one of their quarrels left by a contemporary. 'Turgenev shrieks and clutches at his throat and whispers with his dying-gazelle eyes, "I can't take any more! I've got bronchitis!" and begins striding up and down all three rooms. "Bronchitis!" growls Tolstoy. "Bronchitis is an imaginary disease! Bronchitis is a metal."'[26] The two men had a picturesque quarrel in 1861, when Tolstoy touched Turgenev on the sore point of his illegitimate daughter. Turgenev slapped his face, and Tolstoy challenged him to a duel. This was averted, but in further correspondence Turgenev challenged Tolstoy. All that happened was a breach between the writers which lasted seventeen years.

The list of Turgenev's rows with eminent contemporaries didn't end there. (His embarrassments with Goncharov have already been mentioned.) Partly over his next 'novel', *Smoke*, he quarrelled with Dostoevsky, who duly caricatured him later in *The Devils*.

From 1861, Turgenev had regarded himself as domiciled abroad. *Smoke* is set in the German town of Baden where he had settled, in 1864, to be near the Viardots. The novel presents a young nobleman named Litvinov who has been studying agriculture and technology in Western Europe so as to make himself a more efficient landowner. Waiting in Baden for his sweet young fiancée, he meets again Irina, now the wife of a high-ranking bureaucrat, with whom he had been in love when she was living in Moscow as a girl. She is bored by her luxurious and frivolous existence; she imposes herself on Litvinov; she robs him of his will; she comes to his room and seduces him. When his fiancée arrives, he breaks his engagement, but Irina doesn't have the nerve to run away with him. Litvinov, reasserting himself in a manner rare among Turgenev's men, refuses to remain merely her satellite and returns to Russia, where he eventually marries his former fiancée.

The title refers to Litvinov's thoughts as he looks through the window watching the smoke of the train which takes him back to Russia:

> 'Smoke, smoke', he repeated several times: and it suddenly seemed to him that everything was smoke: everything—his own life, Russian life, everything human, especially everything Russian.[27]

This passage links his despair over the evaporation of his love affairs with his reaction to two sets of Russians he has met at Baden—a gaggle of intellectuals presided over by the stupid Gubarev with his Slavophile notions, and a prattling phalanx of civil-service Generals in which Irina moves. It would not be fair to say that Turgenev fails to relate his bitter satire on these Russians abroad to the love affair which provides the brief and simple 'story' of the book, because Irina's dissatisfaction, which makes her hanker for Litvinov, is seen as the reaction of a girl with good qualities against the emptiness of Russian official life. But the book is badly unbalanced by the prominence given to Potugin, an elderly hanger-on of Irina's whose connection with the story is tenuous but whose rabid 'Westernist' opinions seem to reflect Turgenev's own bitterness against the nation which had failed to understand *Fathers and Sons*. Potugin, though he claims to love Russia, identifies Europe with all 'culture' and 'civilization', asserts that Russians have never invented anything—not even 'the samovar, the bast shoes, and the knout'—and pours scorn on Russian music and painting.

We must not assume that Turgenev always agrees with Potugin, but by giving him so much space he clearly favours him, and to shove general ideas at the reader in this clumsy way is both artistically and intellectually a bad mistake. And Litvinov, the strong silent hero, is much more of a cipher than Insarov. It has been suggested that Turgenev was trying to create a tough-minded nobleman to match his powerful *raznochinets*, Bazarov. If so, the fact that he can give this 'type' barely more than theoretical existence suggests that he was losing his grip on reality and even his interest in it. '*All* is vapour and smoke', Litvinov thinks; and in that case, reality itself can't be trusted. Turgenev's shorter stories from 1862 onwards show a new interest in the supernatural, and there are strange hints in *Smoke* itself that Irina's power over Litvinov involves witchcraft. Turgenev was for the moment retreating towards rhetoric, abstraction and fantasy. The Romantic in him was temporarily out of control.

Dostoevsky met Turgenev at Baden in 1867 with a two-year-old debt to him still unpaid, and fell out with him almost finally; no doubt his unease over the money he owed him contributed, as well as the opinions Turgenev had given to Potugin. But in making the piece of prose which the odious Karmazinov reads aloud in *The Devils* a morbid fantasy of love and the supernatural, Dostoevsky hits shrewdly at Turgenev's weakest side.

Smoke for all its faults is still moving, and it was a great success with readers in French, German and English translation as well as in Russian. And several 'long short stories' of the next few years—*Lear of the Steppes* (1870), *Spring Torrents* (1872), *Punin and Baburin* (1874) are not only up to his very best level, but represent extensions of his range as a writer. That all three are set in the time of Turgenev's youth does not mean that they merely reflect the nostalgia of an ageing man. Given a firm historical perspective, they are played over by ironies deeper and calmer than we find in the 'novels'. Turgenev's 'Lear' is a provincial landlord of the 'old school', uncultivated, inarticulate, and yet lovable. In the light of memory this huge, crude man is forgiven as perhaps he could not have been when his type was still commonplace. As in Shakespeare's play, he divides his land between his daughters, but their unkindness drives him from home. He returns in rage to pull his old house down in a scene which combines pathos with terrible comedy. He dies, crushed by the top central beam. But his daughters live on, to demonstrate both certain effects which can only be obtained by reaching far back into the remembered past, and Turgenev's persisting power to create memorable women. The elder becomes a formidably efficient landlord greatly respected in her neighbourhood and, we are told, a happy woman. The younger, more strangely, leaves home and is glimpsed years later as an awesome figure, 'chief mother' of a sect of thousands of flagellants. 'Not simply the serenity of power—the satiety of power was visible in every feature. The careless glance she cast at me told of long years of habitually meeting nothing but reverent, unquestioning obedience.'[28]

Spring Torrents at first sight seems almost a reworking of *Smoke*. In 1840, in the German town of Frankfurt, a young Russian named Sanin falls in love with an Italian girl whose mother keeps a pastry-shop there. They are engaged to be married, but Sanin is devoured alive by a remarkable Russian woman, Maria Nikolaevna, daughter of a serf millionaire, and he deserts his Gemma to follow her. The Western girl and her family are lovingly portrayed, but their appeal can't keep Sanin from succumbing to a girl who, as she masters him (mistresses him?) seems to represent all the coarseness, vitality and irresistible power of a still half-savage Russia.

Turgenev, now over fifty, was coming to terms again with his Russian identity. As the first Russian writer to make a great name in the West, as the friend of distinguished French writers, including Flaubert, and as the idol of young Henry James, he was looked to in Europe as a spokesman for Russia. He was now ready to prophesy again on the destiny of his native land. In 1872, he planned a new novel which was to deal with the newest wave of political activity in Russia.

Two different kinds of influence were at work there. Turgenev's old comrade, the exile Bakunin, stood for anarchist violence. The idea of an élitist insurrection led by educated men appealed to some young Russians. Others, moved by the ideas of P. I. Lavrov, who urged peaceful propaganda among the peasants, formed a remarkable movement. In 1873 and 1874 hundreds of girls and young men 'went to the people', earning the name of *narodniki* or 'Populists'. They spread revolutionary propaganda among peasants who at best could rarely understand what these intellectuals were saying, and at worst were actively hostile. The police, of course, were watching. Between 1873 and 1877 1611 propagandists were arrested, of whom 15 per cent were women. Of those condemned to prison or exiled, less than a third were of noble birth—children of priests were amazingly numerous, and together with those of non-noble officials, of merchants, Jews and urban workers, made up the remainder.[29]

The mass trials of Narodniks in 1877/8 created great public interest and even sympathy. When, on the day after they ended, a young woman named Vera Zazulich fired at the police chief of St Petersburg because he had ordered an imprisoned student to be flogged, the jury acquitted her at her trial. Meanwhile, the radicals who had remained free had learnt from their mistakes, and in 1876 the first Russian revolutionary party was founded, taking the name of *Zemlia i volia*, 'Land and Liberty'. It operated not only among peasants but also among workers in city factories. In 1879 a division emerged between those who favoured peaceful propaganda and those who wanted political action and terrorism. The latter split off as *Narodnaia volia*, the 'People's Will', and directed themselves to the task of assassinating the Tsar. After several failures, a bomb thrown in the street killed him in 1881.

Turgenev explored in *Punin and Baburin* memories of the naïve rebels of the 1840s, before turning in *Virgin Soil* to present his view of those of the 1870s (though he set the novel anachronistically in 1868). The briefer tale covers a great sweep of history, from the day in 1830 when the noble narrator, as a small boy, first meets the gentle, poetry-loving serf Punin and his devoted protector the stern republican Baburin, to 1861 when Baburin, in exile because he was implicated in the Petrashevsky circle, dies of pneumonia caught while celebrating the emancipation of the serfs. Baburin also protects an orphan girl, Musa, whom he plans to marry. She runs off with a student, seeking more life than the ageing pair can offer her, but Baburin rescues her again after she is deserted and she marries him and goes to Siberia with him, sharing completely in his ideals and in the educational work he begins there. If Punin represents the charm and imagination latent in the peasantry, and Baburin their potential strength of character, Musa shows us a spirited young girl for whom 'Love' is replaced by 'Politics' as the centre of aspiration. In this respect, she anticipates Marianna in *Virgin Soil*.

His last 'novel' took Turgenev only three months to write when he finally got down to it in 1876, but it is his longest and in many ways his most ambitious work of fiction. He had been able to study the new generation not only on his frequent trips to Russia, but also in Paris, where he gave his time and money generously to compatriots who called on him. Nevertheless, on its appearance in 1877 the book was widely attacked as a failure, and Turgenev himself meekly concurred in the verdict that he had failed to present his revolutionaries accurately because he was now out of touch with day-to-day life in Russia. Once again, while the right complained of the novelist's sympathy for agitators, the left sneered at his failure to get his facts straight. Most modern critics seem to agree that *Virgin Soil* is inferior to Turgenev's earlier novels; it might be fairer to say that it repeats certain failings found in them but is rather different in kind from them. Whereas other novels centre round a dominant central figure, here there is, in the group of revolutionaries, a multiple focus of attraction, and these people themselves are sharply contrasted not only with representatives of conformist Russia, but with each other. Of all Turgenev's extended fictions it is least like a 'long story' and most like a big 'novel'.

The 'love story' for once isn't dominant; the revolutionaries' schemes match it in interest. It is very similar in pattern to the 'love story' in

Rudin, and the young man involved in it, Nezhdanov, is yet another 'Russian Hamlet', unable to resolve the conflict between his urge to write poetry and his theoretical commitment to revolutionary politics. Like Rudin, he is a good talker, he spouts ideas which he doesn't at bottom believe in, and is a man unable to fall truly in love. A leading 'Liberal' official named Sipiagin takes him down to his estate as tutor for his son. Nezhdanov links up with the local revolutionaries and attracts Sipiagin's niece and fretful dependent Marianna. The bitter relationship of this girl with her aunt gives a sharp edge to her character which is not wholly ingratiating, but her politics are naively idealistic. She runs away with Nezhdanov determined to live like a peasant with the peasants. But Nezhdanov finds he can't commit himself wholly to her, and his first effort at propaganda ends in shameful failure when mocking peasants make him drunk on their coarse vodka. He commits suicide before the authorities come to arrest him. Marianna, however, escapes and marries Solomin, son of a deacon, super-efficient manager of a factory, gradualist in politics but a friend of the revolutionaries.

It is emphasized that Marianna does not give herself sexually to Nezhdanov. Her political commitment is clearly separate from, and preponderant over, her sexual drive, and is therefore more truly free than Elena's. Her marriage to Solomin matches her with a man of mediocre class but great practical gifts—when last heard of, he has set up a factory run on cooperative lines. As an engineer and political 'realist' he is the man of the future whose presence in the book creates its fundamental optimism. Shubin's question in *On the Eve*—'when are we going to produce some real people?'—seems to be answered in this novel when his counterpart, Paklin, says of Solomin:

> ... I tell you that people like him are the real men! It's difficult to understand them at first, but, believe me, they're the real men. The future is in their hands. ... They are robust, strong, dull men of the people. They are exactly what we want just now. ... Solomin's heart aches just as ours does; he hates the same things that we hate, but his nerves are of iron and his body is under his full control.[30]

Solomin is not an especially attractive character, but he reconciles many of the contradictions which have exercised Turgenev's conscience in and out of his fiction. He is wholly Russian, a 'man of the people,' yet trained in Western technology. He is a radical, and yet a good-mannered gradualist, a man of will and yet a man of kindness. At last Turgenev has managed to imagine a strong male character who, unlike Lavretsky, is not condemned to a permanent lack of full happiness and unlike Insarov and Bazarov is permitted to live and work for his ideals. Turgenev strikes through at the end to a clear affirmation of faith in Russia's future. The dedicated artist applauds the man of technology.

One can hear the sneers of Dostoevsky. There are certainly elements of masochism, if not of dishonesty, in Turgenev's proclamation of a hero with no interest in the arts, as if that gray-haired Magdalene of the male sex were appealing to everyone to notice how he could appreciate the practical ability and firm commitment he had never had himself. And one must feel that even if his motives do him credit, Turgenev has faked a solution to Russia's problems. Solomin is not to be dismissed as merely a cardboard cut-out designed to represent a kind of person who didn't and couldn't exist—Edmund Wilson has noted that in him Turgenev anticipated 'the solid side of the Bolsheviks, something of the character of Lenin. . .'[31] But his relationship with the revolutionaries is not altogether convincing, and Turgenev couldn't understand the life of the modern factory as he had once understood that of the serfs. Even if we could agree that the Solomins eventually came to rule Russia (along with other elements all too reminiscent of the henchmen of Tsarist oppression) we would have to remember that the revolutionary movement in fact had forty years to go before it succeeded in overthrowing the state.

But if its positive message must be seen as a generous shot in the dark by a writer determined to find hope, there are many splendid things in *Virgin Soil*. The portraits of the liberal Sipiagin and his wife have a judicious bitterness which goes beyond Turgenev's previous achievements in satirical characterization. Both, at first sight, seem attractive and as the reader is made gradually to realize the hollowness of their progressive postures, Turgenev achieves the maximum of bite with the minimum of caricature. In quite a different vein, he succeeds superbly with Mashurina, the plain heavy and dogged woman with whom the novel opens and closes, a drudge of the revolutionary cause who is wordlessly devoted to the bright and gifted Nezhdanov.

In spite of the cool reception of *Virgin Soil*, Turgenev was fêted on his trip to Russia in 1879 and in the same year he was given a prize which indicated how wide and secure his fame now was, and with it the reputation of Russian literature; Oxford University awarded him an honorary doctorate. He died of cancer of the spine in a suburb of Paris in 1883. He left behind him a relatively small output of writing, but enough to secure his place as one of the dozen major figures in nineteenth-century European fiction.

Both his weaknesses and his greatness have a great deal to do with the detachment of artist from life which he combined with avid observation. The demands of truth, as he saw them, forced the novelist into withdrawal from binding commitments whether political, social or intellectual. 'Systems,' he wrote to Tolstoy in the 1850s, 'are only dear to those who cannot take the whole truth into their hands, who want to catch it by the tail; a system is just like the tail of truth, but truth is like a lizard; it will leave its tail in your hand and then escape you; it knows that within a short time it will grow another.'[32] The artist must be free to interpret truth as he found it. He wrote in his *Literary Reminiscences*:

What one needs is the constant communion with the environment one undertakes to reproduce; what one needs is truthfulness, a truthfulness that is inexorable in relation to one's own feelings; what one needs is freedom, absolute freedom of opinions and ideas, and, finally, what one needs is education, what one needs is knowledge. . . . Learning is not only light, according to the Russian proverb, it is also freedom. Nothing makes a man so free as knowledge, and nowhere is freedom so needed as in art, in poetry. . .'[33]

Turgenev all too often reminds us of the clever, self-pitying, shoulder-shrugging spokesmen he uses in his novels; his intelligence can seem aimless and self-destroying, his detachment another word for cowardice. He didn't, like Tolstoy or Dostoevsky, force his way *through* 'systems' to raw new truths and to a more than bookish kind of learning; he did not, like them expose himself rashly to experience. As Edmund Wilson remarks, he can't, like Tolstoy, convince you that he, and you, have lived inside another person's skin.[34] His people are not large and diffuse, as we seem to ourselves when we think of ourselves; they are neatly defined and small, because somewhat distant. They are like people we remember from long ago, perhaps from a summer holiday. His novels are mostly set in summer, and bird-loud landscapes and long dusks help to give them the appeal, for us, of a vacation. Hence, perhaps, the legend that Turgenev is a 'perfect' artist (he seems 'perfect' because his books are so attractive). Yet in fact, as Frank O'Connor insists, he can't be regarded as a supremely skilful but perhaps minor writer. O'Connor calls him 'a major writer with colossal faults.'[35]

V

'Colossal' goes rather too far. The flaws matter only in so far as the reader is annoyed by them, and for those convinced of Turgenev's greatness, they aren't decisively important. But by noting 'faults' we can discover what is of more moment, Turgenev's limitations.

If we look at the *Sportsman's Sketches*, some of which are indeed very hard to fault, we can list at least four things which Turgenev is superbly good at. Firstly, he can 'bring a character to life' in a very few touches— face, clothes, characteristic expressions and gestures. Few novelists can achieve such vividness with so little fuss. Allied to this is a gift for broad effects of humour and satire. It was not for nothing that he belonged to the first generation to be bowled over by Gogol, but whereas Gogol's eye is that of an equal or underling slyly observing absurdities among all classes, Turgenev's is that of an aristocrat measuring people of the upper classes by how far they fall short of the standards of good taste, well-mannered behaviour and fine intelligence which he himself represents. In a genial mood, his accounts of mildly eccentric landowners with their mannerisms and unconsciously comic tricks of speech point forward to Chekhov and remind us a little of Dickens. At other times, his satire becomes spiteful and almost pettish.

He is a very great master of landscape description. It would be very hard to match, for instance, the presentation in his sketch 'Kasian from the Beautiful Lands' of a wood where labourers have felled and are felling trees (and we must always remember that Turgenev is by all accounts a very rich prose stylist whose effects will be especially difficult to render in English). In this passage, Turgenev combines, with no apparent strain, an astonishing range of impressions—the shape of the clouds, the fungi, the flowers, the breeze, the heat, the insects, the smell of wood chips, the faint clatter of axes, as well as the trees, living and dead. Nothing seems to be there for any purpose except to evoke what the wood is actually like, yet the richness of the description and its compactness give it a 'poetic' quality which makes the reader feel that Turgenev is communicating something profound about the whole nature of life. The young shoots rise above 'blackened and squat stumps of trees' on which adhere 'round, spongy fungoid growths with grey edges'—in the midst of life we are in death, we think, yet there is no heavy-handed nudging of the reader towards such reflections.

Finally, Turgenev can compose out of a few characters, met, made vivid and briefly shown in action against a clearly visualized scene, works which are not 'stories' in the conventional sense but which make the reader feel he has experienced a great deal of life through a few short pages. 'The Singers' and 'Bezhin Meadow' are justly famous; in each, the sportsman, in his wanderings, encounters a group of people and watches and listens for a while; nothing much out of the ordinary happens; then he goes away. But the contest between two singers in a country pub suggests many thoughts about art, about the creative gifts of the peasantry, and about the paradoxes of human nature. In 'Bezhin Meadow' the hunter gets lost at night and his blunderings bring him to rest at a place where peasant boys sit watching horses and swapping eerie stories; that's all, except that we learn at the end that the most impressive of the lads has since been killed in a fall from a horse, and the threat of senseless destruction which seemed to lurk in the landscape where the hunter was lost appears to be confirmed.

But the reader may be less readily convinced by 'The Hamlet of the Shchigrovsky District', where a nasty satirical picture of a gathering of provincial gentry is followed by the long monologue of one of them, an embittered intellectual who tells the narrator his life story. This is not because the material is uninteresting, but because the form of the sketch seems contrived. And in 'Meeting', where the sportsman sees and hears in a wood in autumn the parting between a betrayed peasant girl and her lover, a flashy young valet, we are more damagingly aware of the contrivances by which Turgenev aims to squeeze pathos out of a commonplace scene. The landscape setting becomes portentously 'symbolic'. The detachment of the narrator from what he describes seems morally dubious —what right, after all, has he got to eavesdrop in this way?

It should be said that in the best of the 'long short stories' which Turgenev wrote later this kind of 'artfulness' is rarely obtrusive. If outbreaks of it mar *Spring Torrents*, the drily moving *Quiet Spot* of 1854 and the marvellous *First Love* of 1860, in which a man retells in middle age the story of his boyish infatuation for a girl who became his father's mistress, seem almost free of it. But the 'novels', more ambitious works, are quite often flawed by writing too obviously worked up so as to prey on the reader's emotions. In *Home of the Gentry*, for instance, it is hard to forgive Turgenev for the use he makes of Lemm, Liza's too 'touching' old music teacher.

Two further elements contribute to the unevenness of the 'novels'. Turgenev, the master of the simple, direct 'love story' and of the 'thumb-nail sketch' commits himself to exploring political themes in a historical context. He would not be the great writer he is if he did not make this attempt. To a very impressive extent, he succeeds. But his aims create acute difficulties for a novelist who tries to fulfil them within the scope provided by a brief 'story' covering only a few weeks (or, as in the case of *Smoke*, a few days). As we have seen, in *Home of the Gentry* the biography of Lavretsky, which is designed to give him the requisite historical depth, is disproportionate both to the length of the novel and (alas) to the intrinsic interest of the man's over-straightforward personality. And in order to bring his characters' political bearings out into the open, Turgenev sometimes offers us set-piece debates which likewise seem out of balance with the love story.

It must be stressed that such things jar on us only because Turgenev *is* such a delicate artist; a more robust and vulgar manner like that of Dickens or Dostoevsky can take such a range of intentions easily in its stride. In the lightly-engineered fiction of Turgenev, the reader will be jolted and irritated by transitions between different modes of writing which in the *Sketches* are generally kept separate. While some characters will be conceived with comprehensive, if detached, sympathy, others will be mauled by satirical caricature. And the 'politics' or the 'history' may, while interesting in themselves, seem only half-digested into the story's flow, or may dam it altogether for a relatively large number of pages.

Turgenev's 'concision', which Henry James thought his 'great external mark'[36] does paradoxically make him at times clumsy in handling the rich material he selects. But, after all this has been said, it is amazing that he can create so much life and meaning in such short books. He is able in his best-conceived characters to draw together love and history, politics and tragedy, charm and unbending realism in a 'concise' fashion that no one, perhaps, has ever matched.

His own remarks suggest two different, but not mutually exclusive, bases for such 'types.' He wrote in 1880:

... I have aspired to the extent that my powers and ability have permitted, conscientiously and impartially to depict and embody in suitable types both what Shakespeare calls: 'the body and pressure of time' and that rapidly changing physiognomy of Russians of the cultured stratum, which has been pre-eminently the object of my observations.[37]

Here the basis is clearly seen as historical. We know that Turgenev would begin with a character in mind, sometimes based on a living person, who seemed to him to have 'typical' traits, then study similar people, and then create a story which would reveal this contemporary 'type' in interaction with other characters who in themselves are more or less 'typical'. Sometimes such 'typing' is very well done on a very small scale. Kurnatovsky, for instance, the official who briefly figures as Elena's suitor in *On the Eve* is a sharp sketch of a new style bureaucrat, ready to call himself a 'proletarian', full of talk about 'principles', factories and science, but hard and shallow, as we know, because Elena reacts against his 'official sort of smile'.

Turgenev's famous lecture on 'Hamlet and Don Quixote', written in the late 1850s, makes it clear that he thought also in terms of his types displaying 'eternal' elements in human nature. Quixote and Hamlet, he points out, both appeared in print in the same year, 1606. (We note Turgenev's habitual obsession with historical time.) Quixote is the idealist with a faith in something bigger than himself and outside himself, whereas Hamlet is the egotist who lives only for himself yet cannot believe even in himself, though his knowledge of his own weaknesses is a strength. Whereas Hamlet's character will tend to produce tragedy, Quixote's lends itself to comedy. Turgenev claims that 'all human life is nothing more than the eternal reconciliation and the eternal struggle' of the 'ceaselessly divided and ceaselessly interfused elements' represented by these characters. Hamlet expresses the 'basic centripetal force of nature, by virtue of which every living thing regards itself as the centre of creation', but if nature could not exist without this force, it also needs 'the other, centrifugal force' represented by Quixote, 'by whose law everything exists only for another':

These two forces of stagnation and movement, of conservatism and progress, are the basic forces of everything that exists. They explain to us the growth of a flower, and they offer us a clue to an understanding of the development of the most powerful of nations.[38]

In the dialectical basis of his view of life, as in his admiration for Shakespeare and Cervantes, Turgenev stands closer to Dostoevsky than we generally realize.

It is easy to find 'Hamlets' in Turgenev's fiction, as it is in Chekhov's; this 'type' may be eternal, but it seems to have made itself unusually at home in nineteenth-century Russia. Critics have hunted Quixotically for Quixotes in Turgenev's fiction, without finding any to convince us—

Elena, for instance, is both introspective and, in effect if not in intention, selfish. And fond though Turgenev was of contrasting a pair of friends in his stories, Punin and Baburin being an obvious example, it's never easy to see each of these friends as clearly representing one of the contrasting principles. Turgenev in fact tends to create characters who (like flowers, if we believe what he says) exemplify simultaneously both forces; the nature of man in his works is double.

Nowhere is this more apparent than in the greatest of all his 'types', Bazarov in *Fathers and Sons*, who is both Quixote and Hamlet, both comic and tragic.

VI

Fathers and Sons is, apart from *Virgin Soil*, Turgenev's most ambitiously conceived novel. Yet there is no 'plot', and the story is complex only by Turgenev's own standards.

In 1859, Arkady Kirsanov brings his university friend Bazarov to stay with his family in the country. His father, Nikolai Kirsanov, is an ineffectual liberal in his forties, whose excellent intentions towards his serfs, coupled with his own incompetence as an estate manager, have only impoverished his property. He has recently had a second son by a serf-girl, Fenichka, who runs his house for him. His brother Pavel is an Anglophile dandy—a 'Westerner' of Turgenev's own generation whose army career has been ruined by his love for a fascinating Princess; he is one among many such victims of *femmes fatales* in Turgenev's works.

Bazarov's materialism has cast a spell over Arkady, who tries to imitate his blunt opinions. Bazarov is a *raznochinets*, the son of a former army surgeon with only a handful of serfs to his name; it is certainly significant that Turgenev gives him origins similar to those of his dead friend Belinsky. He smokes cheap cigars. He catches frogs and dissects them in his room. He admires German science and pours scorn on the backwardness of Russia. He despises Pushkin and mocks Romantic love:

'What are these mysterious relations between a man and a woman. We physiologists know what they are. You study the anatomy of the eye, and where does that enigmatic look you talk about come in? That's all romantic rot, mouldy aesthetics. We had much better go and inspect that beetle.'[39]

Arkady smilingly describes his friend as a 'nihilist': that is, 'a person who does not take any principle for granted, however much that principle may be revered.' Nikolai, whose love for his son is reciprocated across the gap between their ages, is dismayed when Arkady, with 'an affectionate look of pity', takes a book of Pushkin's out of his hands and replaces it with Büchner's famous work. '. . . All over the province,' Nikolai laments to his brother, 'I am known as a *radical*. . . I try in every way to keep abreast with the requirements of the age—and yet here they are saying I'm over and done with.'[40]

Well over a quarter of the book is taken up with the stay of the two young men at the Kirsanov's estate, in which nothing more remarkable happens than a furious argument between Bazarov and Pavel in which the older man is goaded, paradoxically, into the expression of Slavophile ideas and Bazarov's bent for revolutionary activism is subtly manifested. 'Aren't you just talking like all the rest?', mutters Pavel. 'We may have our faults but we are not guilty of that one,' Bazarov mutters back between his teeth, hitting at the generation of Rudins, Pavels (and Turgenevs) who did nothing but talk.[41]

Bazarov has a low estimate of the peasants and their institutions. But the servants like him. Children take to him. And his dynamism emerges by contrast with the timidity of the older men. Nikolai doesn't have the nerve to marry Fenichka, while Pavel (and this is established with matchless delicacy) hankers wordlessly after his brother's mistress. Essentially lovable though both men are made to seem, they are foolish people without their feet on the ground, and Bazarov seems to oppose them with the force of reality itself.

In the second phase of the novel Bazarov and Arkady visit the neighbouring town, where Turgenev finds occasion for some rather broad satire of the bureaucracy, and for some rather silly sniping at an 'emancipated woman', Avdotia Kukshina. When this plain, untidy woman, full of intellectual pretensions, claims that she has invented a new sort of mastic 'To make doll's heads so that they can't break', Turgenev's spite itself seems childish.

At the Governor's ball, Arkady is smitten by the beauty of Madame Odintsova, a rich young widow. Bazarov is also attracted, though he characteristically exclaims, 'What a magnificent body! Shouldn't I like to see it on the dissecting table!' The young men go to stay at her estate; while Arkady has no interest for her, she tantalizes out of his 'nihilist' friend a declaration of love and is then shocked by his passionate embrace. The young men move on to stay with Bazarov's parents, and two longish chapters reveal these kind, simple people to us. They are devoted to their son, who repels their well-meant but clumsy attempts to please him. The old man's craving to gain his son's respect parallels that of Nikolai Kirsanov and develops the theme suggested by the book's title.

When Bazarov's impatience drives the 'sons' off again, we are two-thirds of the way through the book. The main characters have been balanced in three groups: there are three Kirsanovs, together with Fenichka, three Bazarovs; and Madame Odintsova with her sister Katia. Apart from the briefly glimpsed provincial town we have seen three contrasting estates—the Kirsanovs' Marino, substantial but ill-managed, the sumptuous Nikolskoe, and the petty village of Bazarov's parents. The range of life we have met exceeds that of most short stories, even if it is relatively slight by the standards of the nineteenth-century novel. It compares with that in Jane Austen's books, but while Turgenev shows an equal interest in the minutiae of human relationships, his intellectual interests far exceed Jane Austen's, and the events which come with a rush in the remaining seven chapters are of a kind almost unthinkable in her placid world.

Everything has been quietly but thoroughly prepared for this gallop of incidents; for once, Turgenev's pacing is assured. While Bazarov has been trapped into love by Madama Odintsova, Arkady's gentler nature— he loves the arts though he can't admit it to his friend—has been drawn to Katia, who plays the piano well. The relationship between the two young men is now strained by their fundamental differences in temperament.

Arkady goes to Nikolskoe without his friend. While he is away, Bazarov in a second moment of rash male desire kisses Fenichka. Pavel sees this and challenges him to a duel, but when he is wounded he gallantly excuses his opponent to his brother. Bazarov of course has to leave and visits Nikolskoe where, as Arkady proposes to Katia, he and Madame Odintsova wind up their relationship with cool speeches. Bazarov proceeds home and lives restlessly with his parents. He begins to doctor the local people, and cuts himself while he is dissecting the body of a peasant who has been killed by typhus. He dies of pyaemia, but not before Madame Odintsova has paid him a last visit and kissed his forehead.

The closing chapters combine the most conventional of happy endings for Arkady, for Katia and for Nikolai, who, at his brother's insistence, marries Fenichka, with a sad one for Pavel, who goes to brood out his days in Europe, and deep grief for Bazarov's parents. There is nothing finer anywhere in fiction than the scenes in which Turgenev makes us feel their unbearable loss while Bazarov himself bravely confronts his death. But if this is Turgenev's greatest piece of writing, it is set alongside some of his poorest, the arch and sickly-sweet love scenes between Arkady and Katia and the nauseating last paragraph in which Turgenev tries to round things off with a bout of contrived religious feeling:

> But are those prayers of theirs, those tears, all fruitless? Is their love, their hallowed selfless love, not omnipotent? Oh yes! However passionate, sinful and rebellious the heart hidden in the tomb, the flowers growing over it peep at us serenely with their innocent eyes; they speak to us not only of eternal peace, of the vast repose of 'indifferent' nature: they tell us, too, of everlasting reconciliation and of life which has no end.[42]

One's real consolation is to imagine what Bazarov would have said about all that.

Turgenev had in fact invented a character who, unlike any other in his books, is big enough to challenge his own creator. Author and reader grapple with Bazarov together in baffled fascination. He can be cruel, but he is never merely mean. His remarks are often shocking, but are always funny. Madame Odintsova fears him, but Pavel finally respects him. Arkady weeps when they part though in the end, as Bazarov himself prophesies, his death seems to make no difference to anyone but his own parents. He is 'superfluous' in the sense that his gifts find no proportionate outlet, but he towers over everyone else in the book.

The world Turgenev makes him move in has no clear centre which he can attack. Almost the only links between the novel's four localities are provided by Bazarov and Arkady, and this structural feature seems to emphasize a point about the Russian provincial society which the book portrays. Out of the group of students which accepts him as a leader, Bazarov loses credibility as a political force. Arkady's drift away from him emphasizes his utter loneliness. While the Kirsanov serfs warm to him, those in his father's village regard him as an eccentric—'Bazarov the self-confident did not for a moment suspect that in their eyes he was after all nothing but a sort of buffoon.'

When Arkady tells old Bazarov that his son will be a great man, we see him as a revolutionary rather than as a country doctor. But he is not, and cannot be, shown in action on any political front, and his attitudes suggest that he could go no further than purely élitist conspiracy. In a conversation with Arkady which reveals the 'fathomless depths' of his conceit, he anticipates, it has been pointed out, the self-proclaimed 'man-Gods' of Dostoevsky. He needs 'fools' like Arkady, he says, because 'It is not for the gods to have to bake bricks.'[43] Various incidents cut him down to size. Arkady's easy good nature exposes by contrast the harshness of his attitude to his parents, and while his duel with Pavel reveals his courage, it also shows, since he doesn't approve of duelling, how his principles can break down in practice. This is more amply illustrated in his dealings with Madame Odintsova. He shouldn't, by his own lights, fall in love with her.

Because he has no political outlet, his revolutionary drive emerges most clearly in his moments of sexual passion. The vigorous kiss which he gives Fenichka strikes through all the ambiguities of her relationship with Nikolai like a crowd mocking a liberal politician with his own words —if she's not married, what's the harm of it? However, in assailing Odintsova, even though his 'almost animal expression' succeeds in frightening her, he can only fight a drawn bout with a more powerful and deadly 'liberal' inertia. It is this female 'Hamlet', coldly intellectual, sometimes moved by 'noble aspirations' but always flinching back from them, hankering after an experience of love but incapable of giving herself to passion, who emerges as the true 'nihilist' and even, in a sense, as the true 'materialist', since material comfort is in the end her dominating principle. And though her final visit may, ironically, seem a victory for him, he can neither destroy his passion nor compel her to succumb to it.

Odintsova forces him to confront his own self-contradictions. He falls into thoughts which echo Hamlet's:

The tiny bit of space I occupy is so minute in comparison with the rest of the universe, where I am not and which is not concerned with me; and the period of time in which it is my lot to live is so infinitesimal compared with the eternity in which I have not been and shall not be ... And yet here, in this atom which is myself, in this mathematical point, blood circulates, the brain operates and aspires to something too—What a monstrous business! What futility![44]

As his self confidence turns inward as self pity, he begins to see himself as the victim and not the master of history. Earlier, he snorted when Arkady begged him to understand and excuse Pavel as a product of the period in which he grew up: 'As to the times we live in, why should I depend on them?' Now he seems to accept that he cannot be more than the creature of his own times, and even to acknowledge that 'illusion' may promote happiness, when at their final parting he tells Arkady to hurry up and get married and have plenty of children. 'They'll have the wit to be born in a better age, not like you and me.'[45]

We learn about his fatal carelessness in cutting up a corpse through his own words, and they leave interpretation very open. Bazarov has been seen as 'sacrificing himself' in the interests of the health of the peasants, but since the man in question is already dead, this doesn't seem to work: Bazarov's real interest, as this bears out, is dissection, not cure, and it is perhaps more tempting to see the corpse as a symbol of the death-in-life of Russian provincial society, which infects and destroys the bold and ruthless analyst of its failings. We must suppose that it is disillusionment which robs him of his usual self-control, so that his failure to take proper precautions is a form of unwilled suicide. But as he dies, his personality reasserts itself, and the courage with which he diagnoses his own illness, the realism with which he faces death and the sarcastic wit which stays with him to the last re-emphasize at the end what remarkable human qualities he has. The reader is made indignant at the waste of him.

The poignancy achieved here, though it is exceptional in its keenness, is of a kind which Turgenev has often achieved. It might remind us of 'Bezhin Meadow'—we are made unusually sensitive to the caprices of what seems an arbitrary Fate. Since Bazarov also (like his opponent Pavel) represents a whole generation, the casual malignance of chance is allied to a more consistent pattern where the sons in each generation must challenge the fathers and neither generation can wholly transcend its specific limitations. There is also, in this novel, as in all Turgenev's work, a bitter-sweet feeling which Madame Odintsova experiences vaguely as 'a sense of life passing by' but which for Nikolai Kirsanov settles firmly around the image of his dead wife with whom he was so happy—'Why could not one live those first sweet moments deathlessly forever?' No novelist has ever been more sensitive to the march of time. The clock ticks on and on. The beautiful evening, the song of a gifted singer, the hours of first love and the courage and hopes of a generation are all devoured by unheeding time. The feeling awakened in the reader is often indistinguishable from the nostalgia frequently expressed by the characters, and Turgenev's habitual trick of setting even his most topical novels—*On the Eve, Fathers and Sons, Virgin Soil*—just a few years back in the past seems to be adopted so as to give him more room for favourite effects of pathos and irony; it is important that we should know how others remember the dead, or forget them.

Turgenev himself began to feel in his thirties that he was growing old and his real life was finished, and this prompted him, in his letters, to rather ignoble self pity. But if all his fiction achieved were to provoke in the reader a feeling broadly akin to 'nostalgia' we should not rate it so highly. Nor could we learn so much of value from it if it were effectively dominated by pessimistic emphases on the hostility of nature to man and the fickleness and cruelty of Fate—that 'irony of Jehovah' which Turgenev had detected in the death of Stankevich. Turgenev at his best is not morbid. He believes firmly that each generation of sons can actually do better than its fathers. Arkady, partly because he has been exposed to Bazarov's realism, will surely be a better estate manager than Nikolai. But Turgenev never succumbed to the mechanistic 'liberal' ideas so common in the West in his day which suggested that 'progress' was a simple matter of serial progression. If 'progress' can come out of Turgenev's world, it will come through challenge, and tragic conflict. The youthful passion of an Elena, a Bazarov or a Marianna cannot by itself transform the world, but without it the world cannot be transformed. The Rudins and Bazarovs fail, yet even so they shift the situation in which they have operated in positive new directions. The vitalities of the past nourish the present, even if at times they seem to root it to the spot in helpless nostalgia. Shubin's was for Turgenev the most important of all questions: 'When are we going to produce some real people?' And the answer directs us hopefully to the future—'Wait a bit, they'll come.'

In effect, Turgenev comes to terms with the decline of his own class. He is critical of men like the Kirsanov brothers who may be said to represent its most attractive aspects, but he does not see them as historically null. Without the nobleman-idealists of the reign of Nicholas, the plebeian rebels of the reign of Alexander II could not have taken the challenge to Tsarism so much further. For a truly bleak view of the provincial nobility, we must look to *The Golovlovs*, by Mikhail Saltykov-Shchedrin, a masterpiece which has been relatively neglected, perhaps partly because its author's other works are not easily found in translation.

VII

Saltykov was born in 1826 into a noble family in the province of Tver north-west of Moscow. He entered the civil service as a youth, and was exiled in 1848 to the distant town of Viatka for publishing two short stories with a radical political outlook. But, such were the inconsistencies of Tsarism, that during and after his seven years' exile Saltykov continued to rise in the service, and in 1858 became vice-governor of a province, though meanwhile, under the pen-name Shchedrin, he began to publish satirical sketches pillorying the Tsarist social order. He resigned in 1868 and became co-editor with the poet Nekrasov of *Notes of the Fatherland*, a periodical (founded in 1839) which replaced the now-suppressed *Contemporary* as the main organ of the literary left. His satires were extremely popular, and Turgenev was moved to write of him in 1881, 'it sometimes seems to me that the whole of our literature rests on his shoulders.'[46] Saltykov was Dostoevsky's journalistic counterpart on the left and most of his fiction is said by Mirsky to suffer from excessive topicality. He died in 1889, five years after *Notes of the Fatherland* had in its turn been closed down by the authorities.

The Golovlovs appeared in 1872–6. It finds scope for laughter, compassion and even a kind of poetry in the self-destruction of an appalling provincial family which Saltykov uses to typify the irreversible decline of their entire class—'minor gentry scattered all over Russia, with nothing to do with themselves, divorced from the stream of life, and without a position of leadership. Under serfdom they could subsist, but now they simply sit on their ramshackle estates, waiting to disappear.'[47]

The Golovlovs' doom is suspended for a while as the cunning and parsimonious matriarch, Arina Petrovna, extends the family estate from a mere 150 'souls' to one of 4000, in spite of her husband's drunken incapacity. But, obsessed with her business affairs, she denies her children love, and her life-long labours go for nothing. Her eldest son Stepan ('the blockhead') comes home to die of drink in his forties. The younger brothers, Porfiri and Pavel, are given the estate by their mother in a Lear-like division after their father dies. Pavel too drinks himself to death and the odious Porfiri, nicknamed 'Judas', inherits the lot. But one of his own sons commits suicide and the other dies a prisoner on his way to Siberia, because Judas won't give him money to replace the 3000 roubles he gambled away from the funds of his regiment. Arina Petrovna curses Judas and dies in miserable senility. Judas's nieces Anninka and Liubinka have gone on the stage to escape the dreadful boredom of the Golovlov estates. They degenerate from kept mistresses to prostitutes before Liubinka kills herself and the dipsomaniac Anninka comes home to Golovlovo mortally ill with consumption. Even Judas is now brought face to face with the total emptiness of the family's existence. He too embraces the doom of the Golovlovs and takes to drink, and he and Anninka rage and snarl over the family's history together until finally conscience and compassion make, too late, for a reconciliation. Judas, amazingly, pats his dying niece on the head and says, 'Poor little girl, my poor little girl'. Then he freezes to death in a snowstorm, having left the house in the night to walk to his mother's grave and, he hopes, die there.

Each Golovlov in turn retreats into absolute isolation. They have no happy memories. They can only find peace first in fantasy and then in suicidal drunkenness. Finally, with Judas's self-isolation, the servants take over and make merry. All this is too squalid to provide 'tragedy', though the doom of a family is an ancient tragic theme. But 'satire' isn't the right word either. Saltykov makes us feel sorry for these people, though the dry, level, plain manner of the book never jerks at our sleeves to demand sympathy.

There are patches of gruesome Gogolian detail. The old father dies just before the Emancipation thanking God for calling him now so that he won't have to rub shoulders with serfs when he faces his Maker. Judas's ceaseless, pointless calculations of profit and loss in imaginary deals remind us that he had a bureaucratic career before he became master of Golovlovo and extend the scope of the book's criticism from the back woods to the foot of the Tsar's throne. Both he and his mother are fairly close relations of Gogol's Pliushkin. But neither is 'grotesque'—they are, rather, horribly commonplace. Judas, who dominates the book, has been compared to the great hypocrites of fiction, to Molière's Tartuffe and Dickens's Pecksniff. Yet as Saltykov himself explains, you can only be a hypocrite if you know what principles are, so that you can pretend to have them. Judas knows nothing of principles. He is authentically superstitious, truly devoted to the empty rituals of the Church and of private prayer, and his endless wheedling flow of conventional pieties and inappropriate proverbs, so far from ingratiating him with people, makes them shun him.

When his housekeeper bears him an illegitimate son, Judas takes refuge from the flat contradiction which this event offers to his habitual piety by simply refusing to recognize that the event is really his responsibility. Even his rather wicked old servant Ulita, the midwife, is appalled by his attitude. He gets her to take the baby off to the Moscow foundling home, telling her 'I want him to grow up to be a good man, a good servant of God and a loyal subject of the Tsar. So, if God decides to make him a peasant, I want him to know how to work the land, to plow, to mow, to chop wood, all that sort of thing. And, if God decides he should have another trade, let him learn that—or even go into a learned career, because, you know, some babies in the foundling homes even grow up to be schoolteachers!'[48]

The baby in fact will probably die of neglect. Judas takes to an extreme of absurdity an idea implicit in the acceptance of any class system which is supposed to be supported by God's will. ('The rich man in his castle, the poor man at his gate, God made them high and lowly and ordered their estate,' as the nineteenth-century English hymn runs.) With his meaningless verbiage, pointless extortion and litigation, pretended activity but actual idleness, Judas clearly exists on one level as a symbol not only of the parasitic gentry but also of the Tsarist social order. Yet his ludicrous failure to relate words to life—as Saltykov presents it, his verbosity is a habit akin to the family's drunkenness, another way of evading reality—is, ultimately, deeply pathetic. So is the fate of Anninka, the only Golovlov with enough imagination to see that life should be lived in a better way. Her loveless childhood and useless education have given her neither the intellectual nor moral resources needed to escape; she is sucked back to Golovlovo which, as she sees, is death itself. . . 'It was here that children had been fed stale salt meat.'[49]

Food is important in the novel. If the Golovlovs don't strike us as bloodless monsters, this is partly because their appetites are normal enough, even if Arina denies them enough to eat. The spiritually famine-ridden family talk ecstatically of splendid mushrooms, huge carp, enormous melons. The barrels of pickled cucumbers going slimy in Arina's cellar vividly express the whole Golovlov way of life—it is both disgusting and wickedly wasteful. Other elements likewise enrich with imagery a story which might have seemed in danger of becoming a bald recital of nasty facts. Saltykov handles superbly the house itself—its prevailing silence and its abrupt noises. His 'shots' of the landscape have a cinematic vividness. We stand with the doomed Stepan in the mean little room to which Arina has confined him and we look out at the October rains and mud in which peasants, black dots, are at work. Stepan, we're told, perhaps gives no thought to their labour. He turns the landscape into a dismal fantasy. The grey weeping sky seems 'suspended just over his head, threatening to press him down into the gaping, muddy waves.' The clouds overhead barely change from hour to hour; one low, dark one is like a priest in a cassock with outstretched arms.[50] The image subtly relates to the novel's preoccupation with the stultifying aspects of Orthodox Christianity. It is real forgiveness which Judas and Anninka grasp at the end, but the church has not helped them find it. Together with its sharp historical focus and its solid world, *The Golovlovs* packs a sense of moral outrage. Judas betrayed Christ. The Golovlovs' way of life betrays true human values. The book is neither cynical nor despairing; it is pervaded by the conviction that the travesty of life which it describes can be transcended.

ROMANTICISM

'Romanticism' is best defined here as the cultural expression of a shift of consciousness in Europe which began in the North West of the continent in the mid-eighteenth century and was associated with the challenge of the bourgeoisie to aristocratic values, with an unprecedented rapid growth of population and with the French and Industrial Revolutions. Essentially, 'Romanticism' involved the creation of new vistas of faith, hope and charity to replace those of a Christianity which now seemed to educated people too superstitious to be accepted or, if purged of spooks, too abstract to be gratifying. Various cults came together in various combinations to fuel the characteristic Romantic fervour; amongst them the cult of the 'picturesque' in nature, the cult of the 'feelings', the cult of the 'noble savage' and the cults of certain old writers, above all Homer and Shakespeare, whose spirit and methods ran counter to the formalist 'classical' aesthetics which had prevailed in the early eighteenth century.

The human Will, Nature, Love, the Greeks, the Nation, the Child, the Golden Age, the People and the Great Man were amongst the new deities worshipped in opposition to each other or in an infinite number of permutations. Art itself was a pretty awesome new God. This religious-cultural movement drew on the free-thinking of the preceding Enlightenment but resisted the materialism and utilitarianism which were natural outcomes of Enlightened thought. In the writings of such crucial figures as Goethe, Scott, Byron, Stendhal and Pushkin we see an internal conflict between sober sociable calculation and quasi-religious passion. 'Neo-classicism' is one sort of Romanticism which seeks to build order from chaos, and it is no paradox to say that Pushkin is both a Romantic and a Neo-classical writer.

In Britain the great Reform of 1832 signals the end of the Romantic age. In Europe the break comes around the abortive revolutions of 1848, which were followed by industrialization and by relative peace and composure. The shift in Russia is not seen before about 1860. The new culture —we might as well call it Capitalist—whether its base was mainly bourgeois or mainly, as in Russia, bureaucratic, combined homage to values distilled from Romanticism with a more fundamental allegiance to money. Marxism challenged this new culture on the strength of an alternative synthesis of humanism and economics.

I feel entitled to regard Turgenev and Dostoevsky as 'Romantics' because they were formed as thinkers and writers before Capitalist and counter-Capitalist syntheses had congealed to give easy answers to lazy-minded people. The fundamental conflicts of the Romantic age are still freshly present in their work. Dostoevsky, as we can easily show, still projects as late as 1880 a Romantic conflict between civic order and just rebellion which Schiller had set out a whole century before.

Chekhov's temperament, like his work, reflects a 'Victorian'-style compromise. His God, when he has one, is in alliance with Social Utility. Tolstoy's position, however, is unique. God for him is still the abstraction, installed and formally worshipped by the Enlightenment. His Christ is a Universal Man invented to represent Universal ethics. Though he found some ideas of his own in the Romantic philosopher Schopenhauer, his basic intellectual formation owes everything to writers (especially Rousseau) who had preceded but had helped to inspire the main religious-cultural movement. His Rousseauism therefore allies his work very strongly with that of certain Romantic writers, but he is never in tune at all with the religious fervour of the Romantic heyday.

English-speaking readers may have to re-educate themselves a little if they are to understand Romanticism in a European context. The Romantic writers now most highly valued by the English themselves—Wordsworth and Keats—had little influence abroad, and any concept of Romanticism based primarily on their work will be unhelpful in discussion of French, German or Russian writers. But British writers, neglected now at home, were crucially influential all over the continent: Richardson, Sterne, Macpherson, Scott and Byron.

4
UNDERGROUND MAN
Dostoevsky to *Crime and Punishment*

Though Fedor Dostoevsky's family claimed noble rank it was in fact a product of the limited opportunities for 'upward social mobility' available in Nicholas I's Russia. His father was a doctor in charge of the women's outpatients department at a Moscow hospital. He had defied his own father, a priest who had wanted him to follow him in the church, by deciding to study medicine. Though he never beat his own children, had a real interest in literature, and was able to convince Fedor that he loved him, he was a man of violent temper and a drunkard, full of grievances against a world which seemed not to value him as highly as he thought he deserved. Fedor was born in October 1821. His mother was the daughter of a Moscow merchant and raised seven children before she died of tuberculosis in 1837. Two years later, when Fedor was seventeen, his father was brutally murdered by serfs from one of the two villages he owned, who had been exasperated by his cruelty.

The family was not well-to-do and the wealthy relatives Dostoevsky had to turn to for support as he grew up were Moscow merchants, his mother's relatives. Ambiguous social status and incessant worries about money were the soil in which his talent flourished. Georg Lukács observes that the essential point about his characters is that they are all like people at a railway station—men and women who are not at home but are in transition.[1] Whereas Pushkin, Tolstoy and Turgenev, from the heights of their secure social position, could see with Olympian clarity where everyone belonged in Russian society, and could confidently present quasi-feudal relationships between master and man and formal good manners within the noble class, in Dostoevsky's world all relationships are fluid. His outlook is not exactly 'plebeian'. His education, as he discovered in prison, marked him off from most of his fellow countrymen. His attitude towards aristocrats in his fiction hovers between democratic contempt and reluctant admiration, and, bar criminals, his work is only rarely and briefly concerned with the peasantry. But Dostoevsky knew a different Petersburg from Tolstoy's capital of glittering balls and arid conventions; he shared the life of de-classed urban masses in which penniless army officers, civil servants high and low, businessmen shady and self-important, mixed and muddled with noblemen down on their luck, tradesmen, merchants and artisans, in the isolating crowdedness of the modern metropolis. His closest literary affinities are not with his fellow-Russians, apart from Gogol, but with Balzac and Dickens, the poets of city life. Even the country towns which figure in *The Devils* and *The Brothers Karamazov* are conceived as places where high and low people mingle together. Nobody, in his fiction 'knows his place'. Everyone is seeking to discover it.

His early family life rubbed his nerves raw. His father's temper led to terrible 'scenes' at home, and his novels would be full of such scenes. If he could forgive his father, everyone was forgiveable, and if one had to select essential 'messages' from his fiction, one of them would be this: all men are lovable and capable of love. His mother's piety rooted his love of Christ, which would struggle throughout his life against the atheistic and nihilistic promptings of his unappeasable intellect. When the boy Fedor first travelled to Petersburg with his elder brother Mikhail, at the age of sixteen, he watched a government courier driving off from a country coaching station and smashing his fist down again and again on the neck of his driver, who in turn flogged the horses. In this miniature of the Tsarist order he experienced what he later called his 'first personal insult'.[2] Fascination with cruelty, rebellion against it, would mark his greatest writings.

His father had placed him in the Army Engineering College. The institution was grotesquely at variance with his dawning literary ambition. Painfully conscious of his own relative poverty compared to the affluence of certain richer students, Dostoevsky was aloof and unpopular. But he somehow passed his exams in 1841 and became an Engineer Ensign. His improvidence and gambling soon drove him into debt. He had to submit his Romantic idealism to a hard school of experience on the sleazy underside of Petersburg. His fiction would move in the nightmarish gulf between radiant ideal and disgusting reality.

The masterpieces of Lermontov and Gogol, both of whom might, like himself, be called 'Romantic realists', appeared in time to help to form him. Lermontov's proto-nihilist 'hero' would influence his own heroes deeply. Gogol showed him how farce could be meaningful and proved that the 'little man', the urban underdog, could be a subject for rich fiction.

But Dostoevsky's insatiable reading took him deep into contemporary European literature. His intellectual and technical originality mustn't be overestimated. To investigate his debts to Cervantes, Scott and Dickens, Schiller, Goethe and Shakespeare, Balzac, George Sand and Victor Hugo, would take a scholar's lifetime. His taste in reading was primarily Romantic. His own writing began at the very moment when a new urban society, dominated by new values which made money the measure of everything, confronted the appalled eyes of a Romantic generation. If Tolstoy was to take to the point of dissolution and beyond the ideals and intellectual habits of the eighteenth-century Enlightenment, Dostoevsky is the writer who exposes, inflates, shatters and reconstitutes the range of Romantic ideals and modes of writing. The paradoxes of Romanticism inform all his fiction. Sentimentalism and a taste for Gothic horror combine with a Romantic readiness to face all aspects of reality. The Romantic cult of individual genius struggles with a Romantic trust in the wisdom of the common people, and Romantic despair seesaws with a Romantic faith in the destiny of Russia. What Turgenev most obviously carries on from Romanticism is its dressing of Schubertian lyricism; Dostoevsky chops up afresh the ingredients of the salad.

One work which made an unforgettable impression on him was *The Robbers*, an early play by Friedrich Schiller (1759–1805). It explains the references to 'Karl Moor' in his very last novel, *The Brothers Karamazov*. This ardent and implausible work of 1781 tells of a 'great sinner', the son of a nobleman, who turns brigand when his father disowns him, and leads a band which commits atrocious deeds defying both church and state in the name of Robin Hood-style social justice. The seeds of all Dostoevsky's major heroes can be found in the speeches of Karl, who declares that 'two men like myself could ruin the whole edifice of the moral world' before he submits himself in proud repentance to the judgement of God and the authorities; of his fellow-robber Spiegelberg, vain, weak and nasty, who sees crime as the avenue to 'everlasting fame'; and of his atheist brother Franz von Moor, an obvious ancestor of Ivan Karamazov. The beautiful, gifted Karl whose followers commit such base actions under his leadership anticipates Dostoevsky's key idea of the 'double', the mean alternative self which dogs the footsteps of even the best man. Like Schiller, Dostoevsky was obsessed with the freedom of the human will, and like Karl von Moor's creator he would find no convincing way of reconciling the human thirst for happiness and perfection with the pressing claims of religion and social order. A Schiller-like combination of philosophy and melodrama would be the basis of his most important fiction.

II

When Dostoevsky left the army in 1844, he became a professional writer earning such living as he could from publishers. Unlike Gogol, able to subsist on near-sinecures and Government handouts, or Turgenev and Tolstoy, secure in the income from their estates, Dostoevsky didn't have the time which only money can buy. His career was a struggle between his artistic conscience and his need for cash. But his first novel, *Poor Folk*, had been rewritten several times before a friend showed the manuscript to the young poet Nekrasov who in turn took it to Belinsky.

The great critic was deeply moved and hailed Dostoevsky as a new servant of Art and of the Truth. His praise, echoed by others, went to Dostoevsky's head. But *Poor Folk* was indeed a considerable achievement for a writer of only twenty-three.

It is an intensely 'literary' work. Presented throughout as an exchange of letters between a poor elderly clerk, Makar Devushkin, and a young orphan whom he has befriended and on whom he lavishes what little money he has, it exploits a convention founded a hundred years before by Samuel Richardson, the grandfather of all sentimental fiction. When his neighbours joke that Makar is a 'Lovelace' they probably know, but he doesn't, that that is the name of Richardson's most famous character. Makar reads and deeply admires Pushkin's story, *The Postmaster*, but is outraged by Gogol's *Overcoat*. What right, he asks, has Gogol to make fun of a man so much like Makar himself? The novel is in effect a reply to Gogol. While Gogol has presented his starveling clerk as a mechanical creature grotesquely lacking in ordinary human feeling, Makar sees himself as a man like other men, with a right to his own 'fine feelings' and to the respect of his fellows. And, writing this stream of letters to a girl who lives within sight of his window, he becomes very self-conscious about his own literary style.

On its inferior level, *Poor Folk* is as much concerned with the problematic two-way relationship between literature and life as *Eugene Onegin*. What makes the maudlin sentimentalism of Makar's letters bearable is Dostoevsky's knowingness about the chasm which separates gush from reality. Varvara, protesting so as to display her refined feelings when Makar lavishes sweets upon her while he himself goes around in broken boots, is a deliciously odious creation, and her final unashamed exploitation of Makar as an errand boy as she acquires lace and jewels towards her wedding confirms her as first and not least among Dostoevsky's young women of high-strung nerves and gruesome virtue.

Makar's tenement where quite rich people live higgledy piggledy with very poor ones and where garbage pails filled with reeking refuse stand by every door is made solidly vivid. So are the streets he walks in where snub-nosed Finnish women rub shoulders with drunk workingmen and a locksmith's apprentice passes with oily grime on his face. This is a 'realler' Petersburg than Gogol's. But an ambience of chaotic mystery and incomprehensible intrigue surrounds the two letter-writers. The shadowy Mr Bykov who eventually marries Varvara is, we understand, the centre of intrigues which have somehow (we never learn how) robbed her of her good name and thrust her into destitution, and when he eventually finds out her present circumstances she tells Makar:

I cannot understand for the life of me how it is he knows so much about us. I keep making all sorts of wild guesses. Fedora tells me that Aksinia, her sister-in-law, is a friend of Nastasia the laundress who has a nephew working as a hall porter in the office building where a friend of Anna Fedorovna's nephew is employed. But could rumours possibly have reached him that way? But it's quite possible that Fedora is wrong.[3]

The tangles of mystery which we find in Dostoevsky's novels do in fact reflect an important feature of life in the big city, where chance meetings and casual connections take the place of the settled relationships of older kinds of life in countryside and small town. In Petersburg, no one really knows anyone, yet anyone might turn out to know anybody else. The village, the family, the merchant or priestly caste, give a man, at their best, warmth and security. Makar is a typical city man isolated from such community, and, having found Varvara, he tries to create with her a little community of his own. The experiment fails, but before we express our pity for Makar, we should ask ourselves what right an elderly man has to monopolize the life of a young girl whom he sets up as a kind of platonic mistress? His desperate desire that she should always live near him in the Petersburg squalor is tantamount to a wish that she should always be poor and never marry.

Each of the two is, in fact, exploiting the other, but the balance is unequal since youth and the possibility of a very different life are available to Varvara but not to Makar. This predicament is tragi-comic and insoluble. Dostoevsky's insights are already discomforting. In the world of *Poor Folk* young and old, rich and poor, cannot co-exist without hurting each other. The great city has worn the scabbard off the knife. Life cuts cruelly away at Makar's romantic dream.

Poor Folk, thanks to Belinsky, was already a critical success before it appeared in print early in 1846. Next month, Dostoevsky's second novel, *The Double*, came out in a magazine. Belinsky didn't like it; rightly, he thought it too long, but he also deplored Dostoevsky's lapse from 'realism' into 'fantasy'. The story was not well received, and Dostoevsky himself decided that he hadn't achieved what he had set out to do, though he always believed in the importance of his basic idea.

The notion of a man's meeting his own spit-image had been used before by Romantic poets and novelists. The most obvious debt of *The Double* is to Gogol, who prefigures its theme in *The Nose*. Goliadkin, the 'hero' has several features in common with Chichikov. Such borrowings don't spoil the story; after the slow movement of *Poor Folk* it is like a dry and brilliant scherzo, too long-winded but very clever and funny.

Goliadkin is yet another luckless Petersburg civil servant. Humiliated by his expulsion from the name-day party of the daughter of a bureaucrat of higher rank, a girl to whom he has made rash advances, he encounters his own double in the city's snow-swept streets. This creature takes a job in Goliadkin's own office, makes himself popular, and usurps the credit for work 'Goliadkin Senior' has done. Though his appearance, name and origins are identical, others somehow have no difficulty in distinguishing the two Goliadkins. Junior is cocky whereas Senior is shy. He is ingratiating and eloquent, whereas Senior can barely bring a sentence to a grammatical conclusion. He is socially accepted in the drawing rooms of superiors where Senior feels himself surrounded by enemies. When eventually a Doctor comes to take Goliadkin Senior away to the madhouse, the double, gloating and almost dancing, leads the procession and flings open the door of the carriage.

Though solemn claims have been made for its anticipating the discoveries of modern psycho-analysis, only a reader totally humourless or neurotically hyper-sensitive could find *The Double* harrowing. It is a masterpiece of 'black comedy' in which Dostoevsky early shows that he knows more, perhaps, than any other novelist about at least one aspect of life, embarrassment. Goliadkin, presented 'from the inside' but without a trace of sentimentality, represents, with his gaucheness and inability to communicate, a commonplace of human nature. The scene in which, having imagined that his idol Klara is about to elope with him, he hires a carriage and makes it wait while he stands sopping wet in the rain behind a woodpile and fends off the damp and puzzled driver is as wildly amusing as anything in Gogol, but is liable to evoke echoing memories in most readers; it has the ring of banal reality.

The tale, of course, has its serious point. Goliadkin hates his other self, whom we must assume to be a figment of his own imagination. The resourceful and aggressive double represents what Goliadkin would like to be; he has what it takes to be a success. But in his impishly callous treatment of Goliadkin Senior, this double shows the ugly face of the bureaucratic world which is the only one which Senior knows about. Sycophancy, cunning and self-importance are the keys to advancement. A gift for intrigue is indispensable. Goliadkin, absurd though he may be, is too human to like his double, who embodies the values of Tsar Nicholas Flogger's civil service, though he is almost touchingly open to the double's insincere overtures of friendship.

At several points, Goliadkin takes a decision and then at once acts in a totally contrary way—this is another symptom of the duality of human nature as Dostoevsky understood it. For the moment, however, he does not analyse this duality deeply; he presents it directly and simply on a level of near-farce. As we shall see, 'doubling' in his mature fiction takes much more complex forms.

Dismayed by his second book's poor reception, Dostoevsky railed against himself in a letter to his brother Mikhail for his own 'unbounded vanity and ambition'.[4] Vanity and self-will would play in his work the same kind of role as *poshlost* in Gogol's, ineffectualness in Turgenev's and intellectual arrogance in Tolstoy's. In each case the writer exposes a salient vice of his own with fierce insistence. Dostoevsky's vanity had become a standing joke in Petersburg literary circles and Turgevev (whom at this time Dostoevsky admired enormously) was especially expert at making fun of it. The skinny, sickly little writer with his pale twitching lips and uneasy grey eyes was a model for his own touchy heroes.

And the radical circles he moved in gave him his insight into what Lenin would call 'infantile leftism'. Belinsky's atheism and Socialism were, of course, far from infantile, and they impressed the young writer. But early in 1847 he joined the group surrounding a young official named Mikhail Petrashevsky. Here he met young idealists who were playing with a whole toy-box of ideas derived from the French 'Utopian' socialists—Fourier, Cabet, Pierre Leroux and George Sand. Petrashevsky's view that society should realize in practice the Christian precept of brotherly love was too wishy-washy for Dostoevsky, who gravitated towards a more militant group which met in the flat of a minor poet named Durov, where violent speeches were made against serfdom and the censorship. This group of seven or eight impatient liberators, anticipating the rebels Dostoevsky would present in *The Devils*, set about acquiring a secret printing press.

A spy was present in April 1849 when Dostoevsky read out Belinsky's banned 'Letter to Gogol' at a meeting of the larger Petrashevsky circle. On the 23rd of that month, more than a score of men were arrested and conveyed to the Peter and Paul Fortress. Dostoevsky was among them. He denied the aim of revolution, and declared at his trial that he had 'never been a socialist.' But he added, 'Socialism is a science in a state of fermentation, it is chaos, it is alchemy before the advent of chemistry, astrology before the advent of astronomy, though I cannot help feeling that out of the present chaos something harmonious, sensible and beneficial will eventually emerge for the good of mankind, just as out of alchemy emerged chemistry and out of astrology, astronomy.'[5]

Dostoevsky spent eight months in the fortress. Without his knowledge, he was sentenced to death, and then reprieved by the Tsar. This led to the most famous of all exhibitions of Nicholas I's sadistic contempt for his fellow men. In December 1849, Dostoevsky and eighteen others were led from prison to the Semyonovsky parade ground where they heard their death sentences read out. Three men were tied to posts. Three others were called forward. Dostoevsky was next to go. But the guns didn't fire. The retreat was sounded and the announcement of a reprieve was made. Dostoevsky's sentence was to be four years in a Siberian prison, then service in the army as a private.

When he and his fellows arrived in the Siberian town of Tobolsk, wives of Decembrists exiled a quarter of a century before gave them active sympathy. 'Wonderful people,' Dostoevsky called them, '. . . hardened by twenty-five years of sorrow and self-sacrifice.' At Omsk, where he arrived in April 1850, he lived out his four years' sentence in a prison under the command of a brutal, drunken major. Stifling in summer, viciously cold in winter, without any provision for privacy, this environment tested him to the limit. On top of it, he had to endure the hatred his fellow prisoners showed for the few noblemen among them.

Yet in *Crime and Punishment* Siberian prison life offers Raskolnikov the chance of redemption. Four years of constant concourse with murderers gave Dostoevsky a unique opportunity to study and come to terms with aspects of human nature which very few writers have encountered. For someone so self-critical, it was not difficult to accept that his suffering was both merited and salutory, and he came to believe that the whole Russian people craved suffering as a fundamental need. At the same time he resented the callous treatment of himself and his fellow prisoners and the experience could only sharpen his sense of injustice. Already a temperamental extremist, Dostoevsky was pushed simultaneously towards an extreme of acceptance, passive endurance of pain, and the other pole of active resentment of tyranny. His later fiction dramatically projects the co-existence of these extremes within himself.

After his release, he wrote to the woman, widow of a Decembrist, who had presented him with a New Testament at Tobolsk, telling her of his own craving for faith:

> I am a child of this age, a child of unbelief and doubts to this very day and shall be (I know it) to the very day when I am laid in my grave. This longing to believe has cost and still does cost me terrible torments; it is a longing that is all the stronger in my heart the more arguments I have against it. And yet God sometimes vouchsafes me moments during which I am completely calm; at such moments I love and I find that I am loved by others; at such moments I have laid up in myself a symbol of faith in which everything is clear and sacred to me. This symbol is very simple. It is: to believe that there is nothing more beautiful, more profound, more sympathetic, more reasonable, more courageous and more perfect than Christ, and not only is there not, but, I tell myself with jealous love, there cannot be. Moreover, if anyone were to prove to me that Christ was outside truth and that truth really was outside Christ, I would still rather remain with Christ than with truth.[6]

The last remarkable comment turns up nearly twenty years later in *The Devils*, where it is attributed to Dostoevsky's 'great sinner' Stavrogin. The conflict between Christianity (faith) and atheism (scientific knowledge and reason) emerges in shifting relationships with the allied conflict between conservatism and rebellion. At one point, Christianity itself may be a challenge thrown at the existing social order and cynical atheism that same order's intellectual prop. At another, the reverse may hold. It would be very foolish to look to Dostoevsky for the *answer* to any political or theological question. His greatness is not that of a consistent and systematic thinker. It is that of a man with a passion for ideas—it has been observed that he *felt* ideas—who creates dramatic settings in which ideas fight each other. Nothing in his fiction should be quoted, in or out of context, as his settled opinion on any subject.

From Omsk Dostoevsky went to Semipalatinsk, a town of some 6000 people near the border with China, to serve as a private soldier. Here he lived until 1859. He wanted to get back to Russia and he shamelessly composed loyal patriotic verses and persuaded his superiors to forward them to the authorities in Petersburg. By the end of 1855, he had been rewarded with promotion to non-commissioned rank and less than a year later he became a second lieutenant. Meanwhile, he pursued a love affair with Maria Isaeva, the young wife of a drunken civil servant. When the latter died, he was able to marry her, in 1857. This consumptive woman with a young son was terrified when her new husband succumbed on his wedding night to an epileptic fit. He had been having such fits for three years and suffered from them throughout the rest of his life. His marriage to an ailing and unfaithful woman was unhappy from the start.

But he was writing again and getting work published. Influential contacts worked for him with the authorities and in 1859 he was allowed to resign from the army. Before the end of the year he was back in Petersburg, that city which he so deeply loathed and loved.

III

In the autumn of 1860 he launched a new journal, *Time*, with his brother Mikhail. His status as an ex-political exile gave him natural links with the radical camp; his love of a Russian Christ might have allied him with the Slavophiles. For the moment, he steered a middle course, accepting the work of Peter the Great in opening Russia up to Western influence, but broaching what was to be a favourite idea of his own that Russia was destined to 'become the synthesis of all those ideas' which European nations were developing. '. . . Everything that is hostile will find its reconciliation and further development in the Russian national spirit.'[7] This vaporous formula did have one pertinent practical implication; it meant that Dostoevsky's own avid borrowings from Western fiction might be seen as a perfectly natural expression of the Russian gift for synthesis.

Time sent roast beef and wine to students imprisoned in the Peter and Paul Fortress for radical agitation, and Dostoevsky (by his own later account) was personally on good terms with Chernyshevsky. But he soon fell into open war with the *Contemporary* and his hatred of the utilitarian and materialistic ideas of the left became obvious in his fiction. This was far from meaning that he himself became a conformist. The ideas of the young radicals, which tended towards the ruthless bullying of mankind 'for its own good', were in many respects more in tune with the capitalistic ethos of Western Europe than were those backward-looking notions which the Tsarist regime itself was now overriding in its 'modernization' of Russia. A journey abroad in the summer of 1862, when he visited Germany, France, England, Switzerland, Italy and Austria confirmed Dostoevsky in his diagnosis of a moral sickness in modern man.

Petersburg at this time had a population approaching 600,000. The

London conurbation contained over five times as many people. It was a terrifying vision of what Petersburg might become. In London, the vastest city of the day, Dostoevsky saw going on 'a fight to the death between the general Western European individualistic principle and the necessity of somehow or other living together, of somehow or other establishing a community and settling down in one anthill. . .' The alternative to an 'anthill' was 'cannibalism'. The wonders of the Crystal Palace, the setting in London of a great exhibition of industrial products, coexisted with the polluted Thames, smoke-filled air, foul slums, and the splendours and horrors of the Haymarket where prostitutes jostled under brilliant gas light in front of magnificent public houses ornamented with mirrors and gold. Dostoevsky was deeply in tune with such excesses, and contrasted London favourably with the world of the cowardly bourgeoisie of Paris. But the Crystal Palace became a symbol for him of the glittering lure of material prosperity which threatened true human values. He rejected Western individualism in the name of brotherhood, and argued that the Russians retained brotherly instincts now absent in the West. He rejected the orderly ant-hill of London in favour of the suffering, feeling Russian soul.[8]

His wife was mortally ill with consumption. Dostoevsky began a liaison with Pauline Suslova, a young literary girl who associated with extreme radicals. In the spring of 1863 *Time* was banned by the authorities. They were busy suppressing a new rebellion in Poland, and misunderstood an article about the matter written by one of Dostoevsky's collaborators. He faced financial ruin. He went abroad, partly to follow Pauline, partly to try his luck on the roulette tables of Germany. He found that his mistress had fallen in love in Paris with a young Spanish student who spurned her. He and Pauline travelled together to Italy, rowing and wrangling with each other. Nevertheless Pauline helped him out when he lost every penny at roulette on his way home.

Further blows followed. His wife's death early in 1864 shocked him in spite of their quarrels and infidelities. His loyal brother Mikhail died only a few months after they had started a new magazine, *Epoch*. He couldn't carry on alone and the journal soon ceased publication. Meanwhile, he accepted responsibility for 10,000 roubles of his brother's debts. It took courage for a sick and ageing man to carry on the struggle, but in fact his maturity as a writer begins in this period of grief and ruin.

Notes from Underground, published in *Epoch* during its brief existence, was a clear attack on Chernyshevsky and the radicals. Two novels were squeezed into existence by his desperate financial straits. In 1865, Dostoevsky signed a contract with an iniquitous publisher named Stellovsky who stipulated that unless Dostoevsky delivered a new novel by 1 December 1866 he would lose the copyright of all his published and unpublished works for ever. Dostoevsky again tried his luck at roulette. He lost again. At rock bottom he sold an unwritten novel, *Crime and Punish-*

ment, to Katkov, editor of the *Russian Herald*, for a pitifully low price. It began to appear in January 1866 and was a great success. Meanwhile, Dostoevsky had somehow to finish the other novel for Stellovsky by November. At the advice of friends, he hired a stenographer. On 4 October a girl of twenty named Anna Snitkina reported for work. By 30 October, *The Gambler* was finished, and on 8 November Dostoevsky proposed to Anna. They were married three months later. She was, as she had to be, a girl of strong character and gave him such physical and emotional support as he had never had before.

IV

Crime and Punishment is usually seen as the first of Dostoevsky's major novels. The elements which he pulled together in it are separately present in various works of fiction published between 1859 and 1866.

The Village of Stepanchikovo (1859, translated by Constance Garnett as *The Friend of the Family*) is the work of a writer groping after a Russian reality he had lost touch with in exile and not quite grasping it. It is a novel of some length. A good-natured landowner, Colonel Rostanev, falls under the spell of a canting religious hypocrite named Foma Fomich Opiskin. Foma is a man of mediocre social background who repays the world for his former humiliations by using a moral tyranny to cow his benefactors. He opposes the colonel's marriage to the children's governess, but after Rostanev has finally mustered the sense to hurl him out through a glass door and send him packing, Foma restores himself to favour by giving his blessing to the marriage, and is able to live on as an honoured 'benefactor' in the Colonel's household.

The central situation reflects Dostoevsky's abiding interest in the psychology of charity, but it isn't made very plausible. Both Foma and the Colonel read like rather strained imitations of Dickens. But the novel, which in fact was first planned as a play, uses a 'dramatic' basis which anticipates the character of Dostoevsky's greatest work. A list of the important influences on his fiction would have to be extended to include, not only the plays of Shakespeare, to which he frequently alludes, but also those of Molière, Racine and Corneille. As George Steiner puts it, 'Dostoevsky's sensibility, his modes of imagination, and his linguistic strategies were saturated by the drama.'[9]

The long scenes at Stepanchikovo in which people trip over, insult each other viciously, scream, faint and in general behave with what becomes a rather predictable unpredictability already give a pretty rich taste of Dostoevsky's outrageous comedy. The room is full to begin with. Hysterical women and bad-tempered men sit around like so many fireworks waiting to be lit, to coruscate or explode. More and more people crowd in, outrage and absurdity are piled upon each other; the final climactically anti-climactic touch is added, in *Stepanchikovo*, when a 'scholar' long expected as a guest by the Colonel turns up, utterly filthy and disgustingly drunk.

The Insulted and Injured (1861) offers not comedy but pathos. Just as Dostoevsky's comedy is shot through with spite, revulsion and even horror, so his pathos, even when, as in this book, it is at its most extreme, tends to become self-consciously, gleefully ludicrous. The principle of excess is at work in both cases. Farce is heaped upon farce, suffering upon suffering, until what most novelists would accept as 'normality' becomes a distant memory and any 'normal' person intruding into the book would seem distinctly odd. The little girl Nellie in *The Insulted and Injured* is not merely orphaned; she is rescued in the nick of time from rape; she is epileptic and furthermore, has a fatal heart condition; finally, she is moving from childhood into puberty, so that she is both sadly childlike and disturbingly 'mature'.

She is the legitimate but abandoned daughter of the memorably evil Prince Valkovsky, polished man of the world and total blackguard. On one obvious level, Valkovsky represents the power to tyrannize, enjoyed by rank and money in a class society. Yet he is neither securely wealthy nor obviously snobbish and on another level he projects himself as an enemy of social conventions who uses them for his own ends and as an idealist whose disillusionment has pushed him into a sort of nihilism which is very much in tune with the ethic of capitalism. . . . 'But what am I to do,' he asks, 'if I know for a fact that at the root of all human virtues lies the completest egoism? And the more virtuous anything is, the more egoism there is in it. Love yourself, that's the one rule I recognize. Life is a commercial transaction, don't waste your money, but kindly pay for your entertainment, and you will be doing your whole duty to your neighbour.'[10]

One of Valkovsky's remarks in particular helps us to define Dostoevsky's special character as a novelist:

> If it were only possible (which, however, from the laws of human nature never can be possible), if it were possible for every one of us to describe all his secret thoughts, without hesitating to disclose what he is afraid to tell and would not on any account tell other people, what he is afraid to tell his best friends, what, indeed, he is even at times afraid to confess to himself, the world would be filled with such a stench that we should all be suffocated.[11]

There are two overlapping traditions in fiction at work in the nineteenth century. One tradition would assume that the unspoken thoughts and desires which Valkovsky refers to are relatively unimportant compared to the shared or shareable values, customs and ideals which hold any society together. We might describe writers who emphasize convention, criticize existing conventions perhaps, but write as if 'good manners' must always be important, as 'normalists'. In England, Jane Austen and George Eliot, in Russia Turgenev and, arguably, Chekhov, are 'normalists' in this sense.

'Normality' in the nineteenth century was still 'aristocratic'. A traditional state of affairs in which land was the basis of wealth was giving way to a revised normality in which people who had made great wealth in other ways expressed their ultimate values by buying land and setting up as 'gentlemen'. (Even Napoleon paid, in his usual monstrous way, such tribute to 'normality'; he humbled kings but made himself an emperor.) The emerging metropolis was, therefore, inherently 'abnormal'. People who had lost the traditional basis of life on the land now had to choose their values, or even invent values, in order to make sense of their lives to themselves. In Dostoevskian terms, they could choose to be either ants or cannibals. Meanwhile, in the city, 'anything could happen'.

Dostoevsky, like Balzac and Dickens, presents us an urbanized world in which the weakening of traditional restraints on behaviour creates an anarchy of values. But neither of these two goes so far as Dostoevsky in using and even relishing the absence of restraint in order to bring to the surface of fiction the 'secret thoughts' and tendencies of man to which we give such labels as 'crime', 'obsession' and 'perversion'. Dickens's Little Nell stands behind Dostoevsky's, and a whole line of capricious 'Romantic' figures, including Pechorin, stand behind Valkovsky. But Dostoevsky's readiness to face the nastiest and most paradoxical aspects of human psychology, those which 'stink' the most, gives him a special status. Some aspects of the twentieth-century world of imperialism and concentration camps, proletarian revolution and atom bombs are directly illuminated by Dostoevsky as they are by none of his contemporaries. The world was becoming as extreme and 'abnormal' as even his own imagination.

Which doesn't mean that *The Insulted and Injured* is a great novel. Its plot links in a pattern of insult and injury Valkovsky, who is wilfully ruining his former steward Ikhmenev; the latter's daughter Natasha who runs away to be the mistress of the Prince's son Alexei, and the narrator Vania, a young writer modelled on Dostoevsky himself, who loves Natasha and befriends the 'orphaned' Nellie. The Prince at the end is triumphant—he has schemed successfully to get his son away from Natasha and marry him to an heiress. But 'virtue is rewarded' in so far as Nellie's influence dissolves the pride of old Ikhmenev, who is reconciled with Natasha. Nellie dies 'in the bosom', as we say, of the reunited Ikhmenev family. But the narrator, who has worn himself out traipsing from one end of Petersburg to the other at the whim of the Ichmenevs and Nellie, is dying alone in hospital as he tells the story. His self-sacrifice is clearly as remarkable (and as 'abnormal') as anything else in the book, but since he tells the story perspective on this is absent and the novel has a dominantly 'sentimental' character.

Another fault of *The Insulted and Injured* repeats itself until his very last novel, where Dostoevsky finally overcomes his strange inability to communicate sexual passion or even physical attractiveness. One of the salient features of his style, always revealed at once by comparison with Turgenev or Tolstoy, is his lack of interest in what his characters look like, in their physical personalities. He will describe someone thoroughly on his first appearance but then, usually though not always, he will ignore his leading physical traits. He works like a dramatist for whom one description serves to tell the producer how to imagine the speaker of the part. Gestures, of course, he refers to; these are indispensable stage directions. But confrontation, argument and declamation are his main material. Without any directly-conveyed sensuality his psychological insights into lovers and their obsessions become dry, unreal and irritating; unlike Racine and Corneille, he doesn't have verse to give them a heightened depth and force. The relationship between Natasha and Alexei, with its rows and reconciliations, masochistic self-sacrifice and perpetual indecision, is very tedious indeed.

The absence of 'stageyness' is one reason why *Memoirs from the House of the Dead* (1862) is markedly different in character from Dostoevsky's other work. It was for a long time his best-known book. Tolstoy, who in general found it hard to come to terms with his great contemporary, said he knew 'no more beautiful book in modern literature, not excepting Pushkin.'[12] As a straightforward account, under thin fictional disguise, of Dostoevsky's experiences in prison, full of the careful observation of physical detail which elsewhere he tended to neglect, it is closer than his other major writings to standard nineteenth-century 'realism'.

It has some of his usual faults. It is repetitive, and while some sequences have wonderful economy and artistry, like the one in which a peasant who has murdered his wife is overheard in the prison hospital telling his own banal, appalling story, others, like the long account of a theatrical performance in prison, are pitched at the level of rather rambling magazine journalism. The fictional dressing is sometimes irritating. The memoirs are attributed to a nobleman who murdered his wife and spent ten years in prison. Dostoevsky of course only served four years and can't (and doesn't attempt to) describe what the ninth year or even the fifth might be like. Nor does the narrator allude to his own 'crime'.

Nevertheless, as the forerunner of so much modern literature describing prison 'from the inside', as well as in its own right, *The House of the Dead* is a very important book. Many episodes and personalities are so vivid that the reader feels inclined and entitled to argue with the author himself about his interpretation. The Jewish prisoner Isaiah Bumstein, for instance, is described with routine anti-semitic touches—'as like as two peas to a plucked chicken . . . cunning and yet distinctly stupid . . . impudent and insolent, and at the same time terribly cowardly'—yet we are told that the others liked him, and his behaviour is so vivaciously reported that the stereotype which Dostoevsky has carelessly imposed on him dissolves into irrelevancy.

Another feature which confirms the book's essential honesty is the fact that it offers us two contradictory impressions of what prison meant to Dostoevsky. On the one hand, the author feels isolated from his fellow prisoners by his class, and suggests that they hate him because he is a 'gentleman'. 'How can you be a comrade?', one friendly prisoner asks him. In return, he summarizes the other convicts as 'sullen, envious, terribly conceited, boastful, touchy'. Yet within the same covers, he praises them as 'perhaps . . . the most highly gifted and the strongest of all our people . . . condemned to perish uselessly, unnaturally, wrongfully, irrevocably. And whose (he asks) is the blame?' Having come into contact through them with the lowest classes, he feels free to exalt the humble. 'Our wiseacres cannot teach the people very much. I will even maintain that, on the contrary, they ought themselves to learn from them.'[13] What emerges for the reader, between these two poles of generalization, is a world of warmly but unsentimentally pictured men. Dostoevsky testifies to the irreducible dignity as human beings of men who have committed terrible murders and have been degraded by the prison environment itself. His own obstinate devotion to the concept of human freewill, with all the agonies which choice entails, comes to seem a natural outcome of prison. He shows us convicts determined to assert their freedom by earning and saving bits and pieces of money which they will blow all at once on illicit vodka, and men ready to commit a new crime simply in order to 'change their lot' and get into a different prison. . . . 'In consequence of our daydreams and our long divorce from it, freedom somehow seemed to us freer than real freedom, the freedom, that is, that exists in fact, in real life.'[14]

Prison had also made Dostoevsky immune to certain liberal pieties. *A Nasty Story* (1862) is a masterpiece of meaningful 'black' farce debunking the vague hopes of 'liberals' in the reforming phase initiated by Alexander II. Over fifty pages or so, Dostoevsky achieves a consistent mastery which he never quite attained in longer fictions. We meet Ivan Ilich Pralinsky, a rather precocious civil-service General in his forties, getting tipsy on champagne at the house of an older colleague and defending the new reforms. Humanity to inferiors, he blathers, is the cornerstone of a regenerated society; but when he gets outside and finds his coachman has driven off without permission, he exclaims, 'the common people are scoundrels,' and sets off to walk home. On the way, he weaves a favourite fantasy of himself as an enlightened and beloved leader of men. Passing a ramshackle house where a party is in progress he finds from a local policeman that the wedding of a very minor clerk in his own department is being celebrated there. In a luckless moment, he decides to patronize this underling by entering his party uninvited. 'If I repeat this five or ten times,' he tells himself, 'I will win popularity everywhere.'

The crisis which follows slily gathers momentum as Ivan Ilich gets drunker and drunker. From the first moment, when he goes into the house and puts his left foot in a dish of galantine, to the last when, after trying to make a noble speech, he keels over and his head falls in a plate of blancmange, his growing physical incapacity is deftly counterpointed with his surviving awareness that he has made an awful mistake. The wretched clerk, Pseldonimov, who is marrying for money an unpleasant girl he doesn't like, remains stonily respectful, even dashing up to wipe away Ivan Ilich's saliva when he spits involuntarily on the dinner table. Other guests

begin to mock the great man to his face. As an account of drunken behaviour, it is completely convincing and extremely funny. But the farce turns
sour when Ivan Ilich is put up on the bridal bed, and the newly married
couple are bedded down on chairs which at this delicate juncture slide
apart, depositing the bride among the cigarette ends on the floor. It is
wonderful that Dostoevsky can salvage from this affair our sympathy not
only for the unappealing Pseldonimov, but also for Ivan Ilich himself. The
story tells us of a chasm between rich and poor which cannot easily be
crossed, and rapidly sketches in a remarkable range of vivid characters. It
is one of the greatest successes in nineteenth-century fiction.

Seen purely as a work of fiction, it is far more impressive than the celebrated *Notes from Underground* (1864), but these do have a very important
place in the clarification and exposition of some of Dostoevsky's most
characteristic ideas. The 'underground man', a Petersburg clerk of forty
who has retired and now lives as a recluse in a shabby room, is an archetype
of the sterile intellectual, with his self hatred, his vindictiveness, his baffled
idealism, his masochism, and his cynical disgust with a world to which
others, but not he, can adjust.

He is painfully clever, and his cleverness isolates him—'Can a thinking
man have any self-respect whatever?' In his ragings against utilitarianism,
he reflects to the full Dostoevsky's own bias. He resents the claim of self-
styled 'scientific' thinkers that everything can be explained by natural laws,
and rejects even the 'civilization' which progressives prize so highly. A
few years later, Tolstoy, in *War and Peace*, was to pose man's consciousness of himself as free against the knowledge provided (as it seemed) by
nineteenth-century philosophizing and by science, that man is not free.
But Tolstoy's manner would be Olympian and his argument would be
crisp and orderly. Underground Man makes freedom a highly personal
matter. Like his creator's, his style is rambling and verbose. (Dostoevsky
wrote in a letter of 1866, 'For the last twenty years I have felt agonizingly—
and I see it more clearly than anyone, that my chief literary defect is—
verbosity, and I simply cannot get rid of it.')[15] But Underground Man's
tirade seems to come from the guts as well as the brain—he seems to *feel*
the ideas which Tolstoy merely understands, and he gives them a topical
and political bite.

> Furthermore, you say, science will teach men (although in my opinion this is a
> superfluity) that they have not, in fact, and never have had, either will or fancy and
> are no more than a sort of piano keyboard or barrel organ cylinder; and that the
> laws of nature still exist on the earth, so that whatever man does he does not of his
> own volition but, as really goes without saying, by the laws of nature. Consequent-
> ly, these laws of nature have only to be discovered, and man will no longer be
> responsible for his actions, and it will become extremely easy for him to live his life.

A Utopian system of government will permit all to live in harmony and
prosperity. 'The Palace of Crystal will arise'—Dostoevsky is remembering
London—but it will not endure:

Really, I shall not be in the least surprised if, for example, in the midst of the future universal good sense, some gentleman with an ignoble, or rather a derisive and reactionary air, springs up suddenly out of nowhere and says to all of us, 'Come on, gentlemen, why shouldn't we get rid of all this calm reasonableness with one kick, just so as to send these logarithms to the devil and be able to live our own lives at our own sweet will?' That wouldn't matter either, but what is really mortifying is that he would certainly find followers: that's the way men are made. And all this for the most frivolous of reasons, hardly worth mentioning, one would think: namely that a man, whoever he is, always and everywhere likes to act as he chooses, and not at all according to the dictates of reason and self-interest; it is indeed possible, and sometimes *positively imperative* (in my view) to act directly contrary to one's own best interests. One's own free and unfettered volition, one's own caprice, however wild, one's own fancy, inflamed sometimes to the point of madness— that is the one best and greatest good, which is never taken into consideration because it will not fit into any classification, and the omission of which always sends all systems and theories to the devil. . . . What a man needs is simply and solely *independent* volition, whatever that independence may cost and wherever it may lead.[16]

Humanity is indissolubly bound up with freedom. Freedom inevitably brings suffering. Therefore, man must suffer.

Dostoevsky can easily bear either a 'reactionary' or a 'revolutionary' interpretation. He can be read as a man denying the value of all dreams of a better world, all hopes of progress. Or he can be seen as a humanist extolling the essentially free nature of man against pseudo-scientists whose doctrines, by insisting that a man can be only what his background makes him, deny all hopes of genuine change or liberation. But however one reads Underground Man, he is essentially and all the time the voice of the 'modern' intellectual. He talks prophetically of babies born in test tubes. 'Soon,' he concludes drily, 'we shall invent a method of being born from an idea.' In the new metropolitan anti-culture, real flesh and blood are somehow slipping away from the reach of clever people like himself who have 'lost the habit of living'. We don't know, he says, 'whose side to be on or where to give our allegiance, what to love and what to hate, what to respect and what to despise.'[17] The intellectual, divorced from the life of the people, can now think of anything, but he can do nothing.

The hero of *The Gambler* (1866), a clever and rather nasty person, has quite a lot in common with Underground Man, but the novel's relative lightness and crispness is a sign of the difference, not altogether unwelcome, which dictation at breakneck speed made to Dostoevsky's style. In scope and setting, the novel suggests Turgenev, and there are hints of Turgenev-style allegory. The heroine is seduced by a scoundrelly Frenchman and finally captured by a stuffy Englishman, and Dostoevsky seems to be satirizing Russia's seduction by an unworthy West. Alexei Ivanovich, who tells the story, is employed as a tutor by a near-ruined Russian general who is staying at an imaginary German spa called Roulettenberg and eagerly waiting for news of the death of his old aunt ('Grandmamma') since he wants to inherit her money and marry a French adventuress. The tutor is in love with the General's stepdaughter, Polina, whose capricious behaviour recalls that of the real-life Pauline Suslova towards Dostoevsky himself. The novel at first taxis round rather tediously with routine intrigue, but it takes off when Grandmamma, a tough and likeable old lady, astonishes everyone first by arriving and then by gambling away a fortune at the roulette table. As with drunkenness in *A Nasty Story*, Dostoevsky here shows his rare power to portray people who have lost control of themselves. In the latter stages of the novel, even the typically bloodless Polina acquires a certain hysterical vivacity and Mademoiselle Blanche, the Frenchwoman, really comes into her own when she seduces the hero immediately after he has won a vast sum at roulette.

To write *The Gambler*, Dostoevsky had to interrupt his work on *Crime and Punishment*, and there are significant thematic echoes. Raskolnikov is a far fuller portrait of an obsessive man than Alexei, but one question the latter asks might well have come from him. Why is it worse to make money by gambling than by generations of honest toil—and exploitation of other people? Furthermore, Dostoevsky's own obsession with gambling relates in a most interesting way to his acute concern with human freedom of will. In a novel of the 1870s, *The Raw Youth*, he makes his young hero voice a conviction of his own, 'that in games of chance, if one has perfect control of one's will, so that the subtlety of one's intelligence and one's power of calculation are preserved, one cannot fail to overcome the brutality of blind chance and to win.'[18] The conflict between will and 'blind chance' in gambling is like the conflict between will and 'environment' which, on one of his many levels, Raskolnikov represents. In each case, man can only sustain himself by faith. The rebellion of Raskolnikov and the faith in God of Sonia Marmeladova involve the same kind of insistence against the odds as the gambler's faith in his 'system'.

V

Crime and Punishment (1866) is an extremely rich novel, combining the melodrama and pathos of *The Insulted and Injured* with scraps of the Dickensian humour of *Stepanchikovo* and with the insight into crime and some of the documentary realism of *The House of the Dead*. But its basic story is one of the simplest and most compelling invented by modern man. Because it has the starkness of a great myth, it is able to strike through to the depths of our hopes and fears. It has the power of a nightmare.

An impoverished young ex-student, Raskolnikov, ill, half starved, but acting, as he thinks, in accordance with a theory which he has developed, murders an unpleasant old woman pawnbroker. With her money, he proposes to make himself independent and give himself the chance to act as a 'great man'—that is one, over simple, way of explaining his action. But he bungles the job, murders also the old woman's saintly sister Lisaveta, fails to steal most of her money and hides in a panic what little he has stolen. His strange behaviour brings him under suspicion by the police, but they have no 'hard' evidence and an artisan 'confesses' to the murder from religious mania. Raskolnikov cannot accept that what he has done is a crime, but out of sheer exhaustion and despair he finally confesses and is sentenced to eight years' imprisonment. With him to Siberia goes Sonia Marmeladova, the daughter of a drunken civil servant. She took to prostitution to help support her family. Raskolnikov befriended them. This pure-minded and religious girl who loves him eventually brings him, in Siberia, to an acceptance of his guilt and conversion to Christianity.

The first two parts of the novel, nearly two-fifths of it, achieve extraordinary power because we see events almost entirely through the eyes of a murderer. We are with him—'inside him', so to speak—during his illness and obsession before he commits his crime, through the murders themselves and in his panic and illness afterwards. The tension thus achieved would perhaps be unbearable if it were maintained much longer, and in fact the remainder of the novel mixes long spasms of extreme suspense, notably when Raskolnikov is being interrogated by the examining magistrate Porfiri, with easy-going humour centring on Raskolnikov's goodhearted friend Razumikhin, a more sinister humour introduced by a womanizing provincial landowner named Svidrigailov, and horrible farce involving the Marmeladovs. Even so, *Crime and Punishment* remains a remarkably unified novel. And all the characters are bound together, in a way Dostoevsky never quite achieves elsewhere, by the vividly-presented life of Petersburg itself.

From the first pages where Raskolnikov leaves his tiny rented room and walks into the stinking crowded streets of the city in the stifling heat of its summer days, we are bound to see him, and the people he meets, as men and women struggling in a squalid and anti-human environment. It is true that Dostoevsky will not acknowledge 'environment' as an excuse for crime or as a decisive determinant of human behaviour—this is his quarrel with the radicals. It is also true that the force of an 'environment' has rarely been so strongly conveyed. Even better-off people are exposed to the city's sickening odours and lurking humiliations, and the Marmeladovs— a drunken father, his consumptive second wife, his daughter walking the streets and his three step-children short of food and clothes and forced to overhear degrading rows—seem as a family aptly to represent the condition of the poor.

Here is Raskolnikov's rented room:

> It was a tiny cubicle, about six feet in length, which looked most miserable with its dusty, yellowish paper peeling off the walls everywhere. It was, besides, so low that even a man only a little above average height felt ill at ease in it, fearing all the time that he might knock his head against the ceiling.[19]

Into this are crammed three old chairs, two tables, and 'a huge clumsy sofa, occupying almost the entire length of the wall and stretching half across the room'.

This room can tell us a lot about the nature of Dostoevsky's art. We accept its 'reality' without question when we read this description, though we may when we return to the book begin to wonder how so much furniture can fit into such a mere cupboard. If we then ask ourselves how it is that half-a-dozen people can squash into it when friends and family come to visit the sick man, we realize at once that the intensity of Dostoevsky's writing depends on what one might call 'realized exaggeration'. Packing people together like this into a room already too small for its owner, Dostoevsky makes us feel at one and the same time the force of Raskolnikov's persecution mania and a heightened sense of the airlessness of the city.

The whole Marmeladov family live in a room only ten feet in length, and one through which other lodgers have to go on their way to better accomodation. We first meet Sonia's stepmother pacing her tiny territory like a caged beast. Both doors are open, so that stench comes in from the stairs and cigarette smoke blown out by the merry-makers nextdoor inflames her hacking cough. But the window is *closed*, although the room is very stuffy. Madame Marmeladova's sufferings are forced upon her. But she makes them more severe herself; she is Underground Man's free creature refusing to do what is in her own interest. She cannot stop people passing through her room. She can, if only to spite herself, keep the window shut.

By contrast Sonia's room is large, but it has a low ceiling and a strange irregular shape. Like Raskolnikov's or her stepmother's, this room can be seen as a projection of her own personality—its relative bareness, airiness and quiet reflect a girl whose essential goodness, simplicity and refinement are qualities Dostoevsky insists on. But this room too connects—via doors kept closed and thin partitions—with other lodgings. Behind one locked door is the room in which Svidrigailov will listen when Raskolnikov confesses to her. Echoing emptiness is, in fact, almost as disturbing as noisy overcrowding. Both emphasize man's plight in the modern city, where he is lonely among thronging thousands.

Because the environment is 'abnormal' the main characters in the novel, a murderer, an alcoholic, a half-mad consumptive, a prostitute and a child rapist—seem not eccentric but representative. Sympathy for them is not only possible, but almost inevitable.

Raskolnikov is very vain, bad-tempered and stand-offish. We understand him to be highly intelligent, but the murder he commits is both extremely brutal and very inefficient. However, we meet him in a state of sickness and despair which from the outset puts us on his side. We watch him giving money he can't afford to the Marmeladovs (another action perversely against self-interest) and we are with him when he learns from his mother's letter the terrible news that his sister is about to marry a well-to-do blackguard in order to help support him. His pride doesn't prohibit love for his family and sympathy for the sufferings of others, and compared to the mob of Amalia Lippewechsels' lodgers, he seems an altogether better man.

Crime and Punishment is like a detective thriller turned inside out. Balzac, Dickens and others had introduced detectives into fiction and Dostoevsky in *The Insulted and Injured* had invented a character, Masloboev, anticipating the modern 'private eye'. But in *Crime and Punishment* we know who the murderer is as soon as the crime is committed. What creates suspense is the fact that we don't know whether Raskolnikov will be caught and punished. Since we are 'on his side', we don't want him to be punished, however much we abhor his crime. The problem for Dostoevsky is to make it seem both to Raskolnikov and to us that it is *right* that he should be punished. He doesn't succeed completely; the passages leading up to the murderer's confession to the police are not altogether convincing and his ultimate repentance in Siberia is so thinly presented that we must, if we want it, take it on trust. Raskolnikov is both an 'underdog' and a rebel against a patently unjust social system. When he confesses to his sister Dunia we are shown that pride underlies his refusal to repent, and pride and vanity are for Dostoevsky cardinal sins. Yet we (and also, surely, Dostoevsky) must see much truth in his claim that the shedding of blood is hardly, by accepted social standards, a manifest 'crime'. In wars it is 'poured out like champagne' and for shedding it 'people are crowned in the Capital and afterwards called the benefactors of mankind.'[20]

So rather than the deed itself, we have to consider its motive. And this raises the very complex problem of deciding what Raskolnikov's motives are so that we can judge them. As he will later do in *The Brothers Karamazov*, Dostoevsky in effect throws the burden of just punishment from the legal system (which is incompetent to judge motives) on to the sinner himself. Right judgement can only be executed by the free will of the murderer, even if, and this is a source of enigma, his will when he commited the crime was not perhaps 'free'. Self-judgement itself becomes an act of rebellion against 'the environment' comparable to the crime which itself expressed revolt. If *Crime and Punishment* is a less authoritative novel, in the last analysis, than *The Brothers Karamazov*, this is because Dostoevsky cannot yet make us feel the force of self-judgement, and Raskolnikov's ultimate will to believe in God and in love is pictured only on the level of a somewhat sentimental happy ending.

Confessing to Sonia, Raskolnikov offers at least five different explanations of his crime.

'I wanted to become a Napoleon,' he says, linking himself with Pushkin's Hermann and with Tolstoy's contemporaneous Prince Andrei. The lesson of Napoleon's career is that in order to realize his inherent greatness, a 'great man' will have to be prepared to murder and rob so as to clear the obstacles out of his path.

Sonia doesn't think he is being frank. He admits he isn't, but, in a Dostoevsky novel, such an admission proves nothing; his people, like ourselves, contradict themselves constantly. Raskolnikov now turns to the poverty of his family as an explanation. He needed the old woman's money to get through the university without worrying his mother. We know how deeply in fact he reacted to the humiliations his mother and sister were exposed to on his account, so this explanation carries weight. But Sonia still doesn't believe him.

His third explanation throws the blame on his 'environment'. Low ceilings and tiny rooms, he says, warp both mind and soul. He was, he indicates, driven out of his mind as his vanity and vindictiveness interacting with his degrading lodgings. But, as he talks on, a fourth explanation emerges, a modification of the first 'Napoleonic' one. He wanted to prove, he says, that he was superior to the stupid people he had to live among. The capacity to murder and rob is in itself the proof of greatness. 'He who dismisses with contempt what men regard as sacred becomes their lawgiver, and he who dares more than anyone is more right than anyone.' And Sonia realizes that this 'gloomy confession of faith' is his 'religion and law'. She produces, and he assents to, a fifth explanation—'You have turned away from God, and God has struck you down and handed you over to Satan.' And Raskolnikov says, 'I know perfectly well that the devil is leading me on.' The devil dragged him into murder and it was only after he had bungled the crime that the devil explained to him 'that I had no right to go there because I was the same kind of louse as the rest.'[21]

The novel is so rich because *all* these five explanations are made to carry weight. The reader has been helped to see Raskolnikov as a good man warped by the conditions he lives in and by the illness which he suffers from; but if this is all, then he was not a free agent when he committed the murder—it was 'society' or certain germs which did it. Nor would he seem to us a perfectly free agent if, as Sonia perhaps believes, there literally exists a devil who led him into it. If we interpret 'the devil' as merely his own vanity, this still admits the determinist explanation that he acted as he did because of the peculiar physiology of his brain. If we substitute for 'vanity' the words 'acute concern for his own dignity' we get a different perspective on his crime. Whether he is 'free' or not, his reluctance to submit to degradation is one of the qualities which we find most attractive in him. His crime can be seen as a mistaken attempt to break out of squalor and achieve fuller human status. But the word 'human' has no meaning, if we can agree with Dostoevsky, unless it implies 'free'. If Raskolnikov is fully human, he must take responsibility for the action he committed or deny his own freedom, which would be a psychological impossibility. Therefore, *he* did wrong, whether we see the murder (as he does) as an intellectual miscalculation or whether we judge his action (as we clearly should do) as one evil in itself. If we see his illness as something which 'happened to him' and see 'illness', however defined, as the cause of his crime, he must, to prove that he is human, *accept responsibility for what happened to him.* Raskolnikov is one of the great representatives of modern man in fiction becáuse like us he is not free and yet has to be free. On the philosophical level, the problem we wrestle with him is one as old as inquiry itself. On the political level, it could be resolved only if a world could be created in which the interference of society and the environment which currently limit freedom of action could be abolished—if, that is, we need no longer be ill, or subject, or poor.

Hope for a free world is defied by the existence of evil, though this does not in itself contradict the existence of human freedom of will. (Indeed one could argue that evil is a condition of freedom.) Before Raskolnikov murders the old woman he has a nightmare in which he is a little boy watching some peasants outside a pub beat an old horse to death. He kisses the dead bloodstained face of the murdered mare, just as he succours, later in the book, the battered Marmeladov run over by a rich man's carriage. Yet he himself smashes a hatchet down 'again and again' on the pawnbroker's head. How can we explain that a man both loathes violence and commits it? Underground Man would say that this is a case where two and two don't make four. It defies science and reason, and Chernyshevsky's adored self-interest. All we can do, Dostoevsky indicates, is to follow Sonia's faith in God and, like her, accept suffering meekly.

Suffering can in itself be a source of pleasure. This is one of Dostoevsky's most important insights, though he illustrates it rather crudely when Marmeladov's wife drags him by the hair and he cries out, 'I enjoy it . . . I enjoy-y-y it.' And if suffering leads to redemption, to court it can be the expression of vanity and arrogance. Dunia, as Svidrigailov tells her brother, is the kind of girl who in the early days of Christianity would have sought martyrdom. And in this she is akin to her vain brother—Porfiri tells Raskolnikov, 'You're one of those men who, even if he were disembowelled, would stand and look at his torturers with a smile, provided he had found something to believe in or had found God.'

But such is the complexity of Dostoevsky's vision that within a couple of sentences Porfiri brings his appeal down to the merely 'environmental' level. 'What you have long needed is a change of air. . . . All you want now is air, air, air.'[22]

And Svirigailov has anticipated Porfiri. 'Oh my dear fellow,' he told Raskolnikov, 'what every human being wants is air, air, air.'[23]

VI

As this clearly significant 'coincidence' shows, the people whom Dostoevsky invents are cross-linked by a system of echoes and correspondences. Like his other major novels, this one is full of 'doubles'.

The affinity of opposites produces a relatively simple kind of doubling in the case of Razumikhin and Raskolnikov. They are, in fact, 'friends' in the rather special sense this word can have in Dostoevsky; that is, they are drawn to each other. But whereas Raskolnikov's disgust with human nature makes him see the old woman he kills as merely a 'louse' and not a person, Razumikhin judges everyone generously. His name means 'Reasoner', though intellectual coolness and clarity are hardly qualities we associate with him. Raskolnikov's evokes the *Raskolniki*, 'Old Believers'* and suggests dogged and opinionated religious dissent, a quality more obviously akin to Razumikhin's stubborn faith in human nature than to his own would-be-austere logic. The two complement each other; we might say they 'mirror' each other.

The 'doubling' of Raskolnikov and Svidrigailov is far more complex. *Vis à vis* Razumikhin, Raskolnikov is a nihilist. *Vis à vis* Svidrigailov, he is a moralist. There is a strange and complete lack of sensuality in his character. (His relationship with Sonia carries not the faintest charge of lust.) Svidrigailov amply compensates for his double in this respect. He raped, we gather, a fourteen-year-old child who then committed suicide. But Raskolnikov can match this, on the spiritual level, with his own morbid attraction to his landlady's daughter, a strange and ailing girl to whom he proposed marriage, but who then died.

Svidrigailov is fair and Raskolnikov is dark; he is rich and Raskolnikov is poor; he is fifty and Raskolnikov only twenty-three. But he insists that there is an affinity between them. And Dostoevsky seems to confirm it in a passage which, unless this link is grasped, might seem to interfere with the unity of the novel; the long sequence in which we are told of Svidrigailov's last night alive and his suicide, and follow his thoughts and actions as we usually follow Raskolnikov's. In effect, Svidrigailov *replaces* Raskolnikov.

Planning to seduce Dunia, Svidrigailov has first to shake off his non-sensual double. Raskolnikov leaves him to go and stare at the river from a bridge and we infer that he is thinking of suicide. He doesn't notice his sister meeting Svidrigailov by appointment on the same bridge. After this we lose sight of him. Svidrigailov fails to conquer Dunia. He then asserts his freedom and, in a sense, 'redeems' himself by *works*. He 'does good' on what might be called the 'environmental' level, by giving his money away to people who need it. Raskolnikov can only be saved by *faith*, that faith which he will come to share with Sonia. The thunderstorm which has been hanging over the novel breaks. Rain floods parts of the city, but the sultry air is at last cooled and washed. On this rainy night, Svidrigailov retreats to a cubby hole as small as Raskolnikov's room. He dreams of the raped child. The other dreamer in the book is, of course, Raskolnikov. The latter once walked in the country near Petersburg and, we learnt, stopped longer to look at the flowers than anything else. Then he fell asleep under some bushes and dreamed of the horse battered to death. In Svidrigailov's dream, the dead girl is covered with flowers and placed in a country cottage like those which Raskolnikov was looking at. As Svidrigailov next

---

*Since *Raskol* means 'schism', the name also suggests a divided mind or personality— 'Splitman' as well as 'Dissenterson', as it were.

morning walks through the mist to shoot himself he is aiming to kill himself under a 'bush', though he in fact does it elsewhere. His act of literal self-murder corresponds, as an expression of personal freedom, to Raskolnikov's symbolic self-murder—'I killed myself and not the old hag', he tells Sonia. Svidrigailov commits suicide while Raskolnikov, also out in the rain, ponders it and rejects it. It is as if the double's self-destruction, allied with the cleansing rain, liberates Raskolnikov to make his confession; as if Svidrigailov's suicide stands as an explanation for Raskolnikov's decision to accept the burden of going on living.

Raskolnikov, in the middle as it were, doubles both the extreme of optimism (Razumikhin) and the extreme of cynical pessimism (Svidrigailov). The latter's view of the after-life—'What if . . . you suddenly find just a little room there, something like a village bath-house, grimy, and spiders in every corner, and that's all eternity is.'[24]—takes to a grotesque extreme the kind of thinking represented by Raskolnikov's notion that other people are 'lice'. But the family of doubles extends to more than three. Svidrigailov (with his 'air, air, air') also 'doubles' for Porfiri in the simplest way of all, and in his desire for Dunia he is matched by her fiancé Luzhin, the most purely unpleasant character in the novel.

Dostoevsky clearly loathes Luzhin. He tries to make him completely contemptible in the weakest scene of the book, where Luzhin ineptly plants some money on Sonia and then accuses her of stealing it from him. But this ambitious, self-satisfied man of affairs has ideas which 'parody' Raskolnikov. Luzhin is a complacent exponent of capitalist individualism. Science tells us, he says, to love ourselves before everyone else:

> And economic truth adds that the more successfully private business is run . . . the more solid are the foundations of our social life and the greater is the general well-being of the people. Which means that by acquiring wealth exclusively and only for myself, I'm by that very fact acquiring it, as it were, for everybody. . . .

This is all too like Raskolnikov's idea that if he kills the old woman he will be able to use her money to benefit mankind. And Raskolnikov tells Luzhin, 'If the principles you've just been advocating are pushed to their logical conclusion, you'll soon be justifying murder.'[25] What Raskolnikov himself has done on the spiritual level is akin to what Luzhin could do on the 'environmental' level; he has pushed the principles of nineteenth-century liberalism, and utilitarianism, to a conclusion which justifies murder.

The female characters also are complexly linked. Raskolnikov at once sees how, if Dunia marries Luzhin for the sake of the money with which he can help her brother, this would be like Sonia's turning prostitute to save her family. Sonia is also linked to Lizaveta, her friend; her gesture and expression when Raskolnikov confesses to her are exactly like those of Lizaveta when he murdered her. Dunia's habit of walking up and down the room with folded arms should remind us of Madame Marmeladova. The latter's passionate love of justice, her vain and quarrelsome temperament, and the extremism of her attempt to break out of her hopeless situation by going straight to the higher authorities, link her temperamentally with Dunia's brother as well. But the absurdity of all the scenes which she creates—even that terrible one when, crazed and dying, she takes her children out to earn their living as street entertainers—means that her relationship to Raskolnikov is in effect one of parody.

We will find an equally elaborate pattern of linkings in Tolstoy's *Anna Karenina*, where, as in this novel, all situations and characters exist in complexly significant relationship with all other situations and characters. But though Dostoevsky's people are very vivid and moving, they aren't 'real' in the way that Tolstoy's are. Each of Tolstoy's people seems 'complete'—each has a sensual as well as an intellectual life. While Sonia is not inefficient as a part of *Crime and Punishment*'s whole, she is shorn of a dimension which we know real people have. Nothing we are told about her helps us to imagine even faintly how she goes about her business as a prostitute; we don't even really know what her attitude is to it. As with Raskolnikov's room, we must not ask questions; we have to accept what is in effect an implausibility, or exaggeration, the concept of a saintly prostitute.

We might go further and say that ultimately the other characters only 'exist' in relation to Raskolnikov, who stands at the centre of the web of coincidences and chances which brings them together. It is tempting therefore to see them all as aspects of a single human personality. Together, they form a portrait of human nature, in conflict with itself, irreconcilably 'double'. Raskolnikov at the centre of the web transcends and in a sense summarizes them all, and Razumikhin says of him that it is as if 'there were two people of diametrically opposed characters living in him'.[26] His devil inspires him to murder and his good angel draws him to acts of quixotic charity. He has affinities both with the raped child and with Svidrigailov, raper of children. He can be banal as Luzhin or spiritual as Dunia. He can be seen as a profile of human nature in which good, mated with faith and love, will finally triumph over evil, or as a disturbing embodiment of the truth that good and evil always exist in combination with each other and are essentially relative terms. We may see him as an earnest dissenter, an 'old believer', seeking after truth and justice and far finer than Luzhin the bureaucrat-businessman, Porfiri the policeman-inquisitor and Svidraigailov the pervert-nobleman, three figures who rather obliquely represent the status quo of Tsarist Russia. Or we may see him as a tragic exemplar of the Satanic vanity which raises man up against God's will and justice.

But however we view him, he represents human nature *in revolt*. 'So you do believe in the New Jerusalem?' Porfiri asks him. 'I do.' 'And do you believe in God?' asks Porfiri. 'I do.'[27] He believes in God yet rebels against him. What if his vision of the New Jerusalem also exists in defiance of God? As we shall find in Dostoevsky's last novel, the two may indeed be incompatible, even in the original light cast by a 'Christian' anarchism.

REALISM

It seems sensible to call *Crime and Punishment* a 'realistic' novel. Yet its methods are sharply different from those of *Fathers and Sons* and still more from the 'slices of life' technique adopted, as we shall see, by the young Tolstoy and later sometimes used by Chekhov. Are there any worthwhile generalizations which we can make about 'Russian realism'?

'Realism' is a fiendishly tricky term but one which, as Arnold Kettle has observed, 'like one's relations, it is not always possible to accept or ignore.'* Even to begin to discuss adequately the justly influential usage of the word by Georg Lukács in his writings on the nineteenth-century novel would involve us in highly contentious questions about the 'real' nature (so to speak) of 'reality'. There is no space here to review the ideas of Plato, Aristotle, Kant, Hegel, and Marx, to name only a few, even if I were in the least competent to do so. Yet on commonsense grounds we will surely agree that it is proper to talk about the nineteenth-century novel as primarily 'realistic'. In Europe and America, as in Russia, its greatest exponents were people who, in a tradition which stretched back to Cervantes and Defoe, aimed not merely to please their readers, but also to bring to their attention features of human life which were not always obvious and might frequently seem base and unpleasant. Stendhal, one of the very greatest of these writers, called the novel a mirror set in the roadway as life passed by.

Russians, as usual, carried an already existing Western notion to an extreme. That the novelist could have a serious role as commentator and moralist was generally assumed by writers in France and England. To suggest, as Russian critics did, that the novelist had a special and onerous responsibility to describe distinctively 'national' life and to criticize it with saintly truth and severity was, of course, to go much further. Chernyshevky's famous remark of 1855—'With us literature constitutes the whole intellectual life of the nation'—is one which no Western European could have made.

The power of censorship in Russia underlies Chernyshevsky's position.

---

* *The Novel in the Mid-Nineteenth Century*, Open University Press 1973.

Russian 'reality' itself was different. Not only were the Russian political and social structures in contrast at many points with those of England, but the artist who sought to illuminate them faced much greater problems.

Many attempts have been made to generalize about the special character of 'Russian realism' which arose from the unique features of Russian life. Mirsky (169–172) is, as usual, worth heeding. It is noteworthy that he excludes not only Gogol but also Pushkin from a range of generalizations designed to cover major writers from Aksakov (born 1791) to Gorky (born 1868)—both of these latter, incidentally, are men whose best-known works are fictionalized autobiography. He dates the birth of the 'realist' school in the 1840s and sees Belinsky as its prophet—'Never did a literary development so exactly answer to the expectations entertained by a leading critic.'

Mirsky emphasizes firstly the 'equal, level, human treatment of all humanity. . . . People are not good or bad; they are only more or less unhappy and deserving of sympathy.' He then stresses three elements taken over from Gogol—a great attention to detail, especially in describing people; the admission into fiction of 'the vulgar, base, unprepossessing, and unedifying aspects of life'; and a 'satirical attitude towards the existing forms of life.' Besides this Mirsky notes, of course, the 'relative neglect of narrative construction and narrative interest' (of what I have preferred to call 'plot'). He claims—but this hardly seems true of Turgenev, of Goncharov or even of Gorky—that 'the realists avoided all fine writing.' In conclusion he stresses the concentration on themes from contemporary or almost contemporary Russian life; and the recognition by novelists of a duty to tackle the social issues of the day.

Some of these points apply to *War and Peace*, to take one prominent instance. A couple arguably don't. It is set 'sixty years since' and in several respects seems to idealize the old life of the Russian nobility. It is hard to think of a single major work, bar some of Chekhov's stories, which Mirsky's formula represents exactly. Each of the elements he points to can, furthermore, be found in individual Western writers of the same period, sometimes to an equally great extent. Russian 'realism' in fact both imitates and extends existing European modes and approaches. And the differences between individual Russian writers are as striking as those between the Russians as a group and the English 'school'. Dostoevsky's methods are closer to those of Dickens (or of Balzac) than to Tolstoy's.

So we return to the intractable problem, how to define 'realism'. If Turgenev is a pre-eminent 'realist' then Dostoevsky's fiction demands some extra term—we must speak of 'Romantic realism' or, as he suggested himself, of 'higher realism'. And Tolstoy is different enough from all predecessors and contemporaries, in Russia and elsewhere, to draw us willy nilly into talk of 'Tolstoyan realism'.

5
TOLSTOY TO *WAR AND PEACE*
Man against History

To quote a passage from his own *Two Hussars*, Tolstoy's life began

> Early in the nineteenth century, when there were as yet no railways or macadamized roads, no gaslight, no stearine candles, no low couches with sprung cushions, no unvarnished furniture, no disillusioned youths with eye glasses, no liberalizing women philosophers, nor any charming *dames aux camélias* of whom there are so many in our times, in those naive days, when leaving Moscow for Petersburg in a coach or carriage provided with a kitchenful of home-made provisions one travelled for eight days along a soft, dusty or muddy road and believed in chopped cutlets, sledge-bells and plain rolls . . .[1]

It began, in other words, when Russian noblemen still remained almost self-sufficient on the produce of their own estates. And if those words, like the story from which they are taken, convey a kind of dry relish of the old ways, this goes along with plenty of evidence which suggests that Tolstoy remained to the end by disposition a feudal patriarch.

But he lived on until 1910. The paramount symbol of the changes which came about in his lifetime was the railway, and he would use it as such in *Anna Karenina*. The railway came from the West along with Liberalism, English fashions, lawn tennis and mass-produced soap, and it invaded many Oblomovkas. The further change went the more Tolstoy moved towards the people who still told folk-tales and for whom the produce of the soil was still labour realized and not a range of items for commercial exploitation. He moved towards the peasants, and the proud conservative landowner emerged as a prophet of the simple life.

His life overlapped with those of Pushkin as well as of Pasternak, of Walter Scott as well as of George Orwell. He is the representative European writer of his age. In *Anna Karenina* he created what many will regard as the definitive 'nineteenth-century novel'. In *War and Peace* he completed what some call a modern epic; and in *Resurrection* he produced a prototype of the 'committed' novel. We still belong to his period. The battle scenes in *Sevastopol* and *War and Peace* have hardly been outmoded by any writer on twentieth-century world wars; the highest praise for such descriptions is still to call them 'Tolstoyan'. Anna's predicament still speaks directly, it seems, to Western women of the 1970s, and Tolstoy's condemnation of capitalism as 'anti-natural' makes more obvious sense in days when 'pollution' is a bogey-word than it did when he took up his lonely prophetic stance.

Yet paradoxically all his achievement is built on the intellectual life of the eighteenth century. His rationalistic satire recalls Voltaire and Swift. His attitude to nature develops from that of the eighteenth-century prophet Rousseau. And Rousseau's *Confessions* were the starting point of a writer whose own novels, with their self-exploring heroes, are saturated in critical self-analysis. From the eighteenth-century English novelist Sterne, of the *Sentimental Journey*, Tolstoy learnt how to fashion scenes both ironic and touching, brief and exquisitely pointed—his novels, huge as they are, are built out of short and delicate episodes.

Besides these writers his grandparents could have read, he learnt from Russians of his own class. Pushkin, Lermontov and Turgenev, all aristocrats, gave him a good deal. Of foreign contemporaries, he seems to have found Stendhal most useful—he thought him the first man who had ever described a battle properly. And Stendhal, though 'liberal' in his views, was deeply ironic in his attitude to contemporary life and, like Tolstoy, harked back in style and temperament to the eighteenth-century enlightenment.

Every cell in Tolstoy's brain and every nerve in his body resisted the dominant tendencies of the late nineteenth century. He remained as immune to Turgenev's liberalism as he did to the over-excited, plebeian manner of Dostoevsky. 'Progress', industrialism, bourgeois democracy and bourgeois commercialism all seemed to him intrinsically absurd. Newspapers didn't fever his mind as they did Dostoevsky's; they simply provided redundant evidence for the obvious truth that the world was going crazy. 'New ideas', the fuel Dostoevsky ran on, couldn't hold his attention. Like his own heroes, he made his philosophy for himself.

His ideas are 'home-made', like old-fashioned tallow candles, like furniture crafted on the estate by serf-carpenters, like pickled mushrooms and jam made out of fresh-gathered berries. He buys a few thoughts from outside from time to time, but basically aims to remain self-sufficient within his own inherited resources. On his estate, in his little kingdom, he does not argue, he broods. His broodings, like those of his heroes, drive him back to the elemental things which compose his way of life; to the family and its children, heirs to the noble name, to the peasants who grow the food, and to abundant nature itself. The scope of his kingdom does not seem small to him. The Enlightenment had believed that the laws of nature, both human and inanimate, were simple, unified, universal and could be discovered by the human intellect. Tolstoy believed that whatever was true about himself was true also for all mankind. But his thought never became closed or detached. He did not argue much with other thinkers, but he did address the facts. And these facts, as he saw them, paradoxically convinced him that the peasants who were 'natural' but who did not 'reason' lived better than the class which read and thought while its members exploited them.

Tolstoy never retreated into nostalgia. He observed change aloofly but keenly, and he fought his war with it out in the open. He confronted a world of facts with his home-made candour and never ceased to adjust his judgements to what he saw. And his home-made vision saw things which others ignored. He has, almost uniquely among writers, the gift of portraying people and things as if no-one had ever noticed them before. He convinces the reader, for page after page, that he is living through what Tolstoy describes, that no 'art' is involved, and that life is 'like this.'

But of course only extreme artistic skill could create this entrancing illusion.* That manner which seems so straightforwardly frank is the product of many re-writings; thanks to the labour of his peasants, Tolstoy had time to rewrite.

R. F. Christian has analysed Tolstoy's style in *War and Peace*,[2] and finds that apart from 'simplicity' and 'lucidity' its main distinguishing feature is 'repetition'. Characters who seem complete and 'round'—who are, in fact, as 'alive' as people in fiction can be—are evoked again and again by reference to one or two significant external details. An individual word, as numb as 'reception-room' or as potent as 'wept', will be repeated five times in as many lines. Tolstoy, Professor Christian says, was 'particularly addicted to a classical, rhetorical arrangement of his material in groups of three—three adjectives, three nouns, three verbs, three prepositions. Take for example the following sentence. . . .

> On his return to Moscow from the army, Nikolai Rostov was welcomed (A) by his home circle as (1) the best of sons, (2) a hero and (3) their darling Nikolenka; (B) by his relations as (1) a charming, (2) agreeable and (3) polite young man; (C) by his acquaintances as (1) a handsome lieutenant of hussars, (2) a good dancer and (3) one of the best matches in Moscow.

In this case Tolstoy doesn't seem to be trying to convince us of the truth of any general intellectual proposition. We accept this way of writing as 'natural' enough—we are used, after all, to rhetoric—and the impression of easy balance given is aesthetically pleasant without being obtrusive. But the reader must be on his guard. Tolstoy was from the outset an unusually fierce moralist. He wields the word 'natural', for instance, like

---

*I am indebted to a lecture by Robin Wood on *Anna Karenina* for a pertinent extension of this point. He remarked that what we call 'realism' in fiction can be described as 'illusionism'.

an axe to cut what is good from what is 'unnatural' and evil. Readers not alert to the hard thought underlying the innocent-looking surface of his work may swallow Tolstoyan judgements they ought to question. No one is likely to miss the moments where a Turgenev is soliciting tears or a Dickens commanding indignation; Tolstoy is in effect less open about his intentions.

Readers may fear that to go to Tolstoy with both eyes open to his technique and his cunning may destroy that sense of direct communion with life which they rightly enjoy in his fiction. Yet oddly enough the fourth reading of *War and Peace* with pencil in hand can be even more moving than the first splendid experience of it. What we call 'realism' in fiction is always the product of a three-way relationship between the original 'life' from which the novelist selects his material, the personal disposition and special world view of the writer himself and the private experience and (we assume) unique angle of vision of the reader involved. The novelist who sees most and sees most clearly will give most to the reader who sees more than others, not only of life, but of what the novelist is up to. Tolstoy really lived in the Russia he describes. He is, and is bound to be, present in the books he creates. The interest of getting to know Tolstoy better can be as keen after a while as the pleasure one gets from his supreme powers of 'objective' observation.

He was, after all, a very extraordinary man. He was aristocrat and manual labourer, soldier and pacifist, devoted family man and victim of the institution of marriage, lecher and ascetic, spendthrift and extoller of frugality, gambler and patient stylist, intellectual and anti-intellectual, rationalist and sensualist, Christian and materialist, reactionary and would-be revolutionary liberator. And he was *emphatically* all these things. It is a truism that whatever a novelist knows of the deeply 'inward' life of his characters must come from his own scrutiny of himself; there is only one person any man can get fully inside. If Tolstoy creates a wider range of 'live' people from the inside than any other writer of fiction, this is because he is so diverse himself. But at the centre of all this self-contradiction, trying to control it and in fact succeeding in bringing an astounding amount of it into clear, sharp focus is a calm, strong presence of deeply reflective, home-made rational thought. And if any thinking can smell of logs and the wind, Tolstoy's does.

II

Count Lev Nikolaevich Tolstoy was born in 1828 at Yasnaia Poliana, about 130 miles from Moscow. This estate had come to his mother from her father, the proud and domineering old Prince Volkonsky on whom Tolstoy based Prince Bolkonsky in *War and Peace*. Like Nikolai in that novel, Tolstoy's father, Nikolai, had restored the family fortunes by marrying his Maria. Lev had three elder brothers, Nikolai, Sergei and

Dmitri; these four were new twigs on a family tree which had its roots in the fourteenth century.

Deaths unsettled and dominated his childhood. When he was not yet two his mother died. He was too young to remember her, there was no portrait of her, and for his whole life she would be for him an elusive image of infinite tenderness, goodness and love. When he was eight, his father died suddenly, after the boys had moved to Moscow for their education. Their grandmother became head of the family and soon died in turn. In 1841, his legal guardian Aunt Aline died too and the boys were taken from their Aunt Toinette (the original of Sonia in *War and Peace*) to live in the old Tartar town of Kazan with yet another Aunt named Pelageia.

When in *Childhood*, his first important story, Tolstoy described his hero Irtenev's impressions after the death of his fictional mother, he could not draw on direct memory, but had to create them out of similar experience—and of that he had all too much. The little boy, alone in the room with the coffin, stares at the wax-like yellow face of the dead woman with its expression of unearthly calm. In his reverie he forgets himself and feels a 'kind of exalted, ineffably sweet, sad happiness'. Then someone comes in. The boy feels he ought to cry to show that he isn't callous; so he cries:

> As I recall my impressions now it seems to me that only that momentary forgetfulness of self was genuine grief. Before and after the funeral I never ceased to cry and be miserable, but it makes me ashamed when I think back on that sadness of mine, seeing that always in it was an element of self-love—now a desire to show that I prayed more than any one else, now concern about the impression I was producing on others, now an aimless curiosity which caused me to observe Mimi's cap or the faces of those around me. I despised myself for not experiencing sorrow to the exclusion of everything else, and I tried to conceal all other feelings: this made my grief insincere and unnatural. Moreover, I felt a kind of enjoyment in knowing that I was unhappy and I tried to stimulate my sense of unhappiness, and this interest in myself did more than anything else to stifle real sorrow in me.[3]

This is the voice of 'Tolstoyan Man', *Homo Tolstoyensis*. Though only first person narrators and 'heroes' will display the traits of 'Tolstoyan man' so fully, his nature will be shared by almost all Tolstoy's characters. He is self-absorbed and egotistical even when he is not self-analytical. His inner nature—which is essentially 'good'—is hardly ever in harmony with the things he does, with the words he speaks or even with the thoughts he thinks. Outwardly he is prey to impulse and circumstance. He weeps when someone dies, but in pity for himself or so as to impress others with his grief. His appetites, especially sexual ones, will lead him to do things he knows he ought not to do. His tongue will utter words he knows not to be true. Yet the inner core of the self is both 'good' and 'free'. This might be called his 'conscience'—certainly it is full of consciousness of the self, 'self-consciousness'. Paradoxically, however, the self is 'best' and 'freest' when it forgets itself, when, like Irtenyev's here, it is lost for a moment in 'genuine grief', or when it is absorbed in hunting or in hard physical work or in love for another person. It craves for, and sometimes finds, the unconsciousness also present in infancy and in rapture—and in death.

At the age of sixteen, Tolstoy set down on paper the first of many lists he would make of 'Rules of Life'; he embarked on a quest for virtue like one of his own future heroes. But he was constitutionally incapable of sticking to 'rules'. He failed the entry exam to Kazan University. When he got in at the second try, he flopped horribly as a student of Oriental Languages and transferred to the Law Department. Then, when he was eighteen, he withdrew from University without a degree. He was already well set on a course of 'home-made' self education.

The Tolstoy boys divided up their inheritance and Lev took over the management of his portion, Yasnaia Poliana itself, with 4000 acres and 330 peasants. The squalor and sloth of the lives of these serfs shocked him, but his dreams of benefitting them by modernizing agricultural methods ran up against their mistrust and their traditionalism. After eighteen months he could stand no more and went first to Moscow, then to Petersburg. Gambling debts forced a temporary retreat to his estate (where he amused himself by seducing his Aunt Toinette's servant-girls) but by the end of 1850 he was back in Moscow, and amending his Rules of Life to make them rules of social success. '(1) Join a group of card players, to try my luck when I am in funds. (2) Get into the best society and, under certain conditions, marry. (3) Find a good position.... Seek out the society of people more highly placed than I.... Be as cold as possible and let no feeling show.' But his lust made nonsense of such attempts at self control. 'I am living like a beast,' he wrote in his diary. '... In the evening, drew up precepts, then went to the gypsies.'[4]

From debts and a sense of moral degradation he escaped to the snowy peaks of the Caucasus frontier. He joined the regiment of his brother Nikolai there in May 1851 and formally entered the army as a cadet early in the following year. He raided with the Cavalry and fell in love with a beautiful Cossack girl. And he wrote *Childhood*.

When this appeared in *The Contemporary* in 1852, Turgenev hailed the anonymous 'L.N.' as a new master. But Tolstoy stayed in the Caucasus, wenching, drinking and cursing himself for his vices, until he was transferred early in 1854 to the South Western frontier in Moldavia. In Bucharest, Tolstoy wrote in his diary:

> I am ugly, awkward, untidy and socially uncouth. I am irritable and tiresome to others, immodest, intolerant, and shy as a child. .... Whatever I know I have learned by myself—half-learned, in bits and snatches, without any structure or order—and it is precious little withal. I am excessive, vacillating, unstable, stupidly vain and aggressive, like all weaklings. I am not courageous. I am so lazy that idleness has become an ineradicable habit with me. .... I am honourable, that is, I love the

path of virtue ... and when I depart from it I am unhappy and am glad to return to it. Yet there is one thing I love more than virtue: fame. I am so ambitious, and this craving in me has had so little satisfaction, that if I had to choose between fame and virtue, I am afraid I would very often opt for the former.... Today I have to reproach myself for three violations of my rules of life: (1) forgot the piano; (2) did nothing about the report concerning my transfer; (3) ate borscht, in spite of my diarrhoea which keeps getting worse.[5]

Such a swoop from abstractions like virtue and fame to the banality of borscht and diarrhoea indicates a degree of humourless self-obsession which seems exceptional even in a private diary. But it was out of minute self-observation that Tolstoy arrived at his supreme understanding of how elementary physical conditions, well-being or ill-being, affect mood and behaviour and even ideas. *Childhood* already displays his almost unique grasp of the 'concrete' detail.

The very young Tolstoy, making his people burst into tears so often, is palpably reflecting the influence of Sterne, and he seems to have been affected also by Dickens's recent *David Copperfield*.[6] But his own electrifying directness of vision is present in *Childhood* from its very first paragraph, where a German tutor, modelled on Tolstoy's own, wakes up the narrator who, of course, is close to Tolstoy himself, though his family circumstances are sometimes borrowed from those of friends of the writer. The tutor swats a fly. The fly falls on the boy's head. We are, at once, in the middle of life. From this moment, a procession of details sustains our faith in the 'reality' of the far from exceptional incidents described. The fingers of the boy's sister are rosy because they have just been washed in cold water. And when his father gets angry with the steward, we watch the latter's hands for several pages: 'It seemed to me one could guess Yakov's secret thoughts by the movements of his fingers, but his face was invariably placid...'[7]

It is careful selection, of course, which in *Childhood* creates atmosphere and character so vividly and (as we believe) so 'naturally'. The 'concrete' facts which we are given seem to precede our 'abstract' summing up of the characters. But if Tolstoy hadn't been selecting details so as to direct our impressions firmly towards certain 'abstract' judgements, the flow of reminiscence would have been extremely dull. As it is, *Childhood* and its sequels *Boyhood* (1855) and *Youth* (1857) at times hover only just above tedium, in spite of the easy comedy which Tolstoy extracts from the naïveté and self-deception of youth and the specious pretences of grown-ups. The dangers of giving the reader only a plotless 'slice of life' are shown also by one of the short stories which Tolstoy worked on along with his trilogy. *The Snow Storm* (published 1856) recounts an actual experience of his, driving through snow at night and in danger of getting lost and perishing on the steppe. It is, detail by detail, superbly exact and vivid. But there can be no suspense when we realize from the first that the narrator must have survived if he is telling the story, and without suspense forty pages for such an anecdote seems far too long. On the other hand when the young Tolstoy, in *A Billiard Marker's Notes* (published 1855) tries to give point to such a 'slice of life' by making his central figure, an obsessive gambler much like the author, commit suicide, he seems to be arbitrarily murdering the character so as to round off a piece of writing which might otherwise have gone on and on.

Such objections can't so often be made to the *Sevastopol Sketches*, published in 1855 and 1856 to great critical acclaim. Tolstoy arrived in the Crimean town which was threatened by French and English troops in November 1854. He had asked to be transferred there and he proved his great physical courage in his soldiering there until the town fell next autumn. He was still a quite simple patriot and had as yet no settled moral objection to war. His first sketch, describing the town in December, while it is minute in its evocation of the perils of life under bombardment, is full of journalistic praise for the heroism of the defenders.

But in the two later sketches, set in May and August respectively, Tolstoy creates, 'in close up', fictional characters whose Tolstoyan fears and petty vanities work against any generalization about 'Russian valour'. The second, which ran into trouble with the censors, ends by portentously pointing out the incompatibility of such slaughter with the 'one great law of love and self-sacrifice' professed by Christians on both sides.

> Where in this tale (Tolstoy concludes) is the evil that should be avoided, and where the good that should be imitated? Who is the villain and who the hero of the story? All are good and all are bad....
> The hero of my tale—whom I love with all the power of my soul, whom I have tried to portray in all his beauty, who has been, is, and will be beautiful—is Truth.[8]

The third story spoke so frankly of cowardice and corruption in the Army that large portions of it, too, were excised by the censors.

Within a few weeks of the fall of Sevastopol, Tolstoy had decided to quit the army and devote himself to writing. He went to Petersburg and mixed for the first time in literary society. Turgenev welcomed him cordially, but soon found that his taste for orgies with gypsy girls and the scathing rudeness which went with his otherwise admirable candour made him thoroughly nerve-wracking company. Tolstoy, still wearing his officer's uniform, reacted with the scorn of an aristocrat and a military man to the intellectual cliques of Westerners and Slavophiles.

Next summer, he was back in Yasnaia Poliana, determined to free all his serfs and lease the land they farmed to them. They refused to accept his plan. His thoughts turned to marriage and he courted a young woman, Valeria Arseneva, who lived nearby. Matters went so far that when he broke the affair off next winter, indignation against him was general throughout the province. He fled to Western Europe, arriving in Paris in February 1857.

A few weeks later he witnessed there the public execution of a criminal named Richeux. He drew from it conclusions which would resound through all his later writings. 'The truth is that the State is a plot, designed not only to exploit but also to corrupt its citizens. For me, the laws laid down by politics are sordid lies. . . . I shall never enter the service of any Government anywhere.'[9]

He moved on to Switzerland and Italy, and July found him losing his last penny in the casino at Baden—Turgenev arrived in the nick of time to lend him enough money to keep him going. Next month, he was back in Russia, and for all his anger against the depraved and mercenary peoples of the West, his sense of the injustices in Russia itself had been sharpened by contact with freer societies.

His new passion for gymnastics alarmed his serfs. ('I come to the master for orders,' his steward said, 'and I find him hanging upside down by one leg on a bar. . . His hair is all on end and goes flying to and fro, and his face is purple.')[10] He ploughed and scythed with his peasants as Levin would do in *Anna Karenina*. He had a steady liaison with a married serf woman. Hunting bears, he was badly scarred when one attacked him. He published a 'long short story', *Family Happiness*, inspired by his affair with Valeria Arseneva but written from the girl's point of view and imagining what might have happened if he had married. It was warmly received, but Tolstoy now diverted his main energies from writing to education. He set up a school for his peasants on the most libertarian principles conceivable. There was no discipline and no curriculum. But after teaching himself in it for a while, so that his literary friends thought he had gone off his head, he set off West again, in the summer of 1860. One of his brothers, Dmitri, had died of tuberculosis in 1856. Now another, Nikolai, was ill with the same disease in the South of France. Tolstoy was with him when he awoke, asked 'What is it?', and died. He was hard hit, but resumed his travels, studying education in Western countries, meeting Herzen in London and, in Brussels, going to see the anarchist thinker Proudhon who had just finished a study named *War and Peace*.

Meanwhile, the Tsar's proclamation abolished serfdom in Russia, and when Tolstoy returned home he took up an official job as 'arbiter of the peace' to settle disputes between landowners and peasants in his district. After a year of intense activity, in which he outraged the local nobility by what they thought his generosity to the peasants, he resigned. His school, which he was now running again with the help of idealistic young teachers, made him a target for official suspicion, and in July 1862, while he was away, Yasnaia Poliana was occupied for two days by a detachment of policemen searching for evidence of sedition. They found none, and a furious Tolstoy extracted what was tantamount to an apology from the Tsar himself.

Up to 1862 Tolstoy had not accomplished so much that if he had died then we could have regarded him as a major writer. *Family Happiness*, powerful though it is, is somewhat long-winded and concentrates on a single human relationship. Another striking early achievement, *Two Hussars* (1856), is a vivacious 'long short story' which contrasts the dashing, daredevil father, an officer in the 1820s, who sweeps the delightful, silly young widow Anna Fedorovna off her feet, with his mean and calculating son who, in 1848, tries to seduce the widow's sweet young daughter Liza. It explores territory, notably the father's revels with the gypsies, which are outside Turgenev's effective range, but the points which it makes about the pathos involved in the passing of time and in the limited life of a boring provincial town are ones which Turgenev explored with greater depth, if rarely with such freshness.

What we can now see clearly is how all the early stories experiment with material and methods which were to create wonderful fullness of life in *War and Peace*. A distinctive 'Tolstoyan' way of writing fiction was emerging, in contrast with the methods of all other writers. *Family Happiness* presents the 'awakening' of a young girl who needs to fall in love and therefore grasps the first man who comes to hand, so its theme reminds us very directly of several Turgenev heroines and of Goncharov's Olga. But Tolstoy's handling is different; we might call it more 'modern'. Turgenev and Goncharov orchestrate certain Romantic stereotypes of love with great effect and much subtlety, but these stereotypes beg questions—are people really so fully absorbed, ever, into a single experience, even that of idealistic sexual passion? Tolstoy's heroine craves exactly this kind of stereotyped romance, but Tolstoy's dry and exact analysis, coupled with his mastery over objective detail, dissolves the stereotype back into life.

Here is what might have been a stock 'romantic' moment. The lovers go for a walk on a moonlit night. The girl Maria describes it:

> When I looked down the avenue as we walked along I had the impression that in a moment we should be brought to a stop, that the world of the possible would end, that all this must be crystallized forever in its beauty. But we still moved forward, and the magic wall kept dividing to let us pass beyond; and there, too, we found our old familiar garden with trees and paths and withered leaves. And we really were walking along paths, stepping into rings of light and shade, the dry leaves did rustle underfoot and a cool twig brushed my face. And this was really he, walking gently and evenly at my side, and carefully supporting my arm; and it really was Katia walking beside us with squeaking boots . . .[11]

Of course, the stereotypes of 'romantic' love would not exist, and would not move us so much, if they did not have a strong and 'real' basis. It *is* a beautiful night. The moment *is* magical. Tolstoy will show us again in *War and Peace* and *Anna Karenina* how the consciousness of one of his people can, like our own, render dreamlike and wonderful life in the 'real' world. But the world is not and cannot be fully transfigured. The cool twig which brushes Maria's face might, in a different mood, have annoyed her—it is the kind of ambivalent detail Turgenev would tend to leave out. And what other novelist, not meaning to be sardonic, would release into such a passage the squeak of the governess's boots? The part of the girl's mind which notes that detail isn't absorbed into the experience of love. There is more to her life, at this moment as at others, than a single passion can engross.

Tolstoy's first masterpiece, *The Cossacks*, which he worked on intermittently between 1852 and its publication in 1863, is still a 'long short story' rather than a novel. Briefly summarized, the tale sounds like a somewhat enfeebled reworking of Romantic stereotypes developed out of Rousseau and Byron and already exploited and criticized in a Caucasian setting by Pushkin and Lermontov—even though it happens to be very closely autobiographical. Olenin, a nobleman, leaves his debaucheries in Moscow and serves in the Caucasus. Living in a Cossack village he falls in love, just as Tolstoy had done, with a girl named Marianka. Tolstoy had hunted with an ancient Cossack, Epishka, who assured him that sin didn't exist, and this mentor becomes Eroshka in the story. Marianka is courted by Luka, a brave young Cossack. Olenin dreams of marrying her, but on the day when he plans to propose Luka is wounded (probably mortally) by raiding tribesmen. The girl's feeling for her fellow Cossacks emerges as she rebuffs Olenin when he comes to propose:

> 'Marianka!' Olenin repeated. 'I have come'—
> 'Leave me alone!' she said. Her face did not change but the tears ran down her cheeks.
> 'What is it? What's the matter?'
> 'The matter?' she echoed in a rough, hard voice. 'Cossacks have been killed, that's all.'[12]

Olenin gets permission to join the Staff and leaves the village, which is indifferent to his departure.

To the stereotyped situation we must add the disadvantage that Olenin is no more than a timid and rather stupid version of basic Tolstoyan Man, about as uninteresting as it is possible for a central character in a successful story to be. Yet *The Cossacks* does succeed. Partly because they are so commonplace, Olenin's thoughts and desires don't get in the way of Tolstoy's miraculously vivid realization of high snowy peaks, dense and insect-ridden woods, the swift river, the blank steppe and the life of the Cossack village, the dancing, the grape harvest. Tolstoyan realism disintegrates a well-worn Romantic subject and reassembles its elements as fresh life. And to a remarkable extent, he convinces us that we can share the Cossack view of things.

In the three opening chapters, we travel with Olenin south from Moscow and experience with him the shock of seeing the Caucasus peaks for the first time. But then we are taken to the Cossack village before Olenin arrives there, and the character of the life there, with the personalities of Marianka, Eroshka and Luka, are established in the absence of any Russian intruder. It already, 'really', exists before Olenin tries to fit into it his sophisticated needs and his complicated morality.

The Cossacks, with their sexual licence, their frank, bold women, their passion for hunting and drinking, their bent for pilfering, might seem impossible for even the young Tolstoy to harmonize with his own moralism. He cannot, of course, be said to 'approve' of the Cossacks; he makes no attempt to mitigate their violence. Yet it is impossible not to feel that the writer who describes 'Nature' so richly is in effect an accomplice of Uncle Eroshka, who tells Olenin, 'God created everything for the joy of man. There's no sin in any of it. Take a wild animal, for instance. It lives in the Tartar reeds or in ours. Wherever it happens to be, there's its home. Whatever God gives it to eat, so it eats.'[13] The Cossacks, sunburnt, vivid and forceful, in tune with each other even when they quarrel and with the world even when they slaughter men and beasts, dazzle us as they dazzle the pale and furtive Olenin. We know from other writings of this period, such as the rather silly short story *Three Deaths* (1859) in which the death of a tree chopped down is favourably contrasted with that of a querulous rich woman, that Tolstoy not only enjoyed the 'natural' world, but was ready to extol the spontaneous, non-rational life of 'nature' and of 'natural' people as against the fidgetty, selfish and over-thoughtful life of 'civilized' men. The only Cossack in the story who is made to seem ridiculous is Marianka's father; and he has a good deal of education. Yet the achievement of the story itself makes Tolstoy's craving for natural spontaneity seem utterly paradoxical. It is full of the art which conceals art. Tolstoy had fiddled with it for ten years. '. . . By what miracle,' asks Henri Troyat, 'did the finished product acquire that air of a quickly written, smooth and flawless book?'[14]

In spite of the warning he had issued to himself in *Family Happiness*, Tolstoy fell decisively in love, with the sister of a girl he was courting. They were daughters of his old friend Dr Behrs and their mother had been a childhood sweetheart of Tolstoy's. He was thirty-four and Sonia, who cleverly captured him from her sister Liza, was only eighteen. Tolstoy insisted on marrying her only a week after the engagement was announced. In between, he gave her his private diaries to read and she was shocked to learn of his many couplings with other women. The most-documented and most painfully candid marriage in the history of the world was launched in the autumn of 1862.

Next year, with his private life settled, Tolstoy began work on an enormous project. With Sonia's help, he carried it through. She kept him free of small worries, took over the management of his estate, and copied out his untidy manuscripts. The partners showed each other the bitter thoughts they had set down about each other in their private diaries; but by 1869 this strange marriage had produced four children and what many would say is the greatest novel ever written. *War and Peace* ends, not to the taste of all its readers, with a celebration of the joys of family life.

III

The origins of *War and Peace* can be traced to a novel which Tolstoy started about the end of 1860 but soon dropped. He called it *The Decembrists*. It was to deal with a man returning to Russia after thirty years of exile in 1856, when Alexander II pardonned the rebels. The old man was called Pierre, his wife Natasha.

With his new project of 1863, Tolstoy pushed his interest back beyond 1825 itself to the youth of his hero, which he placed in 'Russia's glorious period of 1812.' But the years before had not been so glorious and, as he explained in a foreword he never published, 'I felt ashamed to write about our triumph . . . without having described our failures and our shame.'[15] So he went back still further to 1805, a year of defeat, and pushed forward from there to the climax of his novel in 1812. In the finished work, 'Decembrism' features merely by implication—in Pierre's opinions in the first epilogue, which Tolstoy sets in 1820, and, less directly still, in the dream at the very end of the story in which young Nikolai Bolkonsky sees himself and Uncle Pierre 'marching at the head of a huge army.' Nevertheless, it is important to realize that not only Pierre but also the dead Andrei, the boy's father, are by these hints identified in spirit with that ambiguous revolt of 1825 which was at the same time the last attempt in Russia at an aristocratic coup and the first at a democratic revolution. They are in fact, like Tolstoy himself, old-fashioned free-thinking aristocrats as well as (anachronistically) 'modern' intellectuals.

The first sections appearing in Katkov's *Russian Herald* from 1865 were provisionally titled *1805*. Not until 1867 did Tolstoy find the name *War and Peace* for the ongoing labour, and publication was only completed in 1869. Huge as the book is, its easy flow disguises the amount of work which Tolstoy had given to it over the seven years when it was his main occupation. What seems to the reader a radiant simplicity emerged only after toilsome experiment, rewriting and re-thinking. And because no detail is casually chosen and every minor character has some part to play in relation to the main themes and events, a summary of the story of *War and Peace* is totally helpless to suggest its real nature.

It is 1805. Russia and Austria fight France. Prince Andrei Bolkonsky leaves his pregnant young wife with his eccentric father and plain, clumsy sister Maria and goes off to fight. Young Count Nikolai Rostov also sees action in Austria as a hussar. Meanwhile Andrei's friend Pierre, an illegitimate son of the grandee Count Bezukhov, has inherited the old man's wealth and has been trapped into marriage with the immoral Hélène Kuragina. Andrei himself is left for dead on the battlefield of Austerlitz, but returns, just as his son is born and his wife dies. Pierre fights a duel with his wife's lover Dolokhov and wounds him and then turns for moral relief to Freemasonry. Andrei puts military ambition behind him and interests himself in agriculture. But he feels old and finished until he is revived by a meeting with Nikolai's sister Natasha, a high spirited young girl. He proposes to her, but his father disapproves of the match and Andrei travels abroad for a year to give the situation time to settle. His frustrated fiancée is captivated by Anatole Kuragin, Hélène's brother, and is caught in the act of eloping with him. She is overwhelmed with grief and shame. Pierre tries to console her and confesses his own love for her. The first half of the novel ends here; we have reached 1812.

When Napoleon invades Russia, all Tolstoy's characters are swept up in the struggle to defend the homeland. Andrei is mortally wounded at Borodino; when the Rostovs like almost everyone else desert Moscow as the French approach they carry a train of casualties with them, including Andrei. Pierre, who stays behind to assassinate Napoleon, is captured by the French and marches as a prisoner in their terrible retreat. The homely irrational wisdom of his fellow captive, the peasant Karataev, helps to reconcile him to life. He returns a changed man, to find that his wife Hélène, confounded by her own complex erotic intrigues, has committed suicide. Meanwhile Nikolai Rostov, by a romantic coincidence, has rescued Maria Bolkonskaia from her defiant peasants, and falls in love with her. Andrei in his last days is fully reconciled with Natasha, but his death leaves the way clear for Nikolai to marry his sister. Pierre marries Natasha, and we meet both couples enjoying domestic bliss in the first epilogue. There is also, of course, the notorious second epilogue which summarizes Tolstoy's much-disputed views of 1812 in particular and of history in general. The novel, right to the end, uniquely mingles public with private affairs, minute domestic details with descriptions of battle and vivid narrative with controversial theorizing. We are almost as intimate with Napoleon and the Russian commander Kutuzov as we are with the imaginary heroes and heroines.

Tolstoy, of course, uses coincidence to interlock the affairs of his three main families, Bolkonskys, Rostovs and Kuragins, in various love-relationships. But they all belong to the same small class of wealthy aristocrats and their chance meetings therefore seem perfectly 'natural'. Tolstoy noted in 1864, '. . . I now intend to lead not one, but many heroes and heroines of mine through the historical events of 1805, 1807, 1812, 1825, and 1856. I do not foresee in any one of these periods a dénouement in the relationship between these people. However much I tried at first to think up a novel-like plot and dénouement, I was convinced that it was not within my means. . .'[16] His vast, broad current of detail does indeed seem to flow on out of the end of the book. The surviving heroes and heroines are still developing and we can imagine them in utterly new relationships—Nikolai, for instance, might well, as he threatens, help the government to round up his dissident brother-in-law Pierre.

IV

'It is not a novel,' Tolstoy wrote, 'even less is it a poem, and still less an historical chronicle. *War and Peace* is what the author wished and was able to express in the form in which it is expressed.'[17] To Western critics this book and its successor *Anna Karenina* tended to seem formless, if remarkable, productions. George Saintsbury wrote peevishly in 1907 that they were 'hardly works of art at all. It is, however, pleaded for them that they are "pieces of life"; and so perhaps they are, but in a strangely unlicked and unfinished condition.'[18] Henry James, comparing Tolstoy with Turgenev, had remarked, 'The perusal of Tolstoy—a wonderful mass of life—is an immense event, a kind of splendid accident, for each of us: his name represents nevertheless no such eternal spell of method, no such quiet irresistibility of presentation as shines, close to us and lighting our possible steps, in that of his precursor.'[19]

But no one would now seriously suggest that *War and Peace* is not a novel. Tolstoy's achievement, gradually recognized, was to widen the category of the 'novel' and to establish its capacity to handle every conceivable kind of material with an even unhurried verisimilitude and without Dickensian cranking and creaking of 'plot' or the kind of neat 'poetic' finality in which Turgenev specialized. It has been the task of much recent criticism to show that what seemed even to such a distinguished reader as James only a 'loose and baggy monster' is in fact organized on its own formal principles, both subtle and massive. These can be exposed as we try to find words to define the book as a whole. 'Epic' is one well-known candidate. .

There is no doubt whatever that Tolstoy idealizes his own class and its role in 1812. Of the well-known horrors of social life in Russia at that time —the knouting and sale of serfs, the bedbugs and intellectual backwardness—*War and Peace* contains no trace. Tolstoy's amazing 'authority' over the history he relates should be wondered at with one ear open to John Bayley's comment that 'Russia belonged to Tolstoy because Russia belonged, literally, to his class.'[20] In the end he makes Nikolai Rostov— his own father as he ought to have been—into a model Russian landowner, who farms on traditional lines, studies his peasants, banishes the lazy and dissolute ones, and earns gratitude and respect. '. . . And long after he was dead and gone the peasantry cherished a pious memory of his rule. "He was a proper master". . .'[21]

But if the book draws our attention longest to aristocrats of the best type, we find in it also many representatives of corrupt and frivolous noblemen and women. Against them, Tolstoy poises not only his unconvincing Karataev, but also Tushin, a little captain; that delightful declassed nobleman called 'Uncle'; and that truly complete huntsman, the peasant Danilo. None of his other characters have fuller approval from him. They pull the moral centre in the novel towards the centre of Russian society. They are little, irrelevant folk from the point of view of the high command or of high society, but it is their national culture which Natasha expresses when at Uncle's she dances, Countess though she is, just like a peasant woman. Andrei admires Tushin, Pierre is influenced by Karataev, the young Rostovs adore 'Uncle' and the old Count lets Danilo, his own serf, reprimand him for incompetence on the hunting field. Tolstoy's favourite aristocratic characters are, in fact, idealized as men and women who are in tune with the little people and can understand what the brittle Petersburg set ignore and sneer at.

So it may seem to make sense to call *War and Peace* a 'national epic'. In many ways, it recalls the techniques of Homer. Stock epithets and recurrent details—Maria's 'heavy tread', Napoleon's 'white hands'—suggest the methods of the *Iliad*, and we know that Tolstoy himself told Gorky 'without false modesty, *War and Peace* is like the *Iliad*.'[22] George Steiner develops the point strongly:

> ... There lies behind the literary techniques of the *Iliad* and of Tolstoy a comparable belief in the centrality of the human personage and in the enduring beauty of the natural world. In the case of *War and Peace* the analogy is even more dedecisive; where the *Iliad* evokes the laws of *Moira*, Tolstoy expounds his philosophy of history. In both works the chaotic individuality of battle stands for the larger randomness in men's lives. And if we consider *War and Peace* as being, in a genuine sense, a heroic epic it is because in it, as in the *Iliad*, war is portrayed in its glitter and joyous ferocity as well as in its pathos.[23]

But even if we acknowledge the combination of scale and intimacy in the battle scenes and the heroic extravagance of Count Rostov's prodigal banquets and wolf-hunt, the word 'epic' doesn't connect with most of the novel. Pierre's intellectual self-searchings and Sonia's tremulous, calculating love for Nikolai belong to a different mode. And any word which makes Tolstoy seem to accept 'the glitter and joyous ferocity of war' needs to be used with care. Petia Rostov, indeed, is full of joy when he rides with guerrillas against the French; he kills no one and is himself abruptly killed. Not one of Tolstoy's heroes is permitted to kill a man in our presence, not even the bellicose Nikolai. Andrei is twice wounded, never the wounder. Pierre, for all his huge strength and his rages, remains a civilian and is essentially pacific in direction, though paradoxically it is he, wounding Dolokhov, who comes closest to destroying an enemy. It is Dolokhov, man of mischief and sadism, who expresses unwatered relish for killing, and he appalls even the war-like Denisov. Kutuzov, the 'historical' hero of the novel is too old and unwell to fight in person and strives to avoid combat. Right at the end, the martial dream of Andrei's son collapses from joy into confusion as the menacing face of Uncle Nikolai appears in it, and the boy's waking hope of fame and glory is an ironic echo of his father's, which Andrei himself came to see as hollow. The book is on the side of the humanitarian Pierre, the defensive Kutuzov, the murdered Karataev, the domesticated Natasha and the lovingly Christian Maria; and it stands against the ambitious aggressor, Napoleon and the viciously destructive Dolokhov. There is no other way of reading it, though we cannot overlook the approval which Tolstoy, and Pierre, give to the self-sacrificing heroism of Russians in action in *defensive* combat, or Tolstoy's appreciation of the *esprit de corps* of the hussars with whom Nikolai serves; Tolstoy, the old soldier, could not reject as worthless the courage and cameraderie which he had shared at Sevastopol.

The carnage and confusion of the battles must also be weighed against those critics who stress the 'idyllic' character of the book. Elizabeth Gunn shrewdly points out that Tolstoy's setting back of his novel in the time of his grandfathers 'allowed him his idyll ... allowed him to minimize the pain of individual experience', because it secured for him a detachment which he couldn't have in relation to his own life and times.[24] Edmund Wilson argues that *War and Peace* falls short of the highest summits of literature 'because this idyllic tendency does here get the better of the author....'[25]

As Elizabeth Gunn elsewhere observes, it is striking that the Countess Rostova is already forty-five and past childbearing when the novel opens. She and the still-older Count—whose child-likeness is so often stressed— are therefore 'safely out of the sphere of sexual relations' and do not confront Tolstoy with the need to lay bare his profound and uncomfortable understanding of the woes that are in marriage.[26] This is a book dominated by young people and the elder Rostovs, even the old Prince Bolkonsky, are rather like children. Whereas *Anna Karenina*, written ten years later, is involved with the boredoms and burdens and compromises of people past their first youth and overshadowed by middle age, *War and Peace* has the radiance of optimistic youth, and the first Epilogue makes the happiest ending we will find in the work of the great nineteenth-century Russian novelists.

But this idyllic quality mustn't be overstressed. It is true that at times leading characters revel in a world of fairy tale—Nikolai as he drives with the disguised and dressed up Sonia through the snow, Anatole Kuragin as he prepares to elope with Natasha, Petia on the eve of battle. But Petia is killed. Anatole is a shallow hedonist. And Nikolai doesn't marry Sonia in the end as he wants to at that time—it is a rather damning point about her that she is never freer, more lively and more beautiful than when she is hiding her 'real' self in fancy dress.

In any case, Prince Andrei always dispels, when he appears, the reader's sense of easy, youthful well-being. Andrei, frustrated in and out of marriage, over-intelligent, arrogant, disillusioned, can, it is true, be related to a Romantic stereotype—the bored and remote aristocrat, fascinating to women and cruel to them. But as married man, father, officer, politician and, above all, as wounded and dying man, Andrei inhabits a real and painful 'middle-aged' world. And he is very close to Tolstoy himself. Neither Pierre nor Nikolai could have composed the second Epilogue, with its drily satirical flavour, its arrogant rationalism, its aristocratic *hauteur*, but all these are qualities which we find in Andrei.

Andrei, however, seems to have no time for hunting. Tolstoy did. The novelist's own love of life in the open air is expressed above all through Nikolai. Pierre is less completely successful as a characterization than the two other heroes. We are indeed conscious with him of Tolstoy editing out of reality aspects which we would find painful and problematic. We are *told* that Pierre is an obsessive womanizer, but we are not *shown* this side of him in action, so he is left in our eyes boyish, bashful and even 'innocent'. But Pierre is closer than either of the others to the heroes of Tolstoy's other fiction. The 'conscience-stricken nobleman', basically decent but weak-willed and ineffectual, is a type which runs from the Nekhliudov of *A Billiard Marker's Notes* through the narrator of *Childhood* and Olenin in *The Cossacks*, then through Pierre and into its finest shaping in Levin in *Anna Karenina*. Since all these stories are autobiographical in their tendency, we aren't likely to be wrong if we identify Pierre also with some aspects of Tolstoy himself.

If we say that Tolstoy participates equally in Andrei's contempt for the trivialities of high society, in Pierre's attraction to the peasants and family life and in Nikolai's gusto and compulsive gambling, we are emphasizing again how vast and well-analysed Tolstoy's own experience had been compared with that of most novelists. But to separate himself, as it were, into three heroes, is to clarify at the cost of simplification. Tolstoy's 'wonderful mass of life' is not merely life selected—every novelist has to select—but life simplified, life tidied up. (This charge could not be made against *Anna Karenina*, where Levin's tentativeness is Tolstoy's own.) Dickens's Gothic accumulations of frightening and fantastic detail and Dostoevsky's world of furious intellectual debate force us, as Tolstoy doesn't in *War and Peace*, to question the very basis of our own notions of and about 'reality'. Tolstoy's glittering clarification is based on the assumption, which we habitually share, that there is a 'natural' relationship between man and the inanimate world which is harmonious and 'right'. Rather more controversially, he in effect proposes that the 'natural man' in each of us cannot be at ease or truly himself in the complex structures of the modern State, army or 'society'. If we accept his vision without question, it is because our thinking is still based, like his, on eighteenth-century ideas which emerged in an aristocratic social order.

War and Peace then is best called neither 'epic' nor 'idyll'. It is a 'realistic novel' organized so as to persuade us of the correctness of Tolstoy's own view of 'reality'.

V

•

Hussars are moving into battle:

Tattered violet-grey clouds, reddening in the sunrise, were scudding before the wind. It was getting lighter every moment. The feathery grass which always grows by the roadside in the country could be seen quite plainly, still glistening from the night's rain. The drooping branches of the birch trees, wet too, swayed in the wind and tossed sparkling drops of water aslant across the highway. The soldiers' faces showed more distinctly with the passing of every minute. Rostov, with Ilin who never left him, rode along the side of the road between two rows of birch trees.[27]

This, by Tolstoy's exceptionally high standards, is only a routine piece of description from one of the less intense passages of the novel. We might say that it evokes very well the 'beauty' of early morning; but an important thing to notice is that Tolstoy himself would never use the word 'beauty' in such a description. We see the landscape from the point of view of someone riding through it, enjoying its freshness, no doubt, but not thinking about its aesthetic properties. It is 'naturally' witnessed and conveyed. We are, so to speak, riding along with Nikolai and noticing what he would notice.

But we aren't riding to hunt, we're riding to fight. In one of the most obviously 'significant' passages of the novel, Andrei falls wounded on the field of Austerlitz. He sees, as he lies on his back, not men fighting but the sky. 'How was it,' he asks himself, 'I did not see that sky before? And how happy I am to have found it at last! Yes, all is vanity, all is delusion, except these infinite heavens.'[28] Here the force of the contrast between 'nature' and 'war' is obvious. It is not made explicit when Nikolai is moving towards battle, nor, indeed, is the point identical; it is typical of Andrei that he should contrast the loftiest, purest and most empty and alien aspect of nature—the sky—with the vanity of human struggle and ambition. But in both cases we are prodded by Tolstoy to contrast 'natural' harmony with 'social' conflict.

Karataev and, in their different ways, Nikolai and Natasha, move in unthinking harmony with nature and illustrate how things should be. Tolstoy's assumption that the 'natural' self is separable from 'society' and is menaced by it (whereas the family, a smaller unit, is 'natural' to us) is supported by his technique of 'making strange'. One aspect of it can be illustrated from the passage above. 'The soldier's faces showed more distinctly with the passing of every minute.' Of course they do, we might object, it's dawn. But Tolstoy, as so often, forces us to notice what we might take for granted; he brings it before us as if it were something unusual. Simple, elemental detail, well-chosen, gives us the feeling that we *participate* in the natural world. In descriptions of 'social' life detail of the same kind is often used with satiric and destructive purpose to give us the feeling that we are *alien from* the social world.

Mirsky summarizes 'making strange' very well:

It consists in never calling complex things by their accepted name, but always disintegrating a complex action or object into its indivisible components. The method strips the world of the labels attached to it by habit and by social convention and gives it a 'dis-civilised' appearance, as it might have appeared to Adam on the day of creation. It is easy to see that the method, while it gives unusual freshness to imaginative representation, is in essence hostile to all culture and all social form, and is psychologically akin to anarchism.[29]

Tolstoy develops further a routine which Voltaire had habitually used for satirical purposes.* He would carry the technique furthest in *Resurrection*. In *War and Peace* it has its crudest, but most memorable, expression in the scene where Natasha goes to the opera and catches the eye of Anatole Kuragin. Anatole is at home in this 'artificial' atmosphere. Natasha isn't, but it takes her over and converts her 'natural' sexual drive, which in Tolstoy's view should find expression in marrying and having children, into an immoral and 'unnatural' lust which will make her want to have not only a fiancé, Andrei, but a lover, Anatole, as well. She is for a moment perverted by society. This is how Tolstoy describes the stage and how Natasha herself, 'fresh from the country' where she has been her 'natural' self, initially sees it:

> Smooth boards formed the centre of the stage, at the sides stood painted canvases representing trees, and in the background was a cloth stretched over boards. In the middle of the stage sat some girls in red bodices and white petticoats. One extremely fat girl in a white silk dress was sitting apart on a low bench, to the back of which a piece of green cardboard was glued. They were all singing something.[30]

But after the interval, when she has been introduced to Anatole, all that is happening on the stage seems 'perfectly natural' to Natasha. Illusion has conquered reality.

We learn of Tolstoy's characters how they seem to others and how they are in themselves, and, especially with the heroes and heroines, the gulf is made obvious. Andrei strikes Nikolai as a stuck-up staff officer, Princess Maria is judged by others to be plain, clumsy and haughty, while her spiteful old father is widely admired. Yet Tolstoy could not be further from denying that the real self does emerge in outward appearance, if uncorrupted eyes are there to observe it. As his heroes enter the *soirée* where the novel begins, Tolstoy emphasizes Pierre's expression, which is diffident and at the same time *natural* and, by contrast, the weary, bored look in Andrei's eyes and the way he expresses his *ennui* by screwing them up. Natasha's light gait expresses her 'natural' vivacity and energy and Princess Maria's blotchy blushes suggest her dogged honesty; but the nervous twitch of Prince Vasilli's cheeks when he is alone, which gives his face 'an unpleasant expression such as it never had when he was in company', exposes both the nastiness within him and his success in suppressing his true, nasty self when he moves in society. It is a habit of Tolstoy's, and one which can become irritating, to emphasize small gestures which tell us more than the words which the characters use and are, indeed, often at odds with them.

A succession of details of this kind builds up each of the characters in the novel. One exception proves the general rule. Tolstoy introduces and

* See, for instance, his entry under *Guerre* (War) in his *Philosophical Dictionary* (1764) and compare it with the Second Epilogue of *War and Peace*. Affinities both of method and of message seem to me clear as spring-water.

'summarizes' Bilibin, an important minor character, rather as Turgenev or Dostoevsky would have done—we are told what sort of a person he is before we 'see' and judge him in action. But what other novelist could have got away with telling us virtually nothing about the previous lives of his heroes? About Pierre's childhood and travels, Andrei's courtship of Liza, the eight little dead Rostov brothers and sisters, we are given no clues around which we can even speculate. We get to know the main characters as in 'real' life we get to know 'real' people, by watching and listening. When we are given the added knowledge which in 'real life' we can only have of ourselves, and are admitted into their thoughts, they only rarely remember things which take us beyond the facts about them which we have observed already. In 'real life', people grow familiar with each other by talking about their past experiences—but Tolstoy's characters almost never reminisce. Again, he achieves wonderful clarification at the cost of simplification.

But this technique does ensure that we are never tempted to see the fate of any character as 'inevitable'. Turgenev's life history of Pavel Kirsanov marks the character out as one already set on a doomed course. Even with the old people in *War and Peace* we have no such sense of fatality. Everyone feels (to us) free. At any moment they may reveal wholly new facets of themselves to us as they respond to fresh experience. It is the most beguiling confidence trick in literature. For, as John Bayley points out, Tolstoy has judged them all and decided their fates. 'The book (he adds) is a massive feat of arbitration . . . an allotment of fates on earth as authoritative as Dante's in the world to come.'[31]

John Bayley goes a bit too far. Tolstoy's vision admits inequity. Good people, like Tushin, suffer injustice. Petia is killed when still too young to have sinned. But Tolstoy certainly judges, incessantly. The basis of Tolstoy's arbitration is, roughly speaking, this: characters who are in touch with nature and with truly Russian culture, and who are themselves 'full of life', are approved of and, where possible, rewarded. Those who 'lack something' are judged harshly and 'artificial' people are the targets either of broad satire, like that which Tolstoy directs at the ludicrous, scheming Berg and his bride Vera Rostova, or of a more venomous irony.

Those whom Tolstoy approves of are mostly identified with the countryside and with Moscow. Here, he says at one point, 'matter' predominates, whereas in Petersburg 'form is the prevailing factor'. One very minor character says directly, 'In Moscow, it is like being in the country.'[32] The Rostovs, Moscow people, with their unaffected vitality and rich family life, contrast with the Kuragins, Petersburg people, who are selfish, hedonistic and, in Pierre's view 'depraved'.

Russian 'matter' stands against foreign 'form'. The French army is a complex, artificial creation led by Napoleon, the prophet of artificiality. German military theorists are at work in the Russian army causing disaster by their 'artificial' ideas about war. True Russian-ness emerges in real community and simple natural force. Instinct defeats the schemers. Nature conquers the military machine. Justice is done in the war of 1812, just as it is when Sonia, who schemes to secure Nikolai as her husband, is denied the happiness given to Pierre and Natasha who fall, naturally and instinctively, as it were, into each other's arms.

The reader's sympathies are liable to be with Sonia and have to be carefully prised away from her. Tolstoy can't, perhaps, quite bring it off. But he works cleverly in the scene where Natasha, angrily asking 'Are we a lot of wretched Germans?' prevails upon her family to abandon their possessions in Moscow and take wounded men instead, and Sonia, unable to respond to this grand human gesture, busies herself doing her best to get as much of the family property taken with them as possible.[33]

But within Sonia, as with all the richest characterizations in the novel, we find an interesting tension between 'nature' and 'artificiality' which confounds, as it were, Tolstoy's own rather Napoleonic schemes. He is too honest a writer to avoid, even when he is striving hardest to clarify and simplify human life, the expression of its enigmas and paradoxes. No easy equation of the 'natural' with the 'good' can cope with Pierre, with Andrei, or the little princess Liza.

The finest and tensest of all the 'peace' passages deal with the Bolkonskys, whose relationship to 'nature' is ambivalent. The old Prince likes the country and works as a carpenter, with his hands. But he is monstrously dedicated to 'routine'—a Frenchified or Germanic trait—and suppresses his natural feelings towards his daughter and son. And even the simple and affectionate Maria has moments where she displays Bolkonsky *hauteur*, while her religion is not, like Natasha's, wholly spontaneous—it is a matter of principle.

Not that Natasha herself is 'simple'. It is her very spontaneity and thoughtlessness which make her such an easy prey for Anatole. It is natural for children to imitate. It is also, perhaps, part of Pierre's 'naturalness' that he doesn't dance at balls and keeps out of that empty glittering ritual. There is a most significant moment at the Rostov's party, very early in the novel, when little Natasha persuades Pierre to dance:

> Natasha was blissful: she was dancing with a *grown-up* man come from *abroad*. She was sitting in view of everyone and talking to him like a grown-up lady. In her hand was a fan which one of the ladies had given her to hold, and assuming quite the air of a society woman (heaven knows when and where she had learnt it), she talked to her partner, fanning herself and smiling over the fan.
> 'Dear, dear! Look at her now!' exclaimed the countess as she crossed the ballroom, pointing to Natasha.
> Natasha coloured and laughed.
> 'What do you mean, mamma? Why do you say that? It's quite natural—why shouldn't I?'[34]

Here we can see how the vast novel holds together, how, while it seems to lack any structure, it is all structure. Tolstoy's parenthetical question is, ironically, echoed at the moment when Natasha, at Uncle's, is dancing like a peasant girl. 'Where,' he asks, 'had she picked up that manner which the *pas de châle*, one might have supposed, would have effaced long ago?' We supply the answer without much trouble. This most delightful of all fictional children has at its most highly-developed the childish trait of imitativeness. And Natasha's own question—'It's quite natural—why shouldn't I?'—illustrates already her tendency, which is that of a spoilt child, to excuse herself glibly for doing whatever she feels like doing. This will reappear in her reasoning when she is attempting to elope with Anatole. 'If', she tells herself, 'I could let things go so far, it means that I fell in love with him at first sight. So he must be kind, noble and splendid, and I could not help loving him.'[35]

Anatole, who is so thoughtless and lives for the moment is, after all, rather an apt—one might say 'natural'—mate for the thoughtless Natasha whose frustration during Andrei's absence has been so powerfully conveyed. The sensuality of the Kuragins can be branded 'unnatural' only if Tolstoy is already anticipating his notorious argument in *The Kreutzer Sonata* that sex itself is not really 'natural'. He is not quite ready to be so silly yet. Hélène, furthermore, is presented as someone to whom 'artificiality' comes 'naturally'—she seems, like her father, perfectly 'natural' in high society. For a full investigation of the paradoxes of the Kuragin 'nature' we will have to wait till *Anna Karenina*; it is much like the Oblonsky 'nature' which Anna shares with her brother Stiva. Meanwhile, in order to damn these people, Tolstoy has to invest them with an aura of 'unnatural' depravity. Hippolyte Kuragin must flirt with Liza Bolkonskaia when she is pregnant. There must be rumours of an incestuous relationship between Anatole and his sister, though Tolstoy dropped from the finished novel the scene he wrote in draft where he is found in her bedroom holding her hand.[36] Their mother, in her brief appearance, is accorded only one significant emotion and it is a nasty one—'she was tormented by jealousy of her daughter's happiness.'[37] Most important of all, Anatole intends to bebecome a bigamist and Hélène refuses to have children.

At this stage Tolstoy still endorses, as 'natural', sex as a way of building the monogamous family. Natasha's sexual drive can be excused because it is different from the Kuragins'. She is destined to be the perfect mother and she wants sex not purely for its own sake but so as to have children. Many readers, however, have found it easier to swallow Tolstoy's cunning extinction of Sonia—she lacks natural drive and is 'by nature', as it were, an aunt rather than a mother—than his perfectly open treatment of Natasha, who, after all, when we first meet her has in her hand a doll, an imitation baby. Rebecca West accuses him of showing us Natasha 'reposing in her family like a sow among its litter.'[38] And it is true that not one of all the doctrines ever espoused by Tolstoy is more unworthy of him than his insistence, at this time, that the role of women must be defined and virtually circumscribed by their function as home-makers and child-bearers.

VI

Just as he is forced to discriminate carefully between sexuality enjoyed for its own sake and sexuality meant to produce children, so Tolstoy has to distinguish between offensive and defensive war. The reader, furthermore, must feel the rightness of Napoleon's defeat, but not rejoice over the killing of Frenchmen by Russians. At the moment when Natasha is lifted out of her painful personal griefs by a church service at which the priest reads a special prayer for victory, Tolstoy exposes an issue which is more of a problem for him than for his non-intellectual heroine:

> ... She prayed to God with all the feeling and fervour with which her heart was overflowing, though she was not really clear what she was asking of God in the prayer. With all her soul she joined in the petition for a right spirit, for the strengthening of her heart by faith and hope and the breathing into them of love. But she could not pray that her enemies might be trampled underfoot when but a few minutes before she had been wishing she had more of them to love and pray for. Yet neither could she doubt the propriety of the prayer that was being read by the priest on his knees.[39]

Many little touches in the novel are designed to convince us that, as Kutuzov puts it in the almost unbearably moving scene where he is shown the captured French colours, the French 'are human beings too'. 'But', he ends up, 'with all said and done, who invited them here? It serves them right, the b--- b---s!'[40] Like Kutuzov we must welcome the outcome of the war while regretting the slaughter.

Kutuzov is, we are told, 'the representative of the Russian people'. For Napoleon, the state is himself. Kutuzov knows that events take place irrespective of his own will. Napoleon believes that his will by itself can create events. Tolstoy's portrait of him is often deplored as a travesty. Whether this judgement is fair or not is a question which only historians could decide, and they never will decide it; any attempt to present in a novel the most controversial figure in modern history must annoy one school of thought or another.* As a character in a work of fiction, Tolstoy's Napoleon is surely a complete success. He is not crudely satirized. He is given wit and talent. At Austerlitz, as the Russian army founders in the mist and Napoleon from his hill-top sees all clearly, Tolstoy admits that his calculations have been confirmed. But Napoleon's folly in venturing into Russia is beyond dispute and Tolstoy can use such a self-evident fact to undermine the idea that the high command on its eminence can decide the fate of a battle and that a great general can therefore 'make' history.

Tolstoy's objections to what can be called for brevity 'the Great Man Theory of History' are subtly supported in the very first scene in the novel which describes fighting—the passage recording the crossing and blowing up of the Bridge at Enns. All the main elements of his view are here. The

*See Pieter Geyl's classic *Napoleon: For or Against* (1949).

serene beauty of nature is made to contrast with the ugliness of human combat. The handsome and cheerful Nesvitsky, a minor character, is munching a pie on the hill from which the Russian officers have a clear view of what is happening, and the General sends him down with an order that the hussars—with whom Nikolai Rostov is serving—are to cross last and set fire to the bridge. Everything seems very jolly and easy, to us and to him. But down on the bridge itself, all is confusion. Nesvitsky doesn't give the right order. And as the French fire at the bridge Nikolai, having his first taste of war, gazes at the setting sun and the waters of the Danube and wishes that he were anywhere but here, while the good-hearted Nesvitsky, seeing two men fall, exclaims, 'If I were Tsar I would never make war.'[41]

What this scene has established is that war is palpably 'unnatural'. At Austerlitz, Andrei learns through suffering that his ambition—to be a second Napoleon—is horribly false. As he broods over his dreams of glory on the night before the battle, he hears one of the orderlies teasing Kutuzov's cook, Tit. The echo some thirty pages later is one that can't be missed. Nikolai Rostov had a much simpler dream of glory—he wanted to be of direct service to the Tsar. An almost comic little scene shows that, while Tolstoy treats Alexander with what one might call formal respect—after all, he lived in a state ruled by that monarch's nephew—his opposition to the Great Man Theory bears sharply on the Tsar as well. Alexander, sunk in despair and unable even to cross a ditch, is helped over by Captain von Toll after Nikolai, who sees this, has let his chance slip by. Later Nikolai hears a groom teasing the same cook, Tit, with the same words. Tolstoy doesn't have to comment directly on the vanity of all military ambition and its irrelevance to the lives of the common people.

In the first half of the novel, in which war goes on far from Russia and domestic life there is rarely touched by it, Tolstoy prepares us with many small touches and broad strokes for the generalizations with which he will confront us in the second half—first in long digressions, finally in his second epilogue. The 'particular', his 'wonderful mass of life', has been made to seem to precede the 'general'. In the second half, as the war of 1812 seizes and transforms the lives of all his fictional characters, Tolstoy shows us proportionately less of them and more of Kutuzov and Napoleon. 'Historical' and 'fictional' people alike are confronted by great and shocking events. Andrei and Petia achieve a vision of the whole of life and die, and this relates to Tolstoy's theoretical demand that we should find the laws of human history and achieve understanding of them. Others, like Kutuzov, accept these laws, which they instinctively apprehend, and bow to necessity. Only Pierre is allowed a whole vision—that given to him by Karataev—and continuing life.

Napoleon, above all, bows to necessity when he flees from Moscow. Nikolai accepts the pressure of family needs which turns him away from Sonia to marriage with Maria. Maria herself accepts her longing for physical love. Natasha accepts her necessary role as wife and mother. Pierre likewise comes to terms with himself as a family man. But again, Tolstoy's clarification serves to expose paradox and complexity. Andrei accepts, not life, but death, and the spinning shell which fascinates him and kills him 'echoes' the roundness which Tolstoy so dogmatically makes the main physical characteristic of Karataev. Both in different ways suggest the roundness of the spinning world. Petia's wonderful dream of universal harmony—in which the voices of men and women blend in a march of victory with the mundane 'real' sounds of sabre hissing on whetstone and the neighing of horses—takes place on the same night as Pierre's dream when a voice tells him, 'Life is everything. Life is God. Everything changes and moves to and fro, and that movement is God. And while there is life there is joy in consciousness of the godhead. To love life is to love God.' Pierre sees the round globe as a living thing, and a little old man explains, 'in the centre is God and each drop does its best to expand so as to reflect Him to the greatest extent possible. And it grows, and is absorbed and crowded out, disappears from the surface, sinks back into the depths, and emerges again.'[42]

Pierre's dream provides a kind of consolation for the death of his name-sake Petia. (Both were christened Piotr, and they relate at this point much like Dostoevskian 'doubles'.) Petia, like the dead Karataev, is a drop which has 'overflowed and vanished'. He shares, although he is dead, in the coming victory of the Russian people and in the whole of continuing life. As a Rostov he receives full vision not through ideas but through his senses—like Natasha and Nikolai he is naturally musical—whereas Pierre, the intellectual, extracts from what the wholly non-intellectual Karataev has taught him a series of abstract propositions.

The old peasant's wisdom, so much applauded by Pierre as by Tolstoy, essentially consists of *not thinking*. He is at the other extreme to Napoleon, to the German strategists, and to Andrei. Pierre will finally admit to Natasha that while Karataev, he thinks, would have liked their family life, he wouldn't have approved of Pierre's plans to unite all men of good will in a body to reform Russia. Of course not; his 'wisdom' is totally passive and therefore totally conservative. It could accept any status quo.

Andrei, of course, is more practical than Pierre. His friend dreams of reform—Andrei actually takes part in the reforms of Speransky, though he comes to see that minister as 'unnatural' and hollow, another paltry 'Great Man'. Andrei actually manages to free his serfs, but they give a neat example of the incompetence of intelligence and human will when in 1812 they revolt against his sister Maria; Andrei if anything seems to have made the Russian class problem worse. Tolstoy must have realized that to spare Andrei, who is mature, capable and experienced, would have made nonsense of any distribution of justice at the end. Married to Natasha—or to anyone else—his intelligence would have given both him and us no peace. His besetting sin, from Tolstoy's point of view, is logicality—that desire which he inherits from his Voltairean father to bring everything within the bounds of Enlightened reason.

There is an element of detachment and study in everything Andrei does—even receiving a mortal wound. While he is to some extent 'taken out of himself' by the war of 1812, his mistrust of the flesh, of his own physical nature, keeps him aloof from the soldiers who love him. Pierre can delight in the powerful smell of sweat given off by Karataev, but Andrei is disgusted by the sight of his soldiers bathing in a slimy pool and, rather than join them, souses himself with water alone in a barn. ' "Flesh, bodies, *chair à canon*", he reflected, looking at his own naked body and shuddering, not so much with cold as with aversion and horror, incomprehensible even to himself, aroused by the sight of that immense multitude of bodies splashing about in the dirty lake.'[43] The old Countess Rostova is right to feel instinctively that he's the wrong husband for the highly-sexed and naturally self-contented Natasha.

Yet he does love Natasha. And he is Pierre's best friend. And he does understand Kutuzov. He is not remote from Tolstoy's life-embracing characters. He is the most 'heroic' hero Tolstoy ever created—the one most fully equipped to participate effectively in life. But Tolstoy mistrusts the most important part of his equipment—that incisive intelligence which is so much like Tolstoy's own.

Andrei, before Borodino, is Tolstoy's spokesman. He explains to Pierre why the theories of German generals have no relevance to a war fought on Russian soil. He stresses Tolstoy's own point about the importance of morale. He says forthrightly that the higher command don't help in a battle but merely hinder their men. He wickedly suggests that no prisoners should be taken, because such chivalrous gestures merely cloak the truth that war, if necessary, is vile and argues (like a realist novelist) that if people only saw war as what it is, they would never go to war.

But if we have read the book before, we know that the argument that no prisoners should be taken might be used as a justification for the barbarities of Dolokhov. This is a good moment to consider Dolokhov, a minor character of major importance. He is the closest Tolstoy came to creating a 'Byronic' figure, but he is observed with that minute attention which Tolstoy brings to stereotypes and which dissolves them back into the truth from which they sprang. Though we are surprised to discover at one point that he lives lovingly with a widowed mother, and though he asks Pierre's forgiveness before Borodino with what we must take to be 'natural' tears in his eyes, almost everything he does is wicked or unpleasant. Besides becoming Hélène's lover and provoking Pierre into a duel, he fleeces Nikolai Rostov of a fortune at cards and helps Anatole in his attempted abduction of Natasha. His appalling, pointless courage is displayed in that famous scene where we first meet him and he drinks a bottle of rum on a high window sill. But in war no Frenchman behaves so viciously as Dolokhov, no character does more to counteract any impression we might have that Tolstoy is naively nationalistic.

It is, however, important to notice that no character is more like Andrei. It is coldly intelligent rational thought which makes Dolokhov so dangerous. In practice he is a nihilist, brother to Pechorin and close kin to Bazarov and Stavrogin. As we infer from his glibly insincere use of patriotic clichés, he sees through all specious ideals and all social shams, and can act knowingly in accordance with whim and with total lack of consideration for others. What worries Pierre and repels us in the 'shrill' voice of Andrei before the battle, when he tells us 'I have begun to understand too much', is that his intelligence is bearing him close to nihilism.

Andrei has the same kind of complex fascination that Tolstoy would later create with his lovely adulteress, Anna Karenina. He is potentially evil, though in fact a good man. He is potentially a worldly success, but is in fact doomed to die with his promise unfulfilled. He can appreciate all that is best in the best people in the book, but he cannot be content with them or with himself. And he has in common with Maria, but far more than Pierre, a 'religious' temperament. Pierre uses 'religion' to find a way of coming to terms with the world as it is. For Andrei, when he hopes for posthumous fame or embraces his own death, what is beyond experience is always crucial. To him it seems that Natasha's soul is 'pinioned by her body'. And we notice another paradox—this man of the world is in potential a hermit.

Andrei and Pierre express the contrast within Tolstoy himself between the life-lover and the ascetic who despises the limitations of worldly experience. Pierre takes the goodness of all life on trust. Andrei pushes his thoughts, as he lies dying, through to a recognition that 'love is life' but feels that his proposition, 'Everything is—everything exists—only because I love' is 'too intellectual'. He dreams that death is pushing at the door, and that he dies. After this dream he 'awakens from life' into an unearthly detachment which makes him remote from his son, from Maria and Natasha. He realizes that 'death is an awakening'.[44]

At first sight it may seem that Andrei's final acceptance of death is the opposite, the inversion, of Karataev's complete acceptance of life. Yet the two amount to the same thing. Both dissolve everything into nothing. 'Karataevism' taken seriously would rob life of all significance. Loving all things equally would make any particular love impossible. Karataev's life is a sort of living death in which both consciousness and the exercise of the will are avoided. Andrei's death is an awakening—consciousness and the will, which have pained him so much, are obliterated. So the differences between Andrei and Pierre might seem to be no more than contrasts of temperament—Pierre can accept what Andrei must 'see through' and reject. But these different ways of viewing the same allnothingness do have importantly different implications for the way people live. It would, of course, be inconsistent for a Karataevist to make any choice at all. But Tolstoy himself chooses between Andrei (or Dolokhov) and Pierre (and Natasha). Logic is on Andrei's side, life and morality are on Pierre's.

When Andrei dreams that death stands behind the door, that 'death' is at first called 'IT'. A few pages later, Pierre recognizes as 'IT' that 'mysterious callous force which drove men against their will to murder their kind'. He witnessed IT when French soldiers were executing prisoners, and at the Battle of Borodino. Tolstoy in *Resurrection* would finally identify that IT with the modern State, a structure within which decent people act immorally and which seems to them to relieve them of responsibility for actions they would not undertake if left to their own free will. The way he handles Count Rostopchin, the governor of Moscow, in *War and Peace*, already prefigures his later views.

Pierre's thoughts, we might say, make concrete for us the IT which for Andrei is abstract. We are prodded to identify the death-principle which Andrei accepts with the amoral power of the French military machine; if, like Andrei, we accept death as superior to life, then morality becomes irrelevant and the behaviour of a Dolokhov (which, of course, involves his own life in constant risk) will be acceptable. Tolstoy is a practical moralist asking how men can live well together—and he has not yet given way to the Andrei within him and rejected society, the family and even sex itself.

Sir Isaiah Berlin, in a famous study, has seen within Tolstoy a struggle between the hedgehog, who, according to an old Greek saying, 'knows one big thing' and the fox who 'knows many things'. He argues that 'Tolstoy was by nature a fox, but believed in being a hedgehog,'[45] that his genius was for depicting the variety of life which, as a thinker, he was determined to simplify and reduce to large, clear laws. By this argument, Tolstoy's theory of history as he expounds it in the second Epilogue to *War and Peace* is a prime piece of hedgehogism. Having extolled instinct at the expense of reason and having explicitly denied that the intellect can solve our problems for us, Tolstoy now attempts to persuade us that history, so far from being dictated by 'Great Men', operates in accordance with natural laws akin to those of physics—he runs the risk of reminding us of his own sarcastic picture of the ludicrous but pathetic German military theorist Pfuhl.

The significant force in history, as he hopes he has shown in his presentation of the Battle of Borodino, is not the rulers but the peoples they rule, whose movements the historian must study as he might study those of a herd of cattle. It is in the nature of political power that those who appear to be in charge contribute least to what happens:

> Power is the relation of a given person to other persons, in which the more this person expresses opinions, theories and justifications of the collective action the less is his participation in that action.
> The movement of nations is caused not by power, nor by intellectual activity, nor even by a combination of the two, as historians have supposed, but by the activity of *all* the people who participate in the event, and who always combine in such a way that those who take the largest direct share in the event assume the least responsibility, and *vice versa*.[46]

Having reached this impressive, if most debatable, formulation after many pages of argument, Tolstoy admits the limits of reason, as we have seen Andrei do. 'In the last analysis we reach an endless circle—that uttermost limit to which in every domain of thought the human intellect must come if it is not playing with its subject. Electricity produces heat; heat produces electricity.'[47] Life is life. History happens as it must happen. The roundness of Karataev and the spinning of the fatal shell alike express in symbol the circularity of the world itself and of every argument about the world. The circle cannot be broken. There is in action a law, which we might as well call the Will of God, which dictates all our behaviour, and this law of life, not the will of Napoleon or Alexander, accounts for everything. Once again (as so often in Russian fiction) we stand with the nihilists confronting a world in which morality seems meaningless. Tolstoy now has to rescue himself from his Andreism. Many decades before the Enlightened philosopher Kant had likewise stood at the limits of reason, and Tolstoy arrives at a conclusion recalling Kant's which salvages morality from the pincer attack of reason and of natural laws.

Man is not free, yet his humanity somehow consists in his being free. Unlike a particle of matter, man can say 'I am free':

> A man is only conscious of himself as a living being by the fact that he wills: he is conscious of his volition. And his own will—which is the very essence of his life—he is and cannot but be conscious of as being free.... Man sees his will to be limited just because he is conscious of it in no other way than as being free.[48]

Every human action is both free, because the man undertaking it is conscious of his freedom, and a product of 'necessity', because he is subject to the law of Nature. As soon as we stop to think, we are aware of limitations on our freedom. But because our reason is limited, it cannot discover enough causes for our actions to complete the 'circle of necessity' and we cannot imagine an action entirely subject to the law of necessity.

If we start adding names of characters to the argument, we see how closely Tolstoy's epilogue relates to the content of his novel. 'Reason gives expression to the laws of necessity.' Andrei, the reasoner, dies and ceases to be human or free, in accordance with natural law. 'Consciousness gives expression to the reality of freewill.' Pierre lives, and believes that he and his friends can reform Russia. But in order to increase our understanding of our own lives and to make history a science like astronomy, which the Andrei-like Tolstoy wishes it to be, we 'have to renounce a freedom that does not exist and to recognize a dependence of which we are not conscious.' It is an act of choice if we 'renounce' something, so freedom must exist if we are able to renounce our naive faith in it. Paradoxically, we express our freedom most perfectly when we recognize that our actions are governed by the law of nature. Tolstoy thinks in terms of simple, unchangeable laws of necessity like those of Newtonian physics. Without Dostoevsky's inherently dialectical cast of mind, and without a vivid interest in the newer sciences, notably biology, which impose on us the view of a constantly changing nature, Tolstoy tends to write as if God really had created the world complete in six days and given it unalterable laws. He doesn't fully see that the existence of what we call 'human freedom' indicates a force acting upon and even changing the 'law' while acted upon by it.

This helps to explain his conservatism. He extols Kutuzov, old, pacific and expressing what we might call the 'eternal reality' of Russia, and Natasha, who is content with a traditional role for women, and Nikolai, the old-fashioned farmer who submits to the existing state of mind of the peasants. If Nikolai had married Sonia he would have defied the prevailing social pattern in which money and property tend as a rule to determine the choice of partners in marriage. Instead, he conforms to it, since the woman he freely chooses to marry is also a rich heiress. Free action, it would seem, is something that you discover, or rediscover, not something which you can create. To behave well is not so much to act rightly as, like Kutuzov, to refrain from acting wrongly. Ideally, we would remain what we are in early childhood, naturally good in harmony with nature.

But Tolstoy was too much of a moralist to be altogether conservative. His contention that we must stop believing ourselves free is directed at historians. As a moralist, he believed in the kind of freedom which can change reality by changing human behaviour. He had to, otherwise all moral distinctions would tend to disappear as Rostopchin (man of the Russian state) at one point wishes they would. We must, for instance, revolt against the 'law of nature' which makes us murder our fellow men. The last word of *War and Peace* is left to the 'progressives'. That dissatisfaction with the limitations of present experience which Andrei represents is inherited by his son, who idolizes Pierre the deluded believer in reform. The story ends with the boy's ringing if pathetic words—'Oh, Father, Father! Yes, I will do something that even *he* would be content with.'[49]

VII

It is Tolstoy's ideas which give structure to *War and Peace*, because they control his selection of detail. But Tolstoy was too candid to violate life's truth in the interest of his favourite notions. In Karataev he does, indeed, create a theoretical being, though even with him Tolstoy's warmth and skill provide a little life to cover an abstract concept. Otherwise, except in the passages dealing with Pierre's Freemasonry, which suggest a dull job of research conscientiously completed, Tolstoy never fails to evoke so much of life that we can, in effect, judge for ourselves. Scores of characters are 'alive', and they live because they exist in relationship to each other and the relationships which Tolstoy creates express the complexity of 'real life' as we experience it.

Maria may disarm us completely, but she can't overcome the suspicion of the peasants. Hélène may never fool us for one moment, but she is admired by the highly intelligent Bilibin. And so on. Nikolai, the non-intellectual hero, is created for us not by his ideas but by his reactions to nature and to his fellow men, and by the reactions of dogs and men to him. We may be conscious that Tolstoy is using him at one moment as a 'natural' Rostov to expose the 'artificial' Boris, at another as a medium for exciting indirectly our disapproval of war, or for undermining the credibility of the Tsar's claims to 'greatness'. But we continue to see him, as we see ourselves, in relationship to a moving, changing, radiant or disgusting range of men and objects which surrounds him as it surrounds us, which influences him and receives his influence in turn. His 'world' is as 'real' as our 'world'.

To show how the life which Tolstoy offers us eludes even his own power-ful generalizations, we might finally look at one of the most interesting patterns of 'echoes' in *War and Peace*. At several points a 'veil' or a 'barrier' vanishes from in front of a character's eyes. From Andrei's, for instance, before he dies—and this echoes the moment at Borodino where, as the shell explodes, the sound is like 'a window pane being smashed'. Andrei habitually sees life as if through a window; he observes but cannot participate—he can't, we might say, 'get into the swim of things'. But now reality, the exploding shell, bursts upon him. He has yet to participate in death, which for every human being is the final reality.

The brazen intimacy of Anatole's stare at the opera house creates in Natasha a feeling of horror that 'no barrier' lies between him and her. Tolstoy would argue that the barrier should be there, that this kind of cynical boldness violates the 'natural' respect that young men ought to feel for pure girls. But we would surely 'believe' in Natasha less fully, and even respect her less, if Tolstoy didn't enable her, and us, to confront *vis-à-vis* Anatole her own sexual lust—she is a lovely girl who might be naked in bed with a handsome man and would enjoy it. Tolstoy without doubt approves when the French general Davoust, interrogating Pierre, raises his eyes and his look goes beyond 'the circumstances of war and the court-room' and establishes 'human relations between the two men'. This glance saves Pierre's life. But while Tolstoy suggests that what rescues Pierre is a potentially 'universal' human reaction—if only men could recognize, as Davoust does now, the fact that others are men like them-selves, they would not kill them—if we study his scene we realize that it is because Pierre talks French and appeals to Davoust to take his word for it that he is not a spy that Davoust spares him. Pierre behaves like a man of his class, and the bond between the two men is one of shared class and shared assumptions and language, as well as what Tolstoy wishes it to be, one of common humanity and natural brotherhood.[50]

In all the cases just mentioned the characters themselves suddenly see more than they have recognized before. They stare at reality. Neither their words, nor Tolstoy's, nor ours, could completely express what they see. But Tolstoy gives us enough to provide a vivid apprehension of what they stare at. He himself mistrusted words. It is one of the pleasantest of paradoxes that a writer whose characters, good and bad alike, in effect tell lies almost every time they speak should choose to put his mistrust of words across in one of the longest and most complex creations ever built out of words. Prince Vasili may mask his greed at the death-bed of Pierre's father in conventional phrases which don't even deceive the woman he's talking to, Nikolai may tell fibs about his military exploits and Pierre may say 'Je vous aime' to Hélène not because he loves her but because he knows one should say such a thing to the woman one is going to marry. Tolstoy may insinuate in every way possible that words disguise reality rather than revealing it. But the best evidence we could have against this despair of words—which is, of course, a despair of human society, in which words must be used—is *War and Peace* itself.

ANARCHISM

'Anarchism' seems to define acceptably enough the direction in which Tolstoy was moving. To apply this term to Dostoevsky begs questions. But to reject the paraphernalia of 'justice' by which men restrain each other is, of course, to reject the State itself, and there seems to me no doubt that Dostoevsky's views put him at odds with any conceivable legal system. (Though whether his attack differs in kind or only in degree from Chekhov's implicit criticisms is a question I must leave open here—see the latter's stories *Swedish Match, In Exile* and *Murder*. Chekhov is certainly an individualist, but it would seem nonsense to call him an anarchist.)

The development of Anarchism as a distinct body of political theory owed much initially to Western thinkers, notably Godwin and Proudhon. But its most aggressive representative in the nineteenth century was undoubtedly a Russian, Bakunin. Though his direct influence was greatest in South-west Europe, Bakunin's thought clearly originates in an extreme reaction to the (then) extreme autocracy of Tsarist Russia.

Bakunin's best-known pamphlet, we are told, is called *God and the State*, and he insistently linked the defiance of God (atheism) with political revolution. He once wrote, 'God exists, therefore man is a slave. Man is intelligent, just and free—therefore, God doesn't exist.'* Such a statement would not have seemed strange to Dostoevsky's Stavrogin or Ivan Karamazov. And Dostoevsky's own addiction to the autonomy of the human will makes defiance of God likely if not quite inevitable. For all his loathing of the élitist and murderous methods of Bakunin's follower Nechaev, I would argue that Dostoevsky's drive towards the dissolution of all save self-imposed restraints gives his work an anarchist tendency akin to Bakuninism. And Bakunin's obsession with violence, his 'anti-authoritarian collectivism' and his notion that the 'countless' sufferings and 'exemplary' enslavement of the Russian people would give them a special role as leaders of European libertarianism do echo and 'double' important elements in Dostoevsky's thought. It would be

* Alexander Gray, *The Socialist Tradition*, Longman's 1947, 355.

interesting to interpret Dostoevsky, starting with his *Dream of a Ridiculous Man*, in the light of Bakunin's idea that Adam and Eve deserved to be congratulated for defying God's prohibition and eating the forbidden fruit.

But I would not deny for a moment that there are also authoritarian and even 'liberal' tendencies in Dostoevsky's work. I merely stress that unusually powerful passages in *Notes from Underground*, *The Devils* and *Karamazov* have an anarchist direction.

6

REVOLT AND THE GOLDEN AGE

Dostoevsky's Later Fiction

In some crucial respects, Dostoevsky and Tolstoy are much like each other. Both stand out above all other novelists in their unflagging readiness to confront the most difficult questions facing mankind on both the social and the philosophical level. Both seek for salvation through the rediscovery of Christianity and both associate this with an idealized view of the common people of Russia and of their simple faith. Both see the divorce of intellectuals from the common life as a source of frustration and tragedy; but both are so irredeemably intellectual, so incorrigibly sceptical, that their own prescriptions cannot satisfy them. Pretending to restore religion to its rightful place, both load atheism with ammunition. Creating their own Christs, both are in effect heresiarchs. Dostoevsky's uneasy submission to the Orthodox Church damages that institution as much as Tolstoy's rejection of it.

Tolstoy's range is wide enough to include much typically 'Dostoevskian' material—we have looked, for instance, at the mischief of Dolokhov and at Natasha's 'escape', as it might be called, from Andrei to Anatole. But Tolstoy didn't, and couldn't, feel about such material in the same way. Tolstoy's vision is always sensual and aristocratic, Dostoevsky's is always declassed and dramatic. Tolstoy narrates a simple story, creates people who develop but remain consistent, and analyses them with a calm seriousness which doesn't preclude irony but makes it rare for us to laugh while reading him. Dostoevsky is never calm and is often uproariously funny. 'Melodrama', 'farce' and 'tragedy' are words we find we must use when we're describing the great 'scenes' in which so many characters collide with each other in such unpredictable ways. Tolstoy's people exist in consistent relationship with nature and with a settled class society. The relationships between Dostoevsky's men and women are shifting and often elusive. 'Character' in Dostoevsky is never something defined by heredity and social position—it is what people are always creating for themselves, by free choice, subject to the pressure established by the presence around them of other free men and women.

As we have noticed, they are without vivid sensuality, and we might, and perhaps must, object that Dostoevsky's methods involve a separation of mind and body which is untrue to human experience. Dostoevsky refuses to bind the minds and 'souls' of his people to their bodies, and he can be accused of overlooking the constant interaction between mental conditions and, say, the ebb and flow of sexual desire. Illness, however, plays a great part in his work, in certain drastic forms, epilepsy, consumption and a convenient and appropriate malady which his translators call 'brain fever'. Many of Dostoevsky's major characters are, literally, 'sick'.

But if we call Tolstoy's characters 'normal' and 'natural' and Dostoevsky's 'abnormal', we are begging important questions. It is no longer 'normal' for people in modern Europe to live in the countryside, but our language, and with it our habits of thought, pay continuing tribute to an outmoded rural and feudal world-view, from which such words as 'noble' and 'base', 'gentle' and 'vulgar' derive. Dostoevsky's obsessions with sickness and perversion and murder mean that many of his people would be 'abnormal' by any standards. But when, at the end of *The Raw Youth*, Dostoevsky makes a spokesman associate the break up of the traditional family in modern Russia with the decline of the aristocracy, he establishes firmly the point that his work 'really' confronts a social reality which is transitional and elusive:

> ... a multitude of unquestionably aristocratic Russian families are with irresistible force passing in masses into exceptional families and mingling with them in the general lawlessness and chaos. . . . I must say I should not like to be a novelist whose hero comes from an exceptional family! To describe him is an ungrateful task and can have no beauty of form. Moreover these types are in any case transitory and so a novel about them cannot have artistic finish. One may make serious mistakes, exaggerations, misjudgements. In any case, one would have to guess too much. But what is the writer to do who doesn't want to confine himself to the historical form, and is possessed by a longing for the present? To guess—and make mistakes.[1]

Confronted with chaos, a world where 'normality' no longer exists, Dostoevsky, like his own heroes, has to experiment and take risks. In the city, he confronts a modern experience from which there is no way back to rustic innocence. The only way out is forward, towards a New Jerusalem.

How could he wish to go back to the old order in which his father was murdered by his own serfs? Like Tolstoy, he is preoccupied with 'freedom'. Both value it so highly that they are, in effect, anarchists. But their different emphases reflect the different realities they saw. For Tolstoy, we have noticed, freedom seems at times to be something which men rediscover. It is known to them in childhood, can be taken from them by the conventions of adult, urban society, but may be found again in the countryside. For Dostoevsky, a free life is something which men must invent for themselves, and a free society could only be a new kind of life created in the future.

In the late 1860s and for the remaining years of his life, Dostoevsky was unmistakeably a thorough-going right-winger. He was a nationalist who sneered at Poles and Jews, urged Russia on to imperialistic war, defended the autocracy and supported the Orthodox Church. By 1878, he was thought 'safe' enough to be invited by the Tsar to talk to his royal sons about politics. Yet it wasn't until a few months before his death that the secret police stopped opening his correspondence. While Tolstoy the aristocrat in the last years of his life would be humiliated by the eagerness which the authorities showed to protect his possessions against riotous peasants, Dostoevsky, the declassed ex-convict, was infuriated by the failure of all his efforts to avert suspicion from himself.

Tolstoy was, in important senses of the word, a conservative. The word would seem grotesque applied to Dostoevsky. While Tolstoy became the prophet of passive resistance and moral reform, Dostoevsky returns again and again to themes of active rebellion and social revolution, and he can't smother the revolt of his people under Christian pieties which, at bottom, he doesn't accept.

Most critics regard him as primarily the creator of four novels—*Crime and Punishment, The Idiot, The Devils (Possessed)* and *The Brothers Karamazov*—who achieved maturity only in his mid forties. But it would be a pity to overlook such earlier work as *The Double* and *A Nasty Story. The Idiot* is artistically less successful than either, and certain weaknesses are as obvious in his latest work as in his earliest.

He is, as he admitted, 'verbose'. He is rarely content to use one adjective where four will do. And much of his most 'mature' writing wears the appearance of improvisation. He seems to enjoy 'mystery' for its own sake and to create as many areas of suspense and petty intrigue as he can so as to give himself scope for surprises. As he improvises, he is prone to fall back on literary stereotypes. That he is 'melodramatic' need not bother us in itself—at his best he creates great melodrama. But in the scene in *Crime and Punishment* where Dunia defies Svidrigailov, she is too obviously the heiress of countless Romantic virgins nobly defying their aristocratic seducers, just as her eventual husband, Razhumikhin, is rather too close for comfort to Dickens's Traddles and Herbert Pocket. These characters lack the uncomfortable, fresh vividness of his best inventions and we must conclude that Dostoevsky isn't, when he presents them, creating at full pressure. None of his great Russian contemporaries is so uneven.

His great characters can be listed among those figures in fiction whose mere names can be freely used to evoke particular kinds of personality—

Raskolnikov and Stavrogin and all four Karamazovs have this in common with Hamlet and Lear, Quixote, Lovelace, Werther and Rastignac. They are so vivid, of course, because they do have such an acute bearing on the Russia Dostoevsky wrote about—they may seem to us embodiments of 'eternal' aspects of human nature, but their life depends on that of their own time and place. Dostoevsky, like Turgenev, was insatiably topical. He was delighted when, three days before the first section of *Crime and Punishment* was published, the newspapers carried reports of a murder exactly like Raskolnikov's which had been committed 'from nihilist motives' by a student in Moscow. But to set Raskolnikov besides Bazarov will reveal some interesting contrasts of method.

Bazarov is given a class background 'typical' of those of the young radicals and has clearly defined views which are, again, 'typical'. Both background and views are brought out sharply by contrast with those of aristocratic liberals of an earlier generation. A 'historical conflict' is neatly and clearly set out, so that both 'history' and 'conflict' are relatively easy to define and discuss. If we call the Kirsanov brothers 'liberals of the 1840s', we are not seriously oversimplifying the novel.

But we can hardly describe Raskolnikov as simply a 'nihilist of the 1860s'. His views, as Dostoevsky stresses, are those of an individual thinker, not of a group. And while it is tempting at times to see Svidrigailov as 'a representative of the decadent Russian nobility', the idle moneyed perversion which (amongst other things) he embodies could equally well have been found in British business families of the same period. Whereas what we can say about 'class' and 'ideology' can usefully define a Bazarov, Dostoevsky includes these factors only among many others which make his main people as much 'psychological' types as 'social' or 'historical' types.

So impressive is Dostoevsky's imaginative grasp of certain morbid and extreme psychological states that some readers may overestimate his range. He is, precisely, a specialist in extremism. Chastity and prostitution are topics he often tackles, but he has little to tell us about the psychology of an intelligent married woman embarking on adultery, which Tolstoy and Chekhov would explore so piercingly. Marriage, indeed, seems to be too commonplace an institution to interest him deeply. Nor is he concerned with techniques of farming, the psychology of men at their place of work, or even what one might call 'ordinary' deathbeds—subjects on which other great Russians have much to say. But murder and drunkenness, masochism and sadism, obsessive vanity and excessive humility, are themes he can handle again and again with fresh intensity. His books are full of the coughing of consumptives and the cries of tortured children.

Almost none of his characters do any work. Even those who are supposed to be practising various occupations are very rarely shown busy at them before us, and always seem to have time on their hands to crowd into yet another too-small room and engage at any hour of day or night in another appalling, hilarious scene. Almost all of them turn out to be eloquent talkers. Their addiction to confession is as unusual as their exceptional interest in political ideas and in theology. Their passion for daring debate is what above all else gives Dostoevsky's novels their special character. Again, the half-baked platitudes of *ordinary* political discussion figure only as targets for mockery. Dostoevsky's people are rabid Slavophiles or passionate denouncers of Russia, ardent upholders of Christianity or earnest atheists, utter cynics or Utopian dreamers (and quite possibly all these things at once). Myshkin, somewhat out of character, claims, 'If a Russian is converted to Catholicism, he is sure to become a Jesuit, and a rabid one at that; if he becomes an atheist he is sure to demand the extirpation of belief in God by force. . .'[2]

Dostoevsky has often been praised for his 'historical' consciousness, for an acute sense of how Russia's past interacted with present and future and a profound insight into the causes of the ultimate breakdown of the Tsarist order. But he writes in 1870 as if the cataclysm of 1917 were just around the corner. His novels are less 'historical' than 'apocalyptic.' His people tend to talk and act as if the Last Days of the book of *Revelation* were upon them, and so the reign of the saints might accordingly be close at hand. If he is a 'realist' then he must be a realist in a different mode from Turgenev and Tolstoy.

II

Writing to a friend about *The Idiot*, Dostoevsky discusses 'realism' and helps us to understand both the partial success and the overall failure of that novel:

> I have my own idea of reality in art; and what most people will call almost fantastic and an exception sometimes constitutes for me the very essence of reality. The ordinariness of events and the conventional view of them is not realism in my opinion but, indeed, the very opposite of it. In every newspaper you find accounts of the most real facts which are also the most strange and the most complex. To our writers they appear fantastic and they do not even bother about them, and yet they are reality because they are *facts*. . . . They happen every minute and every day and they are not an *exception*. . . . Is not my fantastic 'Idiot' reality and the most ordinary reality at that? Why, it is just now that such characters ought to exist among our uprooted classes of society, classes which actually become fantastic in real life. But it is no use talking about it![3]

The best passages of *The Idiot* are those in which Dostoevsky presents 'almost fantastic' events which do have the force of a symbolic exposure of the 'reality' of the Russia he lived in. The weakest are those where he labours to express ideas—for instance, his wavering conception of Myshkin himself—which ought, in his opinion, to have had some basis in real life, but which fail to convince the reader, presumably because Dostoevsky couldn't locate in reality any such basis. Some of his intuitions were brilliant, some weren't intuitions at all.

Despite the success of his second marriage, Dostoevsky remained under severe strain. Two months after the wedding, he had to leave Russia to escape creditors who might have imprisoned him for debt. Even after he had settled with his bride in Switzerland, his passion for gambling caused new disasters, his epileptic fits harried him, and his first child, a daughter, died in infancy. His struggles with the plot of his new novel are well documented in his notebooks, and his uncertainties are all too clearly reflected in the completed work. *The Idiot*, which appeared serially in 1868, was battered out against a series of deadlines.

Dostoevsky aimed to present in Myshkin a 'positively beautiful man'. Since, as he himself observed, Christ was the only such man, Myshkin must be Christ-like.[4] And if Myshkin is like Christ, then Dostoevsky's view of Christ is unusual, because Myshkin seems infirm and erratic, and his goodness is not healing but destructive.

Myshkin arrives in Petersburg one foggy morning oddly dressed in Western clothes, and apparently penniless. Scion of an ancient family which dwindled away, he is the last Prince of his name. He has been ill for virtually all his life, and a benefactor sent him to Switzerland four years ago to be cured of his 'idiocy'. On the train coming home he sits face to face with Rogozhin, who is his 'double'. The Prince is very pale and fair, while Rogozhin has dark hair. The Prince is mild and modest; Rogozhin is surly and self-assertive. The Prince has never had sexual relations with a woman, but Rogozhin boasts to him of his passion for the beautiful Nastasia Filippovna. In the bold contrasts set out in the first few pages, light and humility are associated with the decayed aristocracy, darkness and aggression with Rogozhin's old-fashioned merchant background, from which he has just inherited a vast fortune. As the novel proceeds, we will be invited to see Myshkin as the pure Spirit, Rogozhin as a representative of the dark, irresistible forces of Nature. If Myshkin is like Christ, Rogozhin is certainly like the Devil. Yet from the first they feel an affinity for each other.

Neither is truly at home in the 'modern' Russia which Myshkin enters. He heads for the home of the Yepanchins. Madame Yepanchina, the wife of a self-made civil servant cum businessman, was by birth a Myshkin, and as a good-hearted 'childlike' eccentric will have a different kind of affinity for the Prince. Her husband, however, is obsessed today with an intrigue. He is a friend of Totsky, a rich sensualist who picked Nastasia Filippovna as his mistress while she was still a child, brought her up to be his mistress, and became her victim when she left her love-nest in the remote countryside and pursued him to Petersburg so as to interfere with his plans to marry. Now after five years Totsky is trying to rid himself of the problem posed by this bold and vindictive girl, and the idea is to marry her off to Gania Ivolgin, Yepanchin's young secretary, with a bribe of 75,000 roubles. Yepanchin himself hopes to take advantage of the marriage to develop a liaison with her. This very day, she will announce her decision on the matter.

The innocent Myshkin brings his little bundle into a milieu obsessed with money and sex—but with money most of all, since money is thought to buy sex. It is a world, young Kolia Ivolgin tells him, of 'trollops, generals and usurers . . . in our age everyone is a sordid adventurer.'[5] Gania, Dostoevsky's attempt to portray, for once, an 'ordinary' man, has some of Raskolnikov's principles, but none of his ideals. He tells the Prince he will use his bribe of 75,000 roubles to make himself a usurer—'King of the Jews'. He says, 'Having made a fortune, I shall—mark you—become a highly original person. The most disgusting and hateful thing about money is that it even endows people with talent.'[6]

The first part of *The Idiot* (rather under a third of the whole novel) is Dostoevsky's most concentrated indictment of the emerging capitalist world. Aristocrat and merchant's son both serve to expose its false values. Myshkin's indifference to rank and his lack of interest in money, as well as his generous sympathy for all he meets, bring out by contrast the sordid mediocrity of General Yepanchin and Gania. Rogozhin's new fortune attracts to him at once a crowd of disreputable hangers on who with him storm into respectable houses, clarifying in the most 'vulgar' fashion the assumption of Petersburg people that money confers rights and power.

Nastasia Filippovna, in this first part, is one of Dostoevsky's most successful feminine characters. With the power and truth of a savage caricature, she is made to typify on the one hand the male attempt to use and sell women as commodities and on the other the free human impulse which can make an exceptional woman rebel against such treatment. Totsky has 'manufactured' her as it were to act the stereotyped role of polished, subservient and disposable mistress. But she has learnt too much and now she confronts him with 'something in the nature of romantic indignation, goodness only knows why and against whom . . .—in short (says Dostoevsky with leering irony) 'something highly ridiculous and inadmissible in good society'.[7]

Myshkin, of course, has an affinity for her as well. He fell in love with her portrait when he saw it at the Yepanchins, and now he turns up un-invited at her birthday party. She asks him if she should marry Gania. 'No, don't', he whispers. She accepts his decision, saying he is 'the first man' she has ever come across in whom she can believe as a true and loyal friend. Against Gania's 75,000 and the General's costly string of pearls, Myshkin has bid love. But then Rogozhin and his mob burst in. He has raised from the usurers 100,000 in ready cash and flings his bundle, wrapped in the *Stock Exchange News* and fastened with the sort of string which is used for tying up sugar loaves, on to the table. This kind of cash-down payment is, of course, old fashioned in the new era of high finance. The crudity with which money itself is handled by Rogozhin as if it were a commodity like sugar and not at all the mystical thing which stockbrokers have made it into, ironically 'doubles' (we might say) the crudity of values in a world where women are bought and sold. Besides Nastasia, we have met the horrible widow Terenteva who makes the drunken old General Ivolgin buy her with petty cash and IOUs—and Rogozhin treads, with his 'huge dirty boots' on the splendid dress worn by one of Nastasia's guests, a German lady who speaks not a word of Russian but is, like an object of art, in fashion. . . . 'It was considered the done thing to invite her to certain parties in a gorgeous dress, and with her hair done up as though for an exhibition, and let her sit there the whole evening like some charming fashion model, in the same way as people borrow a painting, a vase, a statue or a fire screen from their friends for their parties.'[8]

Nastasia rages at all of them, and also at herself. She is not, in fact, an 'emancipated' girl. Her seduction by Totsky has loaded her with self-contempt and she cannot rise above a commonplace view of adultery as sin and degradation. (Nor, it would seem, can Dostoevsky himself—his sexual morality seems at bottom to be conventional.) The Prince offers to marry her 'just as she is, without anything'. She jeers at him, 'Oh well, you've got that out of—novels' but, for a moment, after the astounding news has come out that the Prince himself has inherited a sizeable legacy, she smiles at the idea that she is now a 'princess'—she can share in that most conventional of dreams. However, the Prince's very nobility and idealism convince her that she cannot marry him. 'Ruin a babe like that?' she says, recovering her satirical bile, 'Why, that's the sort of thing Mr Totsky would do.' Accepting and, indeed, revelling in her own degradation, she agrees to go with Rogozhin. But not for his money. She takes the bundle and throws it in the fire, telling Gania it's his if he will snatch it out. This gesture wonderfully concentrates the meaning of Dostoevsky's attack on the money-mad modern world—look, here, the stuff is only paper, yet men will lose all shame in pursuit of it. Gania resists temptation but faints under his ordeal. Nastasia leaves with Rogozhin and the Prince rushes after her. Dostoevsky subtly leaves the last word to the old cynic Totsky. 'No doubt,' says this man of the world, 'what happened there tonight was ephemeral, romantic, and improper, but, you must admit, it was colourful and original, too. Dear me, what one might not have made of such a character and with such beauty.'[9] Despite the suffering which she has revealed, and for which he is responsible, Totsky still assesses her like an *objet d'art*, a racehorse, or, at best, an actress. But then, the deliberate histrionics which Nastasia has indulged in show the extent to which she defines herself, for all her 'romantic revolt', not as herself but in relation to false social standards. Her repeated statements that she will walk the streets or become a washerwoman do not represent a commitment to honest work—they are merely spiteful abuse hurled at her exploiters. Negatively, she knows what she isn't, an object. But she has no positive vision of herself, and so her rebellion has no direction.

III

After its first book, which concentrates so much significant action in one day, *The Idiot* falls sadly both in its level of artistry and in its thematic clarity. Nastasia Filippovna is reduced to the role of a madwoman haunting the story rather than present in it. Rogozhin, in spite of the wonderfully rich scene in which the Prince visits him in his dirty green, gloomy merchant's house, declines into an almost abstract Devil and Double. Dostoevsky's handling of the Prince seems uncertain rather than thoughtfully complex. Away from the familiar Petersburg setting, the novel fritters itself away when we join the characters after six months, in the following summer, at the country resort of Pavlovsk. Myshkin stays in the house of Lebedev, whose coming importance was foreshadowed when we met him as the third traveller with the Prince and Rogozhin in their railway carriage. Civil servant and usurer, sponger, spy, liar, family man, would-be lawyer, interpreter of the book of *Revelation* and serio-comic self accuser, Lebedev might be described as a prime embodiment of Dostoevskian Man, crawling wormishly and volubly between Myshkin's Christ and Rogozhin's Devil. Or he might be dismissed as improvisation incarnate.

His manner of intriguing, in fact, is rather close to Dostoevsky's manner of writing which, in spite of his labours in his notebooks, now seems to be lunging indecisively in too many different directions. 'The plans of this man were always conceived, as it were, on the spur of the moment, becoming more and more complicated, branching out, and getting further and further away from their starting point as he got more and more excited about them.'[10] Twiggy and unintriguing little intrigues surround Myshkin during the five weeks he spends at Pavlovsk before the end of the novel. Myshkin inadvertently becomes a rival for the hand of the 'beautiful' Aglaia Yepanchina, against Gania, in whom Dostoevsky seems to have lost interest, and the transparent Radomsky, who is supposed to be a clever aristocrat and who regards himself as a 'superfluous man in Russia.' But in the end the Prince's overwhelming pity for the mad Nastasia proves stronger than his (presumably) erotic attraction to Aglaia. Scandalously, he jilts the latter and is all set to marry Nastasia when, on her wedding day, she runs away with Rogozhin, whom she knows will murder her; she chooses to be murdered. In his gloomy green house Rogozhin shows the Prince her dead body. They lie down side by side in the dark room and the Prince, stroking the head of the murderer like a child's, falls almost into the role of accomplice. He reverts to idiocy and is packed off back to his Swiss clinic.

N. M. Lary suggests that the novel contains an allegory of Russian history. Nastasia embodies the 'old Russian psyche', and Rogozhin, with his affinity with the Old Believers, comes from the traditional Russia never swept wholly away by Peter's reforms. Gania is the man of the modern age and the Prince the bearer of light or the 'new word' which will save Russia. Aglaia represents the 'new' Russian psyche. Dr Lary concludes:

> The old psyche cannot survive; and at the same time the new psyche is destroyed by the burden of the past. Aglaia, who might have been a personification of a regenerated Russia, marries a Polish Catholic supposedly condemned to live abroad because of his anti-Russian activities, who in the end turns out to be no aristocrat or revolutionary, but an out-and-out scoundrel. In terms of the whole novel, it seems right that neither the old nor the new Russia should have a chance. The country was being invaded with ideas from the West, and as the nihilistic young men of St Petersburg demonstrate, it was less and less able to absorb them. [11]

That the novel conveys despair is beyond question, and one must be aware of an allegorical intention behind such semi-abstract creations as Gania and Radomsky. But the roles of Aglaia as 'new psyche' and Myshkin as 'new word' are hardly clear to the reader. Aglaia is almost totally unreal, even by the standards of Dostoevsky's young women; her caprices infect the novel with tedium and we must be hard put to see this scratchy figure as a symbol of anything. Myshkin, of course, is a more attractive failure.

Dostoevsky seems unable to combine the Christ-like truth and simplicity which he wished Myshkin to have with the doubleness of Dostoevskian human nature; he is at moments too idealized, and at others too 'real'. But one must in fairness say that many readers find him convincingly touching.

To Rogozhin he seems a 'holy fool', to Aglaia (at one moment) a 'democrat'. The world at large takes him for a 'nihilist' while he himself remarks that he has 'always been a materialist'. To Radomsky, who tells him to his face that he is far too intelligent to be considered an idiot, but then leaves him concluding that he is indeed an idiot, his actions seem to be 'Romantic' and Aglaia casts him as a knight devoted to an ideal of beauty—one of his sayings is that the world will be saved by beauty. Echoing Christ he declares at one point that his 'place is not in society', yet on the occasion when the Yepanchins exhibit him as Aglaia's fiancé, Dostoevsky tells us that he has long been 'very eager' to break into the charmed circle of the upper crust, and he represents himself to the assembled bigwigs as a 'prince of ancient lineage' who wishes to save his class from 'vanishing into utter darkness'. When he says, 'Let us be servants in order to be leaders,' he stands forth for a moment like a Tolstoyan 'conscience-stricken nobleman'.

But at the end of the book he is clearly reduced to mere and pitiful idiocy, and as a moral agent he is disastrously inept. His compassion and generosity make Nastasia fear him and drive her to Rogozhin and death. And the vase which he smashes at the Yepanchins' party seems to symbolize not only the beauty which he thinks will save the world, but also his destructive effect on people. Dostoevsky takes unusual trouble to prepare us by hints for this episode. The first hint comes from Varia Ivolgina, eighty pages or so beforehand, when she tells her brother Gania that the Yepanchins are afraid that Myshkin will drop or break something when he comes into the room. Varia's father, the drunk old general, whose monstrous, amusing and pathetic lies are one of the liveliest features of the book, tells Myshkin an elaborate tall-story about how he was Napoleon's page in 1812. Myshkin feels 'strangely timid, as though his visitor was made of porcelain and he was every minute afraid of breaking him.' He pretends to believe the old man, out of kindness, and the General leaves him delighted by his successful imposture. But Myshkin realizes, what proves to be true, that the liar will soon be overwhelmed with shame. '"Haven't I been guilty of a worse blunder by allowing him to be carried away to such an extent?" the prince asked himself uneasily, and suddenly he could not restrain himself and laughed loudly for several minutes.'[12]

His laughter is childlike, and the book is so much concerned with 'childlikeness' that we might see it as one in which 'innocence' confronts the 'experience' of the corrupt and compromised adult world. The Prince has a special affinity not only for young Kolia, but also for Madame Yepanchina, whose childlikeness is often stressed and whose goodness of heart, like his own, can't operate successfuly either in or upon society. He delights in finding child-likeness in other friends—in Aglaia, in Gania, and even in Nastasia. But treating people as if they were children, forgiving them everything, is as insulting in implication as it is to handle them as if they were china. (We think back to Nastasia's vase-like German acquaintance.) The dying Ippolit Terentev complains, shortly before the real vase is smashed, that Myshkin, whom he calls a 'perfect child', is treating him 'like a piece of china'. [13] Madame Yepanchina at once forgives the Prince for the broken treasure, but it has come to symbolize all the preciousness of human pride and the human personality. In letting down Aglaia, Myshkin 'smashes' both a beautiful girl and a whole life, since she makes, on the rebound, a disastrous marriage.

Only among children, like those whom he befriended in Switzerland, can Myshkin's generosity be anything but clumsily destructive. The Petersburg world seems irredeemable, and the irrelevance of Myshkin's anti-Catholic babblings and his appeal to enlightened upper-class self-interest shows how far short Dostoevsky was of finding a 'word' to save Russia. Diagnosis, not cure, is all he can offer, along with the subversive implication that Christianity itself may be impotent and even 'idiotic' at this stage of Russian history. The main characteristic of Russian life at this time is, as he sees it, simply, confusion. This doesn't really excuse Dostoevsky for having written a confused novel and for trying to handle too many characters whom he can't bring fully alive. It is as if he were shuffling characters desperately looking for some combination which will give him, and Russia, a winning hand and provide for hope in his nation's future. But in the end all he can offer is a friendly correspondence between the dull Radomsky and the faintly attractive Vera Lebedeva.

So hope can only be found outside society and outside time. It is not easy, one of his blankest characters, Prince Sh., observes, to achieve heaven on earth. But nothing less could satisfy Dostoevsky. The book of *Revelation* tells of the coming Apocalypse after which 'there will be time no longer'. Lebedev identifies the network of railways spread over Europe as 'the star called Wormwood' which fell from heaven upon the fountain of waters, and when Gania, the complacent 'modernizer', teases him about it, he exclaims that the railways represent 'the whole spirit of the last few centuries, in its scientific and practical application', which is perhaps 'damned'. And Lebedev is at this moment, if comically and parodoxically, one of Dostoevsky's spokesmen—the story he goes on to tell to make the point that there is now no religious idea strong enough to counteract the 'cannibal' tendencies of modern capitalism, has, for all its macabre hilariousness, the ring of Dostoevsky's approval.[14] Time, bringing 'progress', brings only disaster.

Myshkin hankers for escape from time, to a familiar spot in the Swiss mountains where he could spend a thousand years thinking 'of one thing only', but in fact achieves calm, joy and hope only in the moment or two before one of his epileptic fits. Harmony, beauty, the 'highest synthesis of life', are properties of an illness which handicaps the Prince in the time-ridden world and which confronts him with idiocy as its consequence. But at that moment before a fit, as he tells Rogozhin, 'the extraordinary saying that *there shall be time no longer* becomes, somehow, comprehensible to me.'[15] Sickness and hope, idiocy and salvation, are inseparably twinned, and the Prince's final reconciliation with Rogozhin beside Nastasia's corpse further implies, like other passages in Dostoevsky's fiction, that Good and Evil, Christ and the Devil, are twin forces ruling a Manichean world.

But the themes of *The Idiot* will be explored far more hopefully and convincingly in those later and greater novels, *The Devils* and *Karamazov*. *The Idiot* is like a trial run. Dostoevsky attempts to extend the insights he had reached through *Crime and Punishment* but fails to find a satisfactory intellectual direction—which means, because of the nature of his art, that he can't find a satisfactory fictional shape either.

IV

Dostoevsky stayed abroad for over four years, from April 1867 to July 1871, living in various Swiss, Italian and German towns. Paradoxically, the nationalist Dostoevsky draws more than Tolstoy or even than Turgenev on memories of Western art as well as of Western literature. It was in Basle that he saw the painting by Holbein of the dead Christ which figures importantly in *The Idiot*, and Claude Lorraine's picture,

Acis and Galatea, in the Dresden gallery, haunted him especially; he used it in *The Devils*, in *The Raw Youth* and finally in his late short story *The Dream of a Ridiculous Man*. It gave him an idyllic vision of a Golden Age.

The *Eternal Husband*, a shortish novel published in 1870, marks a return to achieved artistry after the uncertainties of *The Idiot*. Deftly constructed and written with an unusually light touch, it exploits again Dostoevsky's mastery over the Petersburg atmosphere. In the stifling summer heat, a nobleman, Velchaninov, hangs around waiting for the outcome of a lawsuit and broods over his past misdemeanours. As if to haunt him, Trusotsky, the husband of a woman he once had an affair with in the provinces, suddenly appears. He proves almost as hard to shake off as Goliadkin's double, and there are indeed obvious similarities to that early story. Trusotsky's wife has just died. In Petersburg he drinks heavily and tortures the child he loves, whom he knows now is not his but Velchaninov's. Velchaninov rescues the girl and finds her a home in a charming family. (The *only* charming family, perhaps in Dostoevsky's work.) She gives him, he feels, a new 'goal' in life, but his moral regeneration is cut short by her death. After some crisp comedy, when Trusotsky takes Velchaninov to meet a very young girl he aims to marry, the two men part. When they meet again by chance two years later, Trusotsky, the comic, balding, disgusting 'eternal husband' has acquired another unfaithful wife, and the suave Velchaninov has returned to his philandering.

The affinity between the 'predatory' Velchaninov and his double is based on the notion that that 'meek' eternal husband needs a wife to idolize as much as the womanizer needs wives to play with. In Petersburg they meet in a phase where each has drifted out of his usual role—Velchaninov is guilt-ridden and robbed of his usual self-satisfaction, Trusotsky is outraged by his sure knowledge that he has been cuckolded, has been jolted out of his 'meekness' and has a hankering to assert himself and revenge himself; he all but murders Velchaninov. The psychological theory underlying the novel is perhaps over-neat, but its working out is always lively and never merely schematic. On its modest scale, *The Eternal Husband* is a masterpiece.

Dostoevsky, however, lost patience with it—he wanted to get on with a project for a huge novel. It would be called *The Life of a Great Sinner*, would express his insight into atheism, and would be as long as *War and Peace*. 'Believe me,' he wrote to his niece, 'I know for certain that if I had two or three years without financial worries, like Turgenev, Goncharov and Tolstoy, I should have written something people would talk about a hundred years hence!'[16]

But harried by his usual shortage of money, he diverted his 'great sinner' into *The Devils*. In 1871, this began serialization in the *Russian Herald*, but the editor refused to print a chapter in which Stavrogin, the 'great sinner', confessed to the rape of a thirteen-year-old girl, and publication was suspended for a whole year. However, by making him popular with the reactionaries, *The Devils* brought Dostoevsky fresh patronage. At the end of 1872, he returned to journalism as editor of the ultra-right *Citizen*. This gave him a chance to start his *Writer's Diary*, a running commentary into which he could throw his reactionary political views, his memoirs of his career, his self-justifications against his critics, his comments on topical matters, and the occasional short story.

In poor health, chainsmoking cigarettes, addicted to black coffee and strong tea and writing in the small hours to escape interruption, Dostoevsky could hardly cope for long with the demands of regular journalism. By a quintessentially Tsarist paradox, he had to serve two days' sentence in jail in 1874 for publishing a piece by an arch-reactionary who had quoted a remark of the Tsar's without permission. By then he had resigned his editorship. He wrote his next novel, *A Raw Youth*, for the left-wing *Notes of the Fatherland*. The editor, Nekrasov, his friend in the 1840s, had come to him personally with a generous offer. In spite of frequent epileptic fits and the first of several trips to Germany designed to counteract his serious bronchial illness, Dostoevsky finished another long book by the end of 1875.

The Raw Youth is an untidy novel even compared to *The Idiot*. Its ludicrously over-complicated plot defies coherent summary, and it suffers from the presence of three Dostoevskian young women who are certainly, in this case, three too many. Its several suicides, its constant puzzling references to obscure intrigues which took place before the novel opened and its half-hearted hits at the young revolutionaries make it read at times like a self-parody. But it is still an interesting book, which deserves fresh translation and new readers. Dostoevsky himself, as we have noted, saw the disintegration of family life as its theme. The story is told by the 'youth' himself, the nineteen-year-old Dolgoruky, who arrives in Petersburg to resume relations with his father, whom he has met only once before, though this nobleman lives in a fairly regular way with his mother, a married serf woman whom he seduced. Morbidly conscious of his equivocal social status, the 'raw youth' hates and loves his father obsessively. Dostoevsky communicates very well the hesitations and perceptions of a lad barely out of school who is disgusted yet fascinated by the world of adult intrigue in which he has to find his feet and whose egotistic dream—to hoard money and become a 'Rothschild'—is pushed aside by his affectionate good nature.

His father, Versilov, lacks the intensity of Dostoevsky's best characterizations, but is a striking conception. An aristocrat with a taste for filth, frustrated both in his sexual passion and in his desire to do good, he combines features of Svidrigailov, Myshkin and Ivan Karamazov. He is a double man, 'split in two' as he puts it, whose passions which drag him into mean and vile actions contend with ideals of self-sacrifice and Utopian Socialism. It is he who evokes Claude Lorraine's vision of the Golden

Age, and his social idealism is intellectually in tune with that of Makar, Dolgoruky's 'legal' father, now a Christian pilgrim. Makar, the most prominent peasant character in Dostoevsky's novels, is even more abstract and idealized than Tolstoy's Karataev. He preaches a doctrine which Dolgoruky calls 'communism, absolute communism', evoking the end of time in an earthly paradise:

> Now we gather and have not enough and squander senselessly, but then there will be no orphans nor beggars, for all will be my people, all will be akin. . . . Now it is no uncommon thing for the rich and powerful to care nothing for the length of their days, and to be at a loss to invent a pastime; then thy days and thy hours will be multiplied a thousandfold, for thou wilt grudge the loss of a single minute, and wilt rejoice in every minute in gaiety of heart. Then thou wilt attain wisdom, not from books alone, but wilt be face to face with God Himself; and the earth will shine more brightly than the sun, and there shall be no more sorrow nor sighing . . . [17]

The Dostoevsky who in 1876 began to publish his *Writer's Diary* as a monthly periodical in its own right was still nothing if not a 'radical'. His belief that Russia's destiny was to save Europe and redeem the world, as the one remaining home of true Christianity was, by the kindest interpretation, a patriotic daydream. No kindness can disguise the outright racism present at times in his hatred of Germans, Poles and Jews. His reaction in the *Diary* to the outbreak of war between Turkey and Russia in 1877—'We ourselves need war for our own salvation, for war will clear the air we breathe and in which we were in danger of suffocating'[18]—exposes in a most unattractive light his fascination with murderous violence. But he goes on to show that he sees war for a noble cause which will create national solidarity as an antidote to the money-madness and individualism of the capitalist order now emerging in Russia. His jingoism in fact seems to consist of a craving for revolutionary violence resisted and diverted outwards as aggression against other peoples. In the same issue of the *Diary*, he published the *Dream of a Ridiculous Man*, his most direct statement about the Golden Age. The fictional author is an 'underground man' who, at the point of suicide, dreams of a communistic society of child-like, peaceable, loving men and women. Coming to them from the present-day world, much like an empire-building sailor stranded on some South Sea paradise, he corrupts them. They begin to hate and exploit each other and to believe that 'knowledge' is a better thing than 'happiness'. They create a society like that of nineteenth-century Europe and in it they discover the beauty of suffering. The 'ridiculous' dreamer becomes a Christ-like prophet pleading with them to crucify him. But when he awakes his faith in life is restored, and he goes back among men to preach the simple doctrine that they should love their neighbours as themselves. He has beheld the 'living image' of a harmonious society and must now believe that it can exist among men.

A vision which mimics the story of the Fall of Man in Eden and which has such obvious roots in the long-standing European cult of the Noble Savage might seem at first sight to install a backward-looking ideal. But since the vision is only a dream and the Ridiculous Man—Underground Man redeemed—is finally committed to a faith in its future realization, it points in effect towards experimental activism. Dostoevsky told the editor Suvorin, among others, that Alesha Karamazov, his one successful attempt to portray a positively good man, was going, in the sequel to *Karamazov* as we know it, to become a revolutionary and be executed after committing a political crime.[19] It is not, as some have suggested, a quirk or a mystery that Dostoevsky should ever have thought of making his gentle hero a political rebel. Positive goodness, for Dostoevsky, must exist in spite of the social and political shape of the world as it is and must express itself, to find effective outlet, in action against the *status quo*.

The serial publication of *Karamazov* in the *Russian Herald* from January 1879 onwards was greeted with great enthusiasm, and Dostoevsky received such public adulation as had never come his way before. In spite of his faint, husky voice, he was a hypnotic platform performer. In June 1880 he gave a speech in Moscow on the occasion of the unveiling of a monument to Pushkin. Other major writers were present, but the triumph was Dostoevsky's. He heard men hail him as a saint and a prophet, even Turgenev forgave and embraced him, and at the end of the meeting, women rushed on to the platform to crown him with a laurel wreath. He taxed his flimsy health with public readings as he worked furiously to finish *Karamazov*. It was completed in November 1880. In January 1881, still only fifty-nine, he died after a series of haemorrhages. For all his last-minute success, he left his family no more than the 4000 roubles still owed him by the *Russian Herald*. He never bought the country estate he had wanted, which would have made him at last a real nobleman.

V

But he had lived long enough to produce, in *The Devils* and *Karamazov*, two novels of unmatched intellectual scope and of impressive, though unorthodox, artistry. Neither has quite the same unity and drive as *Crime and Punishment*, and neither has any equivalent to the Petersburg atmosphere which gives that earlier novel such density of life. But both on balance gain from Dostoevsky's decision to set them in imaginary provincial towns. Dostoevsky's people move in miniature but 'complete' societies, embracing noble and peasant, layman and cleric, and such a broadly realistic framework compensates for the lost fogs and sunsets of the city. His art gains in restraint what it loses in richness, and he solves problems of narration which have always interfered with his fiction.

Without acute dramatic intensity, Dostoevsky's people become unconvincing. He has difficulty in expressing the development of character over time. We might argue that *The Idiot* falls apart because the gap of six months between first and second books is more than Dostoevsky can cope with. His characteristic method is to set up a dramatic situation and then play it out over a brief period of time, explaining where necessary by reminiscence and flashback. But he is not at home, either, in the role of 'god-like', omniscient narrator. He seems to mistrust the species of self-granted authority which enables a novelist to pronounce with confidence on his character's present thoughts and past history. One of the odder features of *The Idiot* is the way in which Dostoevsky quite often intrudes to say that he can't really explain why things happen or what his characters' motives are. He is only at ease when the characters themselves are telling the story, or exposing its development in dramatic exchanges, or when he is following intimately the thoughts and movements of a strongly-conceived major character.

Over short range, as in *A Nasty Story* or *The Eternal Husband*, he can conduct an efficient narrative by staying close all the time to the consciousness of a single character. But in *Crime and Punishment* when we move out of Raskolnikov's field of vision into that of Luzhin or Razumikhin, the artistic level falls drastically. In *Stepanchikovo* he is fairly successful with a first-person narrator who is also a minor actor in the story, but in *The Insulted and Injured* the story-teller has to race all over Petersburg to keep the various dramas on the boil and in *The Raw Youth*, Dolgoruky has to do some rather implausible eavesdropping. *The Idiot* breaks down into narrative confusion after we have ceased, with the end of the first part, to follow Myshkin from place to place.

The discovery which Dostoevsky uses, first with some falterings in *The Devils*, then with more complete assurance in *Karamazov*, is that he can sustain a long novel by mixing two 'voices'. The first is plausibly uncertain—not that of a god-like Dostoevsky, but that of a dry first person narrator conceived as a shrewd but limited provincial intellectual, who is not importantly involved in the story. He functions as witness in great dramatic 'scenes'. The second voice is God-like, but only in its penetration into a single viewpoint, that of Stavrogin or Shatov, of either Verkhovensky or of one of the three Karamazov brothers.

The two voices are passed off as one. We must assume, if we want to be literal-minded, that the amateur historian and amateur psychologist who comments authoritatively on the situation in the town, relays essential biographical information, but stops far short of omniscience, has somehow found materials with which to reconstruct the direct experiences, in his absence, of men who are, at the time of writing, dead. But the shifts from the standpoint of witness to that of participant aren't any more unacceptable in themselves than the device of God-like narration, and they do relieve Dostoevsky of the obligation to explain his characters definitively and thereby deprive them of the freedom which he sees as inseparable from the human personality. His war against the pseudo-scientists of his day who held that character could be explained entirely by reference to social and material conditions and that human nature could therefore be controlled and legislated for in a 'scientifically' ordered state, is expressed in *Karamazov* not only quasi-directly through Alesha's rejection of the arguments of the 'Grand Inquisitor', but also indirectly by Dostoevsky's refusal to 'explain' or even perfectly to 'solve' the mystery surrounding the murder of old Karamazov. 'Motives' remain enigmatic, but human freedom exists as a fact and Dostoevsky has too much respect for it to delimit its potentialities by neat summary. He is able at last to do equal justice to his own anarchist instincts and to the demands of literary form, which might have seemed to be incompatible with them. It is akin to Tolstoy's apparent self-abolition in *Anna Karenina*. The results are coarser in grain, but, perhaps, more honest. In *Karamazov*, neither the Public Prosecutor nor the Defence Counsel is wholly right or wholly wrong about the murder. The reader, who knows more than either, has to make up his own mind.

VI

The Devils was inspired by a real event. A young 'seminarist' named Nechaev had returned to Russia in 1869 from Geneva, where he had been in touch with Bakunin. He posed as the representative of the 'World Revolutionary Movement' and persuaded the few followers who joined him that they were part of a large organization. In November, four members of his Moscow 'group of five' murdered the fifth, a young student named Ivanov, allegedly for refusing to carry out the instructions of the 'Geneva Committee'. Nechaev fled abroad, and was still at large when Dostoevsky wrote his novel.

The Devils was designed from the outset as a denunciation of Russia's new revolutionaries. But Dostoevsky had no personal acquaintance with Nechaev, and while he stuck closely to the facts of the case as they emerged from the trial of his accomplices, he explained to the readers of the *Citizen* after the book was finished that he had not intended to draw a portrait of Nechaev in his Piotr Verkhovensky, but merely to answer the questions, how could such figures arise in contemporary Russia, and how could they gather followers? And he confessed that he himself was an old 'Nechaevist', equating the Petrashevsky circle in which he had been involved with the new groupings of twenty years later.[20]

So his novel is not merely about the young extremists of 1869—it is about conspiratorial politics in general and, selective and malicious though Dostoevsky is, its insights into the relevant psychological types still give its dramas wide bearing today. It is written out of deep self-examination, and it isn't, whatever some critics may say, important primarily as a 'prophecy' of the Russian revolution or as an 'exposure' of Socialism; it has as much to do with Nazism, BOSS, the CIA or the IRA. It illustrates how a mixture of people, some rascals, some idealists, can be cowed into committing an appalling crime by the manipulations of a cynical leader.

The provincial town in which the murder is set is on the whole more 'real' than that in George Eliot's exactly contemporary *Middlemarch*. As an evocation of a whole 'society', *The Devils* has few equals. It is a rainy, windy autumn. The town's slippery narrow brick pavements run alongside streets reduced to mud. Beyond the maze of streets—Fedka the thief says that the town looks as though the devil himself had carried it in a basket and strewn it all over the place—lie the cholera-ridden Shpigulin factory, bare autumn fields, and black old roads with deep ruts. Nowhere else is Dostoevsky so generous with this kind of detail, and nowhere else does he create such a range of sharply sketched minor characters—amongst them the good natured cabby who takes Maria Lebiatkina to the cathedral, the saintly half-wit Semen Yakovlevich, the drunken Police Inspector Filibusterov, the kind-hearted general who stands by Madame Von Lembke at her disastrous fête and points out to her and to us the local chemist who is dancing the can-can in grey trousers. Such abundance is almost Gogolian, and the rooms in which the characters meet, ranging from Shatov's cubby hole to the down-at-heel luxury of the White Hall where the fête takes place, have more variety and particularity than Dostoevsky ever gives us elsewhere.

The town is on one level a microcosm of Russia. But on another it very specifically typifies *provincial* Russia. Intellectual sluggishness is its hallmark. The prime 'devil', Piotr, is mistaken at first for 'a talkative student with a screw loose' and later, after his crime is known, men in the club acclaim him a genius. '"Organization, sir!" they say . . . raising a finger aloft.' A town pervaded by such banal judgements is a perfect place for Piotr himself to operate. Removing Nechaev's murder to here from Moscow, Dostoevsky can create a memorable image of a whole society in the throes of a disaster which it survives, we might argue, only because it is too stupid to understand what has happened.

Not only is the milieu uniquely detailed, character is established in a leisurely way which is unusual in Dostoevsky's fiction. The opening phase, before Piotr arrives and the trouble starts, takes approaching a quarter of the book and is dominated by Stepan Verkhovensky, the young man's father. This minor member of the generation of Belinsky, Turgenev and Herzen poses as a great thinker and as a virtual 'exile' who has suffered for his beliefs; the dowdy truth is that he has lived for twenty-two years as the dependent of Madame Stavrogina the rich widow of an army general, plays cards at the club and drinks too much, and presides over a 'circle' of small-town would-be intellectuals at which liberal ideas are aimlessly discussed. The narrator remarks that 'The "higher liberalism" and "the higher liberal"—that is to say, a liberal without any aim whatever—are possible only in Russia.'[21] Stepan has, however, had great influence on Madame Stavrogina's son, who was once his pupil. Nikolai Stavrogin's

Byronic career has taken him through service in the cavalry, two duels, a phase of living among the dregs of Petersburg society and three years of travel in Egypt and Palestine (he has spiritual longings) in Iceland (an aptly cold and barren place) and in Germany (the heartland of Romanticism). In between, he returned to his mother's town as a dazzling dandy, but after a few months committed a series of outrages, pulling a local landowner by the nose and biting the Governor's ear. Just before the plot gets underway at last, he has become involved in Switzerland both with the exiled revolutionaries and with the wealthy and beautiful Liza Tushina.

Madame Stavrogina sets about arranging a marriage with Liza and, since Nikolai seems to have had an affair with her own ward Dasha, proposes to marry the girl off to Stepan. This humiliating suggestion coincides with the arrival in town of the new Governor, Lembke, and his wife; of Karmazinov, a 'great writer' modelled on Turgenev, and of a strange engineer named Kirilov. With a full range of characters assembled and more or less accounted for the pace of the novel accelerates suddenly into perhaps the most eventful of all Dostoevsky's great 'scenes'. Madame Stavrogina brings home a madwoman, Maria Lebiatkina, whom she suspects is married to her son. Maria's brother arrives and behaves uncouthly. Piotr, Stepan's neglected son by a long-dead wife turns up out of the blue, followed by Stavrogin who has become his friend. A scene humming with outrage and hysterics culminates when Dasha's brother, a clumsy Slavophile ex-student named Shatov, strikes Stavrogin in the face with his fist.

The town, of course, fills with rumours, but the main action of the novel is still delayed as, in the second part, we move about with Stavrogin, who now in turn dominates our interest. With him we visit at night what we might call 'his people'—they are Night people—Kirilov, Shatov and the Lebiatkins, all old associates who for different reasons idolize him. Not till the third phase does Piotr take charge of the book, with the help of his willing dupe, the Governor's wife. His aim, as we will finally learn, is to undermine the prestige of the authorities, promote cynicism, scandals and disbelief and then use arson to throw society into despair and give the revolutionaries a chance to take over. Even Madame Stavrogina succumbs to the 'nihilistic' notions which the talkative Piotr has imported. The climax of a series of alarums and scandals is the *débacle* of Madame von Lembke's fete, which the revolutionaries reduce to chaos. It coincides with Liza Tushina's going to spend a night with Stavrogin while Piotr's people fire the suburb where the Lebiatkins live. Stavrogin is now known to be Maria Lebiatkina's legal husband, and when she and her brother are found murdered, the mob which has gathered blame him. Liza appears among them and is lynched. The murder of Shatov by the conspirators who believe that, as a renegade, he will betray them to the police, follows two nights later. But meanwhile Shatov's long absent wife has returned and has given birth in his room to a child who is Stavrogin's.

There is no sequence in Dostoevsky's fiction to match the intense pathos and human truth in the scenes where we see Shatov transfigured with joy at his wife's return, frenziedly helping her to a safe delivery and united in love with her and the baby after the birth; then murdered. Piotr escapes, but one of his group of five confesses to the police and the rest are rounded up. Meanwhile, Stepan, cast off by his patroness and hurt by his son's contempt for him, has taken to the roads, to discover the 'real Russia'. He falls ill and dies at an inn, reconciled with Madame Stavrogina. This sequence is also outstanding for its freshness of detail, its sympathy and its humour. But the last action is given to Stavrogin. He hangs himself.

The novel ends gravely and, as it were, 'conclusively' with a series of deaths which move and hurt us. But there is a curious gap between the atmosphere of Apocalyptic calamity which Dostoevsky has created and the broader effects of what has happened. Piotr's planned revolution doesn't materialize—all that has been achieved is a series of scandals and the deaths of a handful of people. The mad Governor Lembke is replaced, the legal system survives to try Piotr's accomplices and the town itself resumes its stagnation. This novel which seems to be offering a diagnosis of utter social breakdown, and which contains in Stavrogin, Stepan, Shatov and Kirilov four figures we might think of calling 'tragic', in fact deals with a world which is too banal to be taken seriously. As Irving Howe puts it, the book is 'drenched in buffoonery.'[22] The main actors themselves are infected by the prevailing mediocrity and inertia. Shatov and Kirilov are both rather stupid, Stepan is an endearing *poseur* and Stavrogin, whatever we make of what he has done in the past, is characterized when we meet him above all by lack of energy. He knows that Maria's murder will happen, does nothing to stop it, and accepts full guilt for it after it has happened—yet he neither commits it nor even 'wills' it—we would have to say that he 'thinks of it'. Apart from a duel in which he does *not* fire to kill, his only 'action' is his last, to destroy himself—and this clinches his negativeness. 'Satire' would seem the wrong word to apply to a book which lavishes so much sympathetic understanding even on the absurd Governor Lembke and which contains several deeply moving passages. Because we are moved, the book is neither negative nor depressing. But Dostoevsky presents a sub-tragic world in which even Apocalypse goes off at half-cock and the most decisive actor is a mean, rude, mediocre near-lad with a greedy taste for steaks and cutlets and a habit of underestimating the people he is dealing with which means that he could never be a successful revolutionary leader.

VII

The novel's title refers us to the New Testament story which is read to Stepan on his deathbed. Jesus expels devils from a man who is possessed by them, and they enter into a herd of swine which run down a steep slope into a lake and are drowned. Stepan himself interprets this as an allegory in which Russia is the sick man, and the devils are its progressives.

They are we, we and them, and Piotr—*et les autres avec lui*, and perhaps I at the head of them all, and we shall cast ourselves down . . . and shall all be drowned, and serves us right, for that is all we are good for. But the sick man will be healed, and 'will sit at the foot of Jesus', and all will look at him and be amazed.[23]

The simplest, though not the best, reading of the novel must make its 'message' a simple affirmation of Slavophile nationalism.

Stepan thinks he may be the head of all the devils. He is the intellectual father or grandfather of many characters in the book and Piotr of course is actually his son—though paradoxically the irresponsible father who, as Piotr puts it, 'packed him off by parcel post' has had no direct influence on his ideas. Stepan tutored Liza, Dasha, Shatov and, of course, Stavrogin. Each has seized a portion of the Romantic idealism of the 1840s which he offers them and has taken it to an extreme. The two girls have grown up as contrasting types—Liza is all capricious self-assertion, Dasha prepared for absolute self-sacrifice. Shatov, as nationalist and believer in the Russian people, and as the faithful lover of a faithless wife, is also a pretty obvious Romantic. These three clearly exist on a level of aspiration far above that of the townspeople, and to that extent, though their fates are sub-tragic, they are a credit to Stepan's own eloquence and idealism.

Stavrogin is more complex. He is clearly the descendant of a line of Romantic heroes which matures with Byron, and he has another source, much discussed by literary historians, in Dickens's rather Byronic Steerforth. Like others of his breed, he combines great physical allure with ceaseless philandering and sometimes with cruelty. Like Lermontov's Pechorin, he is also an intellectual whose mind has cut its way through all conventional thinking so that he can 'believe' in anything and in nothing. His nihilism is of an exalted quasi-tragic type which is very different from the base scoffing of Piotr Verkhovensky.

It was Stepan, we are told, who in Stavrogin's boyhood aroused in him 'the first and still vague sensation of that eternal and sacred longing which many a chosen spirit, having once tasted and experienced it, will never afterwards exchange for some cheap feeling of satisfaction.'[24] Stavrogin's people—those who have fallen under his influence—are therefore Stepan's intellectual grandchildren. Stavrogin's followers share both his longing for the ideal and his intellectual daring, and they would also suffer from his paralysis of the will if they were as constantly and as coldly intelligent as he is.

Even Lebiatkin can throw off disturbing ideas—'The sun, too, they say, will go out one day'—though he is clearly stupid as well as drunken. He is one of Dostoevsky's most amusing inventions. His grotesque Gogolian rhetoric and his ludicrous poems function as parodies of the Romantic imagination. He is extremely vain about his verses, yet knows that people find them funny and doesn't mind. This doubleness mimics Stavrogin's own. Stavrogin is both a successful (and vain) *poseur* and a confirmed self-hater.

It was Stavrogin who put into Shatov's head the idea that the Russians are a 'god-bearing people', yet he now claims that he was an atheist when he expressed a range of ideas which Shatov shares with Dostoevsky himself. Stavrogin was also, as we might say, quoting his creator (from a letter of twenty years before: see p. 117) when he insisted to Shatov that if it were mathematically proved to him that the truth were outside Christ, he would rather remain with Christ than with the truth. This licenses any form of enthusiastic heresy. The truth can only be outside Christ if Christ is not a divine being but a human one, or a human invention. Shatov himself, challenged by Stavrogin, admits that he doesn't believe in God, but says, 'I shall believe in God'. He later admits to his wife that he isn't really a Russian either. He too is 'double', intellectually committed to an emotional faith or, vice versa, emotionally committed to a belief which his intellect can't accept. Son of a serf but uprooted from the people, he now deifies the people as 'the body of God'.[25]

Shatov in turn doubles with Kirilov, the dogmatic atheist, once his closest friend, who still believes in God. While Shatov stands for the dissolution of the self into the God which is the People, Kirilov proposes self assertion. He plans to kill himself to prove that he himself is God. If God does not exist, then Kirilov as the first man in universal history who refuses to invent a God can become God, proving by his suicide that his own free will is the most powerful force in the universe—this would be one way, at any rate, of interpreting his laconic self-explanations. But Kirilov is also a lover of life. If he takes the Romantic cult of the individual will to an extreme in one direction, he takes the Romantic adoration of the All to an equal absurdity in the other when he says that rape is good because 'all's good' and that he is grateful to a spider for crawling on his wall. But Kirilov's essential kindness and honesty make it hard for us to believe that he would confess to Shatov's murder as Piotr persuades him to do, in fulfillment of an earlier promise that before he killed himself he would sign a testament useful to the revolutionary movement. *Logically* it may make no difference, but the man whom we've met playing ball with a baby seems incapable of such treachery to a dead friend, and Dostoevsky's artistic judgement is at fault.

We can't, in fact, discuss Shatov and Kirilov merely as spokesmen for ideas thought by Stavrogin, and the complex vividness of most of the novel's main characters makes the blatant 'doubling' of Stavrogin with the ex-convict Fedia seem by contrast rather contrived. It is Fedia, the believer who desecrates icons, who executes Stavrogin's thought and murders Maria Lebiatkina.

Maria's relationship with Stavrogin is not that of pupil to mentor—she has arrived independently at her (Romantic) belief that 'God and nature are one and the same thing.' But this madwoman takes to an interesting extreme the idolization of Stavrogin expressed by other characters. ('Why', Shatov has asked him, 'am I condemned to believe in you forever?') When the real Stavrogin appears before her, Maria rejects him as an impostor and accuses him of killing her true 'Prince', her 'falcon'. His crazy wife has created her own Stavrogin, much as, so Kirilov claims, all men have created God.

Piotr too sees Stavrogin as a 'Prince'—and he screams out in anger at one point that he 'invented' Stavrogin. What he means is that he saw the value of Stavrogin as a revolutionary figurehead. He wants to bring him forward as 'Ivan the Crown Prince', rightful Tsar of Russia, the bearer of a new truth, who will appear as a new Christ when the agitators have brought everything to ruin. 'You are my idol! You don't insult anyone and everyone hates you; you look on everyone as your equal and everyone is afraid of you. . . . You're an awful aristocrat. An aristocrat who goes in for democracy is irresistible. . . . You're my leader, you're my sun, and I am your worm.'[26] Piotr casts Stavrogin literally as the God of his own creation, to fill the vacuum left by the collapse of Orthodox Christianity. Yet he seems to stand in real awe of the God he has created.

Piotr's ambition, then, is not the bringing about of a democratic social order. 'I'm a rogue and not a Socialist', he says more than once. His passion is not ideas, but organization. He exclaims that the administration is 'the only thing in Russia that is natural and that's been successful.'[27] The most frightening of his followers is the young officer Erkel, a natural hero-worshipper whose mentality would be equally apt for loyal service to the Tsar or for the tasks of a Nazi camp commandant. For Piotr, it is not that the end justifies the means but that power itself—whether expressed through destruction or through autocratic 'administration'—is the end. But without Stavrogin, as he knows, he is nothing. His kind of busy-ness cannot seize general power without the help of the charismatic appeal which a Stavrogin could provide. He is, from the moment when Stavrogin is expected and Piotr pops through the door instead, clearly Stavrogin's double. While Stavrogin is a man of overbearing silences, Piotr is garrulous, 'pouring forth his words like so many peas.' He is incessantly active, Stavrogin always torpid.

Stavrogin's people, as we have seen, have partitioned the realm of Romantic idealism. Like their hero, they travel along with the revolutionary movement without really belonging to it—Shatov quits, Kirilov stays on the fringe, Lebiatkin merely hands out leaflets. Piotr's committed 'group of five' all in various ways share his own mediocrity and uncouthness. The naive and nervous enthusiast Virginsky, the boorish Tolkachenko, the cowardly Liamshin, Shigalev with his closed mind and Liputin with his nasty gossip are men, like their master, who lack some moral dimension. The group collectively 'doubles' Stavrogin's group.

There are no more significant moments in the novel than those where, first, Stavrogin walks along the middle of the pavement with aristocratic unconcern for Piotr who has to run in the mud to keep abreast with him and, secondly, Piotr in his turn forces Liputin into the mud in the same way.[28] But Piotr is not merely a schematically contrived 'double'. He is wholly convincing as the neglected son of a silly father who has grown up with a spite against the world, and as a man without secure status who idolizes a wealthy aristocrat.

Stavrogin, with his mask-like face, beautiful yet repulsive, is always a character seen symbolically by others and hence by the reader. What he typifies on one level is the dominance and doom of the Russian nobility. Byronism is, by definition, an upper-class *malaise*. Shatov rages at him, 'You're an atheist because you're a spoilt son of a gentleman, the last son of a gentleman.'[29] If the collapse of the Orthodox Church would leave a spiritual vacuum, the decline of the aristocracy deprives Russia of secular leadership. Dostoevsky has already explored this topic in *The Idiot* and will do so again in *The Raw Youth*. Christ-likeness is for Dostoevsky somehow aristocratic. The last Myshkin: the last Stavrogin. All Stavrogin's worshippers die except the base Piotr. His own son by Shatov's wife dies. He kills himself. The inert aristocracy completes its own doom while others still look to it as a traditional source of leadership. Stavrogin on one level represents a Romanticism destroyed by its own internecine contradictions between mind and feeling. On another he typifies a class which has exhausted its energy.

Yet without Stavrogin, both Shatov and Piotr feel powerless. What force, if any, can save Russia?

The intellectuals, Shatov would argue, have turned into devils because they have lost touch with the people. Dostoevsky was an intellectual. He had lost touch with the people.

For hope—and *The Devils* is far more hopeful than *The Idiot*—he turns to an intellectual source, both obvious and surprising. The idealism of the 1840s is, so he indicates, responsible for all the later excesses of Russian radicalism. But it is his own idealism. He is a man of the 1840s. He has nowhere else to go.

Karmazinov in *The Devils* is, quite unmistakeably, Turgenev. But in the 1840s, Dostoevsky had idolized Turgenev for his aristocratic radiance much as his own creations adore Stavrogin. He wrote to his brother in 1845 to tell him he had 'almost fallen in love with' this paragon: 'A poet, a man of talent, an aristocrat—handsome, rich, intelligent, well-educated, twenty-five years old—is there anything nature has denied him?'[30] The base and verbose Dostoevsky (in these respects like Piotr), was, in his own terms, Turgenev's double.

Karmazinov is made memorably disgusting, with his lisp, his vanity, his obsequiousness towards the nihilists and the contempt for Russia which he expresses by claiming that he cares more about the new water system in the German town where he now lives than all the political questions of his native land. At first sight, he stands somewhat apart from the other 'devils', with no clear 'double' relation to Piotr or to Stavrogin. But we can set him beside Stepan as a second representative of the 1840s.

And if he is completely 'negative', Stepan might seem to emerge as his 'positive' counterpart, almost a second Turgenev in the novel (though his more obvious model is the historian Granovsky). Stepan embodies Dostoevsky's warmer responses to his own generation of intellectuals.

The narrator G---v is his confidant. G---v sees through him but loves him, and makes the reader deeply intimate with him. For all his fatuous (but amusing) addiction to French phrases, he does give his dismal town what little intellectual liveliness it has. Unlike Karmazinov, he is capable of real grief, real compassion, real dignity, and even of real flashes of self-criticism. ('. . . All my life I've been lying. Even when I spoke the truth. I never spoke for the sake of the truth but for my own sake.')[31] In Dostoevsky's eyes, it must be an important point in his favour that children take to him. He has, indeed, much of the innocence of a child. The ideas he expresses against the radical utilitarians are in great part Dostoevsky's own, and his frank attacks on those who deny 'beauty' have an absurd courage and dignity. Most important of all, perhaps, he has with Madame Stavrogina the most touching and subtly lifelike relationship between a man and a woman which we will find in Dostoevsky's fiction. What they share is by any standards real love.

As he sets off on his pilgrimage on foot, ludicrously cumbered with walking stick, umbrella and travelling bag, as he talks French to the peasants he meets and congratulates himself for his genius for dealing with the common people, we realize how much we have come to like this constant, easy target of ridicule. His dying affirmation of faith in God and Immortality at first seems a too-neat example of death-bed conversion; but his obeisance to the 'infinite and the immeasurable . . . to the Great Idea' is in fact a reversion to the German-schooled idealism of his generation. Something like this, we must infer, was the Romantic philosophy with which he stirred the boy Stavrogin's soul. Stepan has been a *poseur* and a coward, but he has never at heart betrayed his vague Great Idea.

Of course, Stepan offers no more than verbal gesture—action is beyond the 'higher liberal'. Unbridgeable chasms between words and reality are found everywhere in the novel. Liputin the miser and family tyrant advocates a socialist phalanstery. Madame Stavrogina, that insatiable, domineering benefactor, denounces private charity at the very moment when she is helping to organize a charity fête. Piotr's revolutionary organization doesn't really exist. Stavrogin makes promises he doesn't keep. The town and the whole of Russia are swept by ridiculous rumours and false reports. Dostoevsky mocks his own country bitterly; he still believes in his heart what Turgenev and Belinsky believed, that Russia is a land of backwardness, mud and rhetoric. But amongst all the spouters of meaningless words, Dostoevsky must pick out people whose words aren't evil nor wholly silly. Shatov is one whom he chooses, of course, but Stepan is a far more fully created character, and his final reconciliation with Madame Stavrogina is the novel's best counter to Piotr's vicious negation. No word has really superceded his.

The seeds of Dostoevsky's last and greatest novel are to be found among Stavrogin's people, the heirs of a dying Romanticism. Kirilov's love of life and rejection of God, Shatov's generous affections and Lebiatkin's poetical rhetoric reappear in *Karamazov* amplified and represented by three men who are united by a common 'Karamazov nature', by Ivan, Alesha and Dmitri.

VIII

Maurice Baring, who published in 1910 the first well-informed appraisal of Dostoevsky by an Englishman, refused to tell his readers the 'solution' of the murder mystery at the core of *Karamazov*. 'One's mind,' he wrote, 'shifts from doubt to certainty and from certainty to doubt, just as though one were following some absorbing criminal story in real life.'[32] The novel is, amongst other virtues, devised with Conan-Doyle-like ingenuity, and suspense as to the outcome of the trial in which Mitia Karamazov is accused of murdering his father is an important ingredient in its popularity.

But the story is now so well known that it isn't unfair to summarize it here. Old Fedor Karamazov, a 'very small landowner' but cunning businessman who has built up a large fortune, has four sons. He neglected Dmitri (Mitia), the child of his first, aristocratic wife and Ivan and Alexei (Alesha) his sons by his second wife, who was the orphaned daughter of a deacon. All three have been educated by the charity of others. Mitia has grown into a riotous army officer, Ivan into a brilliant intellectual, Alesha into a chaste novice in a monastery. Perversely, the father has taken most care of Pavel Smerdiakov, his illegitimate son by a half-witted beggar girl called Stinking Lizaveta—he has trained him as his cook and trusted servant.

The story opens just after the whole family have come together in Fedor's petty home town for the first time. Mitya has quarrelled with his father over money and is now his rival for the affections and hand of Grushenka, the kept woman of a local merchant. Another triangle involves Katerina, Mitia's fiancée, who has followed him here. She is a rich noblewoman. She loves Ivan, but still clutches after Mitia as a form of revenge for a past occasion on which Mitia was magnanimous towards her. Smerdiakov falls under the influence of Ivan's atheistic ideas. Ivan asserts that if there is no future life in which we might be judged, then 'everything is possible'—there is no barrier to the most wicked crime— and Smerdyakov believes that Ivan wants him to murder their father so that the blame will fall on Mitia. Half-way through the novel, Fedor is indeed murdered.

All the evidence points to Mitia, but on the night before the trial Smerdiakov confesses to Ivan that he murdered the old man in accordance with what he thought to be Ivan's wishes. Then he hangs himself. Ivan, who is by now a very sick man, attempts a wild confession in court next day and Katerina, so as to save him, produces evidence fatal to Mitia.

The book ends with the convicted Mitia planning to escape and live with Grushenka, who is now firmly committed to him.

The murder story is in effect retold several times. The facts are provided first by Dostoevsky's narrator, who omits Smerdiakov's full part in them; then by Mitia under cross-examination; then by Smerdiakov to Ivan. Finally, at the trial, the Public Prosecutor and the Defence Counsel give their lengthy and, of course, different interpretations of the incomplete body of facts they know. Hence what is by Dostoevsky's standards a relatively simple 'plot' is used as the basis for a very probing examination of the character of the Russian legal process and of the psychology of the main characters.

Other matter—we can't really speak of a 'sub-plot'—is concerned primarily with Alesha. His beloved 'elder' at the monastery, father Zossima, is reputed a saint, and when he dies a miracle is expected. Instead his corpse putrefies with more than usual speed. Alesha is greatly disturbed, but his faith is restored by a meeting with Grushenka. Meanwhile, he has made contact with the Snegirev family—discharged army officer with a crazy wife, a hunchbacked daughter and a sick son, who provide us with Dostoevsky's last cameo of the 'insulted and injured'. Alesha rallies the sick boy's schoolfellows around him, but little Iliusha nevertheless dies, to his doting father's extreme grief. The book ends 'positively' with Alesha addressing the schoolboys and urging them always to cherish the memory of their dead friend and of their present comradeship.

If this final episode in which Alesha appears as a kind of scoutmaster surrounded by little playmates makes an untypically sentimental close to Dostoevsky's career, it must be remembered that *Karamazov* as we have it is only the first part of a projected masterpiece in which Alesha was to be the hero, and that *War and Peace* would have an equally suspect conclusion if it broke off at the end of its first half with Pierre's vision of 'his' comet in the sky. Several passages refer us forward to the rest of the story in which Alesha would have achieved fuller status as a 'hero of our times'.

Nevertheless, *Karamazov* as it stands has imaginative unity. Oddly enough, one way of locating the source of this unity is to point out that critics disagree completely about which of the brothers dominates the book. For one, Ivan and his philosophical questions are the chief factor in the novel's greatness; another will see the immensely likeable Mitia as the main force in the whole; while a third, more mindful of Dostoevsky's own intentions, will emphasize Alesha and the unorthodox Christian ideas which he has learnt from Zossima. The truth is that the three brothers cannot be separated sufficiently for us to lay stress on one or the other. The critics' problem is solved if they are seen as sharing, with their father and with Smerdiakov, a common 'Karamazov' identity.

The father is a gross sensualist but in his way a clever man, and he owns over 100 books. Ivan, Smerdiakov claims, is the son most like him; certainly the deliberate rebel against God takes after the coarsely witty blasphemer. But it is Mitia who most clearly inherits the old man's sensuality, while Alesha, who sees him as 'not vicious, but warped', distills whatever is good in him, and Smerdiakov is the apt product of his worst bestiality. Each is a plausible character in his own right, but it is not just fanciful to suggest that they complement each other in such a way as to form a collective image of the nature of man. Ivan could be allegorized as the Mind, Mitia as Body and Heart, Smerdiakov as Disease affecting Mind and Body and Alesha—not quite as the Soul, he is no mystic—but as Good Nature. But all five men share an obsessive interest, at different levels, in questions of Good and Evil, of God and the Devil. Even Smerdiakov is by aspiration an intellectual, while it is Mitia who quotes poétry at moments of crisis. The Karamazovs, says Katerina, are 'sensualists, money grubbers, and saintly fools'. Smerdiakov alone is without a share in the family's sensuality, but he is a product of it; and Alesha alone wholly escapes its obsession with money.

Only the totality of the novel itself can fully define the Karamazov personality. Cheering, disturbing, comic, tragic, this more than any of Dostoevsky's other books gives us a feeling of direct confrontation with the whole of human nature. However, Karamazov is Man, not in his average state, but in a condition of heightened emotional and intellectual activity. He does not merely represent, he 'typifies', the Russia Dostoevsky saw. Unlike the 'normal' man who in effect knows neither (unlike, that is, the Luzhins, Ganias, Rakitins and other targets of Dostoevsky's scorn) he has direct knowledge of good and evil. He is naive and childlike (even Ivan can be childlike) yet seared and disillusioned (even Alesha can be disillusioned). He is saint or God-mocker or both, he cannot be routine-Orthodox or agnostic. He is a murderer and a lover of life and of all mankind.

'. . . . I'm the same as you,' Alesha tells Mitia. . . . 'The steps are the same. I'm on the lowest one, and you're above, somewhere on the thirteenth. That's how I look upon it. . . . Anyone who has put his foot on the bottom step is bound to go up to the top one.' It would be better, he agrees, not to step on the ladder at all. But he doesn't think he can help it. Each Karamazov is potentially capable of the best and the worst in the others. Ivan tells Alesha he cannot accept the world God has made; Alesha, grieving over Zossima's shameful stinking decay falls for a moment into the same rebellion; Mitia too feels, when he dreams of a baby starving in the snow, that he wants to do something for everyone so that 'no one should shed tears from that moment.' Rebellion, not acceptance, is the Karamazov bent. It is coupled with what Ivan calls a 'thirst for life'—and Alesha agrees: 'everyone must love life more than anything else in the world.' The Karamazov force, Alesha says, is 'earth-bound, unrestrained and crude.' He adds, '. . . I, too, am a Karamazov.' And Ivan asserts that 'the force of the Karamazov baseness' is something which can 'endure àll'.[33]

The Public Prosecutor attempts to sum up the 'broad, unrestrained'

Karamazov nature. It is, he argues, 'capable of accommodating all sorts of extremes and contemplating at one and the same time the two abysses—the abyss above us, the abyss of the highest ideals, and the abyss below us, the abyss of the lowest and most malodorous degradation.' When he claims that the family display 'certain fundamental features of our contemporary educated society', Dostoevsky doesn't, of course, endorse his interpretation directly; but he never demolishes it, either. The depraved father is typical of many fathers, though they are less frankly cynical than he. Ivan and Alesha typify young Russian intellectuals—one believes in nothing yet retains an 'instinctive desire for truth', the other in despair goes back to the faith of the people. Mitia represents 'primitive Russia' itself, ready to squander generously what it has not earned, a 'wonderful mixture of good and evil'.[34] On one level of meaning the Karamazovs are Dostoevsky's summing up of his homeland, embodying its vitality, its limitations and its problems. With Mitia, Russia stands trial.

Old Karamazov is named Fedor. On another level, the Karamazovs present a diagnosis of the nature of Fedor Dostoevsky. Ivan has his untameable mind and suffers the pains of free thought, Alesha expresses his will to do good and the open trustfulness of his own better nature, Mitia his craving for love and beauty. And Smerdiakov is a victim of the epilepsy which made Dostoevsky himself, to his humiliation, unable always to control his own life and actions. 'Realism' and self-expression coexist in this collective characterization. And Dostoevsky's passion for 'doubling' his people at last finds a setting in which it can operate without straining the reader's patience; we accept without question that brothers are like each other. There is no grinding of contrivance in the scene where Alesha sees Ivan at the window of a restaurant and goes in to explore his affinity for a man who is still a stranger to him, as there is when Raskolnikov likewise glimpses Svidrigailov. (The role of restaurants in Dostoevsky's fiction might make a complex and interesting chapter in itself.)

The famous passage in which the sick Ivan has a hallucination and conducts a conversation with the Devil (or a devil) conjured up by his own imagination also has a 'natural' credibility absent in earlier 'doubling' episodes. The devil, Ivan protests, is an embodiment of himself, but only of one side of himself. Ivan is not fully 'declassed', and his haughty conduct often shows. His devil is a down-at-heels nobleman with the irritating facile cleverness and weary Voltairean cynicism becoming a genteel parasite.

Further doubling in the novel is so unobtrusively conducted that we can discuss it as we discuss linkings in Tolstoy and echoes in Dickens. The seminarist Rakitin, a shallow pseudo-Socialist careerist demonstrates by contrast how deep and serious Ivan's thought is. Old Karamazov's impudence, we are told, is at bottom a product of shame; and a combination of cowardice and pride distinguishes his mirror-double, the other father in the book, Snegirev, whose love for his own son is repaid by deep devotion. The rather pitiful sponger Maximov is a more direct, 'parodic' reflection of Fedor's own fawning and his uncontrollable lying.

The Karamazov nature is, of course, male nature. Of the women in the novel, the talkative Madame Khokhlakova with her endearing mixture of romanticism, superstition and half-baked modern ideas has a parodic relationship with all three Karamazov brothers. The scene in which the desperate Mitia calls on her for money and she advises him to try his luck in the Siberian gold mines is one of the funniest in Dostoevsky's work. Mitia, so often comic himself, is the centre of a great deal of un-spiteful humour like this which is very different in spirit from Dostoevsky's more habitual black farce. And his relationship with Grushenka is unique in Dostoevsky's work in its combination of unsentimentalized good nature with convincing sensuality. Grushenka, with her plump curves, the cat-like noiselessness of her movements, her uncomplicated jealousy of Katerina and her altogether credible affection for Mitia is the only young woman in Dostoevsky whom one could bear to meet at mid-day, let alone on a dark night. In her drunken communion with Mitia, she shows herself a fit mate for Karamazov. 'The world's a nice place. We may be bad, but the world's a nice place. We're good and bad, good and bad.'[35]

Katerina is not so well-created; we can't really understand why Ivan should find her sensually attractive. She is, as Alesha points out to her, histrionic, playing a part like an actress on the stage, and she is at her best an adequate actress in certain effective scenes. Grushenka with her very solid body is aptly paired with Mitia—no other male character in Dostoevsky is physically so vivid as Mitia, with the turned-in toenail in his right foot, his filthy underwear and long, firm soldier's stride. Ivan's physique is never described at all, and the virtually disembodied Katerina relates to him convincingly only in an intellectual pattern; her morbid pride, *hauteur* and will-to-power match important elements of his character. Between Alesha and the fourteen-year-old cripple, Lise Khokhlakova, a more complex affinity exists. The 'little she-devil' doubles the near-saint, but his acceptance of Lise's proposal of marriage emphasizes the childlike innocence of Alesha himself, who even at the end of the book has not yet fully tested himself against the experience of the adult world which Dostoevsky was saving up for a sequel.

If there is a warmth in the portrayal of almost all the people in *Karamazov* which Dostoevsky had rarely achieved before, Alesha has a great deal to do with it; he helps to humanize the book throughout. He has no important role to play in the murder story, but inherits from the narrators of earlier novels the function of acting as confidant to other characters. They almost all respond to his truthfulness and generous refusal to judge them, and accordingly show the best in themselves to him. Our affection for Mitia and our respect for Ivan are based initially on what they say to Alesha.

Alesha is not allowed to become mawkishly over-good. Dostoevsky sustains our interest in him by dropping frequent hints of latent sensuality and rebellion in his make-up. He tells 'white' lies, he is willing to give bribes to help Mitia to escape, and while he is often uncannily perceptive about the other characters, he also makes many naive misjudgements. He is a far more plausibly human creation than Myshkin, drawn throughout with an eye both to his limitations and to his potential to develop beyond them.

IX

Karamazov is in some respects more 'documentary' than Dostoevsky's other major novels. He visited a Monastery and studied monks at first hand, he studied the lawcourts, checked with doctors about Ivan's illness and read educational theorists to help him write about schoolboys. But though the book carries authority throughout, it isn't a 'social novel' in the same sense that *The Devils* is. Skotoprigonevsk, with its scattered houses, deserted lanes and network of ditches, has scanty existence in its own right. It seems to be merely an overgrown village, without the huge cast of local inhabitants great and small which the town in *The Devils* afforded. The issues which Dostoevsky addresses are still in their final implications 'political', but not immediately so.

The disintegration of the family is one of them. It is a more hackneyed topic now that divorce is so much more common than it was when Dostoevsky began to explore it. The question raised by the Defence Counsel—echoing, over a hundred years, Schiller's play *The Robbers*— as to whether old Fedor, behaving as he did, was a 'real' father for Mitia, doesn't seem to us so explosive as it may have done to the book's first audience. To regain an appropriate sense of shock, we must notice the implicit parallels between the murder of the father and rebellion against God, our Heavenly Father. For Dostoevsky, the coherence of the family and the cohesion of society both depend on faith in the authority of the father. Once this is questioned, 'everything is possible'. The Tsar was 'father', we must remember, to the Russian people. But if Fedor is a monster, how can we respect him? If the Tsar is cruel, shouldn't we defy him? And if God, as Ivan asks, permits the horrible suffering of little children, should we not oppose him even if he exists?

The questions which Dostoevsky raises about justice are equally resonant and subversive. As the novel shows, he was at best ambivalent towards the jury system introduced into Russia. It is suggested that he was thinking of the acquittal by a jury in 1878 of the would-be political assassin (authority-murderer), Vera Zazulich. But Dostoevsky's jury doesn't free the guilty; influenced by the Public Prosecutor, who wants Mitia to be made an example for all parricides (authority-murderers) it convicts an 'innocent' man.

Yes, but how can we call Mitia 'innocent'? He strikes down with murderous force old Grigory who acted as his 'father' when Karamazov cast him off. He admits that he wanted to kill his 'real' father. Ivan's urge to confess to the murder is based on the recognition that to want a crime committed may be as evil as to commit it—and Ivan himself, we notice, is murderous enough to knock a drunken peasant down in the snow and leave him to freeze, though he later returns to help him. Little Lise, who is, admittedly, unbalanced, tells Alesha that everyone 'loves' Mitia for having killed his father and Ivan, who is, admittedly, both unbalanced and sick, screams out to the court, 'Who doesn't wish his father dead?'[36] Freudian psychologists have of course found these moments gratifying, and even non-Freudians can agree that Dostoevsky is striking through to some uncomfortable truths about 'Oedipal' human nature. But the issues which Dostoevsky raises have scope far beyond the disciplines of psychology or jurisprudence.

In effect, Mitia's trial endorses the anarchist reaction that any legal system is both incompetent and irrelevant. Mitia always affirms that he did not kill his father, but he has judged himself more broadly 'guilty', and is prepared at first to go to Siberia. He has judged himself. And his Christ-like wish to suffer on behalf of others is in conformity with the doctrines of Zossima: 'Each one of us is beyond all question responsible for all men and all things on earth. . . .'[37] As in *Crime and Punishment*, the legal process is presented as akin to torture in its violation of human dignity by ruthless questioning. To confirm the superiority of self-judgement to legal process, we are given Zossima's story of the murderer whom he once knew—and who gave him spiritual guidance—whose crime had remained undetected until, with great heroism, he himself confessed it.

All the Karamazovs embody the force of human free will. Dostoevsky's objection to Socialism is not based on rejection of its cries for justice or even on a settled hatred of violent revolt. Alesha, like the common peasants, dreams of the 'kingdom of Christ' on earth, and the coachman who tells Mitia that the Lord will forgive him for being so simple-hearted and believes that all the great men, the rulers, the chief judges and the rich will go to hell, surely carries Dostoevsky's approval.[38]

Dostoevsky endorses the dream of social justice, but despairs of its being realized on earth because it is incompatible with human nature—with the free Karamazov nature. 'Socialism', as he knew it, threatened humanity with tyranny on two different but related levels. On the one hand, the Rakitins—the people whom Mitia calls 'Bernards' after a famous French scientist who laid great stress on heredity and 'environment'—see Mitia himself as the product of social and physiological circumstances and therefore believe that he could not have acted otherwise than (as they falsely suppose) he did. Freudians should observe that Mitia and Dostoevsky would have been equally outraged by their 'psychology'. Nothing must be allowed to rob man of the moral responsibility for what he himself does, and even for what he thinks, which he has because he is free. Secondly, the Socialist state would deny men physical as well as moral freedom in the interests of coherence and harmony. So would a universal 'Catholic' Church.

Zossima and his monks are in tune with Ivan's theory that the State should be dissolved into the Church so as to realize the claim of the *Orthodox* Church to universality. Ivan argues that this would imply that there would be no civil courts and no sentences of penal servitude or death. Excommunication would be the only punishment. Ivan envisages, it would seem, a free association of men who would act freely in 'criminal' ways only at the cost of cutting themselves off from the body of the Church and therefore from all other men and from Christ. Such a universal Church would replace the State with an anarchist communion. But the *Roman Catholic* Church, which Dostoevsky execrated, has historically sought to transform itself into a State. The secular power of the Pope and the punishments decreed by the Inquisition are seen as wicked. Hence, the symbol of totalitarian authority against which Ivan poses his anarchist Christ is not some foreseen Stalin, but the Grand Inquisitor.

Christ, in the fable which Ivan tells Alesha, reappears on earth in Seville in the sixteenth century and is recognized. The ninety-year-old Grand Inquisitor at once imprisons him. Ivan casts the old man as a tragic lover of humanity who accuses Christ of promoting unhappiness. The Redeemer should have succumbed to the temptations offered him by the Devil. By compelling people to believe in him, and thus robbing them of freedom, he could have made them happy. Instead, it is the role of the Church-State to relieve men of the burden of freedom which Christ insists on imposing on them. In the universal Church-State which will eventually emerge, the unfree masses will be happy under an organization which will guarantee them 'bread'. The only unhappy ones will be the 100,000 rulers who will suffer under the burden of freewill and the curse of the knowledge of good and evil. Christ 'asked too much' of man. By leaving him free to sin, he leaves him free to be unhappy.

Christ listens in silence to this argument and finally kisses the Inquisitor on the lips. The old man, who had threatened to burn him, now lets him out, saying, 'Go, and come no more.'[39]

Ivan, in revolt against injustice in a world where little children suffer, cannot accept the 'order' created by God the Father and represented by the physical laws of the universe. He rejects the tyranny of cause and and effect and wants justice on earth here and now. 'I want to see with my own eyes the lion lie down with the lamb. . . I want to be there when everyone suddenly finds out what it has all been for.' He rejects the 'higher harmony' of God's universe in which suffering is necessary. Too high a price has been placed on harmony. The 'admission price' is too high. 'And therefore I hasten to return my ticket of admission. . . .

It is not God that I do not accept, Alesha, I merely most respectfully
return Him the ticket.'[40]

Ivan, of course, is, for all his acuteness—or because of it—immersed
in turbulent self-contradiction. In his free revolt against God he is
Christ-like, because his Christ is an anarchist whose freedom is at odds
with God and God's order, as it is with every State imaginable on earth.
But in so far as Ivan hopes by the exercise of freewill to create an earthly
social order which will enable men to live harmoniously together, he must
intend to deny other men freedom, which as his views define it is inseparable from suffering.

Ivan's rebellion seems to have its intellectual counterweight in Zossima's
doctrine of all-acceptance. We must, Zossima says, seek happiness in
sorrow, God in work. We must love all God's creation, the wild bear
as well as the pretty birds (the lion as well as the lamb). Dostoevsky gives
Zossima his own favourite notion that the world will be saved by the
Christ-bearing Russian people, but of course he can't show us this happening. What he can give us a chance to judge is the application, by his
disciple Alesha, of Zossima's doctrine of 'active love' for our neighbours.

Zossima's religion is not in the least other-worldly, and the faith
which he professes does not depend on miracles. Dostoevsky attacks
the crude superstitions of Orthodox Russia as much through the hilarious
blasphemies of old Fedor and the literal-minded questions of Smerdiakov
(who asks where the light came from on the first day) as through his
delicious caricature, in Zossima's rival the ascetic Ferapont, of the
primitive nonsense the Church still had room for. But Zossima's creed
does ask us to accept that 'active love' can transform the world into a
Kingdom of Heaven and end the age of 'isolation' of man from man which
individualism and the selfish pursuit of wealth have brought about. Its
puritanism and anarcho-communism bring Zossima's message very close
to the heretical Christianity of Leo Tolstoy in his later years. Dostoevsky's
rejection of contemporary capitalism seats him in the same railway carriage
as his rival and double.

But how does 'active love' work in practice? Pretty well, up to a point.
Alesha is universally liked. But while he can soothe his father's sense of
shame he can neither reform him nor give him self respect. He can do
nothing for poor Lise Khokhlakova. He sees that his two brothers are
rivals for Katerina's love. '. . . Whom was he, Alesha, to pity? And what
could he wish each of them . . . among so many contradictions? One
could easily lose oneself in that confusion, and Alesha's heart could not
stand uncertainty, for his love was always active. He could not love
passively.'[41]

Active love for all God's creatures will prove impossible until the
lion really does lie down with the lamb. So Alesha must either waste

himself in impotence and self-contradictions or take sides and actively rebel with the aim of achieving harmony among men. That Alesha
will in fact rebel seems clear from the passage where Ivan tells him
the story of the General who hunted to death, in front of his mother,
a serf boy who had thrown a stone at one of his dogs. What should one
do with him, Ivan asks, shoot him?:

> 'Shoot him!' Alesha said softly, raising his eyes to his brother with a pale, twisted
> sort of smile.[42]

X

Dostoevsky's own unhappy father had been murdered by his unhappy
serfs. The father of the Tsar-Father whom he now loyally supported had
sent Dostoevsky to Siberia, an injustice for which he was grateful. Dostoevsky tends to separate Christ from God, Son from Father, and turn
him into a rebel within the Father's system. His nicest, most Christian
hero, Alesha, will turn into a political rebel. But Christ accepted suffering.
Dostoevsky accepted suffering. One could go on stringing paradoxes
together for several pages more; what must already be clear, however, is
that Dostoevsky's attitudes to authority were profoundly ambivalent.
The rebel may be a saint. But the rebel will be punished.

Towards the 'modern' society emerging in Russia Dostoevsky was
equally ambivalent. His work on one level is a sustained outcry against the
new social order which was being created in Europe in the names of
rationality, utility, 'science' and 'progress', and Russia was becoming
more and more like Europe. But as a Romantic steeped in European
literature he cannot reject along with capitalism the individualism which
makes capitalist ethics possible. And because he is above everything else
an individualist, he in effect revels in the new freedoms of thought and
behaviour made possible by the disintegration of the patriarchal family
and the aristocratic order.

This ambivalence emerges as much as anywhere else in his attitude
towards women. He is hardly more of a 'feminist' than Tolstoy. Time and
again he makes fun of 'feminist' ideas. Yet he accepts and is in a sense at
ease with the growing liberty of women as an actual fact. He never gets far
'inside' one, and he has no portrait to compare with Tolstoy's Anna
Karenina. But histrionic and somewhat abstract as most of his girls are
they do talk and behave like free inhabitants of the new world where
everything may be possible. Like their creator, we take their freedom for
granted.

THE WOMAN QUESTION

The novels of George Sand and Charlotte Brontë mark the arrival of debate over 'women's rights' in European fiction as early as the 1840s. By the eighties writers like Meredith and Ibsen were fanning discussion in the west.

The absurd Madame Kukshina in Turgenev's *Fathers and Sons* (1862) is the first notable emancipationist in Russian fiction, and the cheap satire directed against her had counterparts not long after in the works of Dostoevsky and Leskov. In the latter's *Cathedral Folk* a silly provincial woman 'progressive' who is anxious to make a hit with a well-known radical whom she expects to visit her, dresses up in her worst clothes, disorders the rooms and grabs a handful of earth from a flower pot which she then rubs into her palms—the object being to show how much she despises traditional feminine values of grooming and even cleanliness. Tolstoy never descends to this level, but both he and Chekhov associate 'progressive' ideas in women with dirt and degradation. The slatternly Nadezhda in Chekhov's *The Duel* (1891) is held up for our laughter, and Chekhov has been accused, unfairly I think, of habitually taking a low view of women in general.

Chekhov in fact made the need for improved and equal education for women a frequent, if quiet theme in his fiction. In 1897 there were 104,321 persons in the Russian Empire who had had higher education, and only 6,360 of these were women (Seton Watson, 477). The anti-feminist bias of other great Russians compares at first sight rather poorly with the broad-mindedness of Meredith. But in representing women as by-and-large ill-educated and prone to make fools of themselves in intellectual matters, they were hardly violating the facts. And in practice they not only reflect the perhaps rather 'freer' position of women in Russian society which I point to in my first chapter, but (except for Gogol) give leading woman characters a dynamic sympathy exceptional in Western novels except for those written by women themselves. Tolstoy's Anna is the most wonderful case in point.

A word may be in place here about the treatment of sex in Russian fiction. Before the turn of the century, as in England, and more so than in France, direct depiction of heavings and gropings was eschewed. As in England the novel was regarded as a commodity designed for consumption by the whole family, and the Tsarist censors were in some ways stricter about 'indecency' than about political ideas. But Russian novelists mostly manage to be frank up to and even beyond the bedroom door, stopping short only before they creep under the sheets. Disordered bedrooms, prostitution and adultery are much commoner and are far more directly confronted than in English fiction. The sensuality of women themselves is very often conveyed in ways which leave almost nothing to the imagination, whereas in Britain even the more dynamic heroines seem to have washed their glands away in the bath. Great Russian novelists pay women the tribute, as English novelists of the period mostly don't, of discussing women as if they shared a common nature with men, criticizing without any coyness the ways in which they express sexual impulses and the effects of their limited education. Though Gogol is again an exception, the others have no interest at all in chocolate box pretty-pretties or winsome Little Women—they enjoy most writing about girls with strong characters.

Such girls were perhaps slightly better placed in Russia than in England if they aspired to intellectual distinction. Secondary education for girls was probably as well provided as anywhere in Europe. From 1872 women were able to take regular courses at University level, though political reaction under Alexander III blocked this avenue for a time. It is, in view of all this, an interesting question why Russia should have produced no woman novelist of even the second division status of Mrs Gaskell. I can't answer it.

Another question which stumps me is this: why is it that the great Russians, otherwise able, it seems, to confront somehow all the most perilous issues, have nothing to say, or even to hint, on the subject of homosexuality? (I can remember just one veiled reference, in Tolstoy's late *Resurrection*.) Or am I obtusely ignoring the hints?

7
MAN, WOMAN AND MALE WOMAN
Tolstoy's *Anna* and after

Writing a book, it has been said, is like a long bout of a nasty illness. *War and Peace* was followed by a slow convalescence.

In the autumn of 1869, travelling by train to buy some land, Tolstoy spent one night in the town of Arzamas. Alone in an unfamiliar room, he was seized with terror. Death was in the room with him, and in the face of death, for all his fame, prosperity and good health, life seemed meaningless to him. Prayers were no help. The 'night at Arzamas' haunted him, and played its part in the spiritual crisis which gathered momentum in the 1870s.

As the master writer mowed with his peasants, reopened his school and gave his colossal talents to writing textbooks and stories for children, Sonia was worried and moody. Now that her husband no longer needed her help with a big novel they shared nothing fully together except spasms of copulation which left her, year after year, pregnant again. He brooded over a novel about Peter the Great. In March 1873 he tried seventeen times to start it and gave up seventeen times. Then he remembered an incident of the previous year, when Anna Pirogova, the mistress of a neighbour, had thrown herself under a freight train, possessed by jealousy. Inspired by the typically abrupt opening of one of Pushkin's tales, he sat down and dashed into a new novel. The first part of *Anna Karenina* appeared in the *Russian Herald* a year later.

So Sonia again went to work copying her husband's manuscripts and transferring the copious and often almost indecipherable corrections which he made to his proof sheets. Tolstoy told her that he was inspired, in this new masterpiece, by love of its 'central idea', that of the family; and the ironies prowling around that assertion are too self-evident to need expounding.

The *Russian Herald* published each section as Tolstoy finished it, to rapturous applause. But its editor Katkov refused to accept the final part. Tolstoy had been dismayed by Russia's declaration of war on Turkey in 1877 and made his feelings clear in the novel, where the motives of those who had urged intervention on behalf of the oppressed Balkan Slavs are exposed to restrained but unmistakeable criticism. He had to publish the last section himself, as a booklet, in January 1878. By the time the novel had been carefully revised for a complete edition, nearly six years of work had gone into it. But *Anna* is no longer than novels by Dickens and Dostoevsky which took much less time to finish. Tolstoy remained the aristocrat of writers, able to give his book a density of detail, a perfection of construction and a dazzling artistic polish which hard pressed professional writers couldn't afford to match.

Nor, shackled to their desks, could they call on such a range of direct experience. Levin, in *Anna*, is the closest of all Tolstoy's heroes to himself. His marriage to Kitty is Tolstoy's to Sonia. His intellectual interests (he is a writer, too, though his book is to be a treatise on agriculture) leave him time for farming, hunting and lazy days in Moscow, as Tolstoy's did. The death of his brother Nikolai is 'an exact replica of the death of Dmitri Tolstoy.'[1]

Even the intensity of life which Tolstoy gives to his tragic heroine Anna can be seen as drawing indirectly on his own experience. His first, moralistic intention had been to make her a devilish woman, a *femme fatale* like one of Turgenev's, but coarser, who would victimize two fine men, her lover and her husband. (Traces of this conception can still be seen, very faintly, in the text, which more than once hints that Anna is possessed by a devil.) But evidently he himself fell in love with her, and John Bayley illuminates the novel when he suggests that she is another exercise in self-understanding. For Tolstoy, like his heroine, belonged to the Russian ruling class. Like her, he was uneasy within its conventions. Like hers, his life would become tragic as he tried ineffectually to defy its values.

II

Tolstoy thought that *Anna* was his 'first real novel'.[2] Critics, while assuming in spite of the author himself that *War and Peace* is a 'novel', have often placed *Anna* above it, and those who would deny that it is the crown of all the remarkable achievements of European fiction in the nineteenth century would probably be outnumbered by those who would assent.

It is an unusually complex novel which at the same time appeals to us by its (real) clarity and its (apparent) simplicity. It is a book which touches on many aspects of life and which is loved and remembered for its flow of intimate details—but also because it concentrates our attention with prodigious force on its heroine, the doomed adulteress. Even more than

War and Peace, it seems 'like life itself', so that Tolstoy is praised by some
for removing himself altogether from his novel, yet attacked by others
for 'killing' Anna. The critic's professional ingenuity seems more than
usually inadequate. It would take an analysis three times as long as the
novel itself to begin to do justice to it. No Russian novel has been better
served by critics writing in English, yet none so consistently prompts the
response, yes, Critic X is on to something there but somehow, the way he
puts it, it's not quite right. Like Levin himself, we stumble from partial
revelation through confusion to a new, still incomplete, illumination.
War and Peace, as we re-read it, settles into patterns and seems to reveal
its intentions. *Anna* won't settle and won't tell us what it 'means'.

So convincing is *Anna*'s reality that we miss major inconsistencies until
R. F. Christian tells us:

> that Kitty and Levin spend a year longer on their journey than Anna and Vronsky,
> while Dolly's story is at least six years out of step; that ages are muddled, that dis-
> tances do not tally and that the day on which the novel begins is both a Thurs-
> day and a Friday.[3]

The interweaving of two stories—or, we should perhaps say, of three
marriages—is responsible for these discrepancies. There are plenty of
novels with two or more stories. There can be no other in which the connections between the episodes seem so tenuous in summary and are in fact,
from chapter to chapter, so profound and persistent.

At the outset we meet a Moscow civil servant, Stiva Oblonsky, whose
marriage is in crisis because his wife Dolly has just discovered one of his
many infidelities. They are in their early thirties, as is Stiva's friend Levin,
an earnest country nobleman who comes to see him. Levin is in Moscow
to propose to Dolly's sister Kitty, still a young girl, but Kitty refuses him;
she has fallen in love with a dazzling soldier from Petersburg, Alexei
Vronsky. Anna Karenina, Oblonsky's sister, arrives from Petersburg
to patch up his marriage, which she does very quickly by soothing Dolly.
She utterly captivates Vronsky. These two Petersburg people both glitter
among the duller society of easy-going Moscow. They dance together and
fall in love. Anna takes fright and flees back to her husband, a dessicated
bureaucrat, and her beloved small son Seriozha.

But Vronsky pursues her ardently, and she gives herself to him sexually
and bears his child. After the birth she is very ill, and her husband temporarily forgives her. But she leaves to travel with Vronsky. They sojourn in
Italy, they return to Petersburg, where Anna is socially ostracized, and
then they retreat to Vronsky's country estate. Meanwhile, Kitty has suffered a kind of nervous breakdown after the humiliation of losing Vronsky. She travels abroad, and after her return, she and Levin agree upon
marriage. While Anna's relationship with Vronsky moves towards a
tragic outcome, with her ungovernable jealousy tearing against his wish to
resume an active social life and with Karenin's refusal to give a divorce

precluding any legally settled relationship, Kitty settles down as a house-wife and gives Levin a child. Levin meets Anna, for the first and last time, when she and Vronsky go to Moscow. Soon after, driven by groundless jealousy but also by a more fundamental despair at her own situation, Anna puts herself under a moving train. Life goes on. Vronsky (it is now 1876) volunteers to fight for the Balkan Slavs against the Turks, and hopes to die. Levin, in spite of his workable marriage, has also been temp-ted to suicide by the thought that death makes life meaningless. But at the end of the novel he discovers a new, provisional and untried faith in the Church and in 'living for others'.

Very few scenes directly link Anna's story with Levin's. Levin is Vronsky's rival for Kitty, and meets Vronsky several times; furthermore, he is closely connected to Stiva by friendship and marriage. But before and after their brief meeting, Anna plays no part in his life, nor he in hers. And their stories are radically different in character. Anna's is taut with emotion throughout and full of dramatic confrontations. Levin's, by contrast, is a string of 'slices of life', reaching a kind of climax with his marriage to Kitty and always given interest by his sharply conceived character and his earnest strivings for truth and virtue. The great 'scenes' in Levin's story, except for his trip to succour his dying brother, are not intensive and dramatic but extensive and either humorous or lavishly descriptive. He lives at a pretty even pace the life of a country squire, albeit an eccentric one, and the marvellous passages where he mows with the peasants or hunts with Stiva are the most memorable ones in which he figures. Readers sometimes complain that the Levin story is mostly boring. Why must we be distracted from Anna's absorbing fate by a rather graceless landowner worrying over his relationship with his peasants?

The answer is one of the few points about the book on which we may be reasonably certain. Levin's slowly growing life brings him—and us with him—into touch with the lives of the peasants who produce the food which the other characters eat, and into touch with talkers who are concerned with important arguments about the modernization of Russia, the emancipation of women and the discoveries of natural science. Not only does this sharpen, by contrast, our image of the wealthy 'Petersburg' world in which Vronsky and Anna move, it forces us to view the tragic lovers in the context of a much wider reality than either of them recognizes. The shallow, if amiable, Veslovsky, is hopeless as a shooting companion for Levin in the marshes and outrages him by flirting with Kitty—but a little later we meet him flirting with Anna and very much at home in the rarefied, gadget-ridden life which she and her set maintain even in the countryside. With a gun, Veslovsky is a bungler. On Vronsky's tennis court, he is in his element.

As this example shows, the two stories meet in an unbreakable continuum. Common social contacts draw them together into a single flow. Karenin is present at the dinner party where Levin and Kitty decide to get married. It is Levin's half-brother, the writer Koznyshev, through whom we meet Vronsky on his way to the Balkans. Stiva pops up everywhere, and without the knowledge of him which we gain through seeing him with Levin, we would not understand so well his sister Anna.

When Anna and Vronsky are in Italy, they meet Mikhailov, a Russian artist who is painting a figure-thronged picture of 'Christ Before Pilate'. They view this work in the company of a silly theorist named Golenishchev. Mikhailov has every reason to ignore the judgement of such people, but when Golenischev praises his Pilate—'an official to his very backbone'—he is pleased. This was 'the very idea' he had meant to convey —although Golenischev's remark is 'only one reflection in a million that might have been made, with equal truth.'[4] Much more could be said about this scene—how Mikhailov's subject, the judging of Christ, emphasizes a theme which we cannot miss in the novel, that of the fallibility of men presuming to weigh up the sins of their fellows; how Vronsky's reactions express that interest in superficial 'technique' rather than in profounder matters, which characterizes his outlook on life in general; and so on. There are as many 'meanings' in this passage as there are in Mikhailov's painting, and when we fish for significances in Tolstoy's continuum of life we can catch only a few and must leave behind others equally important. ('An official', for instance: we think of Karenin, as Pilate.)

Mikhailov paints Anna. This portrait is only one of three mentioned in the book. A fine one hangs in Karenin's study. Its expression, after he has learnt of her infidelity, seems to him 'unbearably insolent and challenging.' Vronsky, as a dabbler in painting, attempts one of her in Italian costume. But she is not an Italian; she is a Russian, and Vronsky puts his own aside when he sees Mikhailov's portrait. When Levin visits Anna in Moscow his face is flushed although he himself doesn't think (what drunk man does?) that he has drunk too much. In this unreliable state, he looks at Mikhailov's picture:

> He even forgot where he was and did not hear what was being said: he could not take his eyes off the marvellous portrait. It was not a picture, but a living, lovely woman with black curling hair, bare shoulders and arms, and a dreamy half-smile on her soft, downy lips: triumphantly and tenderly she looked at him with eyes that disturbed him. The only thing that showed the figure was not alive was that she was more beautiful than a living woman could be.[5]

But when Anna comes in she has the 'same perfection of beauty'. The reality is 'less dazzling', but there is 'something fresh and seductive in the living woman' which the portrait lacks.

Perhaps we remember at this point how Kitty saw Anna on the night of the ball when she conquered Vronsky. There were pansies in her black hair, with its 'wilful little curls that always escaped at her temples and on the nape of her neck.' Kitty had thought that a lilac dress would suit Anna. But she realized when she saw her, with her 'full shoulders and bosom, that seemed carved out of old ivory, and her rounded arms with their delicate tiny wrists' displayed and set off by a black gown richly trimmed with lace, that Anna's charm lay precisely in the fact that she stood out from whatever she was wearing. The dress 'was not at all conspicuous, but served only as a frame. It was Anna alone, simple, natural, elegant, and at the same time gay and animated, whom one saw.'[6]

Her dress is a 'frame' as if she were a painting. She is aware of herself as an object of beauty. Just before her suicide, she sees her own feverish face with its glittering eyes in the mirror, recognizes herself, seems to feel Vronsky's kisses on her, and lifts to her lips her own hand and kisses it. In love with the idea that a man should be in love with her, she has become self-infatuated—or rather infatuated with a glamorous object-Anna external to her true self. Even at the ball, Kitty saw 'something terrible and cruel' in her, but Kitty was of course jealous. What we have met, in the Anna framed by her black dress, is someone both forthright and elusive. She seems 'simple', but her dress is luxurious, 'natural' although she must have taken trouble with the pansies which Nature has grown for her. Her wrists are delicate, her whole air elegant, she is Petersburg incarnate; yet she is a solid, full-blooded animal, as passionate as any peasant, and her ungovernable curls suggest both wantonness and 'naturalness'. She is self absorbed, pre-eminently 'herself'. But she is also the vulnerable plaything of the society which she moves in and whose values her way of dressing mirrors. Her vitality strains and pushes against that society, but since she belongs so much to that society, she is thereby set at war with herself. She is both supremely and singly her own self, and 'double', her natural self at odds with her 'social' self. Rousseau's distinction between the 'man of nature' and the 'man of society' is as fundamentally important in *Anna* as in *War and Peace*.

The frame cannot hold Anna. She is always in motion. What Vronsky first sees in her as she alights at the Moscow station is 'the suppressed animation which played over her face and flitted between her sparkling eyes and the slight smile curling her red lips. It was as though her nature were so brimming over with something that against her will it expressed itself now in a radiant look, now in a smile.'[7] She moves like a pool, brimming over, renewed. Her expression cannot be captured except as one in movement between her eyes and her lips. No other woman in the book has such ample vitality. The powdered Princess Betsy with her long pale countenance, Dolly with her thin little braids of hair, and even Kitty—whom Levin first glimpses doll-like from afar at the skating ground, a pretty but slight creature—are all meagre beside her, fully 'real' though they are. Nor is it purely Anna's physical life which is in motion. As she reads an English novel, she envies the Member of Parliament in it making a speech—she would like to make that speech herself.

Of course, this implies that she is imitative, and we may link this moment with Vronsky's mimicry, at different times, of the manner of Italian Renaissance painting and of the life-style of the English country gentleman. But when Anna takes up the study of architecture, she surpasses Vronsky, and it is very significant that her frustration over her situation boils over when he is away playing at Parliaments at the Nobility elections. Not only does Russia have no parliament, women aren't at this time allowed to speak in the English one. When Petersburg ostracizes her and even the immoral Betsy explains that she can't call on her, Vronsky is still free to lead an active life in the open and indeed is welcomed wherever he goes. At the opera, he is courted while she is humiliated.

The fascination of Anna is that she is, we feel, capable of almost anything. In one important perspective, her tragedy is that she is unable to lead even the limited 'full life' open to women, and, more profoundly and simply, that she is a woman. Having become Vronsky's 'mistress' she is consigned to a role in which her sexual attractiveness is her only means of self-satisfaction; if she loses Vronsky, she loses everything. Dolly's situation in the home of the philandering Stiva shows how even the woman who finds satisfaction in the socially acceptable role of mother and housewife is at the mercy of men in a male world, but Anna has moved beyond such a role into one much more narrowing. Since she can only be sure of Vronsky when he is with her and making love to her, she must fascinate him sexually. Committing herself to him, she has in effect dedicated herself to her own body, as we infer when she kisses her own hand. She is developing the mentality of a courtesan. She tries to enchant Levin when he calls, and she succeeds. But there is still more to her than that. Levin finds her intelligent and sincere. These and other qualities which we know she really possesses are now shut into a house where no respectable woman calls.

But then, even if she were still Karenin's wife, they would have no outlet. Russia has no role for such a woman, unless it is throwing bombs at the Tsar. Tolstoy's genius makes us feel the waste of her. No character in fiction is less 'idealized'. She is in the end a frightening, quarrelsome creature obsessed with herself and her own frustration and, like the patient, honourable Vronsky we may find it hard not to recoil from her. Yet she is still a woman of energy and charm, of real capacity and endless potentiality. We loathe and admire her. We cannot merely 'pity' her, though pity is all she gets, even from Levin and Dolly. We have to *become* her, as Tolstoy has become her, and not only watch but participate as her life narrows from the abundance of promise displayed in the early scenes to the treadmill of jealous copulation which she escapes from only by self-destruction.

III

But we must also pity her, because Levin and Dolly do. We are made to see her not only from her point of view, but from theirs. We could not be more 'inside' a character than we are 'inside' Anna when she takes her last journey to death and Tolstoy uses methods which anticipate the 'stream of consciousness' in Joyce and Faulkner. But the novel goes on for fifty pages after her death and in those pages Levin, in spite of temptation, does *not* commit suicide. Nor do he and his friends brood over Anna.

We don't know if Mikhailov is a good painter. We only know that his work impresses Anna, Vronsky and Levin. We can't say that Anna is really a great woman lost to the ranks of greatness. We only know that Kitty is infatuated by her, that Vronsky is enslaved by her, that Karenin, who takes her for granted, misses her in her absence, that her son adores her and that Levin admires her when he is pretty tight. We know also that she is the sister of Stiva, that sensualist who is so much 'himself' when he sprays his body with scent, tears quivering oysters from their pearly shells, whispers wicked things to Betsy and sniffs the leather of a new cigarette case. Stiva, of course, is delightful. We are as relieved as Levin when a guest arrives and it proves not to be the agonized Nikolai but cheerful old Stiva, everyone's favourite, smoothing the movements of society's wheels with his 'almond-oil' smile. But Stiva is also supremely selfish. And Anna, too, is an Oblonsky.

We see Anna as part of a thronging world, and from many viewpoints. Her situation at every point is relative. She is jealous. So is Kitty. She loves Vronsky. So did Kitty. She 'commits adultery' and suffers terribly. Betsy does so too, and is unscathed. Stiva has nothing to fear from the judgements of society; his liaisons, like Levin's wild oats, are accepted as normal for a man. Vronsky only suffers (but less than Anna) because he contracts what his own immoral mother so much dislikes—a serious passion. Vronsky and Anna suffer because they are committed to each other so fully that a 'normal', discreet liaison is impossible. But this doesn't prove that their behaviour is justified.

The dogged Dolly, losing her grief in her housework but still somehow remaining independent, is an even more important counterweight to Anna than the growing, but still girlish, Kitty. No matter how much we may believe that Anna deserves fulfillment, when we see her country household and her unhappiness through the eyes of Dolly we are left in no doubt that Dolly the busy mother is both a luckier and a more valuable woman—in sober fact, in Russia, in the 1870s—than the Anna who is so indifferent to her child by Vronsky. And the husband she has left invites, in his narrower way, the same kind of double response as Anna does. We may loathe in him the consummate bureaucrat altogether adapted to his anti-human work, and yet feel for him as the vulnerable, unloved man who has been unable to give way to his feelings and finds out their value only too late. Anna may see, and make us feel, that with him she lives in a cold world of lies. But she herself lies to him, and hates him.

Anna cannot transcend the life of the book, which is the life of a 'society'. She is trapped in a web of relativities and cannot fly out to stand before us as a clear and simple moral symbol. We may locate her tragedy in this fact; she is only what she can be in the world which she lives in, and she wants to be much more. She cannot help feeling guilty about her adultery. She must still hanker for her beloved son and weigh Serezha against Vronsky. She can't write great books, when she starts to write, because she doesn't have the experience to be a great writer, and she couldn't be a great architect because her education, like that of most women of her time, is so imperfect. Even if she had been a man and a politician, she could only have followed Karenin into the aridities of bureaucracy, or Vronsky into the inanities of 'nobility politics'. The laws of history which govern her existence, like those which governed the war of 1812, are inflexibly limiting. Yet Tolstoy as he wrote about her knew that the world was changing—mostly in directions he didn't like— and doesn't attempt any lordly clarification of the Russian scene in the mid 1870s to match his second Epilogue to *War and Peace*. From the flux of values and conventions, different circumstances could emerge in which she might realize more of what is in her. She is free, as Pierre was, and her freedom like his includes the capacity to imagine a world transformed. As she reads her English novel in the train, she thinks of a different society, of a different world, and of herself taking part in it.

But Levin is free. Vronsky is free. They too pitch hope against limitation. And Anna, for Vronsky, becomes a limitation.

Anna is always insisting that she is not to blame, and after her humiliation at the opera she cries to Vronsky, 'it's all your fault', though in fact he appealed to her not to go. It is the most impressive feature of Vronsky's sharply limited personality that, until just before the end, he does accept the blame for what goes wrong. No one can miss the parallel Tolstoy sets up between Anna and the horse whose back Vronsky breaks in a race. He admits to himself at once that the loss of the race is his own fault. With ironic significance, he is busy selling a pedigree horse when, for the first time, he abdicates responsibility and tells himself that he is 'not to blame in any way' for what proves to be the final crisis of his relationship with Anna.[8]

Men are on top in this world; they ride women like horses. If Vronsky is so ready to accept responsibility, this is in tune with his male confidence and arrogance. If Anna shirks it, this reflects the fact that she has never been educated to see herself as someone accountable for what happens to her. And Tolstoy never explicitly moralizes against Anna.

It might be objected here that the book's epigraph—'Vengeance is mine and I will repay'—implies that Anna gets what she deserves. But in that case, why doesn't Tolstoy punish Stiva and Betsy? He clearly isn't implying—he simply couldn't imply—that sin leads inevitably to punishment on this earth. The motto would seem to suggest, rather, that God has the right to punish, men don't. The 'society' of forty or so exalted people in Petersburg which ostracizes Anna is so amoral, or immoral, in its own standards that it above all has no right to judge her. Levin and Dolly, who might seem to have such a right are, on the contrary, very sympathetic to her. More than once, phrases in the novel remind us of the biblical verdict that only those without sin have a right to cast stones. After Anna's death, that persistent adulteress, Vronsky's mother, proclaims that 'she ended as such a woman deserved to end. Even the death she chose was low and vulgar.' But the likeable Koznyshev retorts, with a sigh, 'It is not for us to judge, countess.'[9]

The judger of *War and Peace* has given way to a novelist who presents moral riddles but can't presume to solve them. Perhaps only the squawk of sour rhetoric he directs against the doctor who examines Kitty at the beginning of the second book can be clearly shown to be in the vein of his assault on Napoleon in *War and Peace*. We can't justly accuse him of 'murdering' Anna to satisfy a moralist's prejudice against adultery. If we leave out of account certain things he said about her outside the book, and concentrate only on the text itself, we must conclude that Anna is presented with full compassion as a woman destroyed by forces within herself which are both created by, and in reaction against, the society in which she moves. Tolstoy's very methods in this novel preclude decisive moral judgement.

IV

His chief people are so 'real' because we see them from so many different viewpoints. Nothing so surely establishes the reality of Levin's strong and looming physical presence as the passage, which only Tolstoy would have dared to write, in which we see him through the eyes of his dog, 'coming along, with his familiar face but ever terrible eyes, stumbling over the hummocks and taking to her an unusually long time. She thought he came slowly, but in reality he was running.'[10]

'She thought' one thing, but reality was another. Tolstoy takes upon himself the novelist's prerogative of omniscience, never more so than at this moment. But the range of viewpoints he feels able to express is so great that we seem to be confronted not with the certainties of fiction but with the enigma of reality. If *Anna* is the greatest of all 'realist' novels this must be partly because it never leaves us in any doubt that there is indeed a solid, murmurous, scented, 'real' world yet never for long imposes one view of it upon us. The world is there, but all its meanings are relative, all its potentialities are left free, and the men and women in it are, as we find ourselves to be, both limited by objective circumstance, and free in their own vision.

As Levin goes to Kitty for the first time as her fiancé, everything in Moscow seems to him beautiful. His own happiness seems to him to be reflected in the happy faces of the cabmen who offer him their services, although they are 'disputing among themselves'. Is all this Levin's illusion? Are the cabmen really cheerful? And if so, is this because his own radiance affects them? When Anna travels through the same city on the last day of her life, she is miserable and sees the life about her as misery. 'Why these churches, the bells and the humbug? Just to hide the fact that we all hate each other, like those cab-drivers so angrily abusing one another over there. Yashvin was quite right when he said, "He is after my shirt and I'm after his."'[11]

The philosophy of Yashvin the gambler is Hobbesian—all men are at war with each other. Levin, on the other hand, finds brotherhood not only among the peasants taken up with common labour, but also with his aristocratic friends in the English Club. We might say, comparing their two views of the Moscow cab-drivers, that Anna's (like Andrei's) is a vision informed by reason which embraces death; Levin's (like Pierre's), is a vision informed by love which embraces life. But the polarizations of *War and Peace* are always replaced with shifting relativities in *Anna*. It is Anna who asks Dolly, when Dolly is shocked by her use of contraception, 'What was my reason given me for, if I am not to use it to avoid bringing unhappy beings into the world?', and it is she whose thoughts, on the brink of suicide, chime with those she overhears a lady speak, 'Reason has been given to man to enable him to escape from his troubles.' And it is Levin who rejects reason, and with it the Yashvin view of life, when he muses, 'Reason discovered the struggle for existence, and the law demanding that I should strangle all who hinder the satisfaction of my desires.... But loving one's neighbour reason could never discover, because it's unreasonable.'[12] Yet in general, of course, we would say that Anna acts by impulse, while Levin is a steady, consistent reasoner.

His reasoning, however, is not in the Bolkonsky manner, assertive, but is characterized by what Professor Leavis calls that 'tense and pertinacious tentativeness of his.'[13] The passage in which he meets Kitty again and wins her gives us important clues both to the character of Levin and to the nature of Tolstoy's novel.

At Stiva's dinner party, Karenin and others are discussing the education of women. Karenin, of course, thinks it dangerous—it seems to imply female emancipation, a shocking thought for a loyal Tsarist bureaucrat. The Moscow liberal intellectual Pestsov retorts, 'It is a vicious circle. Women are deprived of rights from lack of education, and the lack of education results from the absence of rights.' The subjection of women, he says, is so complete that we take it for granted.

The old prince Shcherbatsky, an old-fashioned Moscow nobleman suspicious of Petersburg dandies and all new-fangled nonsense, in general stands for a point of view which the Tolstoy of *War and Peace* would surely have endorsed. We might therefore suspect that Tolstoy is trying to set us on the Prince's side when he halts the discussion by suggesting that for a woman to demand equality is like him demanding the right to be a wet nurse. But one of the bystanders convulsed with laughter is the good-natured Turovtsyn. And we learn a couple of pages later that this man, when Dolly's children were ill, stayed in the house for three weeks helping her to nurse them. Tolstoy at once, therefore, confronts the Prince's joke with a fact that tells against the Prince.

Later on, Levin and Kitty take up the topic of women's rights between themselves. Levin is a natural ally for the old Prince. He insists that the position of an unmarried woman in the family is a good and useful one; every family, rich or poor, needs nurses, paid or unpaid. But Kitty doesn't agree. A girl, she says, may be so placed that it is humiliating for her to live in the family. Levin at once sees her point and capitulates. 'And he saw all that Pestsov had been driving at at dinner about the freedom of women, simply because he got a glimpse of the terror in Kitty's heart of the humiliation of remaining an old maid; and, loving her, he felt that terror and humiliation. . .'[14]

By contrast, Vronsky cannot see that typically male views of the 'woman question' in general bear on the woman he loves in particular. In the final crisis of his relationship with Anna, she is deeply hurt by his laughing at high schools for girls when she is trying to give the little English orphan she has taken up a good education. Levin is like the Tolstoy who wrote this book, humble before the facts he clearly sees. Vronsky is like most of us, arrogant in the face of facts we don't see clearly. *Anna Karenina* helps us to see more clearly than Vronsky. Anton Chekhov was deeply attracted by this novel, and seems to express one of its essential qualities in his famous remark:

> In *Anna Karenina* and *Eugene Onegin* not a single problem is solved, but they satisfy you completely because all the problems in these works are correctly stated. It is the business of the judge to put the right questions, but the answers must be given by the jury according to their own lights.[15]

Dolly saves herself from despair by housework. Levin proclaims the doctrine of *arbeitskur*, health through work, and loses himself in mowing with the peasants. Tolstoy clearly approves of both these characters. But whereas in *War and Peace*, having found a common trait, as it were, between two sheep, we would look for contrasting goats with quite different attitudes, here goats and sheep share a common nature. Karenin too can lose himself in his bureaucratic labours, and Koznyshev in his participation in the warmongering campaign in support of the Balkan Slavs. And when Levin is so caught up in his mowing that he thinks of nothing and wishes for nothing, isn't this very like Anna's relaxation in high society at the Princess Tverskoy's where she 'was not forced to consider what she was to do. Everything did itself'?[16]

Levin envies the peasants for whom labour is 'its own reward'. Karenin is gratified by the sight of his 'well-arranged writing materials'. Anna (like all women, says Tolstoy) enjoys playing with words and hiding a secret—'And it was not the necessity for secrecy, nor its purpose, but the process itself that attracted her.' Just so, it seems to Levin that his friend Sviazhsky is indifferent to the conclusions of his own reasoning—'It was simply the process of reasoning that appealed to him.'[17] And Mikhailov, the artist, is absorbed in the process of creation.

Is Tolstoy in this novel so fascinated by the process of composing it that for once he loses interest in moralizing and in meaning? And is the result of his process therefore itself a 'process'—a work of art experienced by the writer as the charm of writing and by the reader as aesthetic pleasure in the process of reading, both of these being ends in themselves? Ultimately, no, because *Anna* is challenge as well as pleasure. But Tolstoy himself, while he was composing the novel, wrote to a friendly critic in terms which for a moment suggest a purely 'aesthetic' view of art:

> For the criticism of art people are needed who can show the pointlessness of look-ing for *'ideas'* in a work of art and who can guide readers through that endless labyrinth of linkings in which the essence of art resides, and show them the laws underlying these linkings.

The linking, he argued, wasn't achieved through ideas, but through 'organic necessity'—and its nature couldn't be captured directly in words, only 'indirectly, by words describing images, actions, situations.'[18] Yet paradoxically all this must remind us of the very 'ideas' which Tolstoy had spared no pains to state outright in *War and Peace*. Theories (like Pfuhl's, or Koznyshev's) are inherently suspect and irrelevant. But there are laws, of art as of history, which we must find and respect. Both artist and critic are at their best when they discover and accept the 'laws'. Tolstoy, like his own Kutuzov (he might immodestly have said), achieves great deeds by attuning himself with the 'process'. And it is his charac-teristic conservative anarchism which informs the structure of *Anna Karenina*. Let life speak for itself; its linkings are its laws.

He did indeed have great respect for his own achievement. 'The vaults,' he claimed, 'have been built in such a way that you can't see where the keystone is.'[19] Like *War and Peace*, *Anna* is a vast structure airily raised out of short episodes. Several chapters in a row will have straightforward narrative continuity, as we move with Levin, with Anna, with Stiva or Serezha. But then we will switch from Levin to Anna, from Petersburg to the country. In *War and Peace*, as the title itself suggests, contrast as well as continuity was a fundamental principle. But in *Anna* continuity takes over wholly; continuity so subtle that it often defies the naked eye for a time, although the reader senses it. The 'linkings' ensure that when the setting is changed, somehow the subject isn't changed. A couple of paragraphs or so into the next chapter the link will be found.

A relatively simple system of linkings carries us over the end of Book 6 and through the beginning of Book 7. The last chapter of Book 6 shows us Anna brooding at home while Vronsky is at the elections. 'He has the right to go when and where he chooses.' She is jealous of his male freedom, and also fears that his love for her is waning. 'Just as before, only her love and charm could hold him.' But she can't love her daughter by him. He returns when she summons him back on the pretence that their child is ill and he is, of course, annoyed. They decide that Anna must get a divorce from Karenin, and that they will go to Moscow. They go to Moscow.

Kitty and Levin are already in Moscow at the beginning of Book 7. Kitty is pregnant, as Anna was earlier in the book, and like Anna she feels the child moving within her and this fills her with joy. But Anna, as we have just been reminded, now feels indifferent towards the child she bore with so much pain. Anna was tense and miserable in the last chapter, but Kitty for the moment is calm and happy. Levin, however, is restless, like Vronsky. But whereas Vronsky was restless because he felt circumscribed on his country estate, Levin is ill at ease in the city away from his land. Yet he is successful enough in society—with his 'rather old-fashioned, reserved courtesy to women'—to make Kitty at times jealous. She feels possessive, like Anna, though she doesn't make quarrels as she used to do. 'Like . . . but . . . yet . . . like. . . .'

Kitty meets Vronsky by chance at the home of her godmother. By now we have almost forgotten that she was once in love with Vronsky, but we are reminded when she blushes, though she maintains control of herself. She smiles at a joke Vronsky makes about the nobility elections, which he calls 'our parliament'—and we are jogged to remember, if we can, Anna's envy of the English MP she once read about in a train. Levin is at first discomposed when he hears of this meeting from Kitty, but her 'truthful eyes' reassure him, and he decides to make a friend of Vronsky when they next meet.

One cannot merely point to the contrast established in these two chapters between the two relationships, striking though it is; Kitty and Levin are able, as before, to come to an understanding through looks rather than words, whereas when Vronsky smiles and tells Anna 'there is nothing I wish for more than never to be parted from you,' the look in his eyes is that of a persecuted and vindictive man. There are also potent similarities. Both these relationships are tense and both are menaced by jealousy. Both face the dangers inherent in any demanding relationship, inside or outside marriage.

One could use the glib musical analogy and talk of the same themes being played by different instruments or in different keys. But the word 'theme' in its usual literary meaning seems too limiting. 'The position of women in Russian society' may seem an obvious 'theme', but this is inextricably involved with 'marriage' (Tolstoy thought of calling the book *Two Marriages*) and therefore with the position of men and the position of children. Finally it is even linked with the position of horses. At many points these 'themes', if we can still call them that, flow in with and interact with the 'theme' of 'the peasantry'.

At first sight, Levin's preoccupation with the peasantry seems to isolate him from almost all the other characters in the book. But any notion we might have that it is somehow 'irrelevant' must evaporate when we think hard about Anna's dream.

When Vronsky very early in the book is meeting the train which bears not only his mother but Anna to Moscow, our attention is drawn to one of the first passengers to alight—'a peasant carrying a sack over his shoulder.' Shortly afterwards, it is learnt that a guard has been crushed by the train shunting back. Anna, who has just met Vronsky, says 'It is a bad omen', and this provides one of Tolstoy's few wholly unsubtle linkings, since Anna herself, of course, will die under a train. But the dream which occurs towards the middle of the novel is far from easy to interpret.

First Vronsky dreams it. He has recently been hunting. He dreams that a peasant beater employed by the hunters, a dirty little man with a matted beard, is stooping down 'doing something' and muttering strange, incomprehensible words in French. He wakes full of inexplicable horror.

French is the tongue used by noblemen among themselves when they don't want the servants to understand what they're saying. In his dream Vronsky is like a servant; he can't understand the peasant who is talking French like a master.

Anna calls him to her. She thinks she will die in childbirth, and she says she will soon be 'at peace'. (At this point, Tolstoy in one sentence epitomizes his deep distrust of words: "'I don't understand,' he said, understanding her.") Anna tells him she will die because she has had a dream about it, a long time ago. She dreamt that she ran into her bedroom to fetch something and there was a little peasant with a tangled beard stooping down over a sack and fumbling about in it with his hands. The dream is like Vronsky's, but she has seen more and has picked out French words. They are terrible. 'Il faut le battre, le fer; le broyer, le pétrir.' It must be beaten, must the iron; pound it, knead it. She also hears a servant telling her 'In childbirth you'll die. . . .'

The French words clatter like a railway. Iron—what have we heard about iron? Levin's communist brother, Nikolai, was planning when Levin first saw him in the novel to set up a locksmith's cooperative and there was in the corner of the room a bundle of iron bars assembled towards this enterprise. Just a little further on, Anna had a dream in the train when she went from Moscow back to Petersburg; a peasant started gnawing at something on the wall and then there was a terrible screech and clatter as though someone were being torn to pieces. Then a red light blinded her eyes and a wall blotted everything out; she was dreaming of her own death. As, joyfully, on the platform just afterwards, she met Vronsky again, the ferocious wind rattled a loose sheet of iron.

The dream of the peasant and the bag clearly echoes from her earlier train journeys. The bag is perhaps symbolically Anna's womb; the child which comes from it (or so she fears) will kill her. But the French words sound like a slogan. They are the voice of an implacable force; perhaps of the force which is driving Russia, with its new railways, on into industrialization and the new age of iron. They suggest moreover something new being made out of the brutal handling of metal. And again, because the peasant is speaking French, they imply revolution, when the last shall be first: what Nikolai aimed at.

Anna dreams the dream of the peasant and the sack many times again. What makes it so horrible, we are told, is that this peasant 'seems to be paying no attention to her', but is doing something dreadful to her with the iron. At her very last moment of life, she is aware of a 'little peasant muttering something' who is working on the rails on which she has put herself.[20]

The fate of Anna is somehow deeply linked with that of the peasants to whom she herself in fact pays little attention but who grow the bread she eats and build the railways she travels on.

VI

In the 1870s, Russia was going through an industrial boom. Between 1861 and 1873, 357 new joint stock companies were founded: there had been only 78 before. Alexander II's programme of modernization was dissolving Russia's social structure. The landowning nobility remained a powerful vested interest, but the emancipation of the serfs had weakened many of them grievously and while some converted (as Vronsky sets out to do) to successful capitalist farming, more were now forced to look for jobs—in the army, in the burgeoning professions of law and medicine or (like Stiva) in the bureaucracy and in business.[21]

The bureaucratic class in which noblemen meshed with more plebeian elements was now dominant. The decline of the landowning class which had been visible since the days of Oblomov was now very evident indeed. But it would be foolish to talk of the new ruling class as a 'bourgeoisie'. Unlike the middle classes of Western Europe, it had not emerged spontaneously to split the crust of aristocratic hegemony. It was the instrument of an autocratic state bringing in capitalism from above. An astute British observer noted the difference:

> In England, individuals and companies habitually act according to their private interests, and the State interferes as little as possible; private initiative acts as it pleases, unless the authorities can prove that important bad consequences will necessarily result. In Russia, the *onus probandi* lies on the other side; private initiative is allowed to do nothing until it gives guarantees against all possible bad consequences. When any great enterprise is projected, the first question is—'How will this new scheme affect the interests of the State?'[22]

While agriculture stagnated, modern industries were beginning to suck a small but growing section of the peasantry into mines and factories, and into the railway system. At the time of the Crimean War, Russia had had only 750 miles of railway. By the mid 1870s, this had risen to 11,000. The carriages travelled at what now seem moderate speeds of 15 to 30 miles an hour. But by the standards of the old troika rocking over the ruts, the train was a whirlwind.

Levin's aversion to change is pretty constant. Change means the drift to the cities. Change means the speculations of the railway magnates which so outrage him. The hotel where Nikolai dies is full of 'a sort of up-to-date, complacent railway bustle', and it depresses both Levin and Kitty.

Levin takes up, but discards, the Yashvin-like view that self-interest must be the paramount motive in agriculture. He dislikes capitalism root and branch. But Stiva, whose appointment as 'secretary to the committee of the consolidated agency of credit balance of the southern railways' is ironically confirmed at about the same time as his sister dies, is perfectly at ease, as he tells Levin, with the notion that men can become immensely wealthy through mere speculation.

Levin is a worker on his own land. Dolly is also a worker. When she visits Anna's country house, not long after we have watched her making jam on the terrace of Levin's home, the luxury there makes her feel uncomfortable. 'At home everyone knew that six jackets took over eighteen yards of nainsook at one-and-three a yard', and she has saved a lot of money by patching her old dressing jacket. When Anna appears in a 'very simple muslin gown', Dolly looks very hard at it. 'She knew what such simplicity meant, and what it cost.'[23]

Just so, Levin is ill at ease in Moscow because when he buys liveries for his footman and hall porter, he cannot help calculating that the money represents the 'wages of two labourers for a whole summer, that is, about three hundred days of hard work from early morning till late at night. . .'[24] Like Dolly he knows that what things really cost is work, by people.

Raymond Williams draws a brilliant contrast between Levin on the one hand and Stiva, Vronsky and Karenin on the other:

In each of these men the attitude to work, and thence to other persons, is related to their differing yet alike inadequate attitudes to love. For Vronsky, love is like the life of an officer: vigorous, assertive, attuned in the end to the willingness to kill. For Karenin, the official, love is an aspect of an institution, a marriage conceived solely in social terms. For Stiva, the taker of business opportunities, love is the personal equivalent of conscious negotiation and the confidence trick. Levin, by contrast, learns to reject their kinds of society and their kinds of love in a single process. When he is translating a hundred-rouble note lightly spent in Moscow, into the work of men in the fields, he is involved with values in a sense equally opposed to the conventions of fashionable society and the mere flouting of them. In learning this kind of connection with all that lives, he is learning something deeper than either respectability or personal honour. His learning to love Kitty as a wife, and then to love their child, grows within this whole attachment, which is more mature than anything Anna is allowed to live.[25]

Anna remembers the class which creates her wealth only in dreams. She, her brother and Vronsky, are superbly attractive representatives of a new class, official cum capitalistic, which is embarked on a course of speculative 'modernization' leading to disaster. She herself rushes too far. She doesn't merely accept the railways and English gadgets of the latest sort, she accepts contraception. This idea, completely novel to Dolly and abhorrent, of course, to Tolstoy, is one which shocks a diminishing number of people today. But in accepting it, Anna not only seizes an innovation which we may think desirable, though Tolstoy didn't; she defines her position as a woman for whom sex is becoming an end in itself. Open sexual relationships without marriage usually depend on contraception. Her society cannot yet accept such relationships. Change, to make the point over-crudely, is what kills her—not only the external force of modernization represented by the railway train which runs her over, but her own lurching towards something newer still, the freedom of women relieved from incessant pregnancy and childbirth.

Levin, by contrast, is attached to a slower, to an 'organic', pace of change. One owes, he says, a duty to the land. One must work on it without regard to personal profit and be thankful (in these days) if one can hold on to it and pass it on to one's children. One gets married, the peasants approving of this, so as to have children and to ensure the continuity of the noble family. Contraception, the thwarting of childbirth, is also the thwarting of this kind of organic continuity, and Vronsky, who wants legitimate heirs, is sensitive on this point, as Levin would be.

But Stiva argues effectively when he raises one of the questions which Levin still hasn't solved at the end of the book. Why, Stiva asks, doesn't he hand his property over to the peasants, if he feels so strongly about the gulf in income between the railway speculator and the railway mechanic? Levin can only retort with a pompous assertion, that he has no right to give his land up because he owes certain duties both to the land and to his family, which clearly won't satisfy him indefinitely. Kitty, of course, wouldn't go along with him if he decided to give his land to the peasants; she is completely convinced that one must spend large sums of money on useless liveries for servants. Where Raymond Williams must seem too neat is in implying that all is intrinsically well with Levin's marriage. Not only jealousy, but quarrels over values, lie in wait to attack.

No answers, but all the right questions; one comes back to Chekhov. And also perhaps to Nikolai, to that painfully idealistic brother who is closer to Levin both by birth and by temperament than anyone else in the book, and who drops out of the world of his class altogether. *Anna Karenina* seems in a sense radiant with certainty; Tolstoy himself is so sure in his touch, and he establishes, in spite of sickness and suicide, a wonderfully comforting feeling that life—the life of the peasants, of the meadows and of the marsh birds—goes properly on. Organic processes, those of nature, move as a steady norm against which man's tragic progress must be judged. The process of Tolstoy the craftsman, in its complexity and its 'naturalness' seems a perfect fit for life itself. This seems to be the complete victory of realism, the book which is reality, and makes reality seem good.

But because Tolstoy was prophetically attuned to the Russia of his day, to its changing reality, Anna's tragedy is linked with the looming revolution of the urbanized peasant as fully as Levin's problems are linked with those of Tolstoy himself; the links, in short, reach out past the novel's end. *Anna* is rich in meanings and ideas, and all these are suffused with history—the history of Russia—and with personality—the personality of Tolstoy.

VII

Tolstoy's family lived in luxurious style, with throngs of liveried footmen, with French and German tutors. He could afford it; his estates were bringing him in 10,000 roubles a year, and the royalties of his novels gave him a further 20,000.

Like Levin, Tolstoy loved his own class and was proud of it. The ideal of family happiness which he had had in mind throughout *Anna* was one designed to secure its continuity. Yet, as he saw, it could not continue. There was now a revolutionary movement in Russia determined to raise the peasants in violence against their masters. Violence threatened all happiness. But what hope could there be of avoiding it so long as injustice was done to the peasant?

Tolstoy's class had two alternatives. It could either go on as it did now and die disgracefully under the raised sickles of those whom it had exploited, or it could preserve its moral dignity by abolishing itself.

After 1878, Tolstoy dedicated himself to persuading his own class to abolish itself. He saw himself, of course, as a prophet for everyone all over the world. During the 1880s he wrote many moral stories addressed to the poor, simple tales which were in effect parables, though they could not leave his hands without some of the subtleties of literature. But in effect his philosophy expressed his wish that his own class would die out with dignity, reconciled with virtue.

Men should not be violent towards each other because that is morally wrong. Peasants, it follows, should not rise and slay their masters. The poor can live virtuously by staying poor and turning the other cheek as Christ instructed. The rich can live well only by giving up their way of life. They should return their wealth to the poor who have created it and live and work like other men. And, Tolstoy comes to believe, they should practice celibacy if they can.

When Vronsky at last enjoys Anna's flesh, we are told that he feels 'what a murderer must feel when he looks at the body he has robbed of life.'[26] Sex, as the great girl-grasper of Yasnaia Poliana had experienced it and as he now understood it, was a form of aggression by the male against the female.

But if we stop committing sex, the family itself will disappear. Very well, let the family disappear. What then is the role of women to be? The abolition of the family would rob them of what Tolstoy has seen as their proper sphere of life. In his later fiction, he finds two new roles for them. On the one hand, they may be agents of evil. The title of the short story he called *The Devil* refers to the loose woman whose sexual vitality tempts the hero and morally destroys him. Within the home the female obsession with clothes, status and property of all kinds is a force preventing the would-be Tolstoyan moral hero from liberating himself and living simply and well. In Tolstoy's unfinished play, *The Light Shines in Darkness*, the light is the conscience of the hero which tells him to give all his wealth to the poor. The darkness is loud with females telling him this is nonsense. On the other hand, with sex and the family discarded, women may become pure and good, morally and in all else the equals of men. This is how Tolstoy projects Maria Pavlovna and even Maslova in *Resurrection*.

He has struck at the two foundations of Levin's moral mansion. The family becomes a sphere, not of virtue but of war and of degrading armistices sealed under the sheets of the marital bed. The birth of children arising from such vileness becomes a misfortune, and therefore the keeping-up of the land in good condition so as to hand it over to one's heirs also becomes morally worse than null.

All this, on paper, offered Tolstoy a solution at once to his own personal moral crisis and to the political crisis ahead of his class. In practice, however, he remained a wealthy man with a wife who in spite of her decay still allured him sexually and with children whose interests he could not despise and to whose consciences he could not dictate. This was his personal tragedy.

In his attempt to square his own circle, all he could do was become a kind of male woman. His wife took over his business affairs, and with them his male rapacity and guilt. He became the moral guardian of the family, the doer of good works outside the home and the devotee of banal physical labour—all these roles which his Dolly and Kitty had assumed. His marriage, which he had so successfully dominated in its early years, now rang with the clash of equals. And Tolstoy became, like his own mother, and like her imaginary picture Maria in *War and Peace*, the patron of wandering pilgrims who dreamed of joining them on the open road and leading the free life of the pure spirit.

VIII

The early stages of his crisis were very much present while he was writing *Anna* and found expression in Levin's spiritual struggles. Like Levin, he turned to the Orthodox Church in which his peasants worshipped. But its services were in conflict with his own common sense, and he broke with it in 1880. He began to work on the Gospels so as to extract an acceptable message out of them, informed by his belief that Christ was not God, but the son of God, and that the foundation of His teaching was that to achieve salvation it was necessary all the time to think of God and of one's soul, and therefore to set the love of one's neighbour above mere animal existence.

He wrote in his *Confession* of the struggles which had led to his leaving the church. He attacked the teachings of Orthodoxy in his *Criticism of Dogmatic Theology* (1880), rejecting among others the doctrines of the Trinity, of the immaculate conception and of eternal damnation. His *Union and Translation of the Four Gospels* (1882) retold Christ's story the way he thought it should be. (The rewriting of the Bible had been a favourite tactic of Voltaire's more than a hundred years before.) In *What I Believe* (1883) he confronted the world with what he took to be Christ's six basic commandments. 'Thou shalt not be angry, thou shalt not commit adultery, thou shalt not swear, thou shalt not resist evil by evil, thou shalt have no enemies, thou shalt love God and thy neighbour as thyself.' His heresies could not be published in Russia, but they circulated in manuscript and were printed in translation abroad.

He went on a pilgrimage to the Optina Pustyn Monastery in 1881, on foot and dressed like a peasant. But when the monks knew he was there they offered him a velvet hung bedroom, which he didn't refuse. Returning home in a third class railway carriage, he was met at Tula station by his coachman. He could neither wipe away his fame nor get over habits of comfortable living he had had all his life. He shortly succumbed to his wife's urgings that they must set up house in Moscow so that the elder children could study there. He bought a property standing amid factories on the industrial outskirts, but it had a large garden, and cost him 27,000 roubles. He drew water for the family and polished his own boots; later he started to take lessons in cobbling. Sonia wrote to her sister, 'He is a man ahead of his time, he marches in front of the crowd and shows the way it must follow. And I am one of the crowd. . . I cannot walk any faster than the crowd to which I am bound. . .'[27]

Now that his wife could not be his disciple, he needed another devoted confidant. He found one in Vladimir Chertkov, an elegant aristocrat who resigned from the army and gave himself up completely to Tolstoy's ideas. While Sonia, complaining they were short of money, drove him to sign over to her the right to manage not only his property, as she did already, but the copyrights of all his books published before 1881, and began to publish a collected edition, Chertkov collaborated with him in a company which aimed to produce small, good books for the common people at five kopecks each.

In 1886, Tolstoy resumed his career as a major creative writer, publishing his long short story *The Death of Ivan Ilich* and completing the best of his several plays, *The Powers of Darkness*, a tragedy of peasant life which the Tsar found 'too realistic' and 'too horrible' and which was accordingly banned both from performance and publication. Sonia's misery, however, increased. She had given her life to Lev and to their children—the thirteenth and last was born in 1888—and now she was kept at a distance from him and his work while smelly disciples as well as distinguished foreigners came to pay court to the great prophet and added to the burdens of her housekeeping. As a consummate, if unintentional cruelty, he did give her to copy, in 1889, his new long short story, *The Kreutzer Sonata*, which expressed his recently consolidated theory that sex was evil and repudiated altogether the old theory that woman's most noble calling was marriage and childbirth. The work was of course banned, but circulating in manuscript it caused a public sensation, amid which Sonia felt exposed to ridicule and humiliation. Yet, as a still-loyal wife and as a businesswoman she appealed personally to the Tsar to permit publication of the story, which Tolstoy had given her as a present, in her collected edition; and the Tsar agreed. *The Devil* and *Father Sergius*, two further stories presenting sex as vice, which Tolstoy worked on at this time, were neither published nor finally polished.

Sonia, of course, wouldn't let him give his land to the peasants. A compromise was worked out by 1892. Tolstoy effected a Lear-like division of his estate into ten shares which he made over to his wife and their nine surviving children, As a *quid pro quo*, he was permitted to renounce publicly his copyrights to all his work since 1881, which meant that anyone who wanted could print it freely and that publishers, not Tolstoy, would make fat profits. So he no longer carried the guilt of directly exploiting anyone. He lived on the property now legally owned by his wife and children.

IX

The Death of Ivan Ilich is a story constructed to anathematize society and the Russian state which goes beyond this to a denial, in effect, of the value of life itself. Its central figure is an average man of the Petersburg ruling class—a civil servant and worse still (from Tolstoy's point of view) a judge, whose chief interests in life are work, which helps him to forget his unsatisfactory marriage, and playing cards with friends for money. Without strongly-marked personal traits, he is almost an abstract conception, a sour new version of basic Tolstoyan man. The provinces where he worked in the past are unnamed, his family and friends are sketchy malevolent shadows. Ivan Ilich dies at the age of forty-five from a very painful abdominal disease. As he lies suffering, he realizes that his family are impatient for him to die, that no one really sympathizes with him except his kind and helpful servant, the peasant Gerassim, and that his whole shallow, conformist existence has been 'a lie and a deception'. As with Andrei in *War and Peace*, his death is an awakening:

> He searched for his former habitual fear of death and did not find it. 'Where is it? What death?' There was no fear because there was no death either. In place of death there was light.[28]

But whereas Andrei's sufferings and awakening are set against a background of vivid life in which good and evil are mixed, here the contrast resolves itself into one between bad life and good death. The stylized and not very convincing figure of the healthy, cheerful peasant Gerassim is the only substantial indication we have in the story that another and better way of life is possible. The implication is fully intentional—Tolstoy believes that the life of the good peasant is the only meaningful one. His over-simplified moral ideas did not prevent him from writing later on stories which carry them but which are not in themselves over-simplified. The trouble with *Ivan Ilich* is that it is too well designed so as to impose on the reader Tolstoy's over-simplification. It is too simple.

We see what happens from two points of view beside Tolstoy's own sarcastic one. The first is that of Piotr Ivanovich, a still more rudimentary Tolstoyan Man who goes to view Ivan Ilich's corpse and then stays while the priest conducts a service, wishing that he could get off and play cards. The second, of course, is that of Ivan Ilich. Piotr Ivanovich is an uncomfortable payer of meaningless last respects and his depression conditions his unpleasant view of the dead man's family. Ivan Ilich's own view is conditioned by his illness. Neither vision is adequate to convey fairly the characters of the other people introduced. The view of the world which Anna takes on her last journey—'Everything's hateful. . . . Why these churches, the bells and the humbug? Just to hide the fact that we all hate each other. . .'[29]—governs almost every detail in *Ivan Ilich*. For the moment, Tolstoy himself seems as sick and obsessive as Anna.

But in *The Kreutzer Sonata*, Tolstoy showed he could still struggle to a sufficient distance from his own more absurd and anti-human views to write first rate fiction again. Though Chekhov rightly complained that Tolstoy had held forth in it on medical matters he knew nothing about and didn't wish to understand, he added that the story deserved gratitude because it was 'extremely thought-provoking'.[30] So far from imposing Tolstoy's view of life upon us, it challenges us to think for ourselves. Like certain plays of Ibsen, and Hardy's *Jude the Obscure*, which are roughly contemporary with it in time, it confronts the crisis in the European concept of marriage brought about by the growing rebelliousness of women. And it shares with these same works a quality which makes them both extremely uneven artistically and extremely compelling. In their irritable desire to expose lies at the heart of the institution of marriage, all three writers are crude, cruel and repetitive, but their work in subverting cherished post-Romantic fatuities about love and marriage is still important and rawly fresh.

The story is simply summarized. In a railway carriage, the narrator meets Pozdnyshev, who breaks into a discussion about divorce and marriage among his fellow passengers to announce that he is the famous murderer who killed his wife. He then harangues the submissive narrator with the story of his marriage, which he represents as typical of present-day marriages among the upper class—of its rapid decline into mutual hostility punctuated by brief reconciliations in bed; of his wife's attraction, after she has borne five children, by a shallow violinist with whom she plays Beethoven's 'Kreutzer' sonata; and of his murdering her when he surprises her alone with the musician.

According to Pozdnyshev, sex is a vice which experienced debauchees like himself (and Tolstoy) cultivate in the upper-class virgins they marry. Celibacy is better even than the most chaste marriage. The dangers of the manner in which Pozdnyshev (like Tolstoy) wilfully assimilates the 'good' with the 'natural' are illustrated in the freakish passage where Pozdnyshev argues that sex, of all things, is 'unnatural'—'Ask a child, ask an unperverted girl'—and indicates that the natural end of the human race is to wean itself away from its lust and its childbearing and so, decently, die out.

Pozdnyshev (like Tolstoy) despises doctors—they try to prevent children from dying in accordance with God's will. More reasonably, he condemns music. Like Tolstoy, he is deeply moved by it and is suspicious of the mere purposeless agitation, the sense of 'quite new feelings, new possibilities' which the playing of his wife and her lover awakens in him. All students of Tolstoy's work are as clear as Sonia was that Tolstoy endorses Pozdnyshev's views, and his new mistrust of art gives obvious licence to those who dismiss *The Kreutzer Sonata* as inartistic propaganda. R. F. Christian (though he isn't one of these) writes that 'The narrator's role, apart from occasional interruptions, is negligible; he is not important enough to form a barrier between Pozdnyshev and the reader, or between the author and his hero.'[31]

But that isn't true. The narrator is indeed no more than a note-taker. But amongst other things, he notes Pozdnyshev's look and mannerisms. Before the latter gets into his stride, our attention is drawn to his 'unusual glittering eyes' and the 'strange sound he emitted, something like a clearing of his throat, or a laugh begun and sharply broken off.' As he talks, he drinks very strong tea, and he is a heavy smoker who 'greedily' inhales. We don't need to have read other novels by Tolstoy, in which such traits are clearly used to alienate our sympathies from those who have them, in order to recognize at once that however much we may understand and even sympathize with Pozdnyshev we can't be expected to 'identify' with him. We cannot help receiving his opinions as those of a very neurotic man. Tolstoy did not murder his own wife, nor would his principles have permitted him to do so. 'You know,' says Pozdnyshev, 'I am a sort of lunatic.'

Unlike *Ivan Ilich, The Kreutzer Sonata* is respectful before the contradictions and dilemmas of human experience and thought. It would be unfair to blame Tolstoy for never admitting that Pozdnyshev's wife might have had good reason for wanting to escape from his jealousy into a new relationship with a gifted man. Pozdnyshev himself is telling the story. His memory, he himself admits, is fallible. The tale is candidly offered as one told by a self-obsessed and unbalanced man. And we must admire the courage of a writer who dared to present his own views to the public in this way, as well as the clarity with which in spite of the limitations of his spokesman he does expose real issues.

Men, Pozdnyshev tells us, dominate society. They ensure that women get just enough education, of just the right sort, to ensure that they can fulfill the role which men want them to take up, that of 'instruments of enjoyment'. You do not free slaves, Pozdnyshev points out, by abolishing the external form of slavery and arranging that slaves are no longer bought and sold; so long as the many are exploited by the few they are still in effect slaves:

> Well, and they liberate woman, give her all sorts of rights equal to man, but continue to regard her as an instrument of enjoyment, and so educate her in childhood and afterwards by public opinion. And there she is, still the same humiliated and depraved slave, and the man still a depraved slave owner.[32]

No feminist spokesman has ever gone further, though what primarily worries Tolstoy, of course, is the effect of this slavery on men, who are corrupted by immoral power and also exposed to the 'revenge' taken by women who use sensuality as a means of dominating their owners. It is not the 'eternal battle of the sexes' or any such nonsense that he is writing about in the *Kreutzer Sonata*—as the analogy with slavery shows, he confronts a problem of modern society which is involved with the capitalistic and bureaucratic habit of defining and treating people as if they were objects. We cannot bear to exploit human beings, so we turn people into objects and exploit those instead—and this general attitude is inevitably reflected even in the relationships of the marriage bed.

Beside *The Kreutzer Sonata, The Devil* (1889) must seem a throwback. Its hero Irtenev shares a common name with the narrator of *Childhood*, and, as this suggests, is a conscientious but weak-willed landowner like those who figure so plentifully in Tolstoy's early fiction. Even though happily married, he is tempted to fornicate again with the peasant woman he formerly had a liaison with 'for his health's sake'. Two conclusions to the story survive; in one Irtenev kills the peasant woman and in the other himself. Both are melodramatic and unconvincing. But the contrast between the peasant woman's animal vigour and the feeble pleasantness of Irtenev's wife is vividly realized and emphasizes in the most striking way Tolstoy's loss of faith in his own class. *Father Sergius* (1890–1898) would perhaps have been a masterpiece had Tolstoy ever given it final polish, and as it stands it is extremely powerful. A brilliant Petersburg officer throws up his career and enters a monastery when he discovers that his wife-to-be is a former mistress of Tsar Nicholas I. Eventually, he becomes a hermit and when a beautiful divorcee, for a bet, tries to tempt him to bed with her he cuts off his left index finger with an axe and thus withstands temptation. His fame spreads and his spiritual life suffers as he becomes a focus for throngs of pilgrims. He succumbs to the sexual advance of a feeble-minded girl who has come to him to be cured of neurasthenia. He runs away dressed as a peasant, roams the roads, and ends up working as hired man for a well-to-do Siberian peasant. He has broken with formal religion and from Tolstoy's standpoint his simple life of hard work for others is preferable to his former aspirations to sainthood.

Father Sergius's fifty years of moral striving take him from summit to bottom of Russian society. Tolstoy craves the extinction of his own kind of man. But the story is not crudely moralistic. Its combination of hard realistic detail with a folk-lore like fable brings it closer than any of Tolstoy's other major work to the stories of Leskov, a splendid writer who in the 1880s became for a while a convert to Tolstoy's ideas.

NOVELS

Just as the portly appearance of most nineteenth-century English 'novels' reflects the convention of publication in three volumes, so the infinitely variable lengths of Russian masterpieces derive from conditions where stories were initially published complete, or serially, in the 'fat journals', hefty reviews, most of which came out monthly and which sold up to ten thousand copies to members of the small educated public. The results threaten literary critics with a terminological anarchy.

Leskov poses especially fiddlesome problems for those worthy people who wish to define and generalize about the 'nineteenth-century novel'. His *Cathedral Folk* is a fat book which is always called a 'novel' but which is like a collection of shortish sketches, while his *Enchanted Wanderer* is a 'long short story' approaching the length of many present-day 'novels' and with a wider range of character and incident than most of them. It belongs to the same category of amphibian masterpieces as Turgenev's *First Love*, Tolstoy's *Cossacks* and Chekhov's *My Life*.

The term 'novella' at first sight seems convenient, but of course it solves nothing—how long, we would have to ask, is a 'novella'? I am unrepentant about preferring the oafish but honest usage 'long short story' because its sheer bad manners will always remind the reader that definition is impossible. Further discussion may be left to the spiritual descendants of those medieval scholars who argued about the number of angels who (or which) could dance on the head of a pin. My rule of thumb goes like this. A work of fiction under forty or so printed Penguin pages is, self-evidently, a 'short story'. Works of similar character which go on longer are therefore 'long short stories' except when the world has agreed to call them novels. Anything over 175 such pages in length is probably a novel. Publishers who produce long short stories in large print so that they look on the shelf like novels are deceiving the public.

8
LITERATURE AND MORALITY
Leskov, Chekhov, late Tolstoy

Leskov's Russian style, full of slang and puns and freshly-coined words, must clearly present exceptional problems for the translator. But what is left over in English is still potent and delightful. His pages swarm with life, and it is often life of a kind which other novelists rarely show us. He is in love as none of his great contemporaries are with the characteristic tempi of provincial Russia; he finds gusto where they see banality. He pokes fun at popular superstitions, yet he enjoys them, and he writes with affection and respect of ignorant priests, drunken oafs and incompetent policemen. His moral stance, however, is always sturdy and can't be misconstrued; he is a Christian, though neither an intolerant nor a ritualistic one, and the centre of his Christianity is loving forgiveness. In one of his stories, he reminds us of Hamlet's words—'Use every man after his desert and who should scape whipping?' His characters often find themselves at odds with atrocious social conditions and the stupidity of the autocracy, and they are often destroyed by these forces. Yet Leskov's Russia is full of light and colour and fresh air. His people behave with an unself-conscious sense of their own ineradicable freedom.

He was born in Orel province in 1831, and his father was a priest's son turned civil servant. After the death of his parents, he had to leave school at sixteen. He worked as a junior clerk in the Orel criminal court and later transferred to Kiev where his uncle was a Professor of Medicine and where he mingled with learned people. But he was essentially self-taught, and was proud of remaining closer to the ordinary people than other novelists had done. When at twenty-six he left the civil service and went to work for another uncle, a Russified Englishman named Scott, his job took him all over Russia and gave him an unusually wide and varied knowledge of the country.

He began to write, as a part-time journalist, only in 1860. Two years later he went to Petersburg, where he soon fell out with the radicals. He wrote two political novels which they resented and was scorned by the critics as a reactionary, so that, as Mirsky puts it, all his popularity was 'entirely owing to the unguided good taste of the public'.[1]

His best known 'novel', *Cathedral Folk* (1872) certainly shows a fondness for old ways and directs heavy-footed satire at 'progressive' and 'nihilistic' intellectuals; the scheming Termosesov is a conception not far from Dostoevsky's Piotr Verkhovensky, though much cruder. But this is not a tamely conformist book. Its heroes are the clergy at the cathedral of a petty provincial centre called Stargorod, 'Old Town'. Archpriest Tuberozov isn't content to let the Church be no more than the spiritual arm of the State. He preaches a sermon attacking the worldliness and lack of true faith of the officials; this is thought seditious, and he is suspended from his priestly duties. It is significant that at this crisis of his life he turns to the English religious writer John Bunyan. Leskov himself had been influenced by his Aunt Polly, an English Quaker, and like his creator Tuberozov seems close in spirit to some of the gentler forms of Protestant dissent. His subordinate Deacon Akhilla, a Cossack with the build of a legendary hero and the heart of a child, embarrasses him by his noisy escapades, but is utterly devoted to him. Leskov loves them both, and makes it clear that all right-minded people should do so, even at the cost of preferring Akhilla's Orthodox superstitions to the 'scientific' ideas of the local schoolmaster.

Cathedral Folk seems less constructed than bundled together, a medley of laughable anecdotes and scenes of simple pathos drawn from an essentially uneventful provincial life. But its repeated lurchings from expectation to anti-climax are steadied by the touching death of the Archpriest, followed by that of his heartbroken deacon. The book's dry last sentence—'The time had come for an entirely new cathedral staff at Stargorod'—seems to crystallize both Leskov's regret for old ways dying and his acceptance of the inevitability of change.

Leskov attracted conservative patronage—the Empress herself obtained an official post for him, a near-sinecure. But he lost this in the early 1880s for writing a satirical story, and was drawn for a time to the ideas of Tolstoy, who in turn admired Leskov's work and included one of his tales in his first series of cheap booklets for the masses. Leskov's very last work, *The March Hare*, written in 1895, the year of his death, couldn't be published until 1917; it is a sly but emphatic satire of the Tsarist State's efforts to suppress radical ideas. Its story is mostly told by its central figure, a good-natured, ill-educated Ukrainian squireling who, as sub-district police officer, becomes obsessed with the idea of getting a medal for capturing a subversive, and is eventually certified mad. Leskov was certainly not an escapist writer. He once wrote: 'I love literature as something that enables me to express what I regard as truth and what I esteem to be good for humanity at large. . . . The term "art for art's sake" is entirely incomprehensible to me. Art must be of benefit to mankind, for it is only then that it acquires a definite meaning.'[2]

Some of his stories seem at first sight no more than droll anecdotes cleverly told, but the famous *Left Handed Craftsman* (1881) combines hilarious invention with serious point. It is based on a folk-saying—'The English made a flea out of steel, but our Tula craftsmen shoed it and sent it back.' Its manner suggests that of a traditional tale, and on one level it is a laughing tribute to the skill and imagination of the Russian people. But in the telling, two Tsars are cheekily cut down to human size, and the eventual death of the cross-eyed, left-handed genius who helped to shoe the flea, denied admission to Petersburg hospitals when he arrives home from England utterly drunk, makes an unmistakeable comment on the low valuation placed on craftsmanship and on the lives of working people in Tsarist Russia.

Leskov's intelligent jesting reminds us, perhaps, of Mark Twain. So does his favourite method of telling a story in the voice of a rather simple-minded central figure whose own ignorance and superstition flavour the whole with rich humour. *The Amazon*, a tale from the 1860s, splices gossipy self exposure with non-commital but distancing comment by a narrator whom we must take to be Leskov himself. This narrator is both fond of and shocked by the buxom Petersburg procuress who describes to him how she started a prominent courtesan off on her career. In Dostoevsky's hands. Domna Platonovna would surely have been odious. But Leskov *enjoys* this self-pitying provincial widow who after her husband's death accepted that the rule of life is trick or be tricked—a 'woman in whom prayers and fasts and her own chastity, of which she was inordinately proud, and her pity for the unfortunate were combined with barefaced lying. . .'[3] She follows her corrupt trade because it seems forced on her by the 'blind, but terrible force of "the Petersburg circumstances" ', yet she shows she is free to behave quite differently when she ruins herself for the sake of a worthless youth she falls in love with.

Domna Platonovna comes from the Mtsensk district, the scene of Leskov's most famous 'short short story'. Katerina Izmailova, *Lady Macbeth of the Mtsensk District*, is a young and passionate peasant woman who married a wealthy merchant at her parents' bidding and leads a dreary, childless life under her husband's strict authority. In revolt, she lets herself be seduced by Sergei, a handsome and impudent clerk who covets the family fortune. She murders her father-in-law and then, with Sergei, her husband; then they are caught in the act of smothering the boy who is co-heir to the business and are sentenced to penal servitude in Siberia. The scene of the child's murder is agonizing. Yet Leskov in effect compels us, even after that, to sympathize with Katerina, who is betrayed by Sergei for another woman convict as they make their way East, and who finally pulls her rival into the Volga, where both drown. The last image concentrates meaning superbly:

> Sonetka disappeared again. Two seconds later, carried away from the ferry by the current, she raised her arms once more, but Katerina broke from another wave, emerging almost to the waist, and threw herself on Sonetka like a strong pike on a soft little perch, and neither appeared again.[4]

Since both women are in the water, to compare them with fish seems only 'natural'. Yet the image clinches all the vigour and menace of Katerina's character and implies an acceptable moral stance, that of the ordinary decent man. Leskov, like all of us, admires a forceful character, is impressed with such energy, yet condemns murder. He makes this viewpoint seem self-justifying, but only because his far from ordinary skill can find, in the pike, just the image he needs.

The same kind of hard-won simplicity and directness of vision is found in the wonderful passage where Katerina, already a murderer once, makes love with her Sergei in the garden on a sultry night:

> 'Look, Sergei! Oh my darling! What a paradise, what a paradise!' Katerina cried, looking up through the thick branches of the blossoming apple tree into the clear, blue sky where the full moon shone serenely.
>
> She lay on her back under the tree and the moonlight, streaming through the leaves and blossoms, drifted across her face and body forming bizarre spots. The air was still; only a light, warm breeze slightly stirred the sleepy leaves, scattering the faint fragrance of blossoming herbs and leaves. Every breath she drew filled her with languor, laziness, and dark voluptuous desires.
>
> Getting no reply, Katerina was again silent and kept gazing at the sky through the pale pink blossoms of the apple tree. Sergei, too, said nothing, but it was not the sky which interested him. Clasping his knees with both arms, he gazed intently at his boots.
>
> A lovely night! Stillness, light, scented air, and beneficent life-giving warmth. Far away, beyond the ravine, on the other side of the garden, someone began singing loudly; in the bird-cherry thicket near the fence a nightingale trilled once and then burst into song; a sleepy quail in a cage set on a long pole uttered a few shrill calls, and a fat horse sighed languorously behind the stable wall, while a pack of excited dogs ran noiselessly across the common behind the garden fence and disappeared into the hideous black shadows of the ancient, almost dilapidated, salt warehouses.[5]

Katerina's extreme but wholly human sexual passion is in tune with the evening which excites it. Sergei doesn't really love her and doesn't yield himself to the paradisal night. The setting seems to endorse Katerina's passion—and we do reserve throughout the story the feeling that her abundance of life, trapped in a loveless marriage, has a right to escape. But the details which Leskov selects unobtrusively pull us away from participation in Katerina's sensuality towards unease over its consequences. The quail, like Katerina, is caged, and its call is shrill, though the nightingale is free and beautiful. The languors of horses and the mating of dogs are nothing very exalted and the dark warehouses remind us of the unattractive realities of life among the merchant classes at the same time as they loom like omens of evil and decay. We are given a heightened sense of the beauty of the world and of Katerina's fine human qualities, but we are not permitted to forget her animality or her crime.

Lady Macbeth is in form an orthodox short narrative. *The Enchanted Wanderer* (1873) is a far harder work to categorize. It is something like a cross between *Pilgrim's Progress* and *Huckleberry Finn*. On one level it is the exciting saga of a modest hero cast in the traditional folk-tale mould; on another it is a pack of superstitious fibs spilled out by a straight-faced, self-deceiving buffoon; on a third it tells of a good man's quest for salvation. Again, we are distanced by a Leskovian reporter from the man who tells his life-story—Ivan Fliagin, now a monastic novice, who reveals himself in a breathless succession of incidents to be a former serf, thief, male nursemaid, prisoner of the Tartars, horse-trader, reluctant murderer, soldier, civil servant, actor and minor prophet. He has huge strength and a remarkable way with horses. His literal-minded Orthodox piety constantly produces the most paradoxical results, as when the jilted gypsy girl he adores persuades him to murder her so as to save her from the sins of suicide or prostitution. He has the spirit of an 'artist', deeply moved by beauty in horses and women, as well as the spirit of a fighter who, when we leave him at last, seems to be hankering to shed his monastic garb and soldier in another war. He credibly combines extremes of self-denial and self-indulgence, of gentleness and violence, of shrewdness and stupidity. But he is never vengeful or mean, and though he hardly seems to know what truth is, he seems unfailingly candid. He takes for granted the rascals and Tartars, officers and actors he moves among, accepts them for what they are, and defines himself by doing otherwise. Leskov seems to express through him attractive traits of the Russian people which Dostoevsky couldn't have declared through Shatov and which Tolstoy ignored in his Karataev.

Above all, he projects the Russian wanderlust. His travels take him from Caspian Sea to Finnish border. He attributes his adventures to such supernatural agencies as a prophecy made to him in a dream by an old monk he once killed by chance with his horsewhip, and the 'magnetism' cast on him by a down-at-heels gentleman drunk. He never articulates what we may take to be his real motive, a restlessness under all restraints not self-imposed, an urge to keep moving whatever the consequences. The Russia he roams seems much more like Twain's USA than either was like Europe—it is a land of long roads and vast horizons beckoning to the wanderer who can ride well and use his fists. Fliagin, one feels, would be no more and no less at home with Sitting Bull and General Custer than he is with his Tartar Khans and the Russian force in the Caucasus. Expert tamer of Khirgiz wild horses, he tells us that these creatures love freedom so much that he had to pity those who refused oats and water and wasted away; and he is akin to these animals which he maltreats but understands.

In 1883, the editor Leikin introduced to Leskov his prize contributor, a very young writer who greatly admired him. Anton Chekhov described this encounter to his brother:

Half drunk, he turned to me and asked: 'Do you know who I am?'
'Yes, I know.'
'No you don't know. I'm a mystic.'
'I know this.'
Staring at me with his old eyes he prophesied: 'You will die before your brother.'
'Perhaps.'
'I'll anoint you with oil, as Samuel anointed David. Write.'
We parted friends.[6]

Chekhov's style owed less to Leskov's than did that of Maxim Gorky, who matched the old man's exuberance and bright colour. But Chekhov does have a robust yet gentle compassion for his fellow humans which is akin to Leskov's, as well as much of his sense of fun.

II

Leskov was the latest-born of the major writers of fiction who grew up in the reign of Nicholas I. The generations from 1831 to 1860, when Chekhov was born, produced great scientists and composers, brilliant lawyers and historians, but no masters of prose narrative whose names have much meaning outside Russia. Mere accident may have been at work, but it is probable that, as Mirsky suggests, the relatively 'liberal' climate of intellectual life under Alexander II diverted men of great talent from creative writing. Political journalism was now possible. In a modernizing Russia, science and the emerging professions of law and medicine attracted clever young men who were in any case warned off the arts by the prevailing utilitarianism of the Chernyshevsky school of literary-cum-social critics.[7] The deaths of Turgenev and Dostoevsky and Tolstoy's distraction by neo-Christian ideas marked, in the early 1880s, the end of a phase of monumental achievements in Russian fiction, and a relative anti-climax followed. The next quarter-century saw the later masterpieces of Tolstoy, but younger writers achieved most in the short story form. Chekhov and Maxim Gorky (1868–1936) were, of course, great masters of it, and they were followed by a fresh wave of notable talent including Alexander Kuprin and Ivan Bunin (both born in 1870) and Leonid Andreev (1871–1919).

Tsar Alexander III, who succeeded his murdered father in 1881, brought in a new phase of intensified reaction. Many liberal trends were reversed. The Tsar's chief mentor was Konstantin Pobedonostsev, a learned man and friend of Dostoevsky whose ideas mixed populism, nationalism and religious piety with a fanatical devotion to autocracy. As procurator of the Holy Synod, he did his best to repress sectarians, and he influenced the policy of 'Russification' which sought to destroy the cultural individuality of the lesser peoples within the Empire. This was the epoch of 'Jingoism' in Europe, and Russian bureaucrats obeyed its spirit by seeking to impose Russian language and Russian institutions not only on the chronically rebellious Poles and on the Ukrainians and Tartars, but also on the traditionally loyal Baltic Germans. Discrimination against Jews increased and the authorities winked at frequent pogroms.

If Tolstoy's ideas attracted many people, including Leskov and Chekhov, this must have been partly because left wing populism was in retreat and Marxism had not yet surfaced as an alternative. The expression of rebellious ideas became still more difficult, though the populist-Socialist Mikhailovsky was able to maintain even under harsher censorship the utilitarian tradition of literary criticism. Government policy aimed deliberately at keeping people of humble origins out of the secondary schools and universities and showed the reverse of enthusiasm for primary education of the masses. A census of 1897 revealed that only 21 per cent of the population of the Empire could read or write.[8]

'Intelligentsia' is a term of Russian origin which seems to date from the 1860s and refers to all the people who took an interest in general ideas. It was virtually synonymous with disaffection from the Government. As Hugh Seton Watson points out, it is 'most revealing' that when A. S. Suvorin, later Chekhov's friend and publisher, talked once with Dostoevsky, both these right-wingers agreed that if they knew of an impending attempt to kill the Tsar they could not bring themselves to denounce it to the police.[9] Journalists, artists, teachers and professional men were now far more numerous than their counterparts had been thirty years before, but as Chekhov's stories and plays so often suggest to us, their position was desperately cramping. Between ideas and action the gulf was as wide as ever and the 'superfluity' which Onegin and Rudin had once exemplified now characterized an entire class. Only in modest piecemeal attempts to improve the lot of the people did principled and useful action seem possible, and Government policies made these so difficult that it was like trudging up a downward-moving escalator.

Alexander III's government set out to uproot or smother the frail shoots of local 'democracy' planted under his father. In 1889 elected justices of the peace were abolished and 'land captains' were appointed to keep the peasants and their village assemblies in order. In the following year the representation of peasants in the zemstvo's was reduced. Initiative by the zemstvo's was impeded—the official attitude was that all efforts on behalf of the people's welfare should come from the central government. Nevertheless, the zemstvo's were surprisingly active in providing schools and medical services. The idealism which went into such work gave the zemstvo activists the character almost of a political movement, and their employment of doctors, teachers and engineers created a new factor in Russian life—a large class of poorly paid professional people, usually with radical views, who were in a sense heirs of the *narodniks* of the 1870s, bridging the gap between the intelligentsia and the peasants.

But the lot of the peasants generally worsened. The need to find cash to keep up redemption payments for land allocated in the 1860s and to pay the Government's crushing taxes helped to break up the old communal-cum-patriarchal peasant culture, while the population increased and the relative shortage of land meant that wide areas hovered on the brink of catastrophic famine. The period after the Emancipation saw the growth of a sub-class of *kulak*'s ('fists'), lucky peasants who became 'village capitalists', shopkeepers, traders and money-lenders and who feature prominently in Chekhov's stories of rural life. The condition of the peasantry seemed to expose at the same time the worst effects of ignorant traditionalism and of harsh innovation.

By the taxes they paid, the peasants were made to bear the main cost of the official policy of industrialization. Russian industry was making impressive advances. Although by 1900 there were still no more than 2 or 3 million industrial workers in a population of over 90 million, large metallurgical plants had grown up in the Ukraine, where coal mining had also boomed; the cotton industry still waxed around Moscow, fed by raw material from vast areas of Central Asia conquered in the 1860s; and engineering was important in Petersburg. Industrialists worked in corrupt connivance with the Ministry of Finance, which came to follow a deliberate policy of attracting foreign investment that gave French, German and British capitalists an overweening stake in the Russian economy. Production in the modern industries was concentrated in a small number of large factories where foul conditions and shameless exploitation affected many workers simultaneously, and made the advance of Marxist ideas inevitable.

Chekhov produced a near-comprehensive picture of the Russia governed by Alexander III and his inept son Nicholas II, who succeeded him in 1894 and carried on similar policies with less resolution. Edmund Wilson compares Chekhov's later stories with Balzac's enormous survey of early nineteenth-century France—'a kind of Comédie Humaine in miniature.'[10] The eleven stories which he wrote in 1895 to 1897 (they are translated in the 8th volume of the *Oxford Chekhov*) illustrate his remarkable range at the peak of his powers.

Several are very brief. One, *Patch*, is an animal tale about a she-wolf and a mongrel puppy. *His Wife* is a very slight sketch of a doctor's unhappy marriage. *The Savage* portrays a doltish landowner on the southern steppes. These also provide the setting for *Home*, a story which refers to industrialization in the countryside. If these four stories are unimportant, though interesting, *In The Cart* is a brief masterpiece, reflecting Chekhov's concern over the hard conditions endured by rural schoolteachers. The famous *Order of St Anne* (*Anna on the Neck*) features a teacher's daughter who marries an ageing and obsequious civil servant for the sake of her impoverished family; her success in the petty 'society' of her provincial town gains her husband the Order of St Anne, Second Class. We are at first on the girl's side against the world, but this rather Balzac-like tale ends with her driving in a coach with the local millionaire and neglecting her younger brothers and drunken father.

Murder, a longish story, has in common with *Order of St Anne* only Chekhov's abiding disgust at the way people live in provincial Russia. The milieu of glum railway station and decayed coaching inn is superbly realized. The innkeeper, Yakov, is a nonconformist religious fanatic who murders his brother in a quarrel over the eating of oil in Lent and is sentenced to prison on Sakhalin Island. Chekhov writes with a combination of respect and detachment about religious ideas among the lower classes. An acute sense of social and economic history intersects with a Tolstoyan moral direction; mixing, in Sakhalin, with convicts of many races and creeds, Yakov finally grasps the true universal faith and understands the barbarity of his former behaviour. The famous *Peasants* (1897), Chekhov's most controversial work in his own lifetime, is a slice of rural existence at its most degraded; a Moscow waiter comes home to die among his demoralized family. Many intellectuals still cherished the idea that Russian villagers, though downtrodden, were wise and good. But drunkenness and wife-beating, foul diet and overcrowding were what Chekhov himself had seen in the countryside. His frankness worried the censorship, which insisted on cuts, and stirred both argument and high praise among critics and readers.

Ariadne and *The Artist's Story*, both rather shorter, fit in better with the common, distorted image of Chekhov as a poet of doomed love among the decadent rural nobility. The first, however, is one of his funniest pieces and the second, for all its delicate lyricism, reflects sharply on the work of the *zemstvo*'s. Finally, *My Life* (1896) runs to about eighty pages and is one of Chekhov's longest and most important works. It is the story of a provincial Tolstoyan, born into and rejecting the official class, and it gives a vivid and comprehensive picture of society in a horrible town, from butchers and housepainters up to the Governor himself.

The work of this phase nevertheless falls far short of illustrating Chekhov's whole range. Elsewhere he describes people in the capitals, the Caucasus, the Crimea and Siberia, centres stories on Jews and Tartars, merchants and clergy and, notably in *A Woman's Kingdom* (1894), writes searchingly about life in the new factories. No great nineteenth-century writer has a wider variety, and few if any use more different modes and methods, switching from slapstick and ultra-dry satire through gentle comedy and 'poetic' pathos to real tragic force.

Essentially, his viewpoint is that of a member of the 'intelligentsia' with a marked sympathy for the constructive work of the *zemstvos* and of teachers, doctors and engineers. He is utterly antipathetic to the tone and techniques of officialdom and sees clearly the worst side of industrialization. He is saved from despair over his country's fate only by a vestigial confidence that science, education and rebellious goodwill are in alliance with the direction of history and can in the long run make life better. His Russia, Christopher Hill has written, is 'a class-ridden society in which decent human relations were thwarted by considerations of rank, by political and religious oppression, by jealousy and by bumbledom. . . . No one has better captured the malaise, the frustration, the fumbling hopes of a pre-revolutionary society than Chekhov.'[11] The burden of his writings is always, 'We can't go on living like this.'

III

Anton Chekhov was the self-made son of a self-made man. His background and early career are much more like those of Dickens, Meredith and Wells than those of his great predecessors in Russian fiction. His grandfather was a serf who in 1841 bought for 3500 roubles his own freedom and that of his family. His father owned a grocery store in the town of Taganrog on the Sea of Azov, where he passed as a man of some substance. His Orthodox piety tried his family sorely and inoculated Anton against religion, though he always saw meaning and beauty in Christian worship. Pavel Chekhov treated his children severely. Anton grew up so hypersensitive towards suffering that in later years, rather than trapping mice, he used to capture them and release them away from his house. If he wasn't an outstanding pupil at the local secondary school, this must have been because his father made him serve long evening hours in the shop. But the family remained remarkably close and united. All six surviving children received higher education and became proficient professional people.

Taganrog was a town of some 30,000 people dominated by foreign export-import firms and very cosmopolitan in its atmosphere. The railway struck at its prosperity by attracting most of its trade to Rostov on Don. In 1876 Pavel Chekhov was forced to declare himself bankrupt and to leave for Moscow to evade a debtor's prison. While the rest of the family went with him, the sixteen-year-old Anton stayed on alone in Taganrog until he completed his schooling in 1879 and went on to Moscow University to study medicine. His people were living in straitened circumstances in a notorious brothel area, and on his arrival the self-reliant and good-humoured Anton became, what he would remain for the rest of his life, virtual head of his family. To help support them he began to publish, from 1880 onwards, stories and articles in popular humourous journals, and in 1882 his talent was recognized by Leikin, publisher of the best-known of these magazines, the Petersburg *Fragments*. Stories had to be funny and topical and to avoid all serious subjects which might annoy the censor, and it was a great concession when Leikin permitted his favourite contributor Chekhov to increase the maximum length from 1000 to 1500 words.

Before and after he qualified as a doctor in 1884 and began to practise in Moscow, Chekhov dashed off hundreds of little pieces. This training encouraged concision and preciseness of style, but it discouraged ambition and Chekhov's failure, despite several attempts, ever to write a novel may partly stem from these early limitations. He used the pseudonym 'Antosha Chekhonte'. An anecdote like *Surgery* (1884), which brusquely ridicules an incompetent medical assistant, shows the kind of joky matter his readers liked, but, as he wrote on, the pathos and social concern of his mature style began to emerge. Men of good taste began to notice a new talent fattening in the now-lean pastures of Russian fiction. Visiting Petersburg in 1885, Chekhov was surprised to find that Dmitri Grigorovich (1822–1899) a famous veteran novelist of the 1840s, knew and admired his gifts and that Alexei Suvorin, editor of *New Times*, Russia's most widely-read daily paper, also took an interest in him. Suvorin, a wealthy man of peasant origins, became Chekhov's patron and close friend. Chekhov, with *New Times* open to him, began to take more care and write longer stories and in 1888 a collection called *In The Twilight* won him the coveted Pushkin Prize. The committee which gave it to him expressed its regret that he wrote for the cheap press and undervalued his own talent.

The plump, cheerful face which appears in his early photographs is no deception, hard though it may seem to square with the more familiar bearded and sad-eyed image from his last years. Chekhov was hospitable beyond his means and loved jokes and gay company. He was not prudish, either in life or fiction, but he did keep his sexuality under close control. Kuprin, one of the many young writers he influenced, commented that Chekhov's characteristic artistic restraint is like that of a man 'who cannot bring himself to make a declaration of love.'[12] He was certainly no timid virgin, but in life as in writing he found passionate commitment difficult. A fear of losing his independence seems to have mixed with a deeper self-uncertainty in his failure to get married until he was over forty.

Towards the end of the 1880s, such uncertainty started to worry him deeply. Fiction had clearly replaced medicine as his main occupation, though wherever he stayed he was generous with his services as a doctor to friends and to poor people who mostly couldn't pay him. 'Medicine', he joked, 'is my lawful wife and literature my mistress'[13]—and this remark displays division and unease. He grasped for a time at Tolstoy's ideas and wrote some stories to express them. He was disturbed by the attacks made by left-wing critics on the lack of any positive political or moral direction in his work, and on his intimacy with the reactionary Suvorin. His great long short story of 1889, *A Dreary Story*, projects his concern over his own apparent purposelessness into the character of the elderly dying scholar who narrates it. In 1890 he undertook a practical commitment. He left on a journey across Siberia to the Far-Eastern island of Sakhalin which the Russian State was using as a penal colony. He spent three months there making minute research into the dreadful life endured by thousands, which he used as the basis for an important scholarly book, *The Island of Sak-*

halin (1893/4). He travelled back via the Indian Ocean and the Suez Canal, and on his return set about organizing supplies of books to be sent to Sakhalin for the benefit of its population. He found further scope for this kind of positive but small-scale action when in 1892 he bought a country estate at Melikhovo, two and a half hours from Moscow. Besides indulging the passion for planting trees which he shared with Astrov in his play *Uncle Vania*, he doctored the local peasants, served on the *zemstvo* and organized the building of several schools in the area.

He now wrote relatively few stories, but these were often long and thematically challenging. *The Duel* (1891) is a near-novel vividly set on the Caucasian coastline. *Ward Number Six* (1892) is perhaps his most 'political' tale, though *An Anonymous Story* (1892) is actually narrated by a far-left revolutionary who takes up a post as manservant to the son of a leading minister so as to spy on the latter. *Three Years* (1894) gives a remarkable picture of a patriarchal Moscow merchant milieu from which the central character tries in vain to liberate himself psychologically. The theatre had attracted Chekhov since childhood, and his long play *Ivanov* (1887) had been almost as successful as his popular one-act farces *The Bear* and *The Proposal*. *The Seagull* (1896) met with initial disaster at its première, but was revived with tumultuous success in 1898 by the new Moscow Arts Theatre directed by the famous Stanislavsky. Chekhov gave this company his *Uncle Vania* and wrote *Three Sisters* (1900) specially for it. In 1901 he married one of its leading actresses, Olga Knipper, who had for some time been his mistress.

As early as 1884 he had started to cough blood. As a doctor, he knew the symptoms of tuberculosis, but he was for years able to reassure himself that his illness need not be fatal. In 1897, his health broke down. He began to spend most of his time in the Crimean resort of Yalta where he built a house and bought two other properties and the benign climate compensated a little for the provincial tedium. His marriage mixed fulfillment with frustration; Chekhov yearned for his young wife in the Crimea while she, with his full consent, pursued her career in Moscow. As his illness accelerated, he struggled to complete *The Cherry Orchard* for the Moscow Arts Theatre. Its first production in early 1904 was made the occasion for a public demonstration in his honour. At a peak of reputation only surpassed by Tolstoy's, he died in July of the same year in the German town of Badenweiler.

The mature view of the world expressed in his stories of the 1890s and in his four major plays is unmistakeably 'Chekhovian' but hard to adorn with other labels. Politically, he gravitated leftward, coming to terms with the liberal press which had once attacked him, cooling in 1898 in his relations with Suvorin as a result of *New Times'* reactionary line, and finding a close friend in the young Maxim Gorky, a man of revolutionary sympathies. In 1902 he resigned from the honorific Academy of Sciences when Gorky's election to that body was annulled on political grounds at the instance of the Tsar himself. But the controversy over the real nature of *The Cherry Orchard* which has gone on ever since Chekhov himself protested that Stanislavksy had staged it as the work of a 'weeper' though he had written it as a 'merry and giddy comedy', illustrates the elusiveness of his 'tendency'. The play seems at the same time to be a vastly-amused near-farce revealing the inanities of a decadent nobility and a near-elegy for a doomed way of life.

Chekhov had grown up in a coarse and mercenary milieu in a declining and backward town. French, the language which noblemen knew like their own, he did not properly learn until he was nearing forty. For 'rank' he had no respect at all, but he valued very highly gentleness, education and graceful manners because he knew cruder ways at first hand. 'Refinement', in the best sense of the word, was what he wanted all his fellow men to share. To start to understand his work, we must respond fully to the implications of the famous letter which he wrote in 1889 to that other social mountaineer, Suvorin:

> What gently born writers have been endowed with by nature, self-made intellectuals buy at the price of their youth. Write me a story about a young man, the son of a serf, a former shopkeeper, a choir boy, high school and university student, brought up on respect for rank, kissing the hands of priests, belonging to a generation alien to thought, offering thanks for every mouthful of bread, often whipped, going to school without shoes, quarrelling, tormenting animals, fond of dining with rich relatives, playing the hypocrite before God and people without any cause, except out of a recognition of his own insignificance—then tell how that young man presses the slave out of him drop by drop and how he wakes up one fine morning and feels that in his veins flows not the blood of a slave, but real human blood.[14]

IV

Chekhov was a 'slave' by birth who became a qualified scientist and a great artist. Throughout his life he had to work hard to buy the means of a comfortable and gracious life which aristocrats took for granted. One way to approach him is to consider how 'slave', artist, scientist, worker and aristocrat figure in the complex, balletically shifting patterns of his stories.

The common notion that the 'gentle' Chekhov loves and pities all his characters equally is complete, though forgiveable, claptrap. He can indeed appreciate the virtues of many different kinds of men and women. He can equally well express his hatred of their vices; no writer is more adept at making the reader's blood boil with indignation. He loathes obsequiousness and self-abasement, traits of the serf and the shopkeeper. A sketch of 1883, *A Nincompoop*, shows us a governess who humbly accepts the fact that her employers cheat her. 'How easy it is,' muses the narrator, 'to crush the weak in this world.'[15] Chekhov often seems to urge contempt rather than sympathy for those who permit others to exploit them.

Yet in that grim late story *In The Ravine* (1900), one of several harsh presentations of the *kulak* way of life in the countryside, there is no doubt that he means our affection to go to the gentle Lipa, who accepts her cruel fate at the hands of her vital but snake-like sister-in-law Aksinia, a remarkable girl who sets herself up as a petty capitalist. Chekhov is as 'double' as Dostoevsky. The interpretation of his great story *The Darling* (1899) is a notorious crux. Tolstoy, who thought it wonderful, believed that Chekhov had meant to denigrate his Olga, the buxom, warm-hearted 'darling' who has no opinions except those which she borrows from the current man in her life and who, without some male to worship, withers and grows sluttish, but that he could not help bathing her in sympathy. The tale is, in fact, both sardonically funny and very touching, and the same is true of much of Chekhov's finest work. Here and elsewhere, Chekhov balances a rooted contempt for the kind of vegetable, dependent existence which Olga leads against an appreciation of that generous self-giving which can soothe and support the lives of more active people.

The equally famous *Grasshopper* (*Butterfly*) of 1892 contrasts a vain, womanizing landscape painter with a doctor humbly devoted to a faithless wife, Olga, even to the point of acting as *maître d'hôtel* at the arty parties she gives for her male friends. Olga, the dilettante, yearns to meet great men, and the irony of the story is emphatically pressed home; she has a squalid affair with the landscape painter, but when her saddened husband takes a suicidal risk at work and so dies of diptheria she learns from what his colleagues say that he was in fact a 'great' medical scientist. So does this mean that Chekhov exalts the unimpressive but socially beneficial work of scientific research over the vain self-seeking of the maker of pretty but useless pictures? Not really, because Dr Dymov is one of 'the weak in this world'. His self-abnegation is nice but absurd. And in *The Artist's Story* (1896, otherwise rendered as *The House With The Attic*, etc.) most readers will believe that Chekhov is on the side of the landscape painter who narrates the tale against the monstrously virtuous, hard-working Lida, who knows what is good for other people, doctors and schools the peasants and prevents her sweet young sister from marrying the artist, who of course has fallen out with her utilitarian views.

On one level, *The Artist's Story* can be seen as a wrily nostalgic backward look at the world of Turgenev's fiction. The poetry of rural life is presented and snatched away, and Lida, who might have been a Turgenev heroine forty or fifty years before, has given herself to bossy and futile attempts at social engineering. The idyllic setting of the sisters' lives—neglected avenue of limes, pond with its line of willows, cross on the village church reflecting the setting sun, white house with its terrace and attic—reminds us both of many Turgenev scenes and of many other stories and plays by Chekhov. One part of Chekhov is deeply in love with an ideal which had never quite had concrete foundation—with that dream of a truly refined aristocracy which lures onwards the self-made man.

But the magnificent long short story *My Wife* (1892) exposes the rural nobility to fierce slashes of irony. The scene in which an agreeable landowner serves a fourteen-course feast in the midst of an area where the peasants are starving concentrates much of the meaning of the story; no matter how well-meaning noblemen may be in their dilatory efforts towards famine relief, their way of life is in itself immoral. But at least the nobleman has good manners. In *The Duel*, the central contest between Laevsky, a noble weakling and wastrel who excuses himself as a 'superfluous man' and the scientist Von Koren who hates him and believes that such people should be exterminated is made a surprisingly equal one. The story ends (some would say sentimentally, and it certainly isn't very convincing) with Laevsky reconciled with Von Koren and settling down to live better; even the nobility can redeem themselves with hard work. All who know Chekhov's plays will remember the positive value which he attaches to the commitment to work of Nina in *The Seagull* and the decisions to go on living and working taken by leading people in the last acts of *Uncle Vania* and *Three Sisters*.

Yet work is not for Chekhov a good in itself. The drudgery of those rural doctors whom he often depicts is seen as necessary, but coarsening. Chekhov cannot follow Tolstoy in seeing labour itself as spiritually transfiguring; work for him must be a means to some good end. *My Life* exposes, through his own words, the internal contradictions of a Tolstoyan's position. Misail, the son of a bad but successful architect, scandalizes the town by becoming a painter and decorator. But since his job is to refurbish the vulgar rooms of the local rich, his success as an artisan implies that he hasn't so much rejected the dreadful provincial life which he sees through and abhors, as found a new means of living with it. Both Misail and (we guess) his creator can't help admiring the energy of two intruders into this world; Masha the radiant daughter of a rich engineer, who marries Misail, tries to live a simple life on her country estate with him, then deserts him, shocked by the squalor of rural existence; and Dr Blagovo, who seduces Misail's pathetic sister Cleopatra, gives her the only happiness she has ever had, then also departs for foreign pastures. Misail and his sister are hard workers, good people, whose lives lack something which only the gifted and selfish can give them.

But Chekhov is far less close to masochistic admiration of Strong Men and *Femmes fatales* than Turgenev before him. He realizes from the outset that in his own day, in the epoch of Alexander III and Nicholas II, a quest for the Hero would be fruitless. His stories are full of half-cock Elenas, nasty or lightweight Bazarovs and unglamorous Rudins. He cannot wholeheartedly share Turgenev's faith in the ultimate triumph of the left-wing intelligensia. His thinkers and talkers are always more or less weak, more or less tainted with banality. In story after story we watch them, like their creator, enduring a fear that all effort may be futile.

Chekhov's so called 'pessimism' needs to be set in three contexts. The first is international. Any view of his work which sees him purely in terms of Russian tradition and forgets that he was a close contemporary of Ibsen and Wells will over-emphasize the egregiousness of his scientific interests and underestimate his warmth and wistful optimism. The last quarter of the nineteenth century saw a crisis of confidence within the European culture which Russian writers regarded as their own. Industrialization and aggressive imperialism marched step by step with a new science which since Darwin had undermined many traditional bases for belief in God, and they seemed to be marching to disaster. Chekhov's is only one of many worried, warning voices in a culture which was heading, as we now know, towards war, Stalinism, Fascism and the age of aerial bombardment and heart transplants. 'Doctor' Chekhov whose work is so often singled out for its 'scientific' objectivity is, by comparison with the pseudo-scientific Emile Zola, an impassioned moralist and unrepentant aesthete. But like Thomas Hardy he believed that if there were any 'way to the better' it exacted a 'full look at the worst'. Like Ibsen and Strindberg he is deeply concerned with relations between the sexes in the post-Romantic age of the New Woman. Like Conrad he smells anarchic evil haunting the overfurnished rooms of Europe and threatening all civilized values. And, with Maupassant and Kipling, he belongs to a trio of experts who established the short story as a major art form; it is a form best suited to the humorous anecdote and to the cryptically poignant episode, and it must raise more problems than it can talk of solving.

But of course the fact that Chekhov lived in Alexander III's Russia rather than Gladstone's England did give his work different directions and emphases from those of Western writers. Hardy's Wessex was a cruel place, but it wasn't dominated by booze, disease, ignorance and exploitation to the same extent as the appalling village in *Peasants*. Ibsen's *Enemy of the People* may fail in a struggle against provincial corruption, but at least in Norway the possibility of public debate exists. For the ex-revolutionary narrator of *An Anonymous Story* there is in Russia no half-way house between assassination and apathy. The special kinds of sadness which haunt Chekhov's stories breed in a society which was not alone in being quite close to the brink of butchery and turmoil, but was uniquely one in which both aspiration and criticism were generally half-stifled at birth.

Finally, the context of Chekhov's own life must have influenced his responses profoundly. He was ill from his early twenties onwards and could sense that his own life would be a short one. He had struggled from celebrity to the light of fame, squeezing the slave painfully out of himself, only to find himself confronted with the sense of futility pressing on those under sentence of death. In several of his best stories, people sprung from the lower orders brood on the flimsiness of what has been gained. Anna Akimovna in *A Woman's Kingdom* is the daughter of a workman who inherited from his brother a factory with 2000 employees. Now she owns it in her turn and lives in luxury. But she finds herself cut off from the working life she grew up in at the same time as she realizes the hollowness of her 'noble' hangers-on. She is stranded. *The Bishop* (1902) is a late story over which Chekhov took special pains and it tells of a priest whose new dignity isolates him from virtually everyone, including his own mother. He dies of typhus, after experiencing the feeling that though he has attained all he could have hoped for, something is still lacking in his life.

The professor who tells *A Dreary Story* (1889) is also a sick man. Nikolai Stepanovich is probably the most impressive person, so far as his achievements go, to appear in Chekhov's fiction. A scientist of national fame and international repute, a brilliant lecturer, honest, witty and kind, he more than any one else would seem to have risen above the banality of Tsarist Russia. But he is dying, and knows it; and now he discovers that his life is made meaningless to him by the absence of any dominating idea. 'Neither in my judgements about science, the stage, literature and my pupils, nor in the pictures painted by my imagination could even the most skillful analyst detect any "general conception", or the God of a live human being. And if one lacks that, one has nothing.'[16]

Chekhov is a 'reverent agnostic', attracted by the piety of good men. His problem of commitment is initially spiritual; he cannot hitch his morality to a Christian horse like Tolstoy or Dostoevsky, nor can he, like Turgenev, substitute politics for religion. He saw this as a problem of his own generation and in a letter of 1892 went so far as to attribute the shortcomings of the younger Russian writers directly to their lack of faith and direction. The old guard had believed in the abolition of serfdom, in beauty, in life beyond the grave. 'And we? We! We paint life as it is, but beyond that—nothing at all. Flog us but we can do no more. We have neither immediate nor distant aims and in our souls there is a great empty space. We have no politics, we don't believe in revolution, we have no God, we are not afraid of ghosts, and personally I don't even fear death or blindness. He who wants nothing, hopes for nothing, and fears nothing, cannot be an artist.'[17]

Yet he still argued, in 1899, that the business of writers was to keep out of politics and get on with writing—'If we are to wage war, to become indignant, to judge, then we should do it only by the pen.' And at the same period he declared, 'I believe in individuals. I see salvation in individual personalities scattered over all of Russia—they may be intellectuals, or peasants—for although they may be few, they have strength.'[18] Mistrust of all dogmas allied itself in him with what one might call an impatient pragmatism: waiting is bitter, but we must wait and see. He kept shoring up a tentative faith in progress, which he identified both with science and 'God'. He reacted with scorn in 1902 to the way in which some young intellectuals were turning back via Dostoevsky's writings to Christianity. 'Modern culture', he wrote, 'is only the beginning of an effort in the name of a great future, an effort that will continue perhaps for tens of thousands of years, in order that humanity, if only in the remote future, may come to know the truth of the real God, that is, not guess at it or seek it in Dostoevsky, but know it just as clearly as we know that twice two makes four.'[19] He tries to make the best of the vast new perspectives of time opened up by science, which now stretched backwards to life's beginning in primeval slime and forward to the cooling of the sun. A faith in the good future is expressed by a few individuals in his plays and stories—amongst them Gromov in *Ward Number Six*, Dr Astrov in *Uncle Vania* and the narrator of *An Anonymous Story*, who expresses the frustration of all these men when he exclaims, 'But we do want to be independent of future generations, don't we, we don't want to live just for them? We only have one life and we should like to live it confidently, rationally and elegantly.'[20] The problem of the good man in Chekhov's world is that he can only remain honest by remaining an individual, yet as an individual he can do very little. But Chekhov has no patience for people who submit to the banality of Russia because it seems to be unconquerable at this stage in time, or even because it is a necessary prelude to better things. Defiance, if only verbally, must be made.

In view of the context from which his work emerges, the love of life which it displays is amazing. A sense of fun is one aspect of this vitality. Stories like *The Duel* and *My Life*, which sound miserable in summary, are on the page full of pleasure at the world's beauties and often gay with unsentimental humour. Chekhov's work is almost as full as that of Dickens with amusing eccentrics and self-exposing fools. *Ariadne*, for instance, (1895), offers a laughing riposte to Turgenev's obsession with *femmes fatales* and Tolstoy's with the power of sex to deprave. The rather priggish young idealist who tells the story is trapped by his own romanticism into servitude to a sensuous, shallow woman; then, having 'slept' with her, he feels he must stick by her even though he is totally disillusioned. The story ends skittishly as he exults over the news that his mistress is about to marry an empty-headed Prince. Ariadne herself, with her unromantically hearty appetite and her lack of real distinction or glamour, her spiritualist brother with his breath that smells of beef and his eyes like boiled sweets, and the vulgar sponger Lubkov with whom she goes abroad, are all as silly as the narrator himself, but no one comes to any serious harm. Of course, life would be juster if they did, and Chekhov's implicit indignation that such fools can waste so much time and money gives sharp purposeful edge to his comedy.

Landscape and natural description help to prevent his drab subject matter from depressing us. Even the dreary provincial town or squalid remote village can dream of life transfigured and redeemed as sunset blazes from windows and spires or music plays on a summer night. Gorky's famous remark that Chekhov's mind 'like the autumn sun, shows up in hard outline the monotonous roads, the crooked streets, the little squalid houses in which tiny, miserable people are stifled by boredom and laziness and fill the houses with an unintelligible, drowsy bustle',[21] is only accurate up to a point, because Chekhov conveys so wonderfully the freshness of spring and the haze of summer. An early story, *Mire* (1886), opens as a young officer in a snow-white tunic rides up to a distillery on a summer day so fine that even the sooty buildings are not depressing. A nasty tale follows; the young man is seduced and in effect robbed by the sensual Jewish heiress who lives there and who turns out to have captivated most of the neighbourhood's noblemen by her frank and aggressive sexuality, which gives them welcome relief from boredom and hypocrisy. But the gay light of the opening plays over the whole tale. Even *Peasants* is brightened by the glorious open view from above its miserable village. Here and elsewhere, Chekhov anticipates the potent cocktail of natural beauty and human savagery in Isaac Babel's war stories. Joy in life blazes over disgust.

Nevertheless, Gorky's further point that Chekhov above all hated banality seems amply justified. *Poshlost** is his enemy as it had been Gogol's, and the town in *My Life* where all officials take bribes shows how little Russia might seem to have progressed since the days of the *Inspector General*. But Chekhov's view is immensely more mature and humane than Gogol's. The subtlety of *Ionych* (1898) derives from a combination of deep revulsion with deep compassion. 'Ionych', Dr Startsev, is another of Chekhov's social climbers, a deacon's son who becomes a rural doctor. The most 'cultured' family in the nearby town are the Turkins. The mother writes sentimental novels and reads them aloud to her guests. The daughter noisily plays the piano. The father repeats and repeats his feeble jokes. From the first Ionych shows symptoms of greed and vulgarity, but he falls romantically in love with the daughter. She snubs him. He turns to making money and building up a rich private practice. Then she returns chastened from Moscow, where her musical education has proved to her that she has no great talent as a pianist. (She should have stuck to her art nevertheless, like Nina in *The Seagull*.) She wishes to resume the affair with Ionych. They share a moment of honest self-exposure. Ionych denounces the round of money-grubbing and card-playing which now makes up his life. But when she praises him as a fine man devoting his skill to the people, he remembers the banknotes he takes out of his pockets with such enjoyment every evening and 'the flame in his soul' goes out. The cryptic concision here is typical of Chekhov; we may infer either that Startsev is dismayed to realize how unworthy of love and praise he now is, or that his love of money reasserts itself; or both at once. In any case, he becomes a fat bad-tempered profiteer and she reverts to practising the piano four hours every day. The last lines of the story suddenly focus our sympathy on the Turkins. We have laughed at them, yet they are still likeable. It is not their fault, we may feel, as we watch papa waving his wife and daughter off at the station, that they have no talent. Perhaps Ionych and the girl, together, could have made something worthwhile out

*See p. 56.

of life. But it is dangerous to extract this kind of 'moral' from a Chekhov story. We might equally well say that all the characters have throughout displayed their fatuity and that sympathy for such parasites is misplaced. There is plenty of anger and cold satire in *Ionych* to counterbalance the touches of humour and love.

The failure of individuals to make and sustain the contacts they need at the moments when they need them is a recurring motif in Chekhov's work. People who have been or might have been close fork into isolation as when, so poignantly, *A Dreary Story* ends as the old professor watches his beloved ward Katia walk away from him without turning to look back and knows he will never see her again. 'Farewell, my treasure.' Virginia Llewellyn Smith argues that 'in the world of Chekhov's fiction no happy relationship between the sexes is permitted to exist. Love is sought, and not to find it appears to be a tragedy; but when it is found, love becomes a travesty of itself. Chekhov's gloomy view of heterosexual relationships is at once the most immediately striking and the most revealing aspect of his fiction.'[22]

It would be truer to say that Chekhov realizes that no ideal relationship, resolving all problems in 'happiness', can exist between two mortal human beings, that he writes about people who, because life in Russia offers no other hope, expect more from 'love' than it can possibly give them, and that his view of the results is coolly realistic and often extremely funny. He is, of course, alive to the poignancy of frustrated hope. But—*An Anonymous Story* is a case in point—he is often describing people who, like Turgenev's heroines but with less force, try to use 'love' as a way out of a social-political *impasse*. And, though he never describes the sexual act, he is extremely good at conveying the sensual attraction which can support and power feckless romantic illusions.

Chekhov's stories take in a remarkable range of localities, but everywhere we find bored people longing to be somewhere else, and liable to seize at 'love' as a magic which can transform their lives. 'You are doing a great thing with your stories,' Gorky told Chekhov, 'arousing in people a feeling of disgust with their sleepy, half-dead existence.'[23] To suggest that Chekhov is more of a satirist than a tragedian will strike many readers as odd. Yet angry laughter and barely controlled disgust are as important in his work as lyricism and pathos. And behind all the stinks and litter which he so often describes with telling restraint lurk monstrous violence and tyranny. The rich are bored; the poor suffer; the turn of the rich may come.

V

By Chekhov's own supreme standards *Ward Number Six* may seem rather unsubtle, a little forced. But his imagination works harder than usual to create a fable which concentrates message and meaning as that of *My Life* (for instance) doesn't.

A story of some fifty pages, it falls half way in length between his shortest and longest tales. He wrote it in 1892 after his return from Sakhalin where for many weeks he had confronted daily the inhumanity of man to man. Its publication in a liberal periodical which had angered him two years before by accusing him of lacking principles asserted his natural orientation towards the left, and it is generally agreed that it presents a criticism of Tolstoyan ideas. Readers must be careful, however, not to accept the impression which many books convey that Chekhov around this time 'broke' sharply with Tolstoy's views; the deep influence of Tolstoyan moralism is evident in much of his work to the last, and it would be possible, though unfair, to deny Chekhov the status of a great and original writer on the grounds that so many of his stories are thoughtful reworkings of material from *Anna Karenina*, *Ivan Ilich*, and *The Kreutzer Sonata*. He always admired Tolstoy as a writer and, after he first met him in 1895, as a man. Grieved in 1899 when he heard that the old man was seriously ill, Chekhov said that Tolstoy's 'moral influence is so great, that there are people who are ashamed to do evil things simply because Tolstoy lives.'[24]

The central figure of *Ward Number Six* is Dr Ragin, a gentle intellectual who is in charge of the hospital in a petty provincial town one hundred and twenty miles from the nearest railway. The staff rob the patients, and the place is so filthy that it spreads disease rather than checking it. The doctor, a shy man who finds it impossible to assert himself, knows what is wrong yet presides over this institution for more than twenty years without making real effort to improve it. He spends each day before dinner sipping vodka, nibbling at a gherkin and poring over a book, and from the depths of his wide, but theoretical learning he claims that material conditions are unimportant and that a man with developed intellect can be content anywhere; in the long run we will all be dead anyway; what then is the point of curing people by the advanced methods he reads about in journals? 'So it's all a snare and a delusion,' he thinks, 'and between the best Viennese clinic and my hospital there is no real difference at all.' He spends his evenings drinking beer with his sole friend, a ruined nobleman, Mikhail Averianovich, who is the local postmaster, and they regard themselves as the only intelligent men in the town.

But in Ward Number Six, where the mentally ill are confined in abysmal squalor under the regime of a brutal warder named Nikita, lives Ivan Gromov, a young intellectual who was put away when he developed persecution mania. Seeing that there was no justice in Russia, he began to imagine that he might at any moment be sentenced for some crime he had not committed. Now, when Ragin drops into the ward by chance, Gromov rages against his fate and proclaims his love of life. Confronted by Gromov's attacks on his own Stoic quietism, Ragin finds him fascinating company and begins to visit him every day. An ambitious subordinate, Khobotov, takes the chance offered by this eccentricity to get

Ragin eased out of his job. Reduced to near-destitution, Ragin, for the first time, explodes with anger over the way in which Khobotov and the postmaster talk to him like a child. This revolt is taken as confirmation of his madness, and he is lured into Ward Number Six and made to dress in a hospital smock which stinks of smoked fish. The fate which Gromov had feared would happen to him—a wholly unjust deprivation of liberty—has now fallen on Ragin himself. From the window he looks out at a landscape which distills Chekhov's horror at the character of Russian life:

> Darkness was already falling and a cold, crimson moon was rising above the horizon on the right. Not far from the hospital fence, no more than a couple of hundred yards away, stood a tall white building with a stone wall round it: the prison.
> 'So this is reality,' thought Ragin, terrified.
> Moon, prison, the nails on the fence, the distant flame in the glue factory—it all terrified him. Hearing a sigh behind him, Ragin turned and saw a man with shining stars and medals on his chest who smiled and artfully winked an eye. That too struck Ragin as terrifying.[25]

The factory is a sordid and smelly one. The madman in the ward who is obsessed with medals epitomizes Russian official life. The prison dominates the view. Industry, bureaucracy, justice, so Chekhov hints, now appear to Ragin in their 'real' character. Too late he revolts. He tries to insist that he be allowed to go for a walk. Nikita beats him into submission. In his pain he understands for the first time what the patients under his charge have endured. Too late, for he has a stroke and dies.

Ward Number Six is so stark, so stripped of all ingratiating and palliating detail, that we can hardly fail to read it as an allegory. We know that Chekhov was 'always on the look out, as his notebooks prove, not so much for the heights and depths of human nature as for the typically Russian. . .'[26] In the small cast of this story he has assembled a range of swiftly-sketched 'types'. The postmaster who brags of the old life-style of the rural nobility—'How we drank and ate, what frantic liberals we were' —represents the landowning class in decline but still loudly asserting brusque authority. (Ragin's very last memory is of Mikhail Averianich confronting a peasant woman who has brought him a registered packet. 'You can wait,' he yelled at her as he turned to Ragin; this kind of jack-in-office rudeness is something which Chekhov loathes.) Khobotov, plebeian and abrasive, is a Leskov-like hit at a 'progressive' on the make. Gromov, by contrast, recalls Dostoevsky's underground men, with their garbled rush of ideas and pathetic lust for life. He talks of revolt, but he doesn't break out, and his incapacity to act makes him a 'type' of the Russian intellectual, though Chekhov as always respects good manners, which Gromov's education has given him. His fellow-inmates in Ward Six range from the civil servant mad about medals over the other main classes. The Jew is allowed out to beg and then robbed of his money by Nikita; Jews in Russia then were, in fact, forced into unsavoury trades and then bullied and exploited. The paralytic urban worker is a dynamic figure compared to the vegetable-like peasant. Nikita, the old soldier who lounges on the rubbish piled in the ward's lobby, suggests the mindless brutality of the Tsarist State which, like him, believes in 'discipline in all things' and is 'therefore convinced that people need hitting'.

But Ragin is rather more complex. He has great physical strength though he doesn't use it. With his up-to-date knowledge he might seem to typify the professional classes, people who clearly see what is wrong but go on drawing their salaries. His lack of drive is associated with a lack of faith, and we can't take him to represent 'science' because for Chekhov it is probably Gromov, one of his visionaries, looking forward to life transformed and believing that men can make themselves immortal, who speaks in the true spirit of science. Gromov has his future God, but Ragin looks towards the day when human life will die out on a cold earth. This extended view of history makes all action seem absurd.

Ragin's self-indulgence and moral and physical sloth would have been anathema to Tolstoy. Rather than skirmishing directly with Tolstoy's latest ideas, Chekhov seems to have gone back to look at their roots. Ragin's pessimism recalls that of Andrei in *War and Peace*. (One characteristic comment of Chekhov's was that if he had been there to tend Andrei's wound, he would have cured him.[27] Science, as he knew at first hand, had made that particular death unnecessary.) And we cannot miss the obvious smack at the bogus wisdom of Karataev which Chekhov makes when he sketches the peasant in Ward Number Six as a 'nearly globular' creature emitting a 'sharp acrid stench'; this is direct parody of Tolstoy. The peasant has lost all capacity to think, to feel, or even respond to blows, but this is only a step further from what Tolstoy attributed to Karataev, whose conception prefigured the Tolstoyan doctrine of non-resistance to evil.

There are traces of lyricism only in Gromov's prophetic harangues and in the sudden vision of a herd of deer 'extraordinarily handsome and graceful' which springs into Ragin's mind just before he dies. Disgust and unforgiving satire dominate the whole work. Gromov and Ragin, segregated as lunatics, are the best men in town, and neither is very impressive. Yet the story is too angry to be called 'pessimistic'. It could not have pressed home its point if Chekhov had failed to make us sympathize with Ragin and Gromov. The good nature of the one and the idealism of the other are conveyed with just sufficient appeal to bring home to us the full horror of society's denial of human dignity. The anger of Chekhov himself and his correct expectation that his readers will share it offer a kind of hope.

Lenin was much affected by *Ward Number Six*. Lenin's successors have found out how convenient it can be to classify their opponents as mad and commit them to asylums. More than any other work of Chekhov's, this obviously cuts at the quick of modern life.

Yet *Lady With Lapdog* has perhaps things of as much importance to say. Written in 1899, it reflects Chekhov's recently-found happiness with Olga Knipper, though the characteristic Chekhovian anger is still there and the rejection of contemporary society is as radical as ever. It is a masterpiece of less than twenty pages. Gurov, a well-to-do man with a job in a Moscow bank is on holiday in Yalta. Married off early to a woman he doesn't love he is now, at Chekhov's own age, just short of forty, a blasé philanderer whose career of easy conquests makes him speak contemptuously of women as 'the lower breed'. Spotting an unaccompanied young lady with a little white dog, he at once devises and carries out a scenario of seduction and up to a point she plays her expected role well. Anna Sergeevna is so out of sympathy with her husband, a provincial civil servant, that she doesn't even know what his official job is. She despises him as a flunkey and she longs to live, as so many girls in Chekhov's stories have longed to live. But she isn't a girl who can take adultery lightly and the diffidence and angularity of her manner mark her out in Gurov's eyes from the beginning as someone rather different from his previous bedmates. The serious misery which she shows him after her 'fall' in a hotel bedroom breaks through his practised boredom with women's moods. They drive out along the coast together and look at a view which synthesizes, one might say, the visions of Ragin and Gromov, while rooting both in a vivid reality:

> Yalta could scarcely be seen through the morning mist. White clouds lay motionless on the mountain tops. Not a leaf stirred on the trees, the cicadas chirped, and the monotonous, hollow roar of the sea, coming up from below, spoke of rest, of eternal sleep awaiting us all. The sea had roared like that down below when there was no Yalta or Oreanda, it was roaring now, and it would go on roaring as indifferently and hollowly when we were here no more.

This is like Ragin's vision of eternal death, yet it is beautiful and somehow reassuring.

> And in this constancy, in this complete indifference to the life and death of each one of us, there is perhaps hidden the guarantee of our eternal salvation, the never-ceasing movement of life on earth, the never-ceasing movement towards perfection.

This is the message of Gromov, but made unfeverish. Hope glints, rather than blazing, but there is hope.

> Sitting beside a young woman who looked so beautiful at the break of day, soothed and enchanted by the sight of all that fairy-land scenery—the sea, the mountains, the clouds, the wide sky—Gurov reflected that, when you came to think of it, everything in the world was really beautiful, everything but our own thoughts and actions when we lose sight of the higher aims of existence and our dignity as human beings.[28]

Gurov's thoughts don't convey passing self-satisfaction like those of Tolstoy's Levin before his marriage, still less an invincible smugness like that of Chekhov's own *Princess* in the story of that name (1889). They are calm and pondered and, for all their wistfulness, strong.

After Anna goes back to her husband and Gurov has returned to Moscow, he expects to forget her, but can't. Within a few weeks, the love which haunts him produces a disgust with his habitual round of conventional upper-class pleasures. He goes to the provincial town where Anna lives. He sees her again at a second rate theatrical performance and they arrange to meet again in Moscow. Life forms a new routine. Every two or three months she comes to town and they meet at her hotel. Both are past romantic illusion. They are not 'happy'. Their love has become a spiritual need, their relationship the only one in which each can find sincerity and seriousness. Gurov lives two lives:

> ... everything that was important, interesting, essential, everything about which he was sincere and did not deceive himself, everything that made up the quintessence of his life, went on in secret, while everything that was a lie, everything that was merely the husk in which he hid himself to conceal the truth, like his work at the bank, for instance, his discussions at the club, his ideas of the lower breed, his going to anniversary functions with his wife—all that happened in the sight of all.[29]

The distinction between the true and the social self is fundamental in Tolstoy's work. We see here how far Chekhov accepts Tolstoy's world view and yet how far he has modified it towards a more flexible and humane system of ethics. For Tolstoy, of course, the notion that the true self might be found through a furtive adulterous passion would be nonsensical and wicked. Chekhov, however, emphasizes the essential purity of his Anna. She idealizes Gurov and makes him ashamed that he is not the man she takes him to be, while he respects her as he has never respected a woman before. It is not sex but a craving for dignity which binds them together; each sets the image of the other against a stultifying and purposeless society. They gain not happiness but a more vital and human state of unhappiness. Their relationship can 'solve' nothing, but it exposes, to them as to us, the current nature of Russian society.

The story is a supreme example of Chekhov's conciseness. The difficult question why this Anna, unlike Tolstoy's, should have no children to complicate all moral issues, is not so much answered as somehow settled when we are told in passing that her pretext for going to Moscow is that she wants to consult a gynaecologist; without this slight touch, the story might seem sentimental.

Light, cryptic symbolism pervades it, linking the love affair with the society it takes place in. The dog itself helps to individualize Anna while at the same time it gives her a 'typical' quality. It is small and fragile, as she is. It is white, she is pure. It is toy-like and she is still girlish. It is a luxury. She is a well-to-do lady. Like that of the dog, the real life of the colour grey in the story carries hints both intimate and social. No alert reader can possibly miss its importance. When Gurov near the end looks in the glass and sees his hair turning grey and meditates that it is only now that he is growing old that he has fallen in love for the first time, our minds must track back a page or so to the point where we were told that Anna, at this meeting, is wearing the grey dress he likes most. Near the beginning, we learnt that she has grey eyes. In between, we have stayed with Gurov in a provincial hotel bedroom where the carpet is grey and the blanket is grey and (a characteristically outraged Chekhovian detail) the inkstand on the table is grey with dust (no one writes, no one bothers to keep things clean). And we have walked out with him to patrol that long grey fence studded with upturned nails behind which Anna lives. 'A fence like that', he thinks, 'would make anyone wish to run away.'[30]

We will remember also, perhaps, the toothed palings on the fence upon which the professor who tells *A Dreary Story* looks from his summer villa, and if we've ever read it we certainly won't have forgotten the sharp nails on the grey hospital fence in *Ward Number Six*. Such fences, for Chekhov, would seem to symbolize both the isolation in which all sensitive people are aware of living and the prison-like character of life in Russia. But greyness in *Lady with Lapdog* is also beautiful. If life in Russia is grey, this grey is somehow capable of being a different grey; grey the beautiful colour, not grey the absence of colour. An ageing man is transfigured. There is dignity among the filth.

A cryptic but hopeful note is the best one on which to leave Chekhov. Beside his great predecessors, he may seem somewhat minor, a lapdog among the mastiffs. As a miniaturist, he suffers from the limitation that among his people only first person narrators (and only some of those) can suggest anything like the fullness of depth of an Anna Karenina or a Karamazov. The rest are sketched for the most part or, if he doesn't much like them, briskly caricatured. But he transcends this limitation by packed richness of detail and politely insistent symbolism. There can be no justice or point in the complaint that a birch is not an oak. His stories flourish superbly over wide acres of ground. Chekhov certainly, as he feared, lost a source of artistic power through his incapacity to commit himself boldly in ideas, religion or politics. But he also avoided a number of booby traps into which Tolstoy fell.

VI

In 1891/2 an unusually severe drought brought famine to some of Russia's central and south-western provinces. Tolstoy threw himself into on-the-spot operations for relief, setting up free kitchens in the villages. His quarrelling family united behind him and an appeal by Sonia which was printed in Russia and publicized in Europe and America brought in a flood of contributions. Chekhov's sensible but ineffectual efforts to organize relief were paltry in comparison to the prodigies performed by the sixty-three-year-old Tolstoy. Meanwhile the Tsar and his ministers did nothing and tried to halt the scandal by denying that there was famine. Hack newspapers denounced Tolstoy for preaching social revolution; Church and State mustered their forces against him and spies prowled round his kitchens. But the authorities dared not touch him.

Master and Man, published in 1895, showed that Tolstoy remained a supreme artist. A greedy merchant sledges into a snowstorm to buy a forest from a neighbouring landowner, taking his hired man Nikita with him. They get lost several times and finally prepare to spend the night in the snow. The peasant settles calmly down to keep still and doze. His master can't sleep, gloats over his plans to be very wealthy, gets on the horse to ride off, panics as he rides round in circles, returns and finds Nikita freezing to death on the sledge. Suddenly he decides to place his own warm, fur-clad body on top of that of the thinly clothed Nikita. It seems to him 'a good bargain', both will keep warm. Yet his action is also unselfish and in a dream he sees Christ before he dies. Nikita lives.

The moral point of this long parable is as humane and acceptable as that of the story of the Good Samaritan. The peasant, wisely submissive and passive, survives, while his master rebels against nature and perishes. Yet without the master's last action, the peasant would have died. And like Andrei and Ivan Ilich, the merchant dies to awaken. But Nikita, unlike Karataev or Ivan Ilich's Gerassim, is a complex and credible peasant character, kind and trustful of God, yet given to drink. The horse they take with them is as vivid as they are—'You must have been a horse once yourself,' Turgenev had remarked once, after watching Tolstoy talking to an old nag and then hearing him translate the creature's feelings.[31] Moralizing sits lightly on a wonderful compact of detail. As the men drive twice in and out of the same village, they see each time freezing washing hung on a clothes line, and this in the subtlest way creates an ominous atmosphere. When Nikita is pulled from under his dead master, he believes himself dead and is surprised to find, as he thinks, that peasants shout in the next world just as they do in this; we can hardly call this 'comic', yet it removes any trace of religiose sentimentality from the terrible outcome of the story. Within three or four score pages Tolstoy has created two complete-seeming characters and a world for them to inhabit as solid as any in his fiction.

Sonia, enraged when Tolstoy at first wouldn't give her *Master and Man* to publish in her collected edition, rushed out almost naked into the snow and Tolstoy had to follow to save her from the fate of the merchant in his story. He gave way. Next year she imitated another of his tales. Now over fifty, she commenced a sentimental flirtation with a musician which echoed *The Kreutzer Sonata*, though she wasn't physically unfaithful. This must help to flavour the suspicion of music which is so prominent in Tolstoy's notorious *What is Art* (1898).

Though he could touch no subject without making some interesting and pertinent remarks, *What is Art*, a lengthy treatise he took great pains with, shows at its worst the narrowing dogmatism of Tolstoy's last years, as well as exposing his strangely unhistorical ways of thinking. Tolstoy the novelist respected and could present the complex interactions of history as it moved, and had shown this above all in *Anna*. But Tolstoy the systematic thinker remained trapped in the limitations of the Enlightenment. Like men of the eighteenth century he sought for 'universal' solutions to problems which could only be understood and resolved through local and temporal situations.

His ideas nevertheless deserve more respect than they generally get. Art, which draws on the work of such people as stage-hands and printers, must, he argues be an important matter because it insists on such 'fearful sacrifices of the labour and lives of men . . .' What then is art? Tolstoy has no trouble in exposing the inanity of the conventional notion that art is what produces 'beauty'. Its definition he bases not on 'beauty' but on communication—it is an indispensable means of intercourse between man and man and its role is to transmit feeling. 'Good' art expresses the religious ideal of the age which produces it and the words 'good' and 'bad' have the same meaning in literary criticism as in morality. The doctrine of 'art for pleasure's sake' reflects the irreligion of the upper classes since the Renaissance when they stopped believing in God and became, in effect, pagans. The upper classes of Europe now believe that their own art is 'the true, the only, the universal art'—yet not only the people of Africa and Asia, but also 99 per cent of the people of Europe itself are not touched by this art, which lacks the freshness of true feeling, is affected, obscure and over-intellectual and caters above all for the upper-class vices of 'pride . . . sexual desire, and the weariness of life.'

So far, these arguments, despite their oversimplified historical framework, have a great deal of point and power. But, though few would be so absurd as to deny that much of the art of the 1890s is 'decadent', if the word decadence has any meaning at all, Tolstoy's specific targets include Wagner and Ibsen, Mallarmé and Kipling. To include Kipling, one of the few major writers in English to make at that time an immediate impression on ordinary people, among his list of 'incomprehensible' modern artists is to display ridiculous inattention to sociological fact (though to Tolstoy, of course, the urbanized masses of Britain would seem, as compared with rustics the world over, a perverted crowd).

Great works of art, says Tolstoy, are only great because they are accessible and comprehensible to everyone. If peasants are puzzled by Wagner, Wagner is bad. The simple epics, folk tales, folk songs, hymns and parables of every language are great art which can communicate in translation to everyone everywhere. This is because 'every man's relation to God is one and the same.' Hence, we must look in literature for something like the highest common factor in human experience. The function of 'true art' now must be to express the highest religious perception of our time, which

Tolstoy sees as the consciousness that our well-being lies in the growth of brotherhood among men and the creation of a universal commonwealth of peoples. There are two kinds of good art. 'Good religious art' expresses true religion with sincerity. Examples include Schiller's *Robbers*, certain stories of Hugo and Dickens and Dostoevsky, *Uncle Tom's Cabin* and George Eliot's *Adam Bede*. 'Universal art' is harder to find. Molière, for some reason, is perhaps 'the most universal artist of modern times.' Tolstoy rejects all his own work except one 'good religious' fable and one 'universal' story for children.

What is Art is not a dangerous book, it is thoroughly humane, but it is on the whole silly. It is characteristically self-punishing. Tolstoy excludes from his list of 'good' books not only his own novels, his own life's work, but also, except for Dickens, his own favourite writers. Rousseau and Sterne, Stendhal and Turgenev are not attacked, but they are not praised either. The lover of music so easily moved to tears rejects most of the music which moves him. The aristocratic intellectual submits everything to the judgement of the 'unperverted' peasant. Tolstoy, in fact, is advocating again the abolition of his own kind of man.

From 1895 onwards, he was drawn into a new campaign on behalf of the Dukhobors. This sect, now established in the Caucasus, had ideas of chastity, vegetarianism, abstinence from tobacco and alcohol, sharing of goods in common and non-resistance to evil, which were like his own. They wouldn't serve in the army, so the Government persecuted them. Their lands were confiscated, their leaders were imprisoned and thousands were sent into exile in the mountains, where many died of privation. A manifesto on their behalf with a signed postscript by Tolstoy was mailed to prominent figures in the administration. The police swooped and Tolstoy's disciple, Chertkov, was exiled. Tolstoy launched a campaign in the foreign press and the exasperated government finally authorised the sectarians to emigrate to Canada. But private charity couldn't raise enough money for the trip. For years Tolstoy had been working on a third major novel. Now, in the summer of 1898, he hastened to finish the book, sold it to a publisher for an immense sum and made the proceeds over to the Dukhobors. Publication of *Resurrection* began in 1899. It was severely censored but even so was the fullest embodiment yet in fiction of all Tolstoy's dangerous ideas. The Government still refrained from the error of martyring Tolstoy but the Church was less circumspect in the face of Tolstoy's fierce attack. In 1901, egged on by Pobedonostsev, the metropolitans ordered his excommunication to be read in all churches. This, of course, merely increased Tolstoy's stature at home and abroad.

In Moscow the old man was mobbed on the day when the excommunication was published by a huge and enthusiastic crowd of workers and students. Telegrams, letters, flowers and deputations flooded towards his home. Chekhov's right-wing friend Suvorin noted in his diary: 'We have two Tsars, Nicholas II and Leo Tolstoy. Which is the stronger? Nicholas II is powerless against Tolstoy and cannot make him tremble on his throne, whereas Tolstoy is incontestably shaking the throne of Nicholas II and his whole dynasty.'[32]

VII

Resurrection is perhaps the most sustained, eloquent and searching satire upon contemporary society in any language. Critics, missing the holiday atmosphere of the gayer parts of *War and Peace* and *Anna*, often accuse Tolstoy of having lost his love of life. They would do better to compare *Resurrection* with Zola's *Germinal* (1885) which exposes with equal power the prevalence of violence and exploitation in modern life, but in which the characters of both oppressed and oppressors are so deformed that the reader is left almost without hope. By contrast, Tolstoy's vision is kind and optimistic. The natural man still coexists with the man of society, and may yet triumph.

A friend who was a judge gave Tolstoy the basis of his story in 1887; the remorse of its hero had real-life authentication. In the novel, Prince Nekhliudov is a youngish man who has forsaken the high ideals of his student days but preserves an independence of mind which only serves to make him more attractive to his fellow parasites in Moscow high society. He sits on the jury which tries a prostitute named Katiusha Maslova for the murder of one of her clients, a merchant, and the theft of his money. The jury want to find her not guilty, but because the judge is in a hurry to get away and meet his mistress and does not brief them fully, because an old Colonel talks too much and because Nekhliudov himself does not keep his head, they return the absurd verdict that she committed the crime without any motive. Nekhliudov has recognized her as a former servant of his aunts' whom he seduced years ago. Convinced of his own guilt, he takes her case up to the Senate for appeal, meanwhile visiting her in prison, discovering there many other shocking examples of innocence punished, and resolving to marry her. When the appeal is turned down, he follows her to Siberia. Through his influence, she shares on the journey the life not of common convicts but of political prisoners. One of these, Simonson, has quasi-Tolstoyan views, including a devotion to celibacy, but falls in love with her. To spare Nekhliudov the degradation of marrying her, Maslova agrees to marry Simonson, just as word of her final pardon by the Tsar comes through. Nekhliudov, close to despair, reads the Sermon on the Mount and this, we are told, flatly and briefly, gives new meaning to his life.

Nekhliudov functions adequately enough through most of the novel as the man through whose sensitive eyes we observe the iniquities of the legal and social system. Tolstoy makes acute ironic play with the fact that it is because he belongs to the class of oppressors that he is able to pull strings on behalf of prisoners, and is alert to the selfishness inherent

in his project to marry Maslova for the sake of pacifying his own conscience. At one point she cries, 'You had your pleasure from me in this
world, and now you want to get your salvation through me in the world to
come! You disgust me....'[33] But Nekhliudov is not made positively
convincing as a man undergoing a spiritual crisis. He is shown from the
outset as someone with unusually refined moral sensibilities who tries to
behave well and, to the detriment of the novel, succeeds rather consistently
in doing so; for instance, though his offers to give his land to the peasants
are greeted by them with suspicion, he arrives at a settlement with them
remarkably quickly, and though he is tempted by a Petersburg lady who
wants to make him fall in love with her, he dashes away without having
compromised his new-found purity. Since his conscience is so strong
from the outset, his ultimate arrival at a Tolstoyan religious stance doesn't
surprise or move us in the least.

The lack of interesting human substance in Nekhliudov is accentuated
when he arrives in Siberia and Tolstoy is in the difficult position of writing
about characters of a kind he doesn't know very well—young political
prisoners—in a setting he doesn't know at all at first hand. The third
section of the novel is powerful by ordinary standards but laboured by
comparison with Tolstoy's own best work. And while the vegetarian
Simonson who has a home-made theory about everything, including
making fires, is acceptable as an amusing vignette of a limited man of great
integrity—he may hope to live in celibate domesticity with Maslova, but
there are clear indications that his theory will falter in face of her physical
charms—his female counterpart Maria Pavlovna, who lives wholly for
others and has also rejected sex is a creature whom Tolstoy tries to admire
but who makes the reader yearn for the sardonic treatment that Dostoevsky would have given her.

Yet when these important weaknesses have been noted, the achievement
of *Resurrection* remains a towering one. No other work of Tolstoy's has
wider social range, and for the first time he fully confronts in fiction the
revolutionary movement, and the miseries of the urban poor which he
had encountered when assisting with the Moscow census in 1882. The
book is set, rather loosely, in the 1880s. But just as Zola's coal mine in
Germinal becomes a metaphor for the whole of European society and for
its coming cataclysm, so Tolstoy uses the prison system to express the
quintessence of the modern state. Like *Ward Number Six*, but of course
on a far grander scale, *Resurrection* confronts central issues about power
and justice in the modern world.

The book seesaws between Maslova's life with her fellow prisoners
and Nekhliudov's in the world at large. The two milieux intersect whenever
Nekhliudov meets Maslova and in the great central episode where prisoners destined for Siberia march in intolerable heat through the centre of
Moscow to the railway station and Nekhliudov sees two of them die on
the way.

The novel opens with a vista of spring forcing its way through the pavings and smoke of the city in nature's great annual resurrection. Young life is unquenchable 'even in the town' and this elementally, undeniably hopeful image controls the direction of the book which follows. Crucially, we then begin with Maslova. By the time we smell the 'oppressive', 'artificial' scents which fill Nekhliudov's dressing room we have met the 'smell of sewage, tar and putrefaction' in the prison corridors. Neither, of course, is good; what is positive for Tolstoy is the cherry tree making its fragrance present even among the fumes of coal and gas. Both prison and Prince's apartment deny nature.

Within the brilliant, long account of the trial Tolstoy inserts the still more brilliant flashback to Nekhliudov's earlier relations with Maslova when she was a pure and pretty servant at his aunts'. Nowhere does Tolstoy (or perhaps anyone else) convey the drama of sexual awakening so poignantly. These memories climax in a supreme passage. Nekhliudov attends with Maslova the midnight service to bring in Easter Day at the local church. Afterwards, according to Russian custom, all present, rich and poor, greet each other with kisses, crying 'Christ is Risen'. 'On this night,' says an old servant, 'we are all equal.' Amid this foretaste of general, social 'resurrection', the lovers exchange three kisses. But next night, because it is 'what men generally do in these circumstances', Nekhliudov prowls round Maslova's room, and finally seizes her and seduces her. The Easter Service has given the lovers' relationship a dignity which Tolstoy can't dispel unless he makes the immediate aftermath altogether sordid. This he doesn't because as Nekhliudov stands outside Maslova's lighted window in the 'white mist of spring', he hears the ice breaking on the river, and there is no way of making that suggest anything but a necessary and 'natural' release, even though he writes of its 'mysterious sobbing, rustling, crackle and tinkle' and even though when Nekhliudov steps out again after the seduction he is aware of the moon 'shedding a sombre light on something black and menacing.' Tolstoy cannot, in short, deny the 'natural' (if anything is) associations which link spring and resurrection with young love and with the sexual act.

It is against these exciting images of life that we set the horrible image of the dead merchant's organs produced in jars as evidence in court, and the gross details of the medical examination after his body was exhumed:

4. The flesh was of a greenish hue and showed dark spots in places.
5. The skin was variously blistered and in places had peeled off and in places hung in large strips.
6. The hair was dark brown and easily detached from the skin.[34]

We can accept a symbolic association between the disgusting brothel life of Maslova and the corpse of this man who used the brothel. We can also accept Tolstoy's insistence that it was Nekhliudov's seduction which set Maslova on the road to the brothel. But the image of Nekhliudov catching her 'in her stiff unbleached nightshirt, with bare arms' doesn't inevitably imply the drunken whore she became. There would be nothing wrong with that if he had not betrayed her but continued the relationship. What made the marriage impossible was class. It was a class position which Nekhliudov expressed when, parting from her, he thrust an envelope with a hundred rouble note into her bodice. You pay servant girls, like whores for sex. For all Tolstoy's simplistic moral theories, it is not 'lust', as he displays it, which is the prime cause of Maslova's sufferings, it is class. And the act of lust on the night of the breaking ice is in the novel a major image of life to set against much death—against the death-in-life of people in prison and that of people in high society.

Tolstoy, of course, prefers the first to the second. Amid the obscenities, drunkenness and madness he finds among Maslova's prison companions much natural fellow feeling. He gives pity to the hideous red-haired woman who fights in the jail and then cries herself to sleep because she has had all her life 'nothing but abuse, jeers, insults and blows'. He is unforgiving towards the upper class 'invalid' who lolls in a velvet dress and tells polite lies out of sheer habit while a strong, handsome servant has to adjust the curtain for her so that the evening sun will not strike her ageing face and reveal her wrinkles. His straightforward presentation of the poor, with all their faults, gives force to his satire upon the rich.

We see the poor in groups, as we later see the political prisoners in a group. We meet the rich in ones and twos as Nekhliudov calls on lawyers and civil servants in order to use his influence on behalf of the poor. The rich are isolated from each other, as they are from the poor, by the functions which confine them to their offices. The form which the novel takes after the trial implicitly confirms the contrasts which it explicitly points to. The prisoners have a life in common, bad though it may be. But the daughter of the prison superintendent, hammering at the piano in her father's quarters within the jail, is isolated, a sickly, pathetic creature who would like Nekhliudov to come in and relieve her loneliness. One of Tolstoy's most remarkable scenes presents the aged Baron who rules over the fortress in Petersburg where political prisoners are held. After a lifetime spent administering regulations which deny the humanity of others, he is himself dehumanized, vacant of almost everything but obedience; except that it is strangely moving when this man is interrupted as, twisting a saucer on a sheet of paper, he is fooling himself that he is receiving messages sent by the spirit world about the life after death. He is also a prisoner, also a man like us.

The long gallery of officials and rich women down which Nekhliudov takes us blurs in memory into two generalized impressions; one of female sensuality and hypocritical piety, the other of male ambition and insensitivity. This is in spite of Tolstoy's skill in differentiating them, but it represents a valid artistic effect. In essence, he is suggesting, they are all much the same. Each woman has accepted the triviality of 'society' life as her medium, each man belongs to official life with its craving for medals and its substitution of routine for human fellow feeling. All are acting out roles, not expressing what Tolstoy would consider their natural, good selves. Maslova and Nekhliudov, before they meet each other again, are also players of roles. The prostitute, Tolstoy tells us, believes that what she does is good and necessary just as bullying bureaucrats believe that what they do is good and necessary. The priest who swears in the jury at the trial typifies the entire social system. He is proud of having sworn in tens of thousands of men although the Gospel expressly forbids all oaths. And, of course, he draws a salary for his work. Tolstoy's denunciation of the official Church is part and parcel of his attack on the State. But thematically and symbolically it enriches the attack. At the end of the novel Nekhliudov argues to himself that the cannibalism committed by escaped convicts began 'not in the Siberian marshes but in ministerial offices and government departments'; it is a product of a social system for which rich men must be held responsible. The church service in prison not only contrasts with its predecessor in the novel, the liberating Easter Night service, but also shows us a cannibal act ordered by the state. Tolstoy employs his favourite device of 'making strange' as the priest gives children the bread and wine. 'After that the priest carried the cup back behind the partition, and drinking up all the blood left in the cup and eating all the remaining bits of God's body, and painstakingly licking round his moustaches and wiping his mouth and the cup, briskly marched out from behind the partition, in the most cheerful frame of mind, the thin soles of his calf-skin boots creaking slightly as he walked.'[35]

Cannibalism involves treating other people like animals to be eaten or objects to be used. A feature of *Resurrection* which marks a radical departure from the methods of *War and Peace* and *Anna* is the accumulation around the characters of inert detail. Furniture, not before a concern of Tolstoy's, is here brought sharply to our attention. We might remember Gogol; this is another world in which human beings and things are confused, though never so radically as in *Dead Souls*. At one point Nekhliudov wishes to dispose of all his belongings, but his servants, dedicated like everyone else to their roles, insist on his keeping them and, since it is spring, bring out all the unnecessary clothes which are never worn, all the carpets and furniture, and clean them. 'Their only use and purpose, Nekhliudov thought, was to provide exercise for Agrafena Petrovna, Kornei, the house porter, the boy and the cook.'[36] In high society, as Tolstoy portrays it, each man sticks in his place, like a chair or a table, and is as unfeeling. Nekhliudov cannot make adequate contact with his own sister. At lower levels, people flow towards each other, as Maslova and her friend Fedosia support each other in jail.

But no one is wholly bad. All are capable of resurrection. The lawyer Fanarin may be a shallow man, but he does take on without pay the case of a pair of peasants who have been unjustly accused. Tolstoy's view of mankind in general here is, if anything, rather more generous than in some parts of *War and Peace*. Where he has departed from his old views is in identifying flesh and spirit as irreconcilable opposites. Pierre can be virtuous in bed with Natasha, but only celibacy, a victory over the flesh, can, Nekhliudov thinks, liberate his spirit, so if he marries Maslova he won't sleep with her.

Tolstoy himself, so far from defeating the flesh, was still capable, at the age of seventy, of manifesting his passion, as Sonia recorded in her diary, after a ride of nearly twenty miles. In the last pages of *Resurrection* he has Nekhliudov peer into the cots of two pretty young children shown him by their proud mother, and the old Tolstoyan ideal of family happiness reasserts itself against the sterility of Maria Pavlovna. Maslova, further-more, remains irredeemably fleshly. There is no other character in his fiction upon whom Tolstoy lavishes so much physical detail. Psychologic-ally, he handles her well—her revulsion against sex is easily explained by her experiences and her shy presence among the political prisoners is as well conveyed as her half-spiteful, half-adoring reactions to Nekhliudov. But what we remember above all are her full bosom, her curly black hair, her rapid step and her brilliant black eyes with their slight squint. When we set her against the physically vague Nekhliudov, we are tempted to see the war between flesh and spirit as one between her and him, and so far as our sympathies go, flesh must win hands down. The nature which thrusts through the city streets on the first page thrusts also in her walk and her bosom.

The book begins with spring and ends with the first fall of snow in Siberia. It begins with the sexy Maslova marching towards court, and ends with Nekhliudov reading a Bible. There is a movement from imprison-ment to freedom, but also another from fresh new life to winter death. 'Nature', as always, sets problems which Tolstoy can't solve. Another opposition is easier to rationalize. The liberating Christ of Easter equality is opposed to the official Christ of the Church, and his kingdom will come on earth.

But how? Nekhliudov near the end is impressed by an old man who wanders the roads refusing to accept all authority. He will answer to no name save Man, and he identifies himself with Christ. He represents Tolstoy's own yearning for the free life of the wanderer who has evaded all responsibility for the crimes of society. He is also, quite clearly, mad. His happiness may be real, but his defiance is sterile. Tolstoy wants to make Man positive and Society negative. But he can only present people, of course, as what they really are, social creatures.

Resurrection deserves to be judged not in terms of its failure to do what Tolstoy could never have done—show through a realistic novel that his ideas were right—but in terms of the truth and power of its satire on Russian society. Can it really be, Nekhliudov asks, 'that all the talk about justice, goodness, law, religion, God and so on, was nothing but so many words to conceal the grossest self interest and cruelty?' Can it really be 'that all these people had been arrested, locked up or exiled, not in the least because they had transgressed against justice or committed lawless acts but merely because they were an obstacle hindering the officials and the rich from enjoying the wealth they were busy amassing from the people?'[37] The answer, of course, is yes, in so far as there is no clearer or more useful explanation of how the law operated in Russia then and of how it operates now in South Africa. What Tolstoy proposes is true, to some extent at least, of any stratified society.

As Tolstoy sees clearly, such injustice creates revolutionaries, and he so hates it that almost all its enemies seem in effect to be his allies. Amongst his 'politicals', Tolstoy dislikes the Marxist Novodvorov, an *élitist* who would impose revolution from above while creating a new State. But he likes the socialist peasant Nabatov in spite of his atheism; and through Nekhliudov's love for him he invites us to admire the dying Kryltsov, whose experiences in prison have transformed him from a gentle idealist into a man who cries out that the present ruling class should be bombed to death.

Tolstoy's own class must perish. Society must be reborn; his own class must stop having children and die out. So Nekhliudov must be colourless, sterile and negative. His child by Maslova must die. The revolutionaries' spring is also Nekhliudov's winter. The book offers hope, but not for aristocrats. The breaking ice sounds both menacing and delightful.

VIII

Tolstoy finished his short last novel, *Hadji Murad* in 1904, but he didn't publish it; he didn't want any more quarrels over copyrights. He had worked on it from about 1896 and had researched its details with the same care with which he had quarried material for *War and Peace*, though it is only a fraction of that book's length.

It is based on the life and death of a real man, whom Tolstoy himself had met in the Caucasus in 1851. Hadji Murad, long a dangerous enemy of the Russians, quarrels with his leader Shamil and deserts to the imperialist side. But he cannot trust the Russians, nor they him, and, worried about the fate of his family whom Shamil has imprisoned, he finally breaks away to attempt to rescue them. The Russians and their allies pursue him and kill him. He dies bravely in a hopeless fight.

The story's fundamental point seems to emerge in its first pages where Tolstoy describes how, walking in a huge ploughed field of black earth which a landed proprietor has devastated for his profit, he sees a thistle mutilated by a cartwheel but still standing, 'as if a piece of its body had been torn from it, its bowels had been drawn out, an arm torn off, and one of its eyes plucked out; and yet it stood firm and did not surrender to man,

who had destroyed all its brothers around it. "What energy!" I thought.'[38]
This thistle reminds him of Hadji Murad.

Hadji Murad, for all his own cruelty and treachery is a 'natural' man,
simply and habitually religious, who is at odds with the modern state. But
Tolstoy does not moralize upon this theme. Forty years after the suppres-
sion of the Caucasian resistance, he presents the hill-man's way of life,
with its feuds and its ascetic but violent Muslim faith, simply and frankly,
without factitious pathos. His details speak for themselves. These things
have happened, and though we may regret them we cannot alter them.
Tolstoy's fundamentally conservative temperament here expresses itself
not in protest but in statement.

The novel's 'peep-show' method (to use Tolstoy's own description) is
essentially that of *War and Peace* in miniature. Tolstoy begins with Hadji
Murad's desertion and then lets the ripples of this event (as it were) take
us away from his hero as he shows us the conversations and actions of
groups of people on the insurgent and on the Russian side who are
concerned in different ways with him but are ultimately as incapable of
sympathizing fully with his fate as he would be of condoling with theirs.
Tsar Nicholas, whom we meet in Petersburg making a swift decision as to
how to make use of Hadji Murad's defection is still more remote from the
man whose destiny he pretends to arbitrate over than Napoleon is from the
captive Pierre.

Reproducing in miniature the enormous social and geographical range
of his earlier masterpieces, Tolstoy necessarily strips all his characters,
real and invented, down to basic essentials of Tolstoyan man. He dares to
put himself into the mind of a man of a different culture, Hadji Murad
himself, and his method is much like that by which he became Levin's
dog; he assumes that what the eyes see and the brain remembers form the
contents of any creature's consciousness. Butler, the young frontier
officer who becomes a kind of 'friend' of Hadji Murad without really
understanding him at all is a convincing enough abstract of many young
men in Tolstoy's fiction, prone to gambling and careless lust, but decent
at heart. Even Nicholas I, made wonderfully odious in this brief portrait,
is permitted to feel an unacknowledged twinge of conscience as he
remembers his copulation, the night before, with a young Swedish virgin
who has pitched herself at him.

Tolstoy has been accused of, or praised for, contradicting his pacifist
ideas by making his hero in this story an energetic warrior. But *Hadji
Murad* in fact stirs revulsion against war as it does against autocracy. Nor
is it quite the final hymn to life which some critics would like to pretend that
it is. As in *War and Peace*, a craving for absorption into nature, for death, is
in tension with a love of human life. Since the final paragraph reasserts
the image of the mutilated but not dead thistle, though Hadji Murad's
death has ended the story, nature on the one hand and human death on
the other win a combined victory, as they did in *Three Deaths* in the 1850s.

But there is a further meaning to the thistle which makes it a less depressing symbol. It represents the stoical conservatism in Tolstoy himself which prizes still the unselfconscious virtues of older, more 'natural' ways of life—the way of life of the old nobility, or that of old-style peasants, or that of hill tribesmen, lived in easy communion with trees and with horses and with hunted beasts. Tolstoy himself, as it were, is the last thistle in the field, the last voice doggedly holding out against technology, economic 'progress', imperialism and the modern state.

EPILOGUE

To Maxim Gorky, who met him in the Crimea in 1901, when Tolstoy was convalescing after an illness, the old man seemed 'like a God, not a Sabaoth or Olympian, but the kind of Russian God who "sits on a maple throne under a golden lime tree", not very majestic, but perhaps more cunning than all the other gods.'[1]

Few books in any literature can be as moving as Gorky's brief *Reminiscences of Tolstoy* (1919). Gorky, whose real name was Alexis Peshkov and whose pseudonym meant 'bitter', had grown up in the coarse and brutal world of his grandfather, a dyer, in the city of Nizhny Novgorod which has now been renamed after him. *Childhood* (1913), one of the world's great books, is his account of that upbringing. Sent out into the world to make his own way, he had knocked around in various menial jobs and had tramped the long, hungry roads of Russia. Self-educated, he had published his first tale in 1892 and six years later a collection of his stories had made him very famous. He had brought his fellow tramps, as his characters, with him into the daylight of European fiction, and his influence, all over the world (it is, for instance, especially noticeable in certain Indian writers) has been as important as that of any Russian. The main fault of his stories is a tendency towards exaggeration in style and content; their salient virtues are compassion and energy. Equally notable for his courage as a Socialist opponent of Tsarism and for his role after the Revolution as critic, friend and protector of talented writers, Gorky, like Chekhov, is one of the most modest and likeable of major artists.

This shrewd plebeian now confronted an aristocratic master whom he alternately loved and hated, but always admired. Chekhov, of course, was in the Crimea too. 'You know, I cannot stand Shakespeare, but your plays are even worse', Tolstoy had once told Chekhov, to the latter's unaffected amusement, but the old man really loved his sick friend, though he suspected him of atheism, and the younger tolerated his teasing and put up somehow with Tolstoy's fondness for obscene peasant expressions. Gorky was there when Tolstoy asked Chekhov, 'Did you whore a great deal in your youth?' and Anton Pavlovich tugged at his beard and mumbled inaudibly.[2]

Gorky's memoir captures, as if Tolstoy himself were one of the most remarkable characters in fiction, his cunning little smiles, his coldness when he spoke of Dostoevsky or of Christ, his 'very suspicious' relations with God, rather like those of 'two bears in one den', and those aristocratic traits that he couldn't hide under his peasant's beard and 'democratically rumpled blouse', which made the resentful Gorky feel that he was being inspected as if he were a member of a little-known tribe, but which were somehow compatible with a beautiful way of talking, 'saturated in village simplicity.' The man's pride was intolerable. His charm was omnipotent:

> When Lev Nikolaevich wished to please, he could do so more easily than a clever and beautiful woman. Imagine a company of people of all kinds sitting in his room: the Grand Duke Nikolai Mikhailovich, the house painter Ilia, a social democrat from Yalta, the Stundist Patsuk, a musician, a German, the manager of the estates of Countess Kleinmichel, the poet Bulgakov, and all look at him with the same enamoured eyes. He explains to them the teaching of Lao Tse, and he seems to me an extraordinary man-orchestra, possessing the faculty of playing several instruments at the same time, a brass trumpet, a drum, harmonium, and flute.[3]

Yet out in the open air this complete 'man of society', leaping across ditches, sniffing the earth and the moss, seemed at home in the whole of nature. Gorky watched him once sitting on the sea shore, like 'an old stone come to life', apparently in communication with everything around him, and thought, 'I am not an orphan on the earth so long as this man lives on it.'[4]

Tolstoy's serious new illness early in 1902, an attack of pneumonia, upset both Gorky and Chekhov deeply. It might seem almost a pity that he didn't die then, in a phase of close understanding with two of the very few writers who were not limp and wee in comparison with himself. Yet we cannot really wish that the man who had told Gorky 'everything must be written about, everything' should have missed a single second of his experience. The war between Russia and Japan which broke out in 1904 brought him a self-contradictory dismay. He proclaimed his neutrality and his support for the 'workers of both countries', but one of his sons enlisted to fight and the humiliating defeats suffered by his own country on sea and land grieved the veteran of Sevastopol.

Like the Crimean War fifty years before, this new conflict exposed the incompetence of Tsarist organization, and now it was in the face of an Asiatic people which had begun to create a modern state and army only a few decades before. And whereas in 1855 'public opinion' had expressed itself only in rude remarks within the ruling class, now defeat licensed the rage of masses, based less on patriotism than on profound social and economic causes. In January 1905 troops fired on an orderly crowd of workers who had gone to present a petition to the Tsar and killed more than a hundred people. A strike wave involving hundreds of thousands followed. Through the year, peasants revolted, Polish and Ukrainian nationalists made their resentments clear, *Zemstvo* men and professional people voiced their anger. In June after the war with Japan had ended the crew of the battleship *Potemkin* mutinied at Odessa, and in another strike wave in October the workers of St Petersburg set up their own Soviet. In December, a rising in Moscow lasted nearly two weeks. Russia emerged from this year of revolution with its crisis unsolved. The Tsar had granted an assembly with a franchise embracing all classes, but this new *Duma* stood no chance of success when Nicholas II would permit no real inter-ference with his autocratic powers. The first elections in 1906 showed the extent of opposition. Only 32 right-wingers were elected, as opposed to 179 liberal 'Cadets', 94 Socialist Revolutionaries and 18 Social Democrats.

Tolstoy had projected the coming contest of left-wing parties in the contrast between the peasant Nabatov and Novodvorov the Marxist in *Resurrection*. The Socialist Revolutionaries, influential in the country-side, were heirs to the old populist (and terrorist) tradition. Marxism had been slowly gathering strength among town workers since the 1880s and now in Lenin, proponent of the concept of a firmly disciplined revolutionary party dominated by an *élite* of intellectuals, the Bolshevik faction of Social Democrats had the finest of Russian political brains.

Tolstoy's appeals for non-violence in 1905, addressed both to author-ities and rebels, were, of course, obeyed by neither side. But his influence had never been more apparent. He had helped mightily to undermine tolerance for the Tsarist régime among all classes.

While the Tsar stifled the *Duma* by restricting the franchise so as to ensure right-wing dominance in it, Tolstoy's marital problems hovered between tragedy and farce. Chertkov returned from exile in 1907, as dedicated and dogmatic a Tolstoyan as ever. The struggle between him and Sonia resumed. Sasha, Tolstoy's third daughter, still remained at home (Tania and Masha had defied their father's precept of celibacy and had married) and she took her father's side. One prize in the quarrel was Tolstoy's copyrights—should they go to Sonia after his death or should they be public property? Another was the possession of Tolstoy's private diaries. As plots and counter-plots proceeded, and the diaries were read and disputed over incessantly, the writer with a chronic auto-biographical itch was reduced to keeping a secret *Diary for Myself Alone*.

On 28 October 1910 he fled from his home with a doctor friend, leaving a note for Sonia asking her to forgive him all the wrongs he had done her. He went dressed as a peasant; the old dream of a frugal life of contem-plation was to be realized at last. His first goal, reached by train, was the Optina Pustyn Monastery. He wrote to Sasha asking her to send him a pair of scissors, some pencils, a dressing gown, and the three books he had been reading, Maupassant's *Une Vie*, the essays of Montaigne, and the second volume of *Karamazov*.

Sasha joined him on the 30th. Then he escaped southward, hoping to settle somewhere in that Caucasus he had written about so well. The newspapers proclaimed in headlines the story that he had left home. Fellow passengers recognized him. Tolstoy fell ill with pneumonia. He was taken off the train at the obscure station of Astapovo and lodged in the stationmaster's cottage. With him, a great age of prose fiction was dying. His influence would persist in Russian fiction in diverse and seemingly contradictory ways. It would stand behind the laconic stories of Isaac Babel and Pasternak's condensed poetic prose as well as the epic sweep of Sholokhov. In the 1960s Solzhenitsyn would inherit his role as the opponent at the centre, the prophet made so strong by the written word that the authorities could not silence him. But the undisputed primacy of the novel, as the form which had manufactured ideals and dreams for millions and, like the theatre in Shakespeare's day, had engrossed every aspect of life and every debate, becoming itself a major part of the reality which it depicted, was already threatened by the cinema.

Tolstoy had not been hostile to all modern inventions. At one time, he had developed a taste for cycling. In 1909 he had seen his first motion picture. The form appealed to him. He talked about writing a film scenario. 'Just imagine,' he said at dinner, 'with this technique one could reach huge masses of people, all the peoples of the earth.'[5]

Now the film cameras captured the last scenes of his marriage so that all the peoples on earth might one day view them. Sonia, stout and determined-looking, marches up to the door of the stationmaster's cottage. A head appears. They argue. Sonia turns away.

Pressmen and cameramen choked the little town and plain clothes spies mixed with them. The government feared an insurrection and ammunition was distributed to the police. The old man died at 6 am on the 7th November. His last muttered words were, 'The truth ... I care a great deal ... How they....' Sonia didn't hear them. Sasha, Chertkov and the favoured son Sergei Tolstoy, didn't let her in till a few hours before the end.

But the railway workers decorated his deathbed with juniper boughs and a wreath labelled, 'To the apostle of love'. A crowd filed past the body. The church had forbidden any rites, and when the throng began to sing the funeral chant 'Eternal Memory', police rushed in and forbade it.

When they were little boys, Tolstoy's beloved elder brother Nikolai had told him that he knew a secret, and that when it was publicized all sickness would vanish from the earth and all men would love each other. This secret was carved on a green stick buried on the edge of a ravine near Yasnaia Poliana. Tolstoy had asked that he should be buried in that place. On the day that his body went home, troops stood by in the major cities in case of riots. Workers and students demonstrated. State reprisals provoked a long student strike. At the first public burial in Russia at which no priest was present, the crowd sang, knelt, and quietly went away.

Gorky was furious when he heard of Tolstoy's flight. This was no time to create a legend of martyred sainthood. 'I do not want,' he wrote, 'to see

Tolstoy a saint; let him remain a sinner close to the heart of the all-sinful world. . .' But then came the telegram saying he was dead. 'I cried with pain and anger, and now, half-crazy, I imagine him as I knew and saw him—I am tormented by a desire to speak with him. I imagine him in his coffin—he lies like a smooth stone at the bottom of a stream, and in his grey beard, I am sure, is quietly hidden that aloof, mysterious little smile.'[6]

Seven years later, in Europe as in Russia, the world portrayed in the nineteenth-century novel was being shelled and shot and blasted away. The kind of carnage which Tolstoy had described in his account of the battle of Borodino had gone on, not for one day, but day after day for three years. Tolstoy's class was dead. But the peasants of Yasnaia Poliana rallied and repelled a crowd of armed men from neighbouring villages who were marching upon the old home behind a Red Flag. This was one of the few noble houses to be spared. It was not exactly non-resistance which had saved it, but Konstantin Levin's creator had won a posthumous point.

That November, in 1917, one of Gorky's discoveries, young Isaac Babel, joined a friend in a Petersburg building now occupied by the Cheka, the political police of the victorious Bolsheviks. This was a palace once lived in by Alexander III. They sat in the former Tsarina's library and Babel, wearing the Tsar's vast dressing gown, refused one of that monarch's eight-inch-long cigarettes and picked instead a cigar from a box presented by Sultan Abdul Hamid of Turkey. They spent the rest of the night sorting the toys Tsar Nicholas II had once played with. His mother's intimate letters crumbled under their fingers. 'Until daybreak we were unable to tear ourselves away from this silent, fateful story. Abdul Hamid's cigar was smoked to the end.'[7]

REFERENCES

All books cited are published in London, unless otherwise stated. Editions specified are sometimes different from those in the Short List of Books at the end. I have given chapter references to novels because I know that people will be using different translations or editions.

CHAPTER ONE: PUSHKIN'S RUSSIA

1. N. M. Karamzin, *Letters of a Russian Traveller 1789–1790*, trans. F. Jonas (Oxford University Press 1957) 247.
2. ibid., 264.
3. Georg Lukács, 'Dostoevsky', in *Dostoevsky*, ed. R. Wellek, (Prentice Hall, Englewood Cliffs N. J., 1962) 146.
4. A. N. Radishchev, *A Journey from St Petersburg to Moscow*, trans. L. Weiner (Harvard University Press, Cambridge Mass. 1958) 139, 219.
5. ibid., 11.
6. John Parkinson, *A Tour of Russia* . . . (Cass 1971) 97.
7. D. I. Fonvizin, 'The Young Hopeful', in *Masterpieces of the Russian Drama*, ed. G. R. Noyes (Appleton, N. Y. 1933) 73.
8. N. V. Gogol, *Dead Souls*, Chapter 12, trans. B. G. Guerney (Random House, N. Y., 1965) 294–5.
9. M. T. Florinsky, *Russia: A History* . . . (Macmillan, N. Y., 1953) 428.
10. D. S. Mirsky, *Russia: A Social History* (Cresset Press, 1931) 205.
11. H. Seton-Watson, *The Russian Empire 1801–1917* (Oxford University Press 1967) 129.
12. B. R. Haydon, *Autobiography* (Oxford University Press 1927) 283.
13. Baron Von Haxthausen, *The Russian Empire* . . . Vol I (Chapman and Hall 1856) 181.
14. A. G. Mazour, *The First Russian Revolution 1825* (University of California Press, Berkeley, 1937) 55–6.
15. ibid., 220.
16. Marquis de Custine, *The Empire of the Czar*, Vol I (Longman 1843) 192.
17. Florinsky, op. cit., 755.
18. ibid., 789.
19. B. Pares, *A History of Russia* (Methuen 1962 edn) 369.
20. R. Pinkerton, *Russia* (Seeley 1833) 346.
21. T. Raikes, *A Visit to St Petersburg* . . . (Bentley 1838) 322.
22. Seton-Watson, op. cit., 257–8.
23. Florinsky, op. cit., 717.
24. J. Blum, *Lord and Peasant in Russia* . . . (Princeton University Press 1961) 557–8.
25. Haxthausen, op. cit., Vol 2, 229.
26. Blum, op. cit., 369.

27. H. Gifford, introduction to C. Tomlinson, trans., *Versions from Fyodor Tyutchev* (Oxford University Press 1960) 4.
28. Mazour, op. cit., 224.
29. Haxthausen, op. cit., Vol I, 45.
30. R. Lyall, *The Character of the Russians* . . . (Cadell and Blackwood 1823) cxxi.
31. G. Saintsbury, 'Turgenev, Dostoevsky and Tolstoy', in *Russian Literature and Modern English Fiction*, ed. D. Davie (University of Chicago Press, 1965) 23.
32. D. Magarshack, *Pushkin* (Chapman and Hall 1967) 59.
33. E. J. Simmons, *Pushkin* (Oxford University Press 1937) 95.
34. Magarshack, op. cit., 303–4.
35. T. Wolff, ed., *Pushkin on Literature* (Methuen 1971) 327–8, 378.
36. Lyall, op. cit., cxxv.
37. A. S. Pushkin, 'Roslavlev', in *Complete Prose Tales*, trans. G. R. Aitken (Barrie and Rockcliff 1966) 166–7.
38. John Bayley, *Pushkin: A Comparative Commentary* (Cambridge University Press 1971) 5.
39. Magarshack, op. cit., 202.
40. J. T. Shaw, ed., *Letters of Alexander Pushkin* (University of Wisconsin Press 1967) 199–201.
41. V. Nabokov, ed. and trans., *Eugene Onegin* Vol I (Routledge, 1964) 16.
42. ibid., 272–3.
43. ibid., 120.
44. T. Wolff, op. cit., 23.
45. *The Captain's Daughter*, Ch. I, trans. R. Edmonds, in *The Queen of Spades and other Stories* (Penguin 1962) 191.
46. ibid., Ch. 2, 200–1.
47. ibid. Ch. 7, 247.
48. ibid., Ch. 6, 237.

CHAPTER TWO: GOGOL, LERMONTOV AND GONCHAROV

1. I. S. Turgenev, *Literary Reminiscences* . . . , trans. D. Magarshack, (Faber 1959) 119.
2. Alexander Herzen, *My Past and Thoughts*, Vol I, trans. C. Garnett, rev. H. Higgens (Chatto 1968) 95–6.
3. I. Berlin, 'A Marvellous Decade 1838–1848', *Encounter* (Vols 4 and 5, June 1955) 33.
4. ibid., loc. cit., 38.
5. H. Seton-Watson, *The Russian Empire 1801–1917* (Oxford University Press 1967) 257–8.
6. D. S. Mirsky, *History of Russian Literature* (Routledge 1968) 162.
7. Sir J. Maynard, *Russia in Flux* (Gollancz, 1941) 172–3.
8. B. Pares, *History of Russia* (Methuen 1962 edn) 380.
9. Turgenev, op. cit., 110: Herzen, op. cit., Vol 2, 411.
10. R. Wellek, *History of Modern Criticism* Vol 3 (Cape 1966) 243–64.
11. Maynard, op. cit., 175.
12. J. Mersereau, *Mikhail Lermontov* (Southern Illinois University Press, Carbondale, 1962) 16.
13. Turgenev, op. cit., 153.
14. M. Lermontov, *A Hero of Our Time*, trans. P. Foote (Penguin 1966) 19–20.
15. D. Davie, 'Tolstoy, Lermontov, and Others', in *Russian Literature and Modern English Fiction* (University of Chicago Press 1965) 196.
16. Mirsky, op. cit., 158.
17. *A Hero of Our Time*, 69.
18. ibid., 148.
19. ibid., 157.
20. ibid., 180.

21. Mersereau, op. cit., 141.
22. Mirsky, op. cit., 146.
23. Turgenev, op. cit., 149.
24. Mirsky, op. cit., 154.
25. D. Magarshack, *Gogol* (Faber 1957) 132–3.
26. ibid., 126–7.
27. ibid., 157.
28. ibid., 199.
29. ibid., 264.
30. Marquis de Custine, *Empire of the Czar*, Vol 3 (Longman 1843) 181; Vol 2, 255.
31. ibid., Vol I, 121–2; Vol 3, 253–4.
32. Mirsky, op. cit., 151.
33. V. Nabokov, *Nikolai Gogol* (Editions Poetry, 1947) 70.
34. L. Kent, ed., *Collected Tales and Plays of Nikolai Gogol*, trans. C. Garnett, (Pantheon, N.Y., 1964) 574–5.
35. ibid., 462–3.
36. *Dead Souls*, trans. B. G. Guerney (Random House, N.Y., 1965) Ch. 1., 4.
37. ibid., Ch. 8, 202–3.
38. Nabokov, op. cit., 93.
39. *Dead Souls*, Ch. 6, 142.
40. *Dead Souls*, Ch. 11, 281.
41. J. Lavrin, *Goncharov* (Bowes and Bowes, Cambridge, 1954) 9.
42. *Oblomov*, Pt I, Ch. 8, trans. A. Dunnigan (New American Library, N.Y., 1963) 108–9.
43. ibid., Pt 4, Ch. 11, 557.
44. N. A. Dobroliubov, in *Readings in Russian History*, ed. Warren B. Walsh (Syracuse University Press 1963) 446: cf. N. A. Dobroliubov, *Selected Philosophical Essays* (trans. J. Fineberg, Foreign Languages Publishing House, Moscow, 1956) 174–217.
45. Lavrin, op. cit., 55.
46. *Oblomov*, Pt I, Ch. 9, 137–8.
47. ibid., Pt 4, Ch. 9, 547–8.
48. Lavrin, op. cit., 28.
49. *Oblomov*, Pt 2, Ch. 10, 301; Pt 4, Ch. 2, 446.

CHAPTER THREE: THE ART OF TURGENEV

1. P. Kropotkin, *Russian Literature: Ideals and Realities* (Duckworth 1916) 93.
2. *Literary Reminiscences*, trans. D. Magarshack (Faber 1959) 92–3.
3. *Rudin*, Ch. 6, in *The Vintage Turgenev*, Vol 2, trans. H. Stevens (Vintage, N.Y. 1950) 205.
4. R. Freeborn, *Turgenev: The Novelist's Novelist* (Oxford University Press 1960) 9.
5. *Literary Reminiscences*, 108–9, 113.
6. Frank O'Connor, *The Mirror in the Roadway* (Hamish Hamilton 1957) 134.
7. A. Yarmolinsky, *Turgenev* (Orion Press, N.Y. 1959 edn) 143.
8. B. Pares, *History of Russia* (Methuen 1962 edn) 385.
9. Freeborn, op. cit., 38.
10. ibid., 20–21.
11. 'A Correspondence' in *The Diary of a Superfluous Man etc.*, trans. C. Garnett (Heinemann 1899) 288–93.
12. *Rudin*, Ch. 3, 174.
13. H. Seton Watson, *The Russian Empire 1801–1917* (Oxford University Press 1967) 331.
14. D. Mackenzie Wallace, *Russia* Vol 2 (Cassell 1877 edn) 210–11.
15. Seton Watson, op. cit., 335.
16. *Home of the Gentry*, Ch. 45, trans. R. Freeborn (Penguin 1970) 194.
17. *On The Eve*, Ch. 6, trans. G. Gardiner (Penguin 1950) 53.
18. D. S. Mirsky, *History of Russian Literature* (Routledge 1968) 194.
19. *On The Eve*, Ch. 30, 197.

20. E. H. Carr, Introduction to N. G. Chernyshevsky, *What Is To Be Done* (Vintage, N.Y., 1961) xi-xii.
21. R. Wellek, *History of Modern Criticism*, Vol 4 (Cape 1966) 238–45.
22. N. A. Dobroliubov, *Selected Philosophical Essays*, trans. J. Fineberg (Foreign Languages Publishing House, Moscow 1956) 389–441.
23. *Literary Reminiscences*, 168–171.
24. Yarmolinsky, op. cit., 229.
25. F. Venturi, *Roots of Revolution* (Weidenfeld 1959) 299.
26. H. Troyat, *Tolstoy* (Penguin 1970 edn) 186–7.
27. *Smoke*, Ch. 26, trans. N. Duddington (Dent 1965) 225.
28. *A Lear of the Steppes*, Ch. 31, trans. C. Garnett (Heinemann 1898) 147.
29. Seton Watson, op. cit., 422–3.
30. *Virgin Soil*, Ch. 38, trans. R. S. Townsend (Dent 1963) 315–6.
31. Edmund Wilson, *A Window on Russia* (Macmillan 1973) 105.
32. Freeborn, op. cit., 186.
33. *Literary Reminiscences*, 175.
34. Wilson, op. cit., 93.
35. O' Connor, op. cit., 142.
36. Henry James, *House of Fiction* (Hart Davis 1957) 171.
37. Freeborn, op. cit., 47.
38. Freeborn, op. cit., 89–90.
39. *Fathers and Sons*, Ch. 7, trans. R. Edmonds (Penguin 1965) 47.
40. ibid., Ch. 5, 36; Ch. 10, 61.
41. ibid., Ch. 10, 68.
42. ibid., Ch. 28, 237.
43. ibid., Ch. 19, 129–30.
44. ibid., Ch. 21, 150–1.
45. ibid., Chs. 7 and 26, 47, 214.
46. H. Gifford, *The Novel in Russia* (Hutchinson 1964) 97.
47. *The Golovlovs*, Ch. 7, trans. A. R. MacAndrew (New American Library, N.Y. 1961) 295–6.
48. ibid., Ch. 5, 240.
49. ibid. Ch. 7, 293.
50. ibid., Ch. I, 55.

CHAPTER FOUR: DOSTOEVSKY TO 'CRIME AND PUNISHMENT'

1. G. Lukács, 'Dostoevsky', in *Dostoevsky*, ed. R. Wellek, (Prentice Hall, Englewood Cliffs N.J., 1962) 152.
2. D. Magarshack, *Dostoevsky* (Secker and Warburg 1962) 59–60.
3. *Poor Folk*, in *Three Short Novels*, trans. A. R. MacAndrew (Bantam, N.Y. 1966) 129.
4. Magarshack, op. cit., 123.
5. ibid., 151–60.
6. ibid., 191–2.
7. ibid., 250–1.
8. ibid., 268–76; see Dostoevsky, *Summer Impressions*, (trans. K. Fitzlyon, Calder 1955) 55–69, 70–87.
9. G. Steiner, *Tolstoy or Dostoevsky* (Penguin 1967) 131.
10. *The Insulted and Injured*, trans. C. Garnett (Heinemann 1947) 238.
11. ibid., 234.
12. H. Troyat, *Tolstoy* (Penguin 1970) 553.
13. *Memoirs from the House of the Dead*, trans. J. Coulson (Oxford University Press 1965) Pt I, Ch. I, 12; Pt 2, Ch. 10, 359–60; Pt I, Ch. 11, 184.
14. ibid., Pt 2, Ch. 10, 359.
15. Magarshack, op. cit., 329.

16. *Notes from Underground*, trans. J. Coulson (Penguin 1972) 32–4.
17. ibid, 122–3.
18. *A Raw Youth*, trans. C. Garnett (Heinemann 1916) Pt 2, Ch. 6, 278.
19. *Crime and Punishment*, trans. D. Magarshack (Penguin 1951). Pt I, Ch. 3, 45.
20. ibid., Pt 6, Ch. 7, 529–30.
21. ibid. Pt 5, Ch. 4, 428–33.
22. ibid., Pt 6, Ch. 2, 471–2.
23. ibid. Pt 6, Ch. 1, 451–2.
24. ibid. Pt 4, Ch. 1, 305.
25. ibid. Pt 2, Ch. 5, 167, 170.
26. ibid., Pt 3, Ch. 2, 232.
27. ibid., Pt 3, Ch. 5, 278.

CHAPTER FIVE: TOLSTOY TO 'WAR AND PEACE'

1. *Two Hussars* in *Nine Stories*, trans. L. and A. Maude (Oxford University Press 1933) 69.
2. R. F. Christian, *Tolstoy's War and Peace* (Oxford University Press 1962) 148–166: quotation below from 152.
3. *Childhood*, Ch. 27, trans. R. Edmonds (Penguin 1964) 94.
4. H. Troyat, *Tolstoy* (Penguin 1970) 96–7.
5. ibid., 158–9.
6. R. F. Christian, *Tolstoy* (Cambridge University Press 1969) 27–30.
7. *Childhood*, Ch. 3, 20.
8. *Sevastopol in May 1855*, Ch. 16, in *Tales of Army Life*, trans. L. and A. Maude (Oxford University Press 1935) 152.
9. Troyat, op. cit., 235.
10. Troyat, op. cit., 265.
11. *Happy Ever After* ('Family Happiness') trans. R. Edmonds, with *The Cossacks* (Penguin 1960) Ch. 3, 37.
12. *The Cossacks*, Ch. 41, trans. R. Edmonds (Penguin 1960) 329.
13. ibid., Ch. 14, 224–5.
14. Troyat, op. cit., 377.
15. Christian, *Tolstoy's War and Peace*, 22.
16. ibid., 22.
17. ibid., 112.
18. G. Saintsbury, 'Turgenev, Dostoevsky, and Tolstoy', in *Russian Literature and Modern English Fiction*, ed. D. Davie (University of Chicago Press 1965) 27.
19. H. James, *House of Fiction* (Hart Davis 1957) 170.
20. J. Bayley, *Tolstoy and the Novel* (Chatto 1966) 98.
21. *War and Peace*, Epilogue Pt 1, Ch. 7, trans. R. Edmonds (Penguin 1957) Vol 2, 1360.
22. M. Gorky, *Reminiscences of Tolstoy . . .*, trans. S. S. Koteliansky and L. Woolf (Hogarth Press 1934) 57.
23. G. Steiner, *Tolstoy or Dostoevsky* (Penguin 1967) 78–9.
24. E. Gunn, *A. Daring Coiffeur* (Chatto 1971) 56.
25. E. Wilson, 'The Original of Tolstoy's Natasha', in *Tolstoy*, ed. R. Matlaw (Prentice Hall, Englewood Cliffs N.J., 1967) 99.
26. Gunn, op. cit., 32–38.
27. *War and Peace*, Bk 3, Pt 1, Ch. 14 (Vol 2) 771.
28. ibid., Bk 1, Pt 3, Ch. 16 (Vol I) 326.
29. D. S. Mirsky, *History of Russian Literature* (Routledge 1968) 251–2.
30. *War and Peace*, Bk 2, Pt 5, Ch. 9 (Vol I) 663.
31. Bayley, op. cit., 78.
32. *War and Peace*, Bk 1, Pt 1, Ch. 18 (Vol I) 80; Bk 3, Pt 2, Ch. 6 (Vol 2) 839.
33. ibid., Bk 3, Pt 3, Ch. 16 (Vol 2) 1023, 1025.
34. ibid., Bk I, Pt I, Ch. 17 (Vol I) 77.

35. ibid., Bk 2, Pt 4, Ch. 7 (Vol I), 604; Bk 2, Pt 5, Ch. 13 (Vol I) 679.
36. Christian, *Tolstoy's War and Peace*, 45.
37. *War and Peace*, Bk I, Pt 3, Ch. 2 (Vol I) 244.
38. R. West, 'Introduction to "Polikushka"' in *Nine Stories* trans. Maude, xxxiii.
39. *War and Peace*, Bk 3, Pt I, Ch. 17 (Vol 2) 787.
40. ibid., Bk 4, Pt 4, Ch. 6 (Vol 2) 1290.
41. ibid., Bk I, Pt 2, Chs. 6–8 (Vol I) 154–70.
42. ibid., Bk 4, Pt 3, Chs. 10 and 15, (Vol 2) 1249–50, 1261.
43. ibid., Bk 3, Pt 2, Ch 5 (Vol 2) 836–7.
44. ibid., Bk 4, Pt I, Ch. 16 (Vol 2) 1165–7.
45. I. Berlin, *The Hedgehog and the Fox* (New American Library, N.Y. 1957) 11.
46. *War and Peace*, Epilogue Pt 2 Ch. 7 (Vol 2) 1425.
47. ibid., Ch. 7, 1426.
48. ibid., Ch. 8, 1427.
49. ibid., Epilogue Pt I, Ch. 16, 1399.
50. ibid., Bk 4, Pt I, Ch. 10 (Vol 2) 1140.

CHAPTER SIX: DOSTOEVSKY'S LATER FICTION

1. *The Raw Youth* Pt 3 Ch. 13, trans. C. Garnett (Heinemann 1916) 559–60.
2. *The Idiot* Pt 4, Ch. 7, trans. D. Magarshack (Penguin 1955) 587.
3. Quoted in introduction to ibid., 25.
4. N. M. Lary, *Dostoevsky and Dickens* (Routledge 1973) 52.
5. *Idiot*, Pt I, Ch. 12, 163–4.
6. ibid., Pt 1, Ch. 11, 154.
7. ibid., Pt I, Ch. 4, 69.
8. ibid., Pt I, Ch. 15, 188.
9. ibid., Pt I, Ch. 16, 208.
10. ibid., Pt 4, Ch. 10, 630.
11. Lary, op. cit., 65–6, 81–2.
12. *Idiot*, Pt 4, Ch. 4, 533, 543.
13. ibid., Pt 4, Ch. 5, 563.
14. ibid., Pt 3, Ch. 1, 376; Pt 3, Ch. 4, 409–17.
15. ibid., Pt 2, Ch. 5, 258–9.
16. D. Magarshack, *Dostoevsky* (Secker and Warburg 1962) 412.
17. *Raw Youth*, Pt 3, Ch. 3, 381–2.
18. Magarshack, op. cit., 418; cf. *Diary of a Writer*, trans. B. Brasol (Cassell 1947), Vol 2, 660–671.
19. Magarshack, op. cit., 485.
20. *Diary of a Writer*, Vol 1, 142–54.
21. *The Devils* Pt I, Ch. I:9, 47.
22. Irving Howe, *Politics and The Novel* (Stevens 1961) 57.
23. *The Devils*, Pt 3, Ch. 7:2, 648.
24. ibid., Pt 1, Ch. 2:1, 54.
25. ibid., Pt 2, Ch. 1:7, 253–262; Pt 3, Ch. 5:1, 567.
26. ibid., Pt 2, Ch. 8, 420.
27. ibid., Pt 2, Ch. 1:3, 232.
28. ibid., Pt 2, Ch. 6:7, 386; Pt 3, Ch. 4:2, 549.
29. ibid., Pt 2, Ch. I:7, 262.
30. Magarshack, *Dostoevsky*, 118.
31. *Devils*, Pt 3, Ch. 7:2, 645.
32. M. Baring, *Landmarks in Russian Literature* (Methuen 1960 edn) 150.
33. *The Brothers Karamazov*, Pt I, Bk 3, Ch. 4, trans. D. Magarshack (Penguin 1958) 125; Pt 2, Bk 5, Ch. I, 257; Pt 2, Bk 5, Ch. 3, 268–9; Pt 2, Bk 5, Ch. 5, 309; Pt 3, Bk 7, Ch. 2, 400; Pt 3, Bk 9, Ch. 8, 595–6.

34. ibid., Pt 4, Bk 12, Ch. 6, 819–24.
35. ibid., Pt 3, Bk 8, Ch. 8, 518.
36. ibid., Pt 4, Bk 11, Ch. 3, 683; Pt 4, Bk 12, Ch. 5, 807.
37. ibid., Pt 2, Bk 4, Ch. I, 190.
38. ibid., Pt 1, Bk I, Ch. 5, 31–2; Pt 3, Bk 8, Ch. 6, 485.
39. ibid., Pt 2, Bk 5, Ch. 5, 288–308.
40. ibid., Pt 2, Bk 5, Ch. 4, 285–7.
41. ibid., Pt 2, Bk 4, Ch. 5, 218.
42. ibid., Pt 2, Bk 5, Ch. 4, 284.

CHAPTER SEVEN: TOLSTOY'S 'ANNA' AND AFTER

1. H. Troyat, *Tolstoy* (Penguin 1970) 504.
2. ibid., 480.
3. R. F. Christian, *Tolstoy* (Cambridge University Press 1969) 192.
4. *Anna Karenina*, trans. R. Edmonds Pt 5, Ch. 11 (Penguin 1954) 499.
5. ibid., Pt 7, Ch. 9, 728–9.
6. ibid., Pt 1, Ch. 22, 93.
7. ibid., Pt 1, Ch. 18, 75.
8. ibid., Pt 7, Ch. 25, 782–3.
9. ibid., Pt 8, Ch. 4, 812.
10. ibid., Pt 6, Ch. 12, 624.
11. ibid., Pt 4, Ch. 15, 428; Pt 7, Ch. 29, 793–4.
12. ibid., Pt 6, Ch. 23, 669; Pt 7, Ch. 31, 799; Pt 8, Ch. 12, 832.
13. F. R. Leavis, *Anna Karenina and Other Essays* (Chatto 1963) 19.
14. *Anna Karenina*, Pt 4, Chs. 10–13, 413–422.
15. A. Chekhov, *Letters on the Short Story, The Drama and Other Literary Topics* (Bles, 1924) ed. L. S. Friedland, 60.
16. *Anna Karenina*, Pt 3, Ch. 17, 317.
17. ibid., Pt 3, Ch. 17, 319; Pt 3, Ch. 28, 362.
18. Quoted in P. N. Furbank, *Anna Karenina* (Open University Press 1973) 45–6.
19. ibid., 46.
20. *Anna Karenina*, Pt I, Chs. 17–18, 74–79; Pt I, Ch. 25, 102; Pt 1, Chs. 29–30, 115–118; Pt 4, Chs. 2–3, 380–387; Pt 7, Chs. 26 and 31, 785, 798, 802.
21. H. Seton Watson, *The Russian Empire 1801–1917* (Oxford University Press 1967) 404–409.
22. D. Mackenzie Wallace, *Russia* (Cassell 1877) Vol. 1, 4–5.
23. *Anna Karenina*, Pt 6, Ch. 19, 647–8.
24. ibid., Pt 7, Ch. 2, 708.
25. Raymond Williams, *Modern Tragedy* (Chatto 1966) 130–1.
26. *Anna Karenina*, Pt 2, Ch. 11, 165.
27. Troyat, op. cit., 597.
28. *Death of Ivan Ilyich*, Ch. 12, trans. R. Edmonds in *The Cossacks* (Penguin 1960) 161.
29. *Anna Karenina*, Pt 7, Ch. 29, 793–4.
30. A. Chekhov, *Letters*, ed. S. Karlinsky (Bodley Head 1973) 155–6.
31. Christian, *Tolstoy*, 231.
32. *Kreutzer Sonata*, Ch. 14, trans. A. Maude (Oxford University Press 1940) 150–2.

CHAPTER EIGHT: LESKOV, CHEKHOV, LATE TOLSTOY

1. D. S. Mirsky, *History of Russian Literature* (Routledge 1968) 314.
2. Translator's preface to N. Leskov, *Selected Tales*, trans. D. Magarshack (Secker 1961) xvi–xvii.
3. *The Amazon and Other Stories*, trans. D. Magarshack (Allen and Unwin 1949) Ch. 4, 79.
4. 'Lady Macbeth . . .', Ch. 14, in *Selected Tales*, 50.
5. ibid., Ch. 6, 15–16.

6. E. J. Simmons, *Chekhov* (Cape 1963) 60.
7. Mirsky, op. cit., 291–4.
8. H. Seton Watson, *Russian Empire 1801–1917*, (Oxford University Press 1967) 477–8.
9. ibid., 539; the diary entry is printed in I. Berlin, *Fathers and Children* (Oxford University Press 1972) 61–3.
10. E. Wilson, *Window on Russia* (Macmillan 1973) 60.
11. C. Hill, *Lenin and the Russian Revolution* (English University Press 1947) 27.
12. Quoted in V. Llewellyn Smith, *Anton Chekhov and the Lady with the Dog* (Oxford University Press 1973) 158.
13. Simmons, op. cit., 158.
14. ibid., 175.
15. *Selected Stories*, trans. A. Dunnigan (New American Library, N.Y., 1960) 39.
16. 'A Dreary Story', Ch. 6 in *Stories 1889–1891*, (ed. and trans. R. Hingley, Oxford University Press 1970) 80.
17. Simmons, op. cit., 302.
18. ibid., 466–7.
19. ibid., 587–8.
20. 'An Anonymous Story' Ch. 18 in *Stories 1892–1893*, ed. and trans. R. Hingley (Oxford University Press 1971) 250.
21. M. Gorky, *Reminiscences of Tolstoy, Chekhov and Andreev*, trans. K. Mansfield, S. S. Koteliansky and L. Woolf (Hogarth Press 1934) 109–110.
22. Llewellyn Smith op. cit., 9.
23. Quoted in Introduction to *Lady with Lapdog and Other Stories*, trans. D. Magarshack (Penguin 1964) 14.
24. Simmons, op. cit., 490.
25. 'Ward Number Six', Ch. 18, in *Stories 1892–1893*, 164.
26. W. H. Bruford, *Chekhov and his Russia* (Routledge 1948) 21.
27. L. S. Friedland, ed., *Letters on the Short Story . . . (etc.)* (Bles 1924) 207–8.
28. *Lady with Lapdog . . .*, trans. D. Magarshack, 270.
29. ibid., 279.
30. ibid., 274–5.
31. H. Troyat, *Tolstoy* (Penguin 1970) 537–8.
32. ibid., 780–1.
33. *Resurrection*, Pt I, Ch. 48, trans. R. Edmonds (Penguin 1966) 219.
34. ibid., Pt 1, Ch. 20, 100.
35. ibid., Pt 1, Ch. 39, 182.
36. ibid., Pt 1, Ch. 45, 204.
37. ibid., Pt 2, Ch. 27, 386–7.
38. *Hadji Murad*, Ch. 1, trans. A. Maude (Nelson 1912) 19–22.

EPILOGUE

1. M. Gorky, *Reminiscences of Tolstoy, Chekhov and Andreev*, trans. K. Mansfield, S. S. Koteliansky and L. Woolf (Hogarth Press 1934) 14.
2. E. Simmons, *Chekhov* (Cape 1963) 495; Gorky, op. cit., 25.
3. Gorky, op. cit., 62–3.
4. ibid., 59–60.
5. H. Troyat, *Tolstoy* (Penguin 1970) 880.
6. Gorky, op. cit., 57–8.
7. Isaac Babel, 'The Road There', in *Lyubka the Cossack and Other Stories*, trans. A. R. MacAndrew (New American Library, N. Y., 1963) 104–6.

SHORT LIST OF BOOKS

This is not an attempt at a 'Select Bibliography'; it is a short list of books which I can honestly say I have found useful and readable. I have no qualifications to assess the merits of translations and can't presume to offer a list of sound renderings of the novels and stories themselves. In any case, it would soon be out of date. My references will show which I've used, mostly Penguins and Signets; these seem more consistent than the Everymans (Everymen?), some of which are veterans showing their age. I don't mind Constance Garnett at all, and it would in any case be quite impossible to avoid her because her translations of Turgenev, Gogol, Dostoevsky and Chekhov are still the most nearly complete in existence. Someone should take up arms on behalf of Leskov; at the time of writing this, he is completely out of print in Britain. I am enough of an intellectual harlot to have enjoyed thoroughly both Nabokov's runcible line by line rendering of *Onegin* and the metrical translation by Babette Deutsch which he so papally anathematizes. Like many other people, I think Bernard Guilbert Guerney's translation of *Dead Souls* is wonderful; it provides technicolour instead of the black and white of other translators. I have an extremely sweet tooth for Rosemary Edmonds' Penguin versions of Tolstoy, in spite of her strange anti-critical introductions. David Magarshack's Dostoevskys in the same series seem firm things and the Penguin Turgenevs, by various hands, also seem very good. The *Oxford Chekhov*, edited and translated by Ronald Hingley, is a splendid series which will, I hope, soon be completed and offered in paperback. I should also mention Aylmer Maude's complete Oxford edition of Tolstoy; the translations are very readable, though not as convincing to me as Rosemary Edmonds'.

All books listed below are published in London unless otherwise stated, and dates generally refer to first London publication.

1. Contemporary Sources

Custine, Marquis de, *Empire of the Czar* (1843).
Gorky, Maxim, *Reminiscences of Tolstoy, Chekhov and Andreev* (trans. K. Mansfield et al, 1934).
Haxthausen, Baron von, *The Russian Empire* . . . (1856).
Herzen, Alexander, *My Past and Thoughts* (trans. C. Garnett, revised H. Higgens, 1968).
Mackenzie Wallace, D., *Russia* (1877).
Turgenev, Ivan, *Literary Reminiscences* (trans. D. Magarshack, 1959).

2. Works on the Historical and Social Background

Berlin, Sir Isaiah, 'A Marvellous Decade' in *Encounter* Vols. 4 and 5 (1955).
Blum, Jerome, *Lord and Peasant in Russia from the Ninth to the Nineteenth Centuries* (Princeton, 1961).
Bruford, W. H., *Chekhov and His Russia: A Sociological Study* (1948).
Florinsky, M. T., *Russia—A History and an Interpretation* (New York, 1953).
Hingley, Ronald, *Russian Writers and Society* (1967).
Maynard, Sir John, *Russia in Flux* (1941).
Seton Watson, Hugh, *The Russian Empire 1801–1917* (1967).
Sumner, B. H., *Survey of Russian History* (1944).
Venturi, Franco, *Roots of Revolution* (trans. F. Haskell, 1959).

3. Literary Histories

Gifford, Henry, *The Novel in Russia* (1964).
Kropotkin, Peter, *Russian Literature: Ideals and Realities* (1916).
Harkins, William E., *Dictionary of Russian Literature* (1957).
Hauser, Arnold, *Social History of Art* Vol 4 (1962).
Mirsky, D. S., *A History of Russian Literature* (ed. F. J. Whitefield, 1949).
Phelps, Gilbert, *The Russian Novel in English Fiction* (1956).
Slonim, Marc, *The Epic of Russian Literature: from its Origins through Tolstoy* (New York, (1950).
Slonim, Marc, *Modern Russian Literature: from Chekhov to the Present* (New York, 1953).
Wellek, René, *A History of Modern Criticism*, Vols 3 and 4 (1966).

4. Critical Works Covering Two or More Writers

Davie, Donald, ed., *Russian Literature and Modern English Fiction* (Chicago, 1965).
Howe, Irving, *Politics and the Novel* (1961).
James, Henry, *The House of Fiction* (1957).
Lukács, Georg, *Studies in European Realism* (1972).
O'Connor, Frank, *The Mirror in the Roadway* (1957).
Poggioli, Renato, *The Phoenix and the Spider* (Cambridge, Mass., 1957).
Steiner, George, *Tolstoy or Dostoevsky?* (1967 edn).
Wilson, Edmund, *A Window on Russia* (1973).

5. Books or Essays on Individual Writers (Biographies marked B)

PUSHKIN

Bayley, John, *Pushkin* (Cambridge 1971).
Davie, Donald, *The Heyday of Sir Walter Scott* (1961).
Magarshack, David, *Pushkin* (B) (1967).
Nabokov, Vladimir, *Eugene Onegin* . . . (ed. and trans., with a commentary, 1964).
Shaw., J. T., ed., *Letters of Alexander Pushkin* (1967).

LERMONTOV

Mersereau, John, *Mikhail Lermontov* (Carbondale, Ill., 1962).

GOGOL

Magarshack, David, *Gogol* (B) (1957).
Nabokov, Vladimir, *Nikolai Gogol* (1973 edn).

GONCHAROV

Lavrin, Janko, *Goncharov* (Cambridge, 1954).

TURGENEV

Berlin, Sir Isaiah, *Fathers and Children* (1972).
Freeborn, Richard, *Turgenev: The Novelist's Novelist* (1960).
Kettle, Arnold, *On The Eve* (1973).
Yarmolinsky, Avram, *Turgenev* (B) (New York, 1959).

DOSTOEVSKY

Carr, E. H., *Dostoevsky* (B) (1962 edn).
Gide, André, *Dostoevsky* (1967 edn).
Lary, N.M., *Dostoevsky and Dickens* (1973).
Magarshack, David, *Dostoevsky* (B) (1962).
Simmons, Ernest, *Dostoevsky: The Making of a Novelist* (1950).
Wellek, René, ed., *Dostoevsky* (Englewood Cliffs, N. J., 1962).

TOLSTOY

Bayley, John, *Tolstoy and the Novel* (1966).
Berlin, Sir Isaiah, *The Hedgehog and the Fox* (1953).
Christian, R. F., *Tolstoy* (Cambridge 1969).
Christian, R. F., *Tolstoy's 'War and Peace'* (1962).
Gunn, Elizabeth, *A Daring Coiffeur* (1971).
Matlaw, Ralph, ed., *Tolstoy* (Englewood Cliffs, N. J., 1967).
Troyat, Henri, *Tolstoy* (B) (1970 edn).

CHEKHOV

Chekhov, Anton, *Letters*, ed. S. Karlinsky (1973); ed. A. Yarmolinsky (1974).
Hingley, Ronald, ed. and trans. with commentary, *The Oxford Chekhov* (1964-   ).
Llewellyn Smith, Virginia, *Anton Chekhov and the Lady with the Dog* (1973).
Simmons, Ernest, *Chekhov* (B) (1963).

I hope I have named above all the works whose ideas and approaches I have learnt most from. I should pay a final tribute to my constant companion, the wonderful Mirsky, who touches no writer without saying something stimulating.

INDEX